Dominik Besier
Grammar Competition in Second Language Acquisition

Studies on Language Acquisition

Series Editors
Luke Plonsky
Martha Young-Scholten

Volume 70

Dominik Besier

Grammar Competition in Second Language Acquisition

―

The Case of English Non-Verbal Predicates for Indonesian L1 Speakers

DE GRUYTER
MOUTON

ISBN 978-3-11-162177-7
e-ISBN (PDF) 978-3-11-076633-2
e-ISBN (EPUB) 978-3-11-076637-0
ISSN 1861-4248

Library of Congress Control Number: 2022951991

Bibliographic information published by the Deutsche Nationalbibliothek
The Deutsche Nationalbibliothek lists this publication in the Deutsche Nationalbibliografie; detailed bibliographic data are available on the internet at http://dnb.dnb.de.

© 2024 Walter de Gruyter GmbH, Berlin/Boston
This volume is text- and page-identical with the hardback published in 2023.
Typesetting: Integra Software Services Pvt. Ltd.

www.degruyter.com

Contents

1	**Introduction —— 1**	
1.1	The idea —— 1	
1.2	Clearing the ground: Important concepts —— 5	
1.2.1	Second language acquisition —— 5	
1.2.2	Contrastive grammar and language acquisition —— 6	
1.2.3	Non-verbal predicates —— 10	
1.3	The context: Indonesian and English in Indonesia —— 12	
1.3.1	Indonesian —— 12	
1.3.2	English in Indonesia —— 16	
1.4	Outline of this work —— 17	
2	**The theoretical framework —— 20**	
2.1	Basic concepts: Items and operations —— 21	
2.2	Derivation —— 24	
3	**Generative description of Indonesian —— 40**	
3.1	On optionality in Indonesian —— 40	
3.2	The voice-layer —— 47	
3.2.1	meN-voice —— 49	
3.2.2	ter-voice —— 52	
3.2.3	ber-voice —— 54	
3.2.4	zero-voice —— 55	
3.2.5	Transitive markers —— 57	
3.2.6	Structural representation —— 62	
3.3	The D-layer —— 67	
3.3.1	Derivational morphology —— 67	
3.3.2	Modification by adjectives —— 71	
3.3.3	Classifiers —— 73	
3.3.4	yang —— 78	
3.3.5	Zero-nominalizers —— 81	
3.3.6	-nya —— 83	
3.3.7	Demonstratives —— 86	
3.4	The T-layer —— 88	
3.4.1	Non-verbal vs. verbal TAM-markers —— 89	
3.4.2	TAM-markers and grammaticalization —— 98	
3.4.3	T as a category of relative tense —— 109	
3.5	The C-layer —— 115	
3.5.1	Indonesian intonation —— 115	

3.5.2	Topic — 120	
3.5.3	Focus — 121	

4   Non-verbal predicates in English and Indonesian — 127
4.1   Copular clauses — 127
4.1.1   Typological classification — 128
4.1.2   Formalistic classification — 132
4.1.3   Copular clauses and this work — 137
4.2   Non-verbal predicates in English — 142
4.2.1   DPs — 147
4.2.2   Adjectives — 154
4.2.3   Prepositions — 159
4.2.4   Conclusion — 161
4.3   Non-eventive predicates in Indonesian — 161
4.3.1   Adjectival predicates — 164
4.3.2   Nominal predicates — 171
4.3.3   Indefinite nominal phrases with classifiers/numerals — 176
4.3.4   PP-predicates — 181
4.4   Ada vs. adalah (vs. be) — 185
4.4.1   Position — 186
4.4.2   Optionality — 190
4.4.3   Origin — 200
4.5   Conclusion — 215
4.5.1   The category of non-eventive predicate — 215
4.5.2   The number of copulas — 222
4.5.3   The copula type — 223

5   The empirical study — 224
5.1   Theoretical background — 224
5.2   The test — 227
5.2.1   The idea — 227
5.2.2   Purpose of the study — 229
5.2.3   The test design — 229
5.2.4   Test sample — 236
5.3   Results and discussion — 241
5.3.1   Adverb category — 241
5.3.2   Adverb position — 256
5.3.3   The category of the predicate — 266
5.4   Summary — 277

6   Conclusion —— 280

References —— 283

Appendix

Test 1 —— 297

Test 2 —— 301

Index —— 303

1 Introduction

In times of globalization, learning foreign languages is an important asset for the personal success and the economic-political success of a society. As the most important lingua franca in the world, English has acquired an irreplaceable status. However, the acquisition process is influenced and often impeded by various factors. One of these factors is the languages already acquired before, especially one's mother tongue. In general, similar structures in two languages might have a positive effect on the learning process, but more importantly, different structures can present difficulties for the learner.

In Indonesia, English is the most important foreign language learned during compulsory education. This process does not remain without difficulties. One such difficulty that is frequently experienced is the correct use of the English copula *be*. Many Indonesian learners of English show tendencies either to omit (1) or to overgeneralize (2) this constituent.

(1) *Mary sad.

(2) *Mary is go

The first example resembles the Indonesian structure without a copular verb (3).

(3) Maria   sedih.
     Mary   sad
     'Mary is sad.'

Thus, a possible explanation is that the error (1) comes from imitating the Indonesian structure. However, the omission of an item can also occur for many other reasons, e.g., sloppiness. Hence, copula omission like in (1) can result from Indonesian influence but does not have to. Following on from this observation, the goal of this work is to analyze which role Indonesian as L1 plays in the L2 acquisition of English non-verbal predicates. Can we find difficulties for the L1 Indonesian L2 English learner based on structural differences between these two languages?

1.1 The idea

Undoubtedly, language is not random but is based on a set of rules. This set of rules is the grammar. These rules have to be acquired, which is part of language acquisition. It is also undoubted that languages differ in their rule sets, their grammars. Thus, by learning a second language, one must acquire new or different rules. However, this second process is somehow different from the first one as the first grammar rules are already there. Thus, the question is, how does the rule set of the first language (L1) influence the acquisition or the set-up of the set of rules for L2.

How do we acquire this set of rules, or in other words, how does L1 acquisition work? Once again, this is an oversimplification of the process. When children acquire a language, they are never taught rules explicitly (Chomsky 1965: 200–201). Thus, they somehow manage to set up these rules on their own. The two main ingredients for language acquisition or better setting up grammar is the Faculty of Language and input (Radford 2004: 10–13). The Faculty of Language is the innate human capacity to acquire a language (Chomsky 1972: 102). This device is hard-wired in the brain (Chomsky 1972: 102). Still, this concept has to be seen as rather abstract and not something we could easily find by cutting open a brain. In this abstract Faculty of Language, we find the Universal Grammar (UG). This universal grammar is a rather abstract rule set shared by all languages in the world. The rules shared by all languages are called Principles (Radford 2009: 19–22). Besides these universal principles, Universal Grammar also provides the capacity to derive rules by analyzing input (these processes are tacit and implicit). Here, the second factor input comes into play. According to the evidence from the input, rules are added to the grammar. This process has been described as parametrization. In a simplified description, parameters are switched on or off during this process according to the evidence from the input (Radford 2009: 22–30).

But, what does change when we acquire the second set of rules? There are two important questions. First, is the general process still the same, or to put it differently, do the learners still have access to UG? The second question concerns the L1 grammar. Which role does it play? In this work, I follow the Full Access Full Transfer Hypothesis of Schwartz and Sprouse (1994, 1996, see also White 1989). Full Access means that a speaker still has access to UG during second language acquisition. Full Transfer states that the L1 grammar is transferred completely to the L2 grammar. Thus, L1 grammar is the starting point to set up L2.

If the L1 is the set-up at the beginning of the L2 acquisition, there are two possible scenarios for acquiring the L2 rules. First, the L2 rule is identical to the L1 rule. Nothing has to be set up in such a case as it is already available, and acquisition should be facilitated. The second scenario is more interesting as it concerns the case that the L1 rule and the L2 rule are not identical. What happens here?

In Principle and Parameters Theory, parameters are generally seen as binary (Radford 2004: 20–21, Radford 2009: 26). Accordingly, inside this idea, L2 acquisition would mean changing parameters from one setting to another in this scenario. However, language acquisition research has shifted from parameters to features

(Ionin 2013: 506). Thus, we should leave this rather stiff idea and adopt a more flexible picture based on features. The idea is that derivation is based on features. Hence, in acquisition, it has to be figured out which features are relevant and where they come into play in the derivation. To simplify the conceptualization, I will call these rules, which then lead to derivations/representations.

According to the Feature Reassembly Hypothesis (Lardiere 2009a, b), the scenario mentioned above of different L1 and L2 rules could lead to three different outcomes (see Slabakova 2016: 213):
a) A feature does not exist in L1 but in L2; therefore, it has to be added.
b) A feature does not exist in L2 but in L1; therefore, it must be deleted.
c) The features are different; thus, it requires feature reassembly.

If we translate this idea into our term of rules, we get the following picture:
a) A rule does not exist in L1 but in L2; therefore, it has to be added.
b) A rule does not exist in L2 but in L1; therefore, it must be deleted.
c) The rules are different; this scenario requires restructuring the rules with adding and deletion.

However, according to Roeper's Grammar Competition, deleting rules is unnecessary if not impossible (Roeper and Amaral 2014: 12). Thus, rules are just set inactive (Roeper 1999: 171). Nevertheless, the blocking might not always be successful (Roeper and Amaral 2014: 36). Therefore, competition is still possible when the new rule has been acquired (more on that later on).

Considering this idea, we once again have to revise the three possible scenarios as follows:
a) A rule does not exist in L1 but in L2; therefore, it has to be added.
b) A rule does not exist in L2 but in L1; therefore, it must be blocked.
c) The rules are different; this scenario requires restructuring the rules by adding and blocking.

The ideal outcome, of course, would be that the L2 grammar is identical to the L1 grammar of the same language. However, that is normally not the case. Both, the still changing grammar during the acquisition process (see Selinker's [1972] interlanguage) and the end product of a fossilized stage, normally deviate from the L1 grammar of the target language. But how can we describe the differences, and how can we identify whether this is due to the L1?

Although grammar has to be stored in the brain, it cannot be read on certain brain structures. Additionally, grammar competence is tacit knowledge. Hence, it is impossible to ask any speaker for explicit grammar rules. They will not be able to answer that question if they have not learned it in some kind of language class. As a consequence, a common method to describe grammar is to rely on a Grammaticality Judgment Task (see, e.g., Leow 1996). In this method, speakers are asked to identify sentences of their language as grammatical or ungrammatical. Based on the results, the tacit grammar rules can be deducted (Leow 1996). The same approach will be used for the L2 grammar of the English learners in this work.[1] Of special interest are the incidents where the judgments of the L2 learner deviate from the native speaker. This case could be an indication of a difference in grammar. However, not all differences must be based on differences in grammar, and not all differences in grammar must be a consequence of the influence of the L1 grammar. To find the influence of the L1 grammar on the L2 grammar, we should find the following scenario:

(4) a. Deviation from the native speaker
 b. Structural differences between L1 and L2
 c. Imitation of L1 structure

To find such a scenario is the ultimate goal of this work. An experiment conducted in Bandar Lampung with L1 Indonesian L2 English speakers tested whether we find a scenario as in (4) for non-verbal predicates. This experiment and the results will be subject to chapter 5. This whole work is directed to that chapter.

However, in order to test for error patterns based on structural differences, it is necessary to identify structural differences first. Otherwise, implementing the experiment/the test would be useless. This identification is the task of chapter 4. In that chapter, this work will contrast non-verbal predicates in English and Indonesian and show structural similarities but, more importantly, structural differences.

A prerequisite to describing structural differences/similarities is to have a framework for these structures to be described. That is the purpose of the second and the third chapter. The second chapter will provide a general introduction to the theoretical approach applied in this work. The third chapter provides a comprehensive picture of the Indonesian grammar based on that approach.

Thus, this work consists of three major parts that form a build-up, with the former being the prerequisite for the latter, culminating in the experiment on error patterns in chapter 5.

---

[1] Gass (1994) and Leow (1996) have shown that this is a reliable instrument for L2 research. The validity of this method will be discussed in chapter 5.

1.2 Clearing the ground: Important concepts

After outlining the general idea of this work, the goal of these sections is to clarify important concepts, which are required to understand the remaining work. These include the term second language acquisition, the general idea of contrasting languages/grammars in relation to language acquisition, the topic of contrast, namely non-verbal predicates, the languages in contrast (English and Indonesian), and the context of English for Indonesian speakers.

1.2.1 Second language acquisition

Second language acquisition has many different facets that include distinctions that can be made but do not have to be made.

As the term second language (L2) implies, it must be distinguished from the first language, native tongue (L1). Whereas the native language is the dominant language since infancy (Behney and Marsden 2021: 38), the second language is acquired after the first language has been acquired (at least partly). Slabakova (2016: 142–143), following Schwartz (2004) and Meisel (2011), argues that a language that is acquired at the age of 4 or later should be considered a second language since, at this time, the most important structures of the L1 grammar have been acquired. If children acquire two languages before that age, they acquire two first languages (bilingualism).

Second languages cannot only be distinguished from first languages but also third languages. A third language is a language that is learned after two languages have been acquired. This distinction is important for the field of L3/Ln acquisition, as now, not only L1 but also L2 can influence the acquisition of the third language (Slabakova 2019: 148). Outside the field of L3 acquisition, L2 is often understood in a broader sense where L2 is any language that is learned after the native language, and it does not matter whether it is language two, three, four, etc. (Behney and Marsden 2021: 37). This work will use the broader use of the term L2 not distinguishing it from an L3.

Another important distinction in L2 acquisition is the differentiation between child L2 acquisition and adult L2 acquisition. The crucial factor here is the Critical Period (Lenneberg 1967). The idea of the Critical Period is that children acquiring the language before that time follow a different acquisition path than after that period (Lenneberg 1967). Before, native-like competence is quite likely; after, it is very rare (Lenneberg 1967). Whereas Lenneberg (1967: 63) proposed an upper limit of 12 years, Johnson and Newport (1989: 78) found differences after the age of 7. This work will follow the latter and place the threshold around the age of seven.

Before that threshold, second language acquisition is labeled child L2 acquisition; after the threshold, it is labeled adult L2 acquisition (Slabakova 2016: 142). This work will only deal with adult L2 acquisition.

Another distinction that can be made is between a second language in a narrow sense and a foreign language (see Ringbom 1980). Here, the language setting is the crucial factor. Whereas foreign language learning is institutionalized and happens outside the natural environment of that language in the second language setting, acquisition takes place in a natural way with the L2 being the environment language, e.g., due to migration (cf. Ringbom 1980: 5–6). In this work, I will use the term second language acquisition in its broad sense, not making any distinction based on the language setting. Nevertheless, the experiment presented in chapter 5 was conducted in a foreign language setting. Still, I will use the term second language acquisition in its more general sense.

1.2.2 Contrastive grammar and language acquisition

As outlined in the general idea, one important factor in finding L1 influence on L2 grammar is structural differences between L1 and L2. Describing these structural differences requires some contrastive analysis. However, contrastive analysis and language acquisition do not only have a happy history although contrastive analysis undoubtedly provides important insights into language acquisition. Therefore, the goal of this section is to deal with this issue and how contrastive grammar/contrastive analysis is (not) understood here.

Maybe the most famous but also most controversial approach to connecting contrasting grammar and language acquisition is the Contrastive Analysis Hypothesis connected to the work of Fries (1945) and Lado (1957). Before dealing with this approach and its shortcomings in more detail, it is necessary to consider contrastive linguistics independent from language acquisition. Pan and Tham (2007) and Fisiak (1980) show that contrastive analysis has a much longer tradition than the Ladoan and Friesan approach. Foundational ideas of contrastive linguistics are encountered in the work of Wilhelm von Humboldt, e.g., his article 'On the comparative study of language and its relation to the different periods of language development.' In line with von Humboldt, comparative/contrastive works before World War II were essentially theoretical (Fisiak 1980: 2). Pan and Tham (2007) also identify Jespersen and Whorf within this tradition.

Jespersen's (1924/196: 346–347) idea to examine the way a notion or inner meaning, in other words, a universal idea, expressed in different languages in both function and form, is comparable to what Fisiak et al. (1978) describe as theoretical contrastive analysis. The concept of notion or inner meaning could be translated into tertium comparationis, a term that we will return to further below. Whorf, who is believed to be the one who coined the term contrastive linguistics (Pan and Tham 2007: 21), promoted the idea of contrasting languages to highlight the differences among them (see Pan and Tham 2007: 28). Therefore, he was mainly interested in comparing genetically distant languages (Pan and Tham 2007: 31). In his view on language description, he postulated the revision of grammatical categories. He hoped that cross-linguistic contrastive linguistics could help revise terminology and reduce the eurocentricity of these terms (Pan and Tham 2007: 33). Pan and Tham (2007: 32) connect this idea of lexical categories to the more modern term tertium comparationis. There is a strong theoretical interest behind the analysis for both Jespersen and Whorf. This fact highlights that contrastive linguistics is, in the beginning, a branch of theoretical linguistics independent from any application like in language teaching. Nevertheless, the insight of contrasting languages can be useful for the understanding of language acquisition but also language teaching.

The most famous connection between contrastive linguistics and language acquisition and language teaching is the Contrastive Analysis Hypothesis (CAH), introduced as mentioned above by Fries (1945) and Lado (1957). For them, contrastive linguistics could be implemented right away into language teaching. They claimed that difficulties in foreign language learning are generally predictable by examining the difference between the native and the target language. CAH was based on five basic assumptions (Lee 1968: 186[2]):

1. The main reason for errors is the interference of one's mother tongue.
2. Difficulties in the learning process result from differences between target and native language.
3. The greater the difference between the two languages in question, the more challenging the difficulties experienced.
4. Errors are predictable by means of a detailed comparison of the two languages in question.
5. Foreign language instruction should be based on contrastive analysis.

Besides this shift from theory to application, two more shifts are identifiable: a shift from meaning to form and from distant to closely related languages (Pan and Tham 2007).

This strong version of CAH was strongly criticized in the 60s and 70s (Rein 1983). Major objections, as summarized in Rein (1983), concerned the (i) predictability of errors, (ii) the exclusiveness of interference as an error source, (iii) the

---

[2] These assumptions have never been explicitly formulated by any advocate of CAH, but are rather the conclusion of Lee, a critic of this hypothesis (Rein 1983: 22).

question of whether genetically related languages or non-related languages are more difficult to learn, (iv) the very comparability of two languages, and (v) the lack of a theoretical foundation.

Therefore, this CAH version, also known as the strong CAH, had little impact and was soon displaced by Error Analysis (Corder 1967, 1971; Richards 1971; Selinker 1969, 1972) and the concept of interlanguage (Selinker 1972). Nevertheless, this half-baked approach stigmatized the notion of contrastive analysis until today. Although the CAH was too strong and maybe also somehow premature, it is undoubted that the L1 is relevant for L2 acquisition. Those insights in contrastive linguistics can be helpful in language acquisition. Therefore, this work will not refrain from applying insights from contrastive linguistics to language acquisition; however, it dissociates itself from the CAH in the Ladoan and Friesan sense.

Besides the absolute call on exclusivity, maybe the strongest weakness of the CAH was to try to do several steps at a time. Any insight should be directly applied to language teaching. However, the whole process has to be considered longer and more fine-grained. First of all, as mentioned earlier, contrastive analysis/linguistics is purely theoretical in the first step. That was highlighted again in the 1980s, when contrastive analysis experienced a revival, reverting to its roots in the pre-war era to a more theoretical approach. It no longer (only) concerns language teaching but also contributes to general theory on language (Lipinska 1980: 129). This contrast can only be used for insights into language acquisition in a second step. Accordingly, Fisiak et al. (1978) distinguish between theoretical contrastive analysis (CA) and applied CA. Whereas theoretical CA looks at how a universal category X is represented in language A and language B, applied CA deals with the question of how a category realized in language A is presented in language B (Fisiak et al. 1978). Closely related to the concept X is the notion of tertium comparationis, the abstract idea which is contrasted and not yet implemented in any language. In this context, Krzeszowski (1980: 187) talks about equivalent sentences (constructions). For him, 'equivalent sentences (and constructions) have identical input (semantic) structure, even if on the surface these sentences (constructions) are marked differently' (Krzeszowski 1980: 187). We will get back to this concept later by defining the tertium comparationis, the topic of this work, namely non-verbal predicates.

Now, it is time to elaborate on the connection between contrastive linguistics and language acquisition and how it is understood in this work.

With van Buren (1980: 83), I claim that explanatory power should be the goal of all contrastive linguistics. From this perspective, the ultimate goal here is to elucidate certain error patterns of Indonesian learners of English that are explainable by structural differences. It is important to mention that L1 influence is not an exclusive error source. Thus, contrastive linguistics can give us insights into language acquisition but is never sufficient to explain it.

Two important concepts regarding the influence of the L1 on L2 acquisition are the concepts of 'transfer' and 'interference.' Similar to the term contrastive analysis, these terms are not without history. Therefore, it is important to define these terms.

Before considering the concept of transfer in a more modern approach, it is necessary to look at these terms in the traditional contrastive analysis approach. Lado (1964: 222) defines transfer as 'the extension of a native-language habit to the target language, with or without awareness. When the transfer habit is acceptable in the target language, we have facilitation; when it is unacceptable, we have interference.' The main idea of transfer is to use L1 knowledge for the L2. If it produces an error (structural mismatch between the two languages), it is called interference. In his approach of Generative Contrastive Grammar, Krzeszowski (1980) looks at this from a structural perspective. It is necessary to identify all possible structures for a clause in all languages involved in the contrastive analysis. After that, these structures have to be compared in order to identify similarities and differences. Whenever the underlying structure of L1 is used to target L2, we have transfer. It is interference if the transfer is not successful (not the correct surface structure).

In this work, I will follow more modern approaches and see transfer as the application of L1 for L2. No distinction between facilitation and inhibition is made. Thus, the term interference will not be used. To conceptualize the idea of transfer in more detail, it is necessary to take a look at language acquisition in a more general picture. As already outlined above, language acquisition is setting up a grammar here for the L2. In generative Second Language Acquisition theory (GenSLA), three important factors have been discussed: Universal Grammar (UG), L2-input, and here most important, L1-knowledge (Rothman and Slabakova 2018: 419). One major question is whether the L2-learner still has access to UG, and if yes, to what extent? The second question, once again more important for the purpose of this work, is how much L1 knowledge is transferred to the L2 grammar? These questions have been answered in all directions reaching from No-Transfer/No-Access through Partial Transfer to FullTransfer/ Full Access (Sauter 2002). This work here will be premised on the Full Access/Full Transfer Hypothesis (Schwartz and Sprouse 1996), which claims that the L2 learner has full access to UG and fully transfers the L1 grammar to L2. In these terms, the L1 is the initial state for L2 (Amaral and Roeper 2014: 22).

Assuming the framework of multiple grammars[3] (MG) (Amaral and Roeper 2014, Roeper 1999) in language acquisition, the learner adds new rules while not deleting any. All L1 rules, then, should not only be part of the initial stage but remain

---

[3] This approach was initially concerned with language change with an unstable phase with two grammars in competition (see Kroch 1994, 2001 and others), but was later extended first to the individual to account for apparent optionality (Roeper 1999) and then applied to L2 acquisition (Amaral and Roeper 2014).

part of the L2 grammar. Instead of the binary choice of either one rule or the other, multiple grammars allow for several rules/subgrammars in operation simultaneously. Transfer is not predictable and is understood as 'the speaker's inability to block the use of a productive rule from Lx temporarily.' (Amaral and Roeper 2014: 36). This means that the speaker applies a productive rule from one language to another, e.g., an L1 rule to an L2 situation.

As Rothman, Gonzalez Alonso, and Puig-Mayenco (2019: 24) pointed out, transfer concerns representation. With that, they differentiate transfer from cross-language effects (CLE) (Rothman, Gonzalez Alonso, and Puig Mayenco 2019: 24), which concern language processing. This distinction aligns with MG, which focuses on a representational perspective and not on processing (Amaral and Roeper 2014: 27). This work will follow this focus on representation. Accordingly, this work will not formulate certain rules but rather structural representations (tree structures) for certain constructions. For one construction, the speaker has at least one representation in their target language and one in their native language (these structures may be (close to) identical). If the speaker uses the representation of their native language for the target language or vice versa, we are dealing with transfer. If this leads to a judgment contrary to the native judgment, we deal with (L1) competition. With this term, this work avoids the loaded term of interference.

1.2.3 Non-verbal predicates

After dealing with the general idea of contrastive linguistics in connection to language acquisition, it is important to define and narrow the subject of contrast, often called the tertium comparationis. Here it is non-verbal/non-eventive predicates.

Let us take a perspective proceeding from right to left and start with the notion of predicate. For predicates, there are at least two very common yet different definitions. The first one is known from traditional grammar, where the predicate is seen as one of two major parts of the sentences, namely subject and predicate. Consequently, the entire non-subject constituent, prototypically comprising the verb with the object(s), and sometimes even adjuncts, is understood as the predicate. However, sometimes this constituent is further divided into its parts, namely object, adjuncts, and the expression that takes the arguments, prototypically a verb, which is unfortunately labeled predicate as well. As if this much is not confusing enough, there is even a broader understanding of predicate, mainly in formalistic approaches in semantics and logic. Here, the predicate is understood as an expression that gives information on referents (Löbner 2013: 107). The predicate term is the core of predication and takes a certain number of arguments. However, according to this definition, the predicate is not limited to standing in complementarity to the subject; predicates can occur elsewhere, e.g., within the subject in nominal phrases.

The framework used in this work is related to the second definition in formalistic approaches, predicates as function. However, to avoid any misunderstanding, this work refrains from the term 'predicate' as used in the functional sense and uses the term 'function' instead and reserves the term 'predicate' for its traditional sense. Thus, the particular notion 'non-verbal/non-eventive predicate' always refers to the main predicate of a clause, that is, the one that takes the subject as its argument.

Prototypically, the main predicate of a clause is a verb. However, there is also the possibility of having non-verbal predicates, namely nouns, adjectives, and prepositions. A distinction is often made between verbal and non-verbal predicates. Although I do aim at this non-verbal category, the idea of non-verbal is somewhat problematic in the case of Indonesian. 'Non-verbal' indicates a distinction along the lines of syntactic categories based on syntactic behaviour. For Indonesian, it is at least doubtful whether a clear line can be drawn between a verbal and an adjectival category solely based on morphosyntactic evidence. Hence, in order to be able to distinguish between these two categories – what would be a verb and what would be an adjective in English – with reference to Indonesian, this can only be done with semantic categories. A syntactic categorization is not possible. Although it is nearly impossible to list all members of a syntactic category that share only one or two features, the prototypical feature that applies to verbs is that they denote an event. Therefore, the category targeted here should be called non-eventive instead of non-verbal. This term would be more neutral and less misleading. However, as this description correlates to the syntactic category of a verb in English,[4] I stick with the more traditional term non-verbal. However, I rely on the non-eventive characteristics instead of the syntactic behaviour of verbality. Hence, non-verbal predicates as tertium comparationis are expressions that function as the main predicate of a clause and do not denote an event.

Since English generally applies a copula, mainly *be*, with non-verbal predicates, the topic inevitably leads to copular constructions. However, the notion of copular constructions would be, on the one hand, too broad of a topic; on the other hand, misleading, given especially that Indonesian lacks a copula in certain constructions. Additionally, this case study is restricted to predicational copular constructions (in the sense of Higgins 1979).

The contrast of non-verbal predicates will be twofold. On the one hand, it deals with the inner structure of the predicate itself and, on the other hand, with the

---

4 Non-eventive is not identical with stative. I will demonstrate further below that all stative verbs of English are eventive, sometimes only based on the syntactic requirement of transitivity.

necessity of copula(s). Normally, the former determines the latter. Thus, the inner structure of the predicate influences the necessity of the copula. Whereas in English the non-verbal category will be analyzed as homogenous, in Indonesian, three different structures for non-eventive predicates will be proposed. As these structures apply different copulas, a third contrast required is the contrast of the copular forms.

1.3 The context: Indonesian and English in Indonesia

1.3.1 Indonesian

Indonesian or Bahasa Indonesia is the national language of Indonesia, the fourth most populated country in the world. With 198 million speakers (Badan Pusat Statistik 2010) and 23 million native speakers (number increasing) (Simons and Fennig 2017), it is gaining in importance. The Indonesian name *Bahasa Indonesia* (literally language Indonesia) can either mean the Indonesian language or the language of Indonesia. Indonesian is a Malayic language within the Austronesian language family (Simons and Fennig 2017) and belongs to the Malay macrolanguage (Simons and Fennig 2017).

The historical homeland of the Austronesian language family is Formosa. From there, Austronesian spread via the Philippines into the Indonesian archipelago, and from there westward as far as Madagascar and eastward to Easter Island further South and Hawai'i further North (Blust 2013). The homeland of the Malayic languages is Borneo (Sneddon 2003a: 31). About 2000 years ago, groups of Malayic-speaking people sailed west to the east coast of Sumatra, where they settled and Malay developed (Sneddon 2003a: 32). At more or less the same time, the Malay-speaking community started to trade with the Indian subcontinent. Due to the strategic position of the Strait of Malacca on the sea route between India and China, the Malay settlements continued to grow in importance. With the adoption of ideas of philosophy and religion, in the 4th century, the first Hindu-Buddhist Malay kingdoms emerged in the area (Sneddon 2003a: 33). The most important kingdom was that of Srivijaya in Southern Sumatra in the area of today's Palembang. This kingdom had trade relations far to the East, and Malay became a lingua franca throughout the archipelago (Sneddon 2003a: 36). Following the decline of the Hindu-Buddhist states, Muslim traders, also from India, introduced Islam, and Malay sultanates emerged in the area. The most influential sultanate was the Sultanate of Malacca, which had trade relations throughout the whole archipelago, strengthening the position of Malay as lingua franca (Sneddon 2003a: 52).

When the Europeans, Portuguese and Dutch entered the region, they found Malay in a diglossic situation. The low Malay was used as a trade language, and the High Malay was spoken at the courts with a literary tradition, later known as the Classical Malay. Dutch language policy favoured the High Malay and chose this variety both for bible translation (Sneddon 2003a: 84) and for education (Sneddon 2003a: 92). Hence, Classical Malay was put into a prestigious position at the beginning of the 20th century, the time of national awakening. This awakening was mainly driven by a new national intelligentsia who had studied in the Netherlands (Sneddon 2003a: 100).

On the 28th of October 1928, this awakening gave birth to Indonesian in the *sumpah pemuda* (Youth Pledge). On that day, young "Indonesian" intellectuals gathered to announce three goals for their striving for independence: one people (*bangsa*), one fatherland (*tanah air*), and one language (*bahasa*), namely Classical Malay, which should become the language of Indonesia and was then called Bahasa Indonesia (Sneddon 2003a: 101).

In the following years, before and after independence (in 1945), Indonesian was deliberately developed by either influential writers like Alisjahbana or governmental institutions like the *Pusat Pembinaan dan Pengembangan Bahasa*[5] (Centre of Language Development). The goal was to make Indonesian a language suitable for all sectors of life, but especially for politics, administration, and science (Sneddon 2003a: 107). This development was mainly on the lines of modernization and westernization (Sneddon 2003a: 107). Even though most Indonesians had to learn that language (native speakers were estimated to be a million people), the story of Indonesian was a great success. Today Indonesian is the only national language in Indonesia used in administration, politics, education, and science. It is spoken by close to 200 million people out of 250 million Indonesians and continues to grow.

Despite all language planning, Indonesian is far from being a homogeneous language. Throughout the archipelago, we find diglossia, if not polyglossia (see Ferguson 1959), especially if we use the extended diglossia concept (Fishman 1967) and keep other regional languages in mind. Generally, Standard Indonesian is used in formal conversation (politics, administration, law, speeches, lectures, etc.) and non-standard Indonesian in informal conversation (Sneddon 2003b: 521).

As it is typical for diglossia (see Mesthrie 2009), the 'high' variety, Standard Indonesian, has no native speakers, but children raised with Indonesian are raised with the low variety (Sneddon 2003b: 523).

Despite every effort dedicated to the standardization of Indonesian, even Standard Indonesian is not as standardized as one might expect. On the one hand, we find the prescriptive version of Indonesian developed and promoted by the language department (*pusat bahasa*). This language, however, is sometimes so

---

5 This institution is still active today.

aloof that it might not be spoken anywhere, perhaps not even by the people in that department. Often it is limited to the books published about Standard Indonesian. On the other hand, there is the Standard Indonesian attested and actually in wide use by politicians, schools, and formalized public life (administration, court, etc.) This variety is the Indonesian that we will mostly concern ourselves with throughout this work. Since Standard Indonesian is limited to formal situations, no child is raised with that language. In the event that no regional language is spoken at home, parents will use some kind of colloquial Indonesian (Sneddon 2003b: 523). Although colloquial Indonesian is normally strongly influenced by regional languages, in the last decades, a highly prestigious colloquial Indonesian has emerged, the so-called Jakarta Indonesian (Sneddon 2003a: 154–156, see also Sneddon 2003b, Mahdi 1981, Oetomo 1990). This variety is now considered the standard colloquial Indonesian and is also partly promoted in the mass media. It is, therefore, spoken not only in Jakarta but also in other urban areas of Indonesia (Anwar 1980: 154), e.g., in Bandar Lampung, where I conducted my case study. This variety is the second one I will refer to in this work. In general, Standard Indonesian and Standard Colloquial Indonesian are comparable in structure. The main differences are (a) reduced morphology, (b) different vocabulary (often borrowed from other languages), and (c) more freedom in word order in Standard Colloquial Indonesian (see also Sneddon 2003b: 529).

The main differences in morphology are the exchange of the transitive markers *-i* (GOAL-object) and *-kan* (THEME-object) with the Balinese borrowing *-in* (Sneddon 2003b: 529), used for both, the shortening of the *meN*-prefix to an *N*-prefix, comparable to Javanese, and last but not least, a trend of affix omission. If Standard Indonesian with all affixes spelled out is used in informal conversation, the language is stigmatized as *bau baku* (stinks for formality). Such usage, then, is not seen as ungrammatical but only as a register violation. The second important factor is vocabulary. We find much of the so-called paired vocabulary with one form for the high and another for the low variety (Sneddon 2003b: 532). Examples are *tidak* (high variety) in contrast to *nggak* (no, not), or *besar* (high variety) and *gede* (big) (Sneddon 2003b: 532). A word list of 10 items is offered by Sneddon (2003b: 532), which still could be easily extended.

With that information, let us have a look at some examples:

(5) a. *Kita lagi (ng)omomg-in itu.* (Colloquial Indonesian)
 1P PROG CAUS.VOICE-speak-TRANS this
 'We are talking about this.'
 b. *Kita sedang mem-bicara-kan itu.* (Standard Indonesian)
 1P PROG CAUS.VOICE-speak-TH.TRANS this
 'We are talking about this.'

1.3 The context: Indonesian and English in Indonesia — 15

(6) a. *Gue udah bilang ama dia.* (Colloquial Indonesian)
    1s   ANT say   to   3s
    'I have already told him/her.'
  b. *Saya sudah ber-kata kepada dia.* (Standard Indonesian)
    1s   ANT GO.VOICE-word to 3s
    'I have already told him/her.'

Both examples show the important differences in lexis (e.g. *gue* vs. *saya* or *omong* vs. *bicara*) and in morphology (e.g., *-in* vs.*-kan*). The syntactic structure, however, is identical.

These differences provide a picture similar to Javanese with speech levels:

(7) a. *Aku wis mangan* (Javanese, Ngoko register)
    1s ANT eat
    'I have eaten.'
  b. *Kula sampun dhahar* (Javanese, Krama register)
    1s   ANT   eat
    'I have eaten.'

Since both the examples are identical in terms of structure, the differences (affixes and vocabulary) can be subsumed as PF-matters, more concrete as a matter of vocabulary insertion, namely if certain feature bundles are realized overtly or not (reduced morphology) and which vocabulary item is inserted.

Although the syntactic structures are generally identical, standard and colloquial Indonesian still show a difference when it comes to word order. However, this difference is related to information structure and the degree of freedom of how many inversions are possible. Whereas Standard Indonesian has been forced into a strict corset of SVO word order, colloquial Indonesian demonstrates much greater freedom based on focalization and topicalization marked with prosody.

(8) *Udah makan // gue.* (Javanese, Ngoko register)
    ANT eat   1s
    'I [have]$_{FOC}$ eaten.'

However, the strict word order in Standard Indonesian should ultimately be seen as a solely prescriptive rule, so not necessarily ungrammatical in the sense of the internal grammar.

Therefore, structure-wise the two languages should be (more or less) still identical. The main differences lay at PF, social pressure, and stigmatization. Since I am mainly interested in the structure, I will use both varieties throughout this work without always indicating to which variety I refer. This simplification makes sense since a clear boundary between these varieties is hard to draw (Sneddon 2003a: 123).

1.3.2 English in Indonesia

After identifying the first subject of contrast, Indonesian, we have to turn to the second subject, namely English.

English is probably the most influential language in the world. Approximately 350 million people speak it as L1, approximately 350 million people as L2,[6] and about one billion[7] people as a foreign language (Jenkins 2003: 14). It is an official language in 75 territories worldwide (Jenkins 2003: 2). Genetically it is classified as a West-Germanic language within the Indo-European language family (Simons and Fennig 2017).

Kachru (1992) divides the English-speaking world into three circles: the inner circle, the outer (extended) circle, and finally, the expanding (extending) circle. The inner circle comprises the traditional bases of English like Great Britain and Ireland, the USA and Canada, and Australia and New Zealand. These countries have a huge majority of monolingual English speakers. Countries that belong to the second circle are normally countries that have been colonialized by Great Britain or the USA. English is acknowledged as an official language in these countries though usually in a multilingual setting. Often we can find a local variety of English. Examples are Singapore, India, and Nigeria. In the expanding circle, we find countries where English has no official status, but where it is gaining influence due to its internationality. Here, we cannot find a local English variety. Speakers are norm-dependent (Jenkins 2003: 16), imitating an inner-circle country's norm.

Indonesia belongs to this third category. English has never been accepted as an official language (Lauder 2010: 17) but is seen as the 'first foreign language' (Dardjowidjojo 2003: 57 cited after Rini 2014: 26). Indonesians have an ambivalent relationship with English, a status that has been labeled as "language schizophrenia" (Lauder 2010: 13 citing Kartono 1976: 124). On the one hand, it is highly prestigious and associated with modernity (Rini 2014: 34), while on the other, it is perceived as a vehicle by which liberal values are spread (Lauder 2010: 17). Therefore language policy promotes English (international language) and Indonesian (national

---

6 Jenkins (2003) treats English as L2, where it is "an official (i.e. institutionalised) second language in fields such as government, law and education" (10), and as foreign language, when it "serves no purposes within their own country" (14).
7 This number is controversial.

language) in complementarity and not in competition (Lauder 2010: 16). English is thus seen as a tool (Indonesian: *alat*) (see, e.g., Lauder: 13; Rini 2014: 28; Agustin 2015: 358) serving in the fields of international communication, technology, and science (Agustin 2015: 358).

English is compulsory throughout education due to its status as the first foreign language. However, in general, educators do not seem to be content with teaching success (see Lauder 2010; Marcellino 2015). The problems attested in TEFL in Indonesia are numerous. The major issues are low priority (Dardjowidjojo 2003: 57 cited after [Rini 2014: 28]), erroneous material (Lauder 2010: 17), and the lack of teacher proficiency (Marcellino 2015: 64). Consequently, there is an ongoing debate on how to improve teaching English in Indonesian, which also involves the question of which variety should be chosen. Although personally non-aligned as to what kind of English would best suit Indonesian purposes, it is necessary to describe the status quo. Normally British or American English is seen as the standard for teaching (Lauder 2010). Some programs initiated by the Australian government also involve Australian English. Nevertheless, this variety is not seen as prestigious as British or American English (Lauder 2010). Rini (2014: 27) follows a more pragmatic approach, claiming that most Indonesians learn American English since this is the English they are exposed to in movies or music. Unlike in Singapore, Malaysia, or the Philippines, there is no Indonesian English variety (Lauder 2010: 15). There is not even a significant community of English speakers in Indonesia (Rini 2014: 27).

In spite of that, there is a tendency to mix English words into Indonesian. In particular young people follow this trend (Sneddon 2003a: 185). Whereas a lot of positive code-mixing can be observed due to advances in technology, there is also negative code-mixing by using English terms to display one's familiarity with English or, as Lowenberg points it, "to foreground a modern identity" (Lowenberg 1991: 136) since it is regarded as highly prestigious. However, this code-mixing is only superficial concerning vocabulary insertion; however, it remains Indonesian (Rini 2014: 33).

In summary, English in Indonesia enjoys the status of a prestigious foreign language learned at institutions while not normally playing a role in daily conversation or formal situations.

1.4 Outline of this work

As already outlined shortly further above, the following work consists of four chapters plus an introduction and a conclusion. The four chapters (here chapters 2–5) form a built-up heading towards chapter 5, the empirical study.

The second chapter presents the theoretical framework used in this work exemplified for English standard clauses.

The third chapter provides a more detailed description of Indonesian. After a few general observations on the omission of morphology in Indonesian, the description proceeds along the lines of the three important layers of a clause: v (for Indonesian voice), T, and C. The initial section concerns the voice layer. First, the distribution of the four overt voice-markers *ter-*, *ber-*, *meN-* and *di-* is addressed before integrating this into the framework described in the second chapter with a θ, a Cat-head (either Stat[e] or Ev[ent]) and the δ-head, the voice-head. Next, this idea will be projected onto nominal morphology and the general structure of NPs and DPs, respectively. After this excursus, we will turn our attention to the T-layer, introducing Indonesian TAM-markers. It will be argued that we find a continuum of a grammaticalization process from stative verbs to non-verbal finite T-auxiliaries indicating relative tense (anterior, simultaneous, and posterior). In the last section, we will focus on the C-layer, focusing on the notion of topic related to Spec-CP, and focus, as a consequence on T-to-C-movement. This general description of the Indonesian language should be understood as a helpful tool for readers not familiar with Indonesian. In addition, the topic of non-verbal predicates itself requires such a strong foundation. As the topic concerns such a fundamental concept as predication, it concerns most of the general structure.

Based on this strong foundation, the fourth chapter deals with a detailed contrastive description of non-verbal predicates in English and Indonesian. In English, the group of non-verbal predicates corresponds to predicational copular clauses. Here, the copula *be* is inserted to compensate for the non-verbality of the predicate. We will see that non-eventive predicates are equivalent to non-verbal predicates in English. Since the event feature is the decisive feature for the verbal category in English, this feature is selected by v and the verbal feature v by T. Since non-eventive predicates do not have an event feature, the copula is required to make up for this missing feature and therefore the Ev- and the v-layer.

In contrast to that very homogenous group in English, for Indonesian, there are three different strategies: the *no-copula*-type for "adjectives," the *ada*-type for PPs, and finally, the *adalah*-type for nominal predicates. Whereas the no-copula-type does not have a copula position at all, the *ada*-type has a verbal copula *ada* in Ev and voice. The *adalah*-type has a non-verbal copula *adalah* realized in T. However, *adalah* is not a full T-auxiliary but rather a PF operation to avoid ambiguity. Both *ada* and *adalah* are optional and can be left out. Thus, this third chapter combines a discussion of the predication structure of non-verbal predicates and the copulas required for these predication structures. Since the main research question of this work is if and how structural differences in English and Indonesian non-verbal predicates affect the Indonesian learner of English, this description is the prerequisite for the empirical study presented in chapter 5.

This empirical study then will deals with the main research question here, if and how structural differences in non-verbal predicates in English and Indonesian influence L2-acquisition of English non-verbal predicates for Indonesian learners of English. The case study was conducted in March 2018 in Bandar Lampung. In this case study (run at a high school and two universities), the participants tested their perception of English non-verbal predicates with an omitted copula. These erroneous patterns in English were tested for grammatical acceptability by Indonesian learners of English. The test was split into two major parts, the category of the non-verbal predicate (adjectives, PPs, and nominal forms) and the influence of adverbs. The main findings were that ungrammatical English sentences involving predicates realized with the no-copula strategy in Indonesian were more often rated as grammatical by the Indonesian learner of English than any other non-verbal category. Certain adverbs in the second position (between subject and predicate) affect acceptability. All these effects are exactly where we can find a structural difference in the underlying structure of the English sentence in question and its Indonesian counterpart. The main reason is the non-availability of a copula-position in the Indonesian representation for the structures in question. Thus, it will be shown that the structural differences do have an impact on L2 acquisition.

Finally, the findings presented in this work will be summarized and concluded in the concluding chapter.

To avoid misunderstandings and any wrong expectations, it is necessary to clarify what this work can do and, more importantly, what it cannot do.

As outlined above, this work aims to describe structural differences for non-verbal predicates in English and Indonesian and how they impact L2 English acquisition of L1 Indonesian learners. Thus, this work will not deal with any factor outside of these structural differences.

Although this work uses the concept of second language acquisition in a quite broad sense, the experiment was conducted in a quite narrow setting. All the participants in the experiment fit an EFL setting, such as they acquired/learned English in the institutionalized setting school. Therefore, this work cannot and will not say anything about L2 English acquisition by L1 Indonesian speakers outside of Indonesia. Additionally, this work deals with adult L2 acquisition, ergo, after the critical period. Consequently, it will say nothing about child L2 acquisition.

Another limitation of this work is that it has nothing to say about the timing of language acquisition. The experiment in chapter 5 is just a snap-shot. Thus, the work can only provide some answers to the questions if and where we find competition but not when in the acquisition process.

2 The theoretical framework

First-semester students often come to university expecting that they will learn certitudes approaching the status of "the truth". In the course of their studies, they will realize that scientific work cannot provide something like the ultimate truth. It can only endeavour to discover suitable explanations for observed data (hypothesis and theories). All such explanations have to be based on (initial) assumptions. Therefore, during her further studies, the student has to find the personal truth, the framework, and the worldview. With this observation in mind, the goal of the following section is to describe my linguistic worldview, the framework I work in, the assumptions I make, and which I take for granted for the rest of the work.

From a broad perspective, this work is grounded in Chomsky's (1957; 1968; 1993; 1995) framework of generative grammar, with a computational device (syntax) at its core that combines items from the lexicon (more about that later on) and gives this information to the interfaces LF (logical form) and PF (phonological from) which are then processed by modules independent of syntax, namely the sensory-motor-system (phonology) and conceptual-intentional system. Therefore, I follow, in general, the so-called Y-model (Figure 1, here, the Y is upside down):

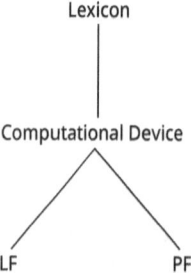

Figure 1: Y-Model.

At the beginning of the derivation is the lexicon, a concept that has been widely discussed and interpreted variously. Two major directions have emerged during the years: a lexicalist approach and a constructivist approach. In lexicalism, the burden of information is stored in the lexicon. In constructivism, the burden is given to computation. This work is on the constructivist end of the spectrum.

With regard to Distributed Morphology (DM) (see Halle and Marantz 1993, Halle and Marantz 1994, Harley and Noyer 1999), this work assumes a split of the traditional lexicon into three sets: the set of morphemes,[8] the vocabulary, and the encyclopedia. The set of morphemes comprises the material relevant for the computation. These morphemes can be divided into l(exical)-morphemes (from now on roots) and f-morphemes (from now on functional heads) (Harley and Noyer 1999: 6). Roots are abstract forms linked to a sound pattern in the vocabulary set and a meaning in the encyclopedia set. Functional heads are morphosyntactic feature bundles.

The vocabulary contains information about the PF-realization of roots and f-morphemes and, of course, of the combination of both. The encyclopedia is related to LF and meaning. Here, concepts linked with, e.g., the roots, are stored.

With Marantz, this work assumes late insertion, meaning that syntax only deals with functional heads (morphosyntactic features) and roots. Syntax has no access to the vocabulary and the encyclopedia, so there is no access to phonological or logical features. Therefore, whenever the term lexicon is used in the remainder of this work, it refers to the set of morphemes (roots and functional heads) available to syntax.

Roots, in contrast to a lexical item in lexicalist approaches (amongst others Grimshaw 1990, Levin and Hovav 1995), do not have any information on word classes, argument structure, etc., but all this information is derived by the same three operations like the rest of the derivation; move, merge and adjoin. A differentiation between l-syntax and phrase-syntax (s-syntax) (Hale and Keyser 1998) is therefore not necessary (Harley and Noyer 1999).

2.1 Basic concepts: Items and operations

Basically, we need two items, roots and functional heads, and the three operations of move, merge, and adjoin to generate the whole syntactic derivation. In sum, then, before proceeding further, it will be necessary to define these five basic concepts:

Merge

Merge is one of the three basic operations that can combine two elements. It is understood as combining (merging) the derivation with another item either from the lexicon (root or functional head) or a phrase generated separately. Merge is driven by feature selection.

---

[8] I will refer to the set of morphemes as lexicon some time.

Move

Move, or internal merge, is similar to merge, the crucial difference being that the merged element is taken from the derivation itself. The Copy-Theory of Movement (see Chomsky 1993) is assumed for this operation. Here the "moved" item is copied, then pasted (merged) into the new position. Normally, only the last copy is assigned phonological features at vocabulary insertion. Since lower copies can be phonologically realized as well (Bošković and Nunes 2007), they cannot be treated as traces. Therefore every copy is syntactically available; however not overt at spell-out. Therefore, movement is not indicated with arrows but simply by copying the element in a higher position and deletion shown by strikethrough.

According to the Chain Uniformity Condition (Chomsky 1995: 253), movement is only possible in a position with the same projection level. So we have to distinguish between head movement (from head-to-head) (see Travis 1984) and phrasal movement (from specifier to specifier). The possibility that, in the end, both movements could be seen as only one type of movement is of no importance for the purposes of this work. Like merge, movement is triggered by uninterpretable features, which must be checked during the derivation (before spell-out) since LF cannot interpret them.

Head-Movement (Travis 1984) is the movement of one head to another head position. After merging these two heads, the result is a complex or derived head (9).

(9)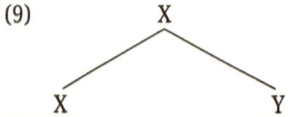

With Matushansky (2006: 95), I assume this head adjoining is interwoven with spell-out. Hence, the derived head is given to spell out (Matushansky assumes a morphological operation). After that, syntax cannot access the constituents inside this complex head, namely Y and its sister X. The only part still accessible to syntax is the highest X. Consequently, syntax will treat it as a head. This inability is also true for the root merged with a functional head, although movement has not been involved yet. Head Movement underlies the Head Movement Constraint (Travis 1984), which states that no head can be skipped.

Phrase Movement is the movement of a phrase to a specifier position. An uninterpretable feature triggers this operation as well. Although only the head of the moved phrase is triggered initially not to violate the Chain Uniformity Condition, the rest of the phrase is pied-piped (Ross 1967) to move the whole phrase. Phrase Movement underlies the concept of locality, so the head that triggers movement

(X) has to attract the closest fitting phrase into its specifier position (Spec-XP) (see Shortest Attract, Richards 2001: 46).

The driving force for the internal and external merge is features. The newly merged head bears an uninterpretable feature. This uninterpretable feature bears no information for the interpretation and cannot be given to Spell-Out. Therefore it has to be checked in the derivation. In order to be checked, it has to agree with an interpretable feature in the derivation (see, e.g., Adger 2003: 71). Although the standard direction of agree is downwards, there is also the possibility of reverse agree (see, e.g., Haegeman and Lohndal 2010; Merchant 2011; Wurmbrand 2012) when the probing direction is upwards. Here an uninterpretable feature is checked by a feature appearing later in the derivation.

Adjoin

The third operation possible is 'adjoin' (see Adger 2003: 89). Adjoin looks similar to merge. However, there are important differences. Adjoin is not driven by uninterpretable features, nor is it even related to projecting heads. In adjoin, a maximal projection (YP) is added (adjoined) to another maximal projection (XP) without changing the status of the latter since the outcome is itself an XP. The XP before and after adjoin has the same distributional behaviour. This operation, therefore, only extends a phrase. The added/adjoined phrase (YP) is called adjunct. Adjuncts provide additional information and are not required by argument structure based on feature checking with a head. In contrast to specifiers, it is possible to have more than one adjunct.

Roots

In contrast to functional heads, roots do not project. They can merge with a functional head employing head-adjoining, similar to the merge assumed in head-movement (see Travis 1984), and are treated as non-projecting heads.

The root is merged with a functional head, here F, to build a head, namely F (10).

(10)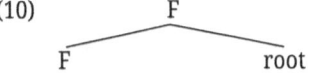
   F   root

Functional heads

With Rothstein (1983) and Heycock (1994), I see functional heads as one-place-functions that assign one special function (theta-role, structural function, pragmatic role) to their specifier. This function is assigned in the specifier position, whereas the complement is only the former derivation merged with the functional head. Therefore I assume the following basic structure (11):[9]

(11)
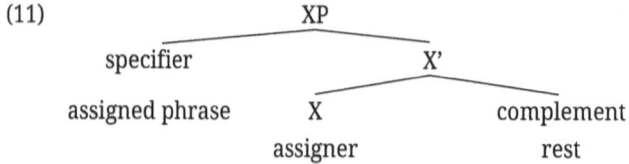

Since merge is triggered by uninterpretable features in the head that have to be checked, the X'-structure requires the X-head to have two uninterpretable features in order to be able to merge twice. However, the nature of these two features is different. The first uninterpretable feature is a subcategorization feature that has to be checked under sisterhood (see the discussion in Collins (2002: 50), see also Chomsky [2000]). Every functional head must have a subcategorization feature, which must be merged first (see also Collins's idea of locality), a process in which no theta-role, syntactic function, etc., can be assigned. This assignment can take place in a second step, if such a feature is available, in the specifier. As a result, the phrase merged into the specifier position is given an interpretable feature relevant to the interpretation, e.g., subject status in Spec-TP. Whereas the first step is required for every functional head, the assignment step is only necessary if a particular 'role' is assigned to an argument.

2.2 Derivation

Following the general outline above of the most basic operations and items, presenting how these elements can be put together is necessary. As we have seen above, we have non-projecting heads (roots) that have to be merged with a functional head. As all functional heads are one-place-functions, they take one argument in their specifier position. From this, a valid question arises, namely, with which func-

---

9 Although these structures should be understood as bare (see Chomsky 1995), still the X-Bar-notation (Chomsky 1968) is used for a more convenient presentation.

tional head should we merge the root first? In formal semantics, all "lexical" categories (nouns, verbs, adjectives, and some prepositions) are treated as functions and, therefore, as predicates. Accordingly, we should start with the predication. In this formal concept of the predicate, the predicate as a function requires certain arguments. These arguments must have one and only one theta-role (see Chomsky 1993: 36) and may have one syntactic function (subject, object). Whereas the syntactic function is only assigned by verbal predicates, adjectives (Meltzer-Asscher 2011), prepositions,[10] undoubted verbs, and even (certain) nominal forms assign theta-roles to their arguments.

Additionally, theta-roles remain stable for a predicate, whereas subject-assignment, for example, can alternate due to voice. Therefore, the theta-role assignment should be more basic (earlier in the derivation) than the assignment of syntactic functions (at least theta-role assignment for the internal argument). However, is theta-assignment a syntactic primitive? Despite the ongoing debate about the number and definition of certain thematic roles, rather abstract theta-roles[11] play a crucial role for several morphosyntactic processes. Amongst others we find applicative structures that promote certain theta-marked phrases to argument status, e.g. German *be-* with a GOAL/LOCATION-role, case-marking (accusative vs. dative) in intransitive verbs along the lines of theta-roles (THEME vs. GOAL), transitivity markers specified for theta-roles (Indonesian: *mengajari* 'to teach somebody (something)' vs. *mengajarkan* 'to teach something (to somebody)') and last but not least voice alternations like in Malagasy[12] (12):

(12) a. AGENT-Trigger
         M-an-sasa ny   lamba   amin 'ny savony   ny   zazavavy.
         AT-wash   the clothes with the soap   the girl
         'The girl washes the clothes with the soap.'
         (Guilfoyle et al. 1992: 380)
     b. THEME-Trigger
         Sasa-na   ny   zazavavy amin 'ny savony   ny   lamba.
         wash-TT   the girl   with the soap   the clothes
         'The clothes were washed with soap by the girl.'
         (Guilfoyle et al. 1992: 380)

---

10 At least if it is treated as a lexical category.
11 Carnie (2007: 220) argues for a differentiation between thematic relations and theta-roles. Whereas an argument can have certain thematic relations it can only bear one abstract theta-role. As a consequence one abstract theta-role can also have different specifications for their thematic relations.
12 The verb form corresponds to the thematic role of the subject which is realized clause-final.

c. INSTRUMENT-Trigger
An-sasa-na   ny   zazavavy   ny   lamba   ny   savony.
IT-wash   the   girl   the   clothes   the   soap.
(Guilfoyle et al. 1992: 381)

Such agreement processes could be best described with features. As a consequence, the constituents which are triggered due to their theta-feature must have acquired this feature somewhere during the derivation. Therefore, theta-assignment is assumed to be done by a special functional head, θ. This θ-head is normally the functional head involved in the very first merge of a derivation.

Before we examine the derivation, a few words about thematic roles are in order. The number of thematic roles has been a matter of wide debate. Although most scholars agree on a number of 5–15 roles (AGENT, THEME, PATIENT, GOAL, RECIPIENT, SOURCE, EXPERIENCER, etc.), there is neither a basic set agreed on nor any agreement concerning the definition of certain categories. With, among others, Dowty (1991) and Foley and van Valin (1985), here two proto-categories are assumed. This work will adopt Reinhart's (2003) feature system of c(ausation) and m(ental state). With these two features, Reinhart categorizes most of the thematic roles like AGENT [+c +m], INSTRUMENT [+c −m], etc. The feature clusters are divided into three classes: the [-]clusters, the [+] clusters, and the mixed clusters (Reinhart 2003: 256). I reduce the classes to two, namely the [-clusters] henceforth Proto-THEME and the non-[-clusters] henceforth Proto-CAUSE. These proto-roles represent an abstract theta-role (see Carnie 2007) and can comprise several thematic relations. Therefore, roles like GOAL, THEME, and PATIENT fall into the Proto-THEME group, whereas CAUSE, INSTRUMENT, AGENT, and EXPERIENCER fall into the Proto-CAUSE category. Whereas the classification of Proto-CAUSE is sufficient for the remainder of this work (a more detailed description is not necessary), a split within the Proto-THEME group is of great utility (especially for the description of Indonesian). Here I make the distinction between two main subcategories, GOAL and THEME.[13] This distinction is easily motivated with ditransitive forms, which can have two objects. One object is normally assigned a THEME-(like) role and one argument a GOAL-(like) role. However, it is impossible for both arguments to have the same theta-role (GOAL-[like] or THEME-[like]). If a nominative-accusative case system is applied, the THEME-(like) argument is assigned accusative case and the GOAL-(like) argument dative case (if available). Harley (1995) proposed to decompose verb forms into three basic forms, namely CAUSE, BE and HAVE. Whereas CAUSE and BE are realized in Harley's Event (comparable to what I will label v or voice),

---

[13] Concepts like BENEFICIENT and RECIPIENT would be part of the GOAL-group, whereas PATIENT part of the THEME-group.

HAVE[14] is a preposition[15] (Harley 1995: 107) and realized as base (Harley 1995: 111). As a consequence, *give* could be decomposed into CAUSE+HAVE (Harley 1995: 110). The alternation of CAUSE and BE goes hand in hand with argument selection, the external argument for CAUSE and the internal argument with BE (Harley 1995: 102). This argument selection can be related to theta-roles. For CAUSE we should expect that the AGENT/CAUSE is chosen, whereas for BE it would be the THEME. The last primitive HAVE can be related with the GOAL. Therefore, the AGENT/CAUSE causes what the base means the THEME **is** what the base means and the GOAL **has** what the base means. An Indonesian form like (8) could be decomposed into all three basic theta-relations.

(13) Ridwan   meng-hadiah-i   Udin   sebuah   mobil.
      Ridwan   CAUS.VOICE-gift-GOAL.TRANS Udin   CL   car
      'Ridwan gave Udin a car as a present.'

The car is what the base means, namely a gift, *Udin* has what the base means, namely a gift (in this case, the car due to the first relation), and Ridwan causes the gift. Therefore, we could generalize and connect the (proto)-roles with prototypical light verbs, namely make for CAUSE, have for GOAL, and be for THEME. Although we might not be able to explain every single instance, I consider this a helpful approximation, which will be especially relevant for the Indonesian case in the next section. Despite all its possible shortcomings and imperfections, I will apply this threefold classification (CAUSE, THEME, and GOAL[16]) throughout this work.

After dealing with the notion of thematic role in its traditional sense, it is time to introduce a further extension of this term. In this work, I assume that abstract thematic relations can be available without assigning them to arguments. I will use the term thematic relation instead of thematic role/theta-role in these cases. This distinction is especially relevant for non-verbal predicates later on.

The root head adjoins to the functional head θ that bears a specific theta-feature (THEME, GOAL, or CAUSE) and builds the derived head. The main function of a theta-assigner is, of course, to assign its theta-role to an argument. If it is the first step of the derivation, one might argue that there is no subcategorization feature involved. This assumption, however, would pose the problem that the argument would be assigned the theta-role in the complement position (14). Then, however, we would have to rule out the possibility of assigning a function to the complement later in

---

[14] Note, the 'verbal' form *have* is BE+HAVE (Harley 1995: 110)
[15] Harley (1995: 103) provides the following structural definition for a preposition: [BaseP [Y] [Base' [Base] [X]]]
[16] Interestingly these three forms are accounted for in approaches like UTAH, with the GOAL as the complement of V, the THEME in Spec-VP and the CAUSE in spec-vP (see Baker 1997).

the derivation. Additionally, there is no reason to assume that a functional head, if involved in the first merge, does not have an uninterpretable subcategorization feature, whereas all other heads do. Later in the derivation, the function assignment has to happen in the specifier position (here theta-assignment in Spec-θP, whereas the former derivation (here indicated with '...') is in the complement position (15).[17] To solve this problem, the first argument has to be merged into the complement position as 'former derivation' and then moved via roll-up-movement (see Kayne 1994) to Spec-θP to be assigned a theta-role (16). Although the roll-up movement is somewhat stipulated and therefore costly, the general gain on uniformity of the structure and, therefore in economy, outweighs the costs of this stipulation.

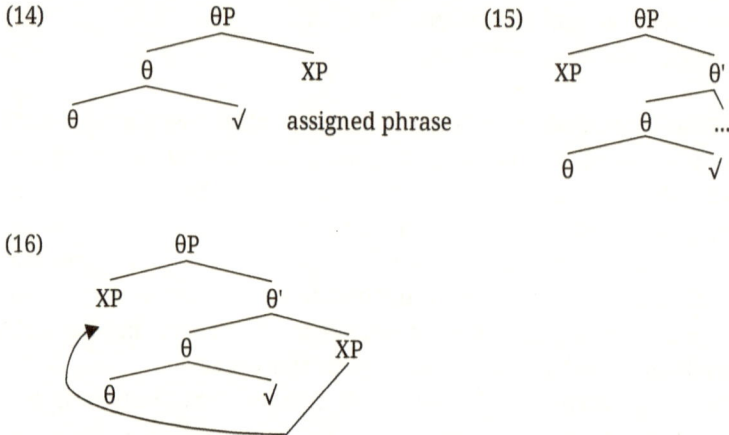

After identifying the first functional head θ, we have to continue with our derivation. Different "lexical" categories can assign thematic roles as we have seen above. But, how do we arrive at these "lexical" categories in our derivation since this is not information stored in a lexicon?

In general, "lexical" categories are based on their morphological, syntactic, and semantic properties. Since the morphological realization must be the result of either a semantic or syntactic property, the latter two are of interest here. It is often claimed that all class members describe the same referent type, so (prototypical) nouns describe individuals, and (prototypical) verbs describe events. However, such an approach is insufficient since many words would not fit into the category they are matched. For this reason, we need syntactic categories. Rauh (2010: 8) defines a syn-

---

17 I will use the structure as presented in (15) with a tentative complement most of the time, especially if only sections are represented.

tactic category as a 'set of linguistic items that can occupy the same positions in the structures of the sentences of a given language.' Whereas this extensional definition (Rauh 2010: 8) only identifies members of a certain category, in a second step, we need to explain what enables words/phrases to be part of a certain category (intensional definition) (Rauh 2010: 8). Every word should have a semantic category and a syntactic category. Since these categories are not seen as syntactic primitives but derived by the same mechanism as phrases are, namely merge and move, we need 'category-assigning' functional heads, one for the semantic category and one for the syntactic category. For an extensional definition, it is enough to take an abstract functional head, for an intensional definition we need to find properties/features in this functional head that actually make it class-defining. For now, we will remain agnostic about these features and just assume an abstract head. On top of the θP we merge a semantic category like event, stative or individual. I label this as Cat(egory)-head with the θ head-moving to Cat. In Spec-CatP an XP can be assigned a certain function depending on the specification of Cat itself (17).

(17)
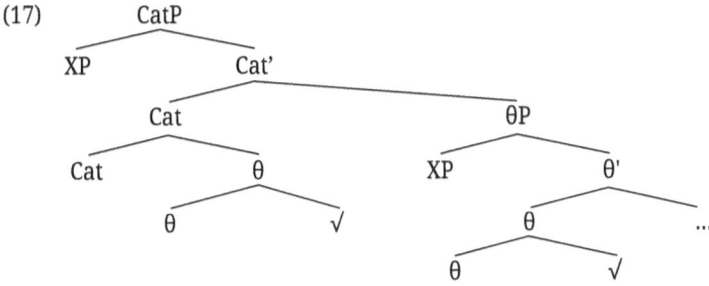

As I mentioned before, this category fits the idea of the referential argument as the referential argument denotes what a construction is about. Some linguists have even attempted to build a correlation between referential arguments and lexical categories. For example, Zwarts (1992: 59) assigns the following referential arguments to the four 'standard lexical categories' (see Table 1):

Table 1: Lexical Categories and their Referential Arguments. (see Zwarts 1992: 59)

Referential Argument	Lexical Category
E(event)	V
R(referent)	N
G(degree)	A
S(space)	P

Moreover, Zwarts (1992: 193) proposes another functional head, namely δ. This δ-head carries the referential force. This idea leaves us with two layers and, therefore, two dimensions. For the three major lexical classes, we can identify the following dimensions in Table 2 (terminology adapted from Croft 1991). The first dimension describes the relationship of the word to what it refers to in the outside world, thus a rather semantic dimension. The second dimension refers to the implementation in the linguistic expression, hence a syntactic dimension. Therefore, Cat representing the first dimension describes the semantic category, such as entity for nouns or events for verbs, and δ representing the second dimension describes the syntactic category, namely reference, modification, and predication (see Table 2)

Table 2: Syntactic Categories.

	Noun	Adjective	Verb
Semantic dimension	Entity	Property	Event
Syntactic dimension	Reference	Modification	Predication

To fit this into our notions of syntactic categories above, the δ-head defines the categorical status and thus the syntactic behaviour. On these grounds, we could say that the δ-head is the syntactic category. To conclude, Cat defines the semantic category, and δ refers to the syntactic category. Resultantly, we obtain the following abstract representation (18):

(18)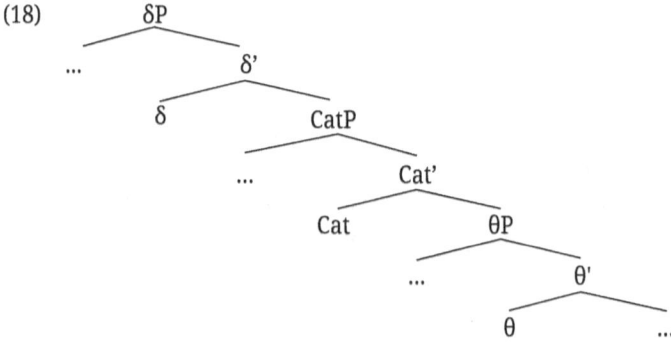

Now, it is time to flesh this abstract structure out with substance: Whereas the Cat-layer is often translated into the lexical labels N, V, A, and P, members of the δ-class are D for nouns, v^{18} for verbs, degree (Zwarts 1992) / intensifier (Napoli 1993) for

---

18 Sometimes T as well is proposed.

adjectives, and R (Zwarts 1992) / intensifier (Napoli 1993) for prepositions. In this work, I will adopt and adapt this system. Since the syntactic category is rather defined by the δ-head than by the semantic category, I will not take the labels N, V, or A but opt for semantically oriented labels like Ev(ent) or Stat(e) instead. An exception is N, which I will use for the category indicating individuals. For the δ-class, I choose the labels D(eterminer) for nouns, little v (Marantz 1997 comparable to Kratzer's (1996) voice, Harley's Event (1995) or Bowers' (1993) Pred) for verbs, and Mod(ifier) for adjectives. DP refers to referents/arguments, ModP to modifiers, and vP to predicates. We now have our building blocks, and we can start putting these together.

Let us take an example, namely, the root *fall*. *Fall* is merged with the theta-assigning head and assigns the THEME-role to its specifier; let us assume John. Next, *fall* head-moves into Cat, in this case with an event feature, so Ev. Thus, it is understood as an event. We now come to the crucial point δ, where we can have a v, a D, or a Mod-head. When we merge v, the form becomes the main predicate of the clause, and the argument is moved into Spec-vP, the pivot of the clause, which can move into Spec-TP later on to receive the subject status.

(19)
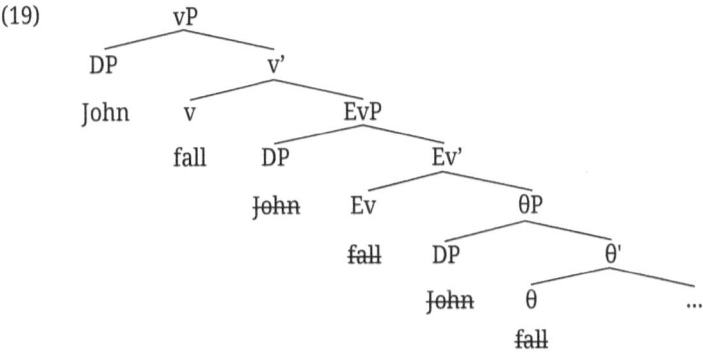

When we merge D, e.g., the definite article *the*, we get a form like *the fall* (20) or *the falling* (depending on aspectual features taken during the derivation). In this case, the argument in Spec-θP would, of course, be abstract and not realized. The initial argument could be realized in Spec-DP in a case like *John's falling* or *John's fall* (21). Although these forms still describe an event and not an individual or an entity, they are not predicates but referents.

(20)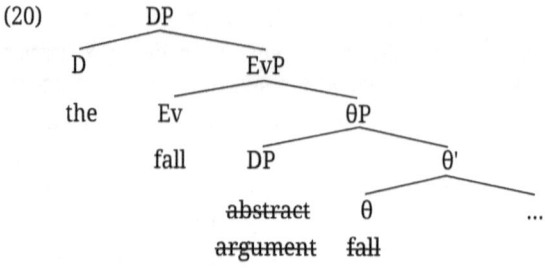

(21)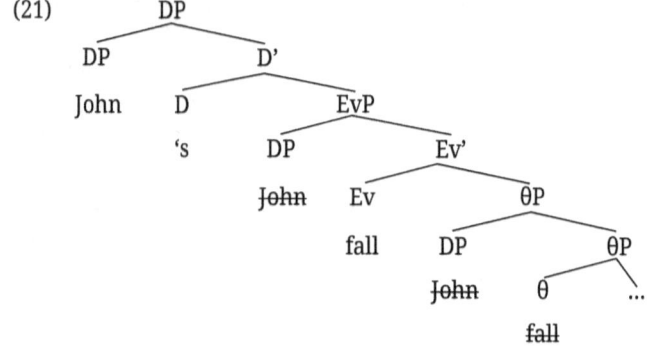

In the last case, we merge Mod, an abstract category assumed for adjectives, and get a form like *falling* in *the falling man*. While this form is still eventive in notional terms, it is not a predication but a modification. The argument introduced in Spec-θP is abstract as well.

(22)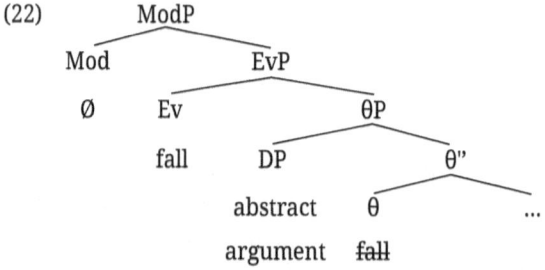

A further important characteristic of the δ-layer is phasehood. With Chomsky (1999, 2008), I assume the computation to be based on phases. At the end of each phase, the derivation is given to Spell-out. Subsequent to the transfer, the computation has no access to the information computed in a lower phase (Phase Impenetrability Condition). The only elements still available for further operations are the phase-end specifier and the head.

The most important phase heads in Chomsky's original approach are C, concluding the domain of Rizzis's (1997) left periphery (we will talk about the C-layer shortly further below), and v, the head indicating a full argument structure. Another phrase that is assigned phasehood is D(P) (for an overview, see Citko 2014). I will adopt this view and add the Mod-head in particular and the δ-head in general.

So far, we have restricted our examination to argument structures with one argument. But, how can we account for two-place predicates? The first group that has to be considered is that of transitive forms. Here, the first (internal) argument must be assigned a special status, traditionally called object. Therefore, I assume the doubling of the general structure of [δP[CatP[θP]]].

(23)

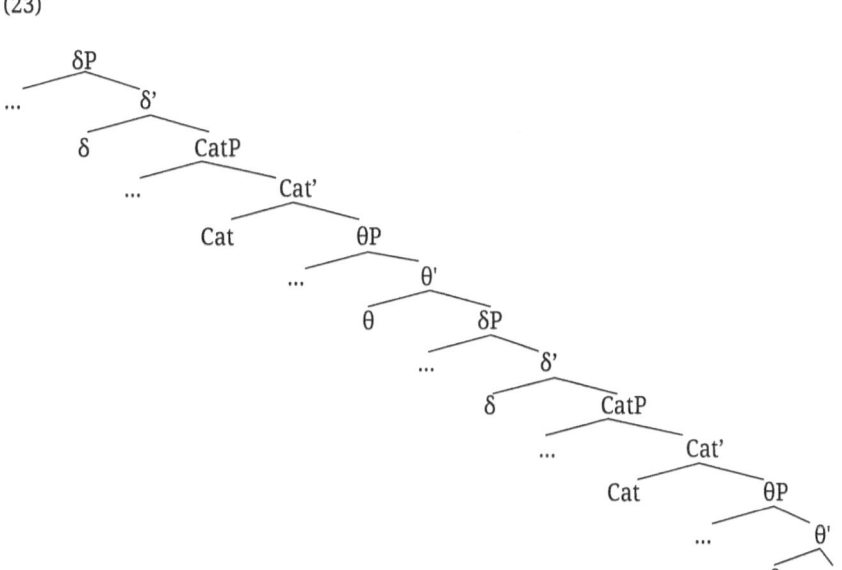

Semantically, a prototypical transitive form like 'hit' is built by causation and a result (cause to be). Whereas the outer argument (higher base-generated) is the CAUSE, the inner argument (lower base-generated) is affected by the result, so the (proto)-THEME. We start with the first θP, where the root 'hit' is merged into the θ-head, and the first argument is merged into Spec-θP, where it is assigned the THEME role. The inner argument should be categorized as a state rather than an event. In general, transitive structures never comprise two events.[19] Whenever we have two events in one clause, we need the light verb 'make' as in (24).

---

[19] In general it is not possible to merge a root twice into the same head, here Ev.

(24) *John makes his mother laugh.*

Here, both the causation as well as the result are events. First, *laugh* merges into the first θ-head and takes *his mother* as its argument in Spec- θP. After that, *laugh* moves via Ev (as Cat) to v (as δ), whereas its argument, *his mother*, moves to Spec-vP via Spec-EvP. This δP is the complement of the higher θ-head. In the higher θ-head, we merge *make* and John into Spec- θP. *Make* moves again via Ev (as Cat) to v (as δ). John is moved stepwise to Spec-vP.

(25)

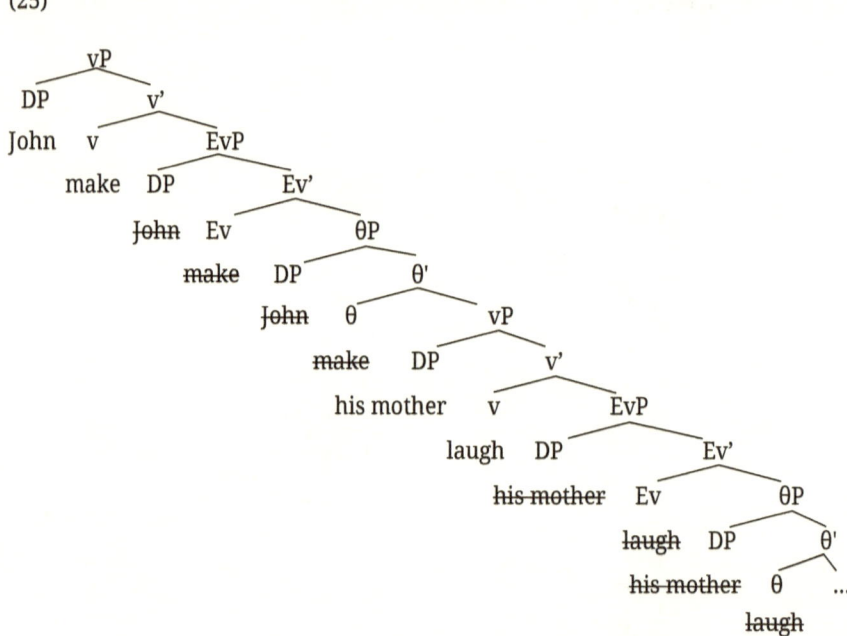

In our transitive structure, the result always represents a state. Hence, we merge Stat on top of θP. After merging this category head, we need the δP. Here, I make use of Bowers' (2002) TransP. This Trans-head selects the StatP (it cannot take an EvP) and bears an uninterpretable CAUSE-feature, which must be checked via reverse agree by the second θP.

(26)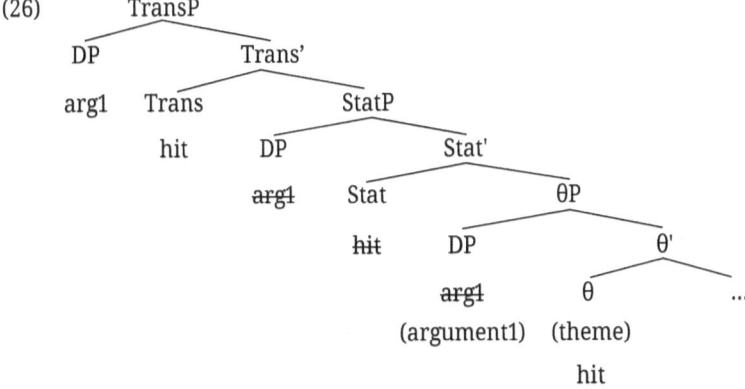

In Spec-TransP, the argument is assigned what has traditionally been called object status. In this work, however, I assume a more neutral term like "secondary pivot" since the argument in Spec-TransP can become the subject via movement to Spec-TP in a passive clause. Although we traditionally say that the object is promoted to the subject position in passive structures, when promoted, the subject is no longer the object. However, if the argument attains object status in Trans-TP and then subject status in Spec-TP, it would have both statuses concurrently. Therefore, I use a more neutral term like secondary pivot. As a consequence of the general phasehood of δP, we need to assume the phasehood of TransP as well.

On top of TransP, we merge the second θP, with the root moving further into θ and the second argument merging into Spec-θP. In this position, the CAUSE role is assigned. The theta-head specified for CAUSE can only be selected by Ev(ent). Since merging a Stat-head for a second time would be ungrammatical, the Ev-head need not be semantically motivated but can also be syntactically motivated (feature checking). Therefore, all transitive forms necessarily have Ev as the second Cat-head and are at least syntactically eventive. EvP is selected by v, and the whole argument structure becomes the predicate (27). Case-assignment is merely seen as PF-matter and therefore not relevant for the syntactic derivation.

(27)

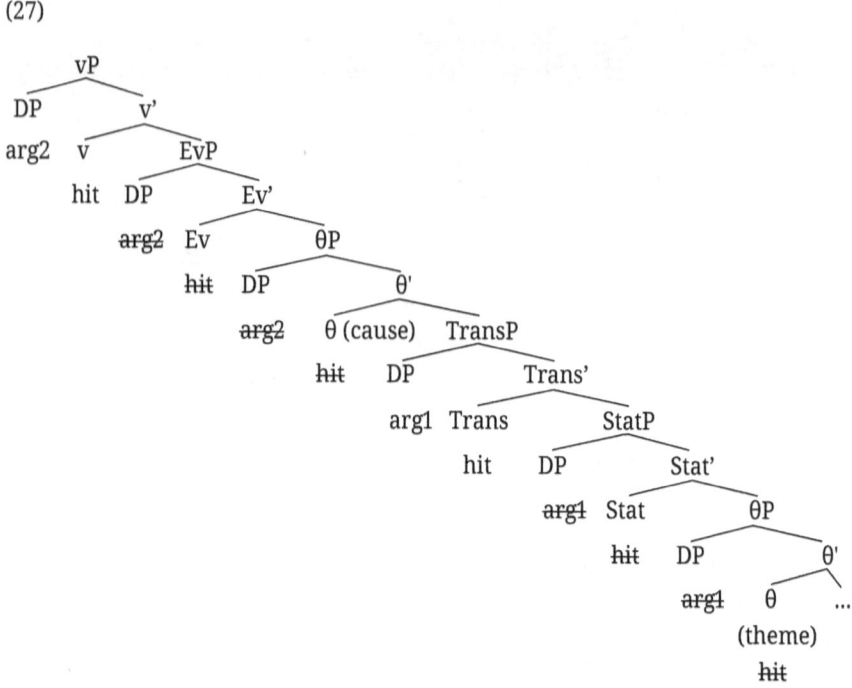

Besides transitive structures like those indicated above, more two-place-predicates are not transitive. These two-place predicates do not assign a secondary pivot/object status and consequently do not allow passivation. One group is unaccusative telic verbs with a PP-complement like *go*. Here we assume the same double-argument structure as above, but with two main differences in the first δ-head. On the one hand, this δ-head (in contrast to Trans in transitive structures) does not trigger the first argument to move into Spec-δP. Therefore the first argument has complement status in a rhematic sense as in Ramchand (2008). On the other hand, this δ does not have an uninterpretable [CAUSE]-feature but an uninterpretable [THEME]-feature. Thus, the higher θ assigns a THEME-role to its specifier, while the lower theta-role assigned in this derivation is GOAL or something comparable. Hence, the Ev-head must be semantically motivated, which fits the class of unaccusative telic verbs, all of which denote an event. The preposition is only a PF-matter similar to case-realization and not part of the syntactic derivation. Although the δ-head described here is different from the transitive Trans, the label Trans is still used due to the lack of a useful alternative.

(28)

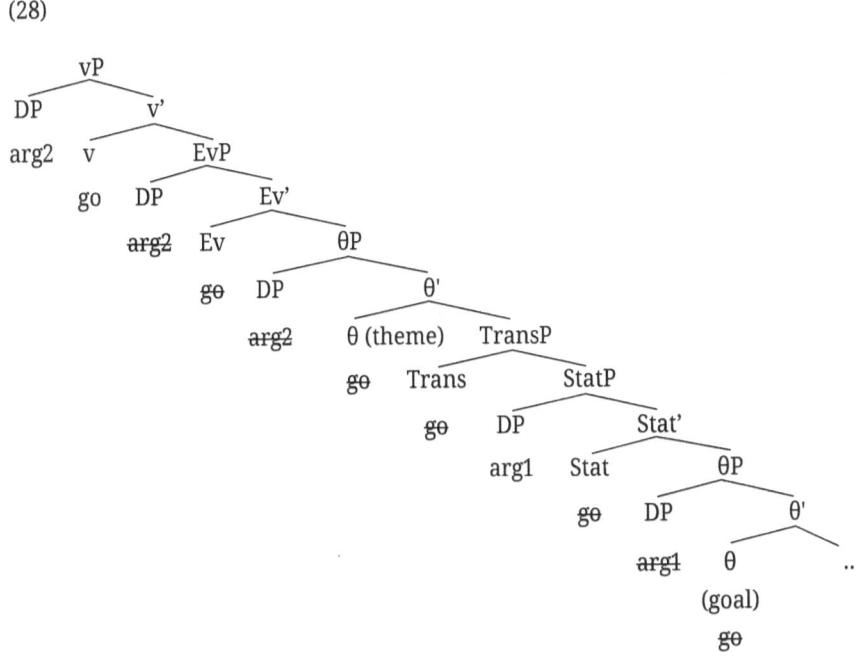

The last group of two-place-predicates is non-verbal two-place predicates. Although we will deal with non-verbal forms in more depth in the coming chapters, it is necessary first to deal with the most important group of non-verbal two-place-predicates, namely prepositions.

Often prepositions are divided into two groups, namely lexical and grammatical prepositions (see, for instance, Rauh 1995, 1996, 2015, van Riemsdijk 1990). Whereas I treat grammatical prepositions as found in the unaccusative telic forms we have discussed before as PF-matter similar to case-assignment, lexical prepositions function as predicates themselves. Concerning the theta-role pattern, lexical prepositions resemble unaccusative telic verbs. The first argument is assigned a GOAL role (or comparable), and the second argument is a proto-THEME role. The difference between prepositions and telic unaccusatives is the referential argument. Whereas prepositions describe relations (and therefore in the broadest sense states), telic unaccusatives describe events. This difference however has a far reaching consequence for the derivation; it is impossible for prepositions to be merged into the higher Cat- and consequently the second δ-layer. Since prepositions are neither semantically eventive nor have a CAUSE-role as external theta-role, merging Ev is impossible. To merge Stat for a second time with the identical head merged into it, namely the preposition, is impossible due to theory internal considerations. Therefore, a preposition cannot continue the derivation after the second theta-role. In order to get the EvP and consequently the v-layer, we need the help of the copula, something that we will talk about in more detail in the fourth chapter. Prepositions, then, are transitive structures that are cut off, after the second theta-role and need the help of the copula for the higher Cat and δ-layer.

(29)

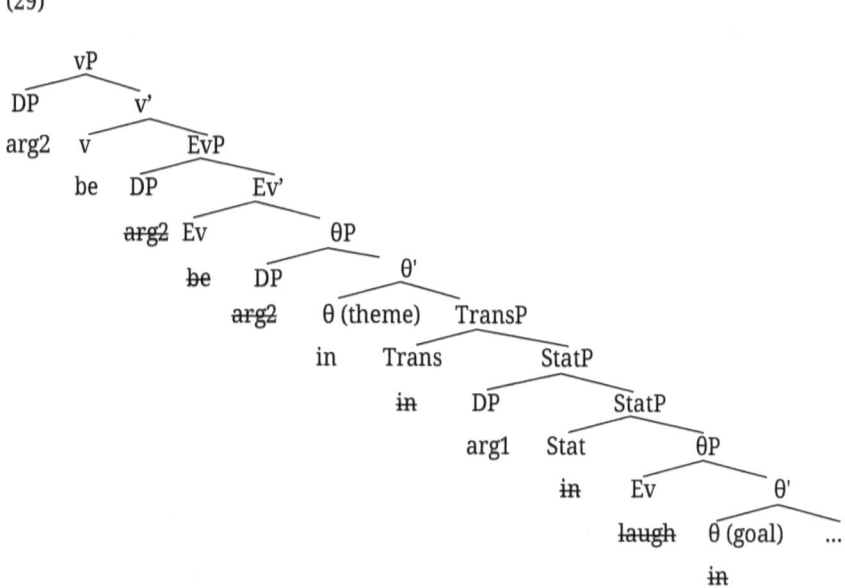

Having clarified the basic operations and the basic elements and taking a closer look at argument structure and syntactic categories, it is now time to turn our attention to the bigger picture, the standard structure of a clause.

A clause generally consists of three domains/layers: the v-layer, the T- or I-layer, and the C-layer. Whereas the v-layer is concerned with argument structure, the T- or I-layer is concerned with placing a proposition into time, and the C-layer deals with pragmatic roles like topic and focus.

Since we have already dealt with the v-layer in the previous section, I will proceed with the T-layer before concluding with the C-layer.

Starting with the split-INFL (former name for T)-hypothesis by Pollock (1989), T/I was no longer understood as one particular functional head but as a domain, a layer including more than one functional head. In general, tense, mood and aspect are grouped in this layer. In his cartographic approach, Cinque (1999) proposes a strict hierarchy with more than forty functional heads inside the T-layer. However, for the purpose of this paper, I assume that every language only chooses certain relevant functional heads. Consequently, functional heads that do not have an overt realization are left out for minimality reasons. In this work, I will comprise everything under the head T if a split is not necessary to understand the argumentation.

To proceed, T selects a vP as its complement, and the pivot in Spec-vP is moved into Spec-TP. This movement is caused in English by the Extended Projection Principle (EPP) (see Chomsky 1982). This principle generally states that every English sentence must have a subject, which is always realized in Spec-TP.

On top of the T-layer, the highest layer of the clause is the C-layer. Rizzi (1997) proposed a split C-layer with a topic and focus position as well as finiteness and force heads. In this work, I generally subsume all aspects of C as C. Only when necessary a distinction is provided between single functional heads inside a certain layer. C is normally of no interest for the English examples in this work. For the Indonesian examples it has more relevance. Therefore, I will deal with the Indonesian C-layer in more detail in the coming chapter.

To conclude this section on derivations, let us consider the derivation of a prototypical English clause like *John will fall*. Starting with the argument structure, the root *fall* is merged into the THEME-assigning θ-head assigning the THEME-role to its argument, here *John*. The θP is merged with the Ev-head. The v-head selects the EvP. The root *fall* moves via every head available until v. *John* moves to Spec-vP, becoming the pivot of the clause. After that, T (*will*) is merged with the vP, and *John* is moved to Spec-TP, becoming the subject. The C-head, merged with the TP, is null. In sum, the derivation can be represented as follows (30):

(30)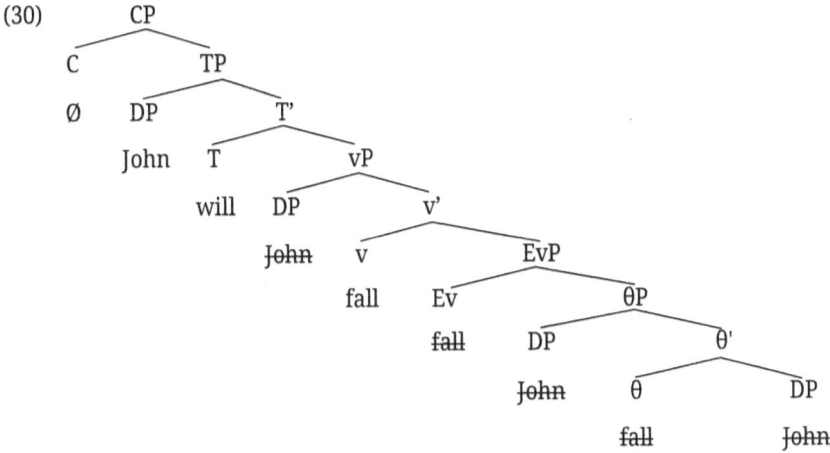

3 Generative description of Indonesian

After setting the general framework, this third chapter will provide a general outline of the Indonesian language in the framework described above. This section aims to provide a more comprehensive picture of Indonesian, especially to the reader less familiar with the structure of this language.

However, before we can discuss the structure of Indonesian, it is necessary to give some kind of preface concerning the general character of this language. Indonesian often shows a high degree of optionality since certain forms can be omitted regularly. Since optionality is highly problematic for a generative description, I will try to account for this with a general tendency to allow the omission of certain elements. Since this tendency is central to understanding the general character of Indonesian, it merits some prefatory treatment before embarking on the description of the Indonesian clause structure.

3.1 On optionality in Indonesian

It is a common misconception that Indonesian has only 'little grammar' and is therefore easy to learn. This prejudice is due to the isolating character of Indonesian with only little overt (inflectional) morphology. Functional markers, in particular, seem to be absent in this language. One important aspect is the lack of obligatoriness (see, e.g., Arka 2013: 25). Interpretation is based instead on morphosemantic features or context, which often leads to ambiguity if sentences are taken in isolation without context. Sentence (31) in Indonesian, unlike (32) in English, cannot be interpreted unambiguously for tense without further context.

(31)   *Adit   datang.*[20]
      Adit   come
      Adit came/Adit is coming/Adit comes.

(32)   Adit came.

The claim is often made that *datang* (in this example) is not specified for tense (relation between the utterance time and the topic time (see Klein 1994: 6) since it could be interpreted variously as having either future or present or past reference (31).

---

[20] The examples (31) and (33) are adapted from Arka (2013: 25).

https://doi.org/10.1515/9783110766332-003

(33) *Besok/Sekarang/Kemarin   saya   datang*
tomorrow/now/yesterday   1s   come
'Tomorrow, I will come. Now I am coming. Yesterday I came.'

Without any additional marker, no future reading is normally available. However, it still seems to be ambiguous for present or past. But, it is also obvious that an event cannot have happened in the past and happen in the present at the same time. While this isolated sentence (29) might be unspecified for tense, it can nevertheless be interpreted with respect to certain temporal relations if uttered in context (31), e.g., given by time adverbials.

What does this say about Indonesian grammar? Does Indonesian lack functional heads, e.g., for tense in the derivation? If so, how is it possible to interpret the sentences correctly at LF? My answer is that relevant functional heads are syntactically available, even if not (always) realized at PF. Dardjowidjojo (1983: 38) states that there is "a marked tendency for (us) Indonesians not to state explicitly what we feel is obvious." In prescriptive grammar, this concept is summed up under the notion of *kalimat efektiv* (efficient sentence). This concept comprises the principle of reducing redundant overt material in the sentence. A prototypical example is the omission of the subject in a subordinated clause if it is identical to the subject of the main clause (34). Another example is the omission of the complementizer *bahwa* (35).

(34) *Saya   kemarin   tidak   datang   ke   sekolah   karena   (saya)   sakit.*
1s   yesterday   NEG   come   to   school   because   1s   sick
'I didn't come to school yesterday because I was sick.'

(35) *Saya   harap   (bahwa)   dia   datang.*
1s   hope   (that)   3s   come
'I hope (that) he comes.'

In both cases, there is no grammatical constraint to have an overt subject or complementizer. Adding such elements makes the sentence merely inefficient. Dardjowidjojo (1983: 39) even goes as far as to claim that inexplicitness is a shared value in Indonesia since explicitness and frankness are "*kasar*[21]" (rough).

---

[21] The dichotomy between *halus* (fine) and *kasar* (rough) is important in Indonesian culture. It is related to one's language, one's movement etc. Whereas *halus* is seen as positive, *kasar* is rated negatively.

The question is how we can grasp such a pragmatically motivated tendency in a generative grammar model. Since the subject, for example, is available for interpretation, the information must be syntactically generated anyway. Thus, the efficiency need concerns the phonological interface. For reasons of economy, the element is given null spell-out. Since it is realized in syntax, LF has no difficulty interpreting it. We can, then, formulate the efficiency tendency as follows (34):

(36) Redundant material tends to be set on Null-Spell-Out.

The important question that needs to be answered is how to decide what material is redundant. According to Arka (2013: 25), Indonesian exploits morphosemantic and contextual information. Roots stored in the lexicon are linked to mental concepts in the encyclopedia. These concepts are highly influenced by world knowledge, of course. For some cultures, prototypical houses have attics; houses are prototypically built on poles in other cultures. In an attic culture, utterance (37) would be highly acceptable due to entailment, whereas utterance (38) would be acceptable in a pole culture. These utterances must be very surprising outside of their culturally appropriate shared knowledge (see Dardjowidjojo 1983: 50).

(37) *He built a house. The attic is very small.*

(38) *He built a house. The poles are very strong.*

This world-knowledge contains information about certain words or logic in general. This world-knowledge assigns a default interpretation. World knowledge could be seen as stored "unchangeable" knowledge, something which is taught (implicitly or explicitly) to the next generation. The second factor is contextual knowledge. This knowledge includes the information given by the situation and the information given by the conversation so far. The combination of both can be seen as providing the common ground. Stalnaker (1978: 320) describes the common ground as "common" or "mutual knowledge". The common ground is information and beliefs shared by speaker and addressee (Stalnaker 1974: 199) based on a learned worldview, a specific situation, and the information uttered so far. All information in the derivation that is already available by the common ground can be set on null spell-out. Let us consider some examples:

(39) *Udin lagi di kamar mandi.*
     Udin PROG in room bath
     'Udin is in the bathroom.'

(40) Dia   mandi.
     3s   bath
     'He is taking/takes a bath.'

The first sentence is overtly marked for progressive aspect with *lagi*. In the context of (39), the second sentence (40) has to be understood progressively as well. Since the information is shared due to the information uttered before, progressive marking is set on null spell-out.

The same principle works for information available consequent to a certain situation. In isolation, sentence (41) can only be understood as *the mother is heavy*. However, in a certain context, it can be used for *it is too heavy for the mother*, e.g., due to the weight of an older child on her lap. In isolation, we would either expect the overt voice-marking *ke-an* (42) (or a completely different sentence). However, in a given context, where the situation is available to both speaker and addressee, the voice-marking can be set to null spell-out while still being understood by the addressee.

(41) Mama   berat.
     mother heavy
     'The mother is heavy. It is too heavy for the mother.'

(42) Mama   ke-berat-an[22].
     mother PT.VOICE-heavy-TH.NOM
     'It is too heavy for the mother.'

The last example of the common ground is shared world knowledge. For two Indonesians, sentence (43) is perfectly understandable for being *anterior*, so the situation time precedes the topic time (here, by default, also the speech time) since it is shared knowledge that the first president of Indonesia passed away more than 40 years ago. In such terms, any overt material that has no additional information for the addressee's parser can or even must be left out since an overt *sudah* (44) has either an emphatic character or provides aspectual information, suggesting that the addressee might not be informed who Sukarno is and/or when he lived or when he passed away.

---

[22] The word *keberatan* can have a metaphorical meaning so the mother doesn't like it or doesn't feel comfortable about the situation.

(43) Sukarno   wafat.
    Sukarno   die
    'Sukarno died.'

(44) Sukarno   sudah   wafat.
    Sukarno   ANT   die
    'Sukarno (already) died.'

However, in a different situation, the *sudah* is required since, for example, the addressee does not yet know that an event has already taken place (45). In this example, the addressee knows that Dewi is pregnant and about to give birth but does not have any information concerning the birth. However, the fact that Dewi has given birth is not completely unexpected to the speaker.

(45) Anak-nya   Dewi   sudah   lahir.
    child-3s.POSS   Dewi   ANT   be_born.
    'Dewi's child has been born.'

But, giving too much information does not only make the sentence odd but can have a different meaning as well. Overt redundant information can make way for emphasis (46).

(46) Anak-nya   Dewi   sudah   lahir   kemarin.
    child-3s.POSS   Dewi   ANT   be_born   yesterday.
    'Dewi's child was born yesterday.'

Since *kemarin* 'yesterday' indicates that the topic time is anterior to the utterance time, *sudah* (anterior) should only indicate that the event (situation time) is anterior to yesterday (topic time), so potentially even the day before yesterday or still before that. However, this interpretation would be surprising. Another way to interpret it is to see *sudah* as an emphasis marker. If *sudah* is not related to the topic time introduced by *kemarin* (yesterday), but to the topic time introduced by discourse, here equivalent to utterance time, *kemarin* would provide the information that the birth happened the day before utterance time, and *sudah* would provide the information that the birth happened before the utterance time. Since prior to utterance time includes the day before topic time, the information provided by *kemarin* is more precise, and the information given by *sudah* is superfluous. *Sudah*, in this case, makes way for an emphatic reading as contrastive to the expectation or assumption of the addressee. (46) should be translated with the full paraphrase: "Different to your expectation or knowledge, Dewi's child was already born yesterday."

TAM-markers do not even refer to a tense or aspect relation at all. The difference between (47) and (48) is not based on aspectual information or relative tense but only shows the speaker's attitude.

(47) *Ridwan sudah 30 tahun.*
Ridwan ANT 30 year
'Ridwan is 30 already (so old).'

(48) *Ridwan baru 30 tahun.*
Ridwan REC.ANT 30 year
'Ridwan is only 30 (so young).'

Another example of avoiding redundancy is the use of classifiers. Classifiers in Indonesian have a non-generic but indefinite reading (Dardjowidjojo 1983).

For example (see Dardjowidjojo 1983: 32) in (48), the classifier is obligatory since (49) would only have the generic reading. Here, the interpretation is influenced by the appearance of the classifier, so it is required.

(48) *Se-ekor anjing meng-gonggong.*
one-CL.AN dog CAUS.VOICE-bark
'A dog is barking.'

(49) *Anjing meng-gonggong.*
dog CAUS.VOICE-bark.
'Dogs bark.'

In example (50), however, the context of *saya* (I) and *mendengar* (hear) blocks a generic reading since the speaker has to hear one certain dog or some dogs (the plural reading is not ruled out per se), although not more closely specified. Therefore, the classifier is optional and normally omitted. It might be relevant if the speaker wanted to highlight that she only hears one barking dog and not several dogs.

(50) *Saya men-dengar (se-ekor) anjing meng-gonggong*
1s CAUS.VOICE-hear (one-CL) dog CAUS.VOICE-bark
'I hear a barking dog/ I hear a dog barking.'

Consequently, Indonesian as a foreign language may be seen as easy and difficult to learn at the same time. On the one hand, the L2-learner is happy not to have to learn many different paradigms as in other languages; on the other hand, they have to grasp the cultural and world-knowledge to understand which information is redundant and which is required. Hence, every L2 learner will find herself in situations where she produced too much and situations where she produced too little.

What has to be highlighted here is that this PF process only concerns elements that are vital for the derivations, and their complete absence would lead to a crash of the derivation. In other words, even if this material is set on null-spell-out, it is still part of the derivation and, as such, relevant for the interpretation. This includes functional heads like T, D, or C, but also the subject. Hence, this PF constraint is not relevant for optional or additional information like adjuncts. In those cases, we would apply pragmatical criteria like Grice's Maxims (Grice 1975), especially the Maxim of Quantity: Only provide as much information as required. To further highlight the difference, let us consider the following sentence pairs with (51) having a (non-)overt T and (52) with an optional adjunct.

(51) Sukarno (sudah) wafat.
     Sukarno ANT   die
     'Sukarno (already) died'

(52) Sukarno wafat (40 tahun yang lalu)
     Sukarno die   40 year REL ago
     'Sukarno died (40 years ago)'

In (51), *sudah* provides information about relative tense that the event happened anterior to the topic time. As this information is obligatorily provided in T, the anterior interpretation is available in both cases, with or without overt *sudah*. With T being obligatory for the derivation, there is no chance to have no information on relative tense. Thus, it is a PF question whether to realize *sudah* or not. As the common ground, here shared world knowledge about Indonesia's first president, already provides the anterior interpretation, an overt *sudah* is unnecessary and rendered null. In (52), in contrast, the adjunct *40 tahun yang lalu* 'forty years ago' provides additional information. However, if this information is omitted, it cannot be traced back from the derivation. Thus, the information is not available for interpretation. Here, the decision on the realization of this adjunct is only based on pragmatical deliberations like Grice's Maxims. From this standpoint, we need to refine our Efficiency Tendency:

(53) Redundant material obligatory for the derivation can be given Null-Spell-Out if the information is available in the common ground.

When dealing with the obligatoriness for the derivation, another concept of importance is relevance. As Gil (2008) pointed out, all languages are vague since the linguistic tools are insufficient to express all the concepts we could perceive or imagine. Some of the information is seen as relevant, and other information is not. A speaker of a language without number marking does not wonder whether the relevant entity is a singularity or a plurality just because other languages have such categories. In the same sense, an English speaker does not wonder whether a plural form is dual or plural only because languages like Arab distinguish between them. This information is, in most cases, not relevant. And where it becomes relevant, other strategies (overt numeral) exist to make this information available (see Gil 2008: 127–129). Therefore, this efficiency tendency is only relevant for (functional) categories available in Indonesian and not all that have been generally attested in linguistics.

In this section, we have seen that Indonesian exploits a deletion strategy at PF to avoid ineffectivity and provide inexplicitness. This strategy, however, should not lead to an inflation of the structure with an endless number of empty categories but rather be utilized to explain why certain aspects of grammars (normally functional heads) are sometimes expressed overtly and sometimes set on null spell-out.

Having completed our brief prefatory digression, we will start digging into Indonesian structure in the next section.

3.2 The voice-layer

In non-cartographic generative approaches, three general layers are assumed: V-layer, I/T-layer, and the C-layer. Whereas the V-layer, or its extended form the v-layer, is relevant for the argument structure, the I/T-layer is closely linked to structural agreement, tense and/or aspect marking, and finally, the C-layer deals with pragmatic roles like topic or focus. I will adopt these three layers but relabel the lowest layer to voice[23], following Kratzer (1996).

Indonesian has a sophisticated voice system. One stem, here *baring* (lie), can be used with four different voice-markers:
(i) **ter**baring
(ii) **mem**baring*kan*[24]
(iii) **di**baring*kan*
(iv) **ber**baring

---

[23] Note that the Indonesian voice-head is different to the English v-head.
[24] The suffix *-kan* refers to a transitive structure and will be dealt with further below.

At first sight, it looks like two voice pairs, that is two active forms (*ber-* and *meN-*[25]), either intransitive (54) or transitive (55), along with two passive forms (*ter-* and *di-*), one with an AGENT (eventive) (56) and one agentless (stative) (57). In terms of thematic roles, passive constructions would have a THEME-subject and either a CAUSE-oblique or nothing. Active constructions would have a CAUSE-subject and either a complement or no complement.

(54) *Anak itu senang ber-baring di pangkuan ibu-nya.*
child DEM happy GO.VOICE-lie LOC lap mother-3S.POSS
'The child lay happily on her/his mother's lap.'

(55) *Ibu itu mem-baring-kan anak-nya yang sakit.*
mother DEM CAUS.VOICE-lie-TH.TRANS child-3S.POSS REL sick
'The mother lay down her sick child.'

(56) *Anak itu di-baring-kan ibu-nya.*
child DEM PASS-lie-TH.TRANS mother-3S.POSS
'The child was laid down by his/her mother.'

(57) *Anak itu ter-baring di rumah.*
child DEM TH.VOICE-lie LOC house
'The child lies at home.' (not necessarily voluntarily, but more likely because he/she is sick)

However, the picture is a little bit more complicated since there are intransitive *meN-*forms (58), transitive *ber-*forms (59), *ber-kan-*forms (60), and another suffix, namely *-i* (61) in contrast to *-kan* (62).

(58) *Adit me-nangis.*
Adit CAUS.VOICE-cry
'Adit cries/cried.'

(59) *Adit ber-buru rusa.*
Adit GO.VOICE-hunt deer
'Adit hunts deer.'

---

[25] The capitalised N refers to a prenasalisation process. The nasal is assimilated to the first sound of the root. For details see amongst others Sneddon 1996, Alwi et al. 2003 and Kähler 1965.

(60) *Pohon ber-tulis-kan nama-mu.*
 tree GO.VOICE-write-TH.TRANS name-2S.POSS
 'The tree has your name written on it.'

(61) *Adit di-ajar-i matematika.*
 Adit PASS-teach-GO.TRANS math
 'Adit is taught math.'

(62) *Matematika di-ajar-kan kepada Adit.*
 math PASS-teach-TH.TRANS
 'Math is taught to Adit.'

If the assumptions above were correct, why are (58) not transitive and (59) not intransitive? Why does *bertuliskan* select a GOAL-subject and not a CAUSE-subject? Why does *di-* sometimes select a THEME-subject (62) and sometimes a GOAL-subject (61)?

To solve these problems, the proposal here is that every prefix selects a different thematic role. For this reason, *meN-* and *ber-* should not be grouped in one active voice category, nor *ter-* and *di-* in one passive category, although they show a certain similarity. So voicing in our Indonesian context is understood as pivot assignment to a special theta-marked constituent[26].

3.2.1 meN-voice

Let us start with the most discussed prefix in the Indonesian language: *meN-*. In traditional descriptions, *meN-* is mainly given a clear active voice marking in contrast to the *di-*marking for passive (see Sneddon 1996 and Alwi et al. 2003). Intransitive *meN-*forms are either explained by the necessity to form a proper verb (Sneddon 1996: 61) or are seen as derivational processes of deriving verbs from non-verbal bases (see Sneddon 1996 and Alwi et al. 2003). However, this view has often been opposed on various grounds.

These non-voice-approaches to *meN-* can be split into two groups: a clitic pronoun marking and an eventive marking.

Fortin (2006) interprets *meN-* as an indefinite clitic pronoun, which is obligatory in the absence of an overt object. This interpretation, although highly interesting, shows two weaknesses. On the one hand, some grammaticality judgments

---

[26] A similar idea has been proposed with thematic agreement by Chang (1997) for Seediq.

for Indonesian sentences relevant to her argumentation may not be shared by all/ many Indonesian speakers. On the other hand, this approach only holds for transitive occurrences of *meN-*. A second homophonic prefix is assumed for intransitive forms like *menangis* (cry). It would be preferable if *meN-* could be explained in both transitive and intransitive forms with only one prefix.

The second approach is much more common. Nuriah (2004) argues for a *meN-* interpretation outside of argument structure. She assigns *meN-* an aspectual function marking eventive action. Whereas in (63), Anto opens a new store, in (64), he opens the door in the morning.

(63) *Anto buka toko.*
 Anto open shop
 'Anto opens a shop.' (a new shop)

(64) *Anto mem-buka toko.* (Nuriah 2004: 34)
 Anto CAUS.VOICE-buka shop
 'Anto opens the shop.' (the door)

A similar idea is proposed by Nomoto (2013). He argues against a voice-marking and favours *meN-* as either an aspectual head or as the specifier of VP somehow in an adverbial position marking eventive action. In another article (Soh and Nomoto 2009), he even argues for a progressive reading. Based on these ideas, Soh (2010) proposes the zero-prefix as the true active marker, whereas *meN-* as indicated above, bears aspectual information. Although the aspectual part of *meN-* is undoubted (I will get back to it later on), total separation from the voice system seems not very likely.

The main argument of Zuriah against a voice-reading is the occurrence of *meN-* with apparently unaccusative predicates. However, Soh and Nomoto (2011) argue that intransitive meN-forms are unergative since all *meN-* forms are atelic and internally caused, both properties of unergative verbs. This unergativity is where the interpretation here hooks in. The main characteristic of unergative verbs is that the only argument is the CAUSE (AGENT). If we consider the Indonesian voice system not as equivalent to the European active-passive distinction but rather as CAUSE or THEME-focus[27] (see Feuge 1991), so as a selection process of one theta-role[28], then *meN-*, being either

---

[27] Feuge (1991) uses the German word Agens and Patiens-Fokus. However, I prefer the more neutral terms CAUSE and THEME.
[28] This fits the larger context of Austronesian languages. Schachter (1995) proposed the trigger idea to analyze the voice-system in Philippinian languages. The trigger is a neutral term for the

unergative or active, selects in both cases the CAUSE (AGENT)[29]. Therefore, *meN*-forms are classified as CAUSE-voice based on the idea of causing in a transitive form and the internal[30] causing for unergatives (see Soh and Nomoto 2011). In this view, the cause of the event somehow lies in the argument itself (internal to the argument). Let us have a look at intransitive forms described by Sneddon (1996: 65–66) in his derivational description: make it a proper verb (65), go to [base] (66), produce [base] (67), and become like [base] (68) and (69).

(65) *Adit me-nangis.*
     Adit CAUS.VOICE-cry
     'Adit cries.'

(66) *Pesawat men-darat.*
     plane CAUS.VOICE-ground
     'The plane lands.'

(67) *Singa me-raung.*
     lion CAUS.VOICE-roar
     'The lion roars.'

(68) *Siska mem-batu.*
     Siska CAUS.VOICE-stone
     'Siska freezes.'

(69) *Tangan mem-bengkak.*
     hand CAUS.VOICE-swell
     'The hand swells.'

On initial inspection, it looks as if some of them should be seen as unaccusative forms[31]. However, according to the atelic (except for *mendarat* 'to land') and, much more important, the internally-caused property, these forms have to be seen as

---

focused argument . The trigger is attracted by thematic agreement, so we have an AGENT-trigger, a THEME-trigger and a GOAL-trigger. I will argue for a comparable structure for Indonesian.
29 For convenience I continue with the term CAUSE. In general I abstract away from a detailed differentiation between every semantic aspect of a certain role, but assume rather abstract theta-roles like proposed by Carnie (2007).
30 The idea of internal and external causation goes back to Levin and Hovav (1995).
31 Perlmutter and Postal (1984) group inchoative verbs in the unaccusative category.

unergative. Whereas for roaring or crying, there is no doubt about the internal causation ergo the unergativeness, it is harder to perceive it for the inchoative processes *membatu* 'to freeze' or *membengkak* 'to swell' and even harder for the example with the plane, especially since European languages normally classify their translation as unaccusative verbs. But as Hellwig (2010) described, translation bears a high risk in semantic fieldwork, especially since it is impossible to predict whether a given intransitive verb will turn out to be unaccusative or unergative (Rosen 1984, Dowty 1991). We cannot find a universal set of unergative and unaccusative verbs in all languages of the world (Rosen 1984, Dowty 1991). Therefore, it cannot be the goal to explain all members of a group concept-wise. Still, we must accept a language's unique system in distinguishing between unergative and unaccusative verbs. Here, we should not forget that some forms prototypically fit the group in the unergative-unaccusative distinction in Germanic languages based on morphological arguments (choice of the auxiliary, for instance). In contrast, others do not follow our intuition, not even as native speakers[32]. In the case of *membatu* (freeze) or *membengkak* (swell), the causation is not focused on the initial cause like a shock or a hit, but on the internal processes in the body that causes somebody to freeze or something to swell. For *mendarat* 'land', we can conceptualize landing as a controlled process compared to a crash, for example. Whereas the controlled process is seen as internally caused, the crash would be externally caused.

3.2.2 ter-voice

In the previous section, we grouped forms like *mendarat* 'to land' and *membengkak* 'to swell' as unergative forms. Although this classification might not be completely convincing so far, it might become more easily conceivable once we continue with the second group, the *ter*-forms. *Ter*-forms are traditionally seen as stative (70) or accidental passives (71) (see Sneddon 1996: 112–113). In contrast to *meN*-forms, these forms are normally telic (the result of a process) and externally caused, leading to the accidental reading in many cases. These events are not caused by the argument itself but by something outside (external) to the argument. Hence, these verb forms must be seen as unaccusative verbs, and the single argument is the THEME.

---

[32] Therefore some scholars propose a looser definition, e.g. primary and non-primary arguments (see Breul and Wegner 2017).

(70) *Buku itu ter-tulis dalam bahasa Inggris.*
book DEM TH.VOICE-write in language England
'This book is written in English.'

(71) *Adit ter-jatuh dari sepeda.*
Adit TH.VOICE-fall from bike
'Adit fell from the bike.'

So *ter-* should be identified as THEME-voice. However, in this *ter*-category, we find examples like (72) and (73).

(72) *Siska ter-senyum.*
Siska TH.VOICE-smile
'Siska smiles.'

(73) *Adit ter-tawa.*
Adit TH.VOICE-laugh
'Adit laughs.'

In most European languages, laugh or smile are classified as unergative verbs; see, for instance, the auxiliary selection of *have* in German (74, 75).

(74) *Sofie hat gelächelt.*
Sofie AUX smiled
'Sofie has smiled.'

(75) *Anton hat gelacht.*
Sofie AUX laughed
'Anton has laughed.'

While these two examples are hardly to be seen as counter-examples of an unaccusative category for *ter*-forms in Indonesian, they show that smiling and laughing are for the Indonesian understanding not active processes but rather the results of an external cause. This idea is interesting, as we all know situations where we cannot refrain from laughing or where we smile despite attempted suppression. We also know how hard it is to either laugh or smile naturally on demand. If we allow Indonesian to categorize their unaccusative forms based on their worldview, we also have to accept the unergative forms that might not have (for our understanding) convincing arguments.

3.2.3 ber-voice

The third voice-marker is *ber-*. Often *ber-* is associated with unergative verb forms (Vamarasi 1999). However, based on the assumption that every prefix selects a distinct theta-role, it must select a theta-role different from THEME and CAUSE. Similar to the idea of unaccusatives and unergatives, Broekhuis and Cornips (2012) proposed the undative form *krijgen* in Dutch. The peculiarity of this form is that its subject bears a GOAL role and its object a THEME role.

If we take a look at Indonesian *ber-kan* forms (76), we can identify the same pattern.

(76) Pohon   ber-tulis-kan   nama-mu.
     tree   GO.VOICE-write-TH.TRANS   name-2S.POSS
     'Your name is written on the tree.'

The tree is not the CAUSE, the one writing something, but the place, on which something is written, the GOAL.

Besides *krijgen*, Broekhuis and Cornips (2012) also identified *hebben* (have) and *houden* (hold) as undative verbs. Especially *hebben* is interesting for our case. Having something can be seen as the result of having been given something; if John gives Mary a book, Mary has a book. Both the indirect object of 'give' and the subject of 'have' can be argued to have a GOAL role.

This have-relation is particularly crucial for our Indonesian case. Many *ber*-forms indicate 'having' what the base means (Sneddon 1996: 61–63) (77–80).

(77) Adit ber-istri
     Adit GO.VOICE-wife
     'Adit has a wife.'

(78) Kaki-nya   ber-debu.
     foot-3S.POSS GO.VOICE-dust
     'His feet are dusty.'

(79) Siska ber-topi.
     Siska GO.VOICE-cap
     'Siska wears a cap.'

(80) Anak   itu ber-nama   Tuti.
     child DEM GO.VOICE-name   Tuti
     'This child is called Tuti.'

The second interesting part of *have* is that many Indonesian *ber*-forms correlate to some forms of the English *have*-group or show a certain similarity.

(81) *ber-senang*
GO.VOICE-happy
'to have fun.'

(82) *ber-cinta*
GO.VOICE-love
'to have sex.'

(83) *ber-baring*
GO.VOICE-lie
'to lie' (similar 'to have a nap')

(84) *be-renang*
GO.VOICE-swim
'to swim, to have a swim.'

(85) *ber-bicara*
GO.VOICE-speak
'to speak, to have a talk.'

(86) *be-kerja*
GO.VOICE-work
'to work, to have work.'

So *ber*-forms should be grouped as undative voice or GOAL-voice.

3.2.4 zero-voice

The last group we need to talk about is bare-roots, roots without an overt prefix. There are two possibilities: the prefixless verb bears the same meaning as a marked form (87), or it bears a meaning different from all available marked forms (88). Although the form seems underspecified, it is not ambiguous.

(87) a. *Adit jatuh.*
  Adit fall
  'Adit fell.'

b. *Adit ter-jatuh.*
  Adit TH.VOICE-fall
  'Adit fell.'

(88) a. *Adit tinggal.*
  Adit stay
  'Adit stays.'

b. *Adit *ber-tinggal*
  Adit GO.VOICE-stay
  'Adit has a stay.'

c. *Adit ter-tinggal.*
  Adit TH.VOICE-stay
  'Adit is left behind.'

d. *Adit me-ninggal.*
  Adit CAUS.VOICE-stay
  'Adit died.'

In the first case, since there is no meaning-relevant difference, the prefix can be deleted in certain contexts, most likely due to the efficiency tendency (see the first section of 3.1). In the second case, the bare forms fit the meaning of the non-available *ber*-form. This approach can even solve the problematic sentences proposed by Nuriah (2004: 34) (89–90).

(89) Anto mem-buka toko.
  Anto CAUS.VOICE-open shop
  'Anto opens the shop.'

(90) Anto buka toko.
  Anto open shop
  'Anto opens a shop'

In Indonesian, a form like *berbuka* is not available. So it is possible that (90) has a null-*ber*- leading to the appropriate translation: "Anto has a shop-opening". Thus, in both cases, the zero-voice is the consequence of the zero-realization of the voice-morpheme. This null-allomorph can either be optional like in the first case (*jatuh* vs. *terjatuh*) or obligatory like in the second case (*tinggal*). In any case, information on voice (theta-role selection) is available even in the null cases.

It is important to mention that the voice markers bear more than just voice information. Like the English passive marking in the participle, where there is some aspectual information for perfectivity, Indonesian voice-markers also bear some aspectual information. *meN-* is eventive (Nomoto 2013) and partly progressive (Soh and Nomoto 2009), *ter-* is strongly resultative (Sneddon 1996: 112)[33], and *ber-* is mainly stative.

3.2.5 Transitive markers

So far, we have seen that Indonesian marks three different voices in one-place-predicates: *ber-* (GOAL-voice or undative voice), *ter-* (THEME-voice or unaccusative voice), and *meN-* (CAUSE-voice or unergative voice). We have not accounted yet for the prefix *di-*, traditionally seen as the passive voice marker. However, before we turn to *di-*, a short digression on the Indonesian suffixes *-kan* (91) and *-i* (92) is in order. Both can be seen as transitive or sometimes applicative (see Shiohara 2012) markers:

(91) *Adit   men-jatuh-kan   Ridwan.*
     Adit   CAUS.VOICE-fall-TH.TRANS   Ridwan
     'Adit made Ridwan fall.'

(92) *Adit   me-warna-i   bunga   di   kertas.*
     Adit   CAUS.VOICE-colour-GO.TRANS flower in   paper
     'Adit coloured a flower on the paper.'

An allomorphic explanation can be ruled out since there are even minimal pairs with either meN-i (93) and meN-kan (94).

(93) *Adit   me-nidur-kan   anak-nya.*
     Adit   CAUS.VOICE-sleep-TH.TRANS child-3S.POSS
     'Adit put his child to sleep.'

(94) *Adit   me-nidur-i   istri-nya.*
     Adit   CAUS.VOICE-sleep-GO.TRANS child-3S.POSS
     'Adit slept with his wife.'

For both suffixes, multiple functions are attested. In general (see amongst others Sneddon 1996; Shiohara 2012; Kroeger 2007), five functions are attested for *-kan*: causative *-kan* with intransitive verbs (95), causative *-kan* with transitive verbs (96), instrumental *-kan* (97), optional *-kan* (98) and benefactive *-kan* (99):

---

[33] Sneddon actually classifies them as state, however they 'refer to the state which exists following an action' (Sneddon 1996, p. 112) which I relabel resultative.

(95) Adit   men-jatuh-kan   Ridwan.
     Adit   CAUS.VOICE-fall-TH.TRANS Ridwan
     'Adit makes Ridwan fall.'

(96) Adit   men-jahit-kan   baju   ke tukang jahit.
     Adit   CAUS.VOICE-sew-TH.TRANS clothes to expert sew
     'Adit had his cloth sewn at the tailors.' (Sneddon 1996: 83)

(97) Adit   me-nikam-kan   pisau ke perut-nya
     Adit   CAUS.VOICE-stab-TH.TRANS knife to stomach-3s.POSS
     'Adit stabbed the knife into his stomach.' (adapted from Sneddon 1996: 79)

(98) Adit   me-lempar-kan   bola.
     Adit   CAUS.VOICE-throw-TH.TRANS ball
     'Adit threw the ball.'

(99) Adit   mem-beli-kan   Ridwan buku
     Adit   CAUS.VOICE-buy-TH.TRANS Ridwan book
     'Adit bought Ridwan a book.'

For -i (see amongst others Kroeger 2007; Sneddon 1996; Shiohara 2012), a locative (100), a recipient (101), and an iterative function (102) are attested:

(100) Adit me-nanam-i   kebun   dengan bunga.
      Adit CAUS.VOICE-plant-GO.TRANS garden with   flower
      'Adit planted flowers in the garden. (Ali had the garden planted with flowers).'

(101) Adit me-ngirim-i   saya uang.
      Adit CAUS.VOICE-send-GO.TRANS 1s   money
      'Adit sends me money.'

(102) Adit me-mukul-i   istri-nya.
      Adit CAUS.VOICE-hit-GO.TRANS wife-3s.POSS
      'Adit hit his wife repeatedly.'

Whereas some scholars argue for a unifying approach of *-kan* (for instance, Son and Cole [2008] or Cole and Son [2004]), I follow Kroeger (2007), who argues for at least two *-kan* morphemes. Whereas the first four functions can be subsumed as a modification of the Lexical-Conceptual Structure (LCS) (see Jackendoff 1990, Levin and Hovav 1995), the second *-kan* changes the syntactic expressions of arguments and only holds for the benefactive case. Kroeger (2007) receives historical support from Sirk (1978) and Mead (1998: 206), who argue in favour of two distinct forms -*kən und *-akən in an early stage of Malayo-Polynesian.

Kroeger (2007) identified the LCS as [CAUSE BE AT] for the first- kan. This structure could be easily translated into CAUSE, THEME, and GOAL, whereas (96) and (97)[34] show all three required roles, (95) and (98) could be easily extended to (103) and (104).

(103) Adit men-jatuh-kan   Ridwan ke lantai.
      Adit CAUSE.VOICE-fall-TH.TRANS Ridwan to floor
      'Adit made Ridwan fall on the floor.'

(104) Adit me-lempar-kan   bola ke Ridwan.
      Adit CAUS.VOICE-throw-TH.TRANS   ball to Ridwan
      'Adit threw the ball to Ridwan.'

(105) Adit meng-ajar-i   saya matematika.
      Adit CAUS.VOICE-teach-GO.TRANS 1s   mathematics
      'Adit taught me mathematics.'

(106) Saya di-ajar-i   matematika   oleh Adit.
      1s   PASS-teach-GO.TRANS   mathematics by   Adit
      'I was taught mathematics by Adit.'

(107) *Matematika   di-ajar-i   saya oleh Adit.
      Mathematics PASS-teach-GO.TRANS   1s   by   Adit
      Intended meaning: 'Mathematics was taught to me by Adit.'

Even in the instrumental function, the object has to be seen as THEME and not as an INSTRUMENT, as it denotes something that is handled or moved (Sneddon 1996: 79–80)[35].

For -i, we can assume the same LCS [CAUSE BE AT], but the GOAL is in the object position (Shiohara 2012). Hence, we have the general structure of CAUSE (AGENT), GOAL, and THEME. This structure works for both the recipient function (101) and the locative function (100), especially when we apply Sneddon's explanation of things being handled or manipulated with the *dengan*-argument. Iterative -i must be treated as a second homonymous morpheme (Shiohara 2012), similar to the second -*kan*.

---

[34] The third argument should not be seen as CAUSE or AGENT but as GOAL or LOCATION (Kroeger 2007: 242).
[35] Sneddon (1996) cites Hein Steinhauer (p.c.)

-*kan* and -*i* are transitive/applicative suffixes promoting either the THEME (-*kan*) or the GOAL (-*i*). If this assumption proves valid, we should have a correlation between the subject of *ber*-forms and the object of -*i*-forms and the subject of *ter*-forms and the object of -*kan*-forms. The following examples show precisely such a correlation:

(108) *Adit me-warna-i bunga di kertas.*
Adit CAUS.VOICE-colour-GO.TRANS flower in paper
'Adit coloured a flower on the paper.'
→ *Bunga di kertas ber-warna.*
flower In paper GO.VOICE-colour
'The flower on the paper is coloured.'

(109) *Bapak itu me-nama-i anak itu Yusuf.*
father DEM CAUS.VOICE-name-TH.TRANS child DEM Yusuf
'The father called the child Yusuf.'
→ *Anak itu ber-nama Yusuf.*
child DEM GO.VOICE-name Yusuf
'The child is called Yusuf.'

(110) *Adit men-jatuh-kan Ridwan.*
Adit CAUS.VOICE-fall-TH.TRANS Ridwan
'Adit made Ridwan fall.'
→ *Ridwan ter-jatuh.*
Ridwan TH.VOICE-fall
'Ridwan fell.'

(111) *Adit men-daftar-kan Ridwan.*
Adit CAUS.VOICE-register-TH.TRANS Ridwan
'Adit registered Ridwan.'
Ridwan ter-daftar.
Ridwan TH.VOICE-register
'Ridwan is registered.'

Further evidence is furnished in that this interpretation holds for the locative alternation attested by, amongst others, Sneddon (1996), Kaswanti Purwo (1995), and Dardjowidjojo (1971).

(112) *Buruh itu me-muat-kan beras ke kapal.*
worker DEM CAUS.VOICE-fit-TH.TRANS rice to ship
'The workers loaded the rice onto the ship.'

(113) *Buruh   itu   me-muat-i   kapal dengan beras.*
      worker   DEM   CAUS.VOICE-fit-GO.TRANS   ship   with   rice
      'The workers loaded the ship with rice.' (Sneddon 1996: 96)

It can even account for the difference in *-kan-* and *-i-*forms for verbs of motion (114–115). In this *i*-case, the policeman comes to the house of Ali. Therefore, the house is not moved but the goal of the action. In (115) the rice has been brought to Indonesia, thus it has been moved and is therefore the theme,

(114) *Polisi   men-datang-i   rumah Ali*
      police   CAUS.VOICE-come-GO.TRANS   house Ali
      'A policeman came to Ali's house.'
      (Kaswanti Purwo 1995: 98)

(115) *Indonesia   mem-datang-kan   beras   dari Thailand*
      Indonesia   CAUS.VOICE-come-TH.TRANS   rice   from Thailand
      'Indonesia imported rice from Thailand.'
      (Kaswanti Purwo 1995: 97)

The third argument comes from ditransitive verb forms. As Dardjowidjojo (1971) pointed out, either the direct object (DO) or the indirect object (IO) can be placed immediately to the right of the verb and be passivized. Since the DO prototypically correlates with the THEME and the IO with the GOAL, we should expect *di-i* forms with the GOAL in the subject position and *di-kan* forms with the THEME in the subject position. Examples (116–118) show exactly this pattern.

(116) *Adit   me-nyerah-kan   pekerjaan itu   kepada Ridwan.*
      Adit   CAUS.VOICE-surrender[36]-TH.TRANS work   DEM   to   Ridwan.
      'Adit gave the work to Ridwan'

(117) *Adit   me-nyerah-i   Ridwan   pekerjaan   itu.*
      Adit   CAUS.VOICE-surrender-GO.TRANS   Ridwan   work   DEM
      'Adit gave Ridwan the work.'

---

[36] In intransitive forms like *berserah* "surrender" and *menyerah* "surrender, give up, give in", the root *serah* has a meaning related to surrender. In the transitive form *menyerahkan* it is better to translate it with "give".

(118) *Ridwan di-serah-i pekerjaan itu.*
       Ridwan PASS-surrender-GO.TRANS work DEM
       'Ridwan was given this work.'

For transitive forms without *-kan* or *-i*, a similar process as with bare roots must be assumed. The suffix *-kan* or *-i* has been deleted at PF. Whereas prototypical transitive forms like *membunuh* (kill) no longer allow *–kan*, less prototypical or less frequent forms like *mengantar* or *mengantarkan* (to pick up) still show the optionality stage. For other verb forms like *menulis* (to write) or *membaca* (to read), LCS-changing *-kan* is blocked by the homophonous benefactive *-kan*. The same is true for *memukul* (to hit) or *menikam* (to stub), where the iterative *-i* blocks the recipient[37] *-i*.

After establishing the theta-role selection function of the morphemes, it is now time to look at structural representations in the following section.

3.2.6 Structural representation

Heycock (1991: 43) and Rothstein (1983) propose predicates to be one-place syntactic functions. In other words, a predicate assigns a theta-role to one and only one argument, its subject. With Stowell (1978), I assume that the licensing position is the specifier position. I follow the position of Hale and Keyser (1998), Harley (1995), Halle and Marantz (1994), etc., in that thematic roles are not stored with the lexical item inside the lexicon but that their assignment is a result of configuration. Instead of assuming certain positions, complement vs. specifier distinction as in UTAH (see Baker 2003), I assume functional heads to be predicates that assign only one theta-role. This assignment is based on an uninterpretable feature that needs to be checked. Since heads normally have a second uninterpretable feature – a subcategorization feature has to be checked first (see chapter 2) – the theta-role is assigned in a second step and, therefore, to the specifier. Hence, a root is merged into the first head, let us call it θ, which makes the root a theta-role-assigner (in traditional grammar V) and assigns a theta-role, e.g., THEME, normally to its specifier. It is important that all arguments merged into the specifier positions are not lexical roots but maximal projections of a functional head. I will deal with these in more detail further below. For reasons of simplicity, I assume the functional head D and call them DPs. Thus, for the sentence *Udin terdaftar* 'Udin is registered', we start with *daftar* being merged into the θ-head, becoming a THEME-marking head. Since it is the first step in the der-

---

[37] The instrumental *-kan* forms indicate that the victim is seen rather as GOAL of the action than as THEME. The instrument used is the THEME as the thing being handled.

ivation, Udin is merged as complement first and then moved via roll-up movement to the specifier position where it receives the thematic role THEME (119).

(119)[38]

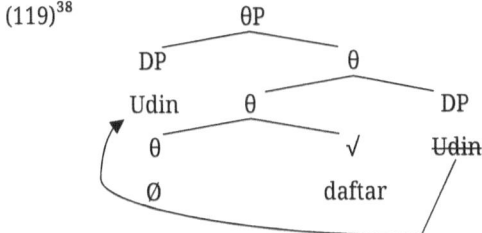

As outlined at the beginning of this chapter, we need two more heads above θP, namely CatP and δP. The Cat-head assigns a certain semantic category to the theta-assigner, which could be something like state, event, or individual. For Indonesian verbs, this head matches the aspectual information of the overt verb morphology, namely Result[39] for *ter-*, Stat(e) for *ber-*, and Ev(ent) for either *meN-* or *di-*. The δ-head for Indonesian 'verbs' is voice. The phase-head voice selects the THEME argument and assigns pivot status to the argument by moving it into Spec-voiceP. Like Marantz' v or Harley's Event, voice makes the whole form a categorical verb. At PF, the head-combination for Cat and δ is decisive for the insertion of the correct voice morphology. For a better understanding, the overt morpheme is shown in the structure although it is not inserted earlier than vocabulary insertion. For the sentence *Udin terdaftar* (Udin is registered), we arrive at the following structure (120):

(120) Udin ter-daftar.
 Udin TH.VOICE-register
 'Udin is registered.'

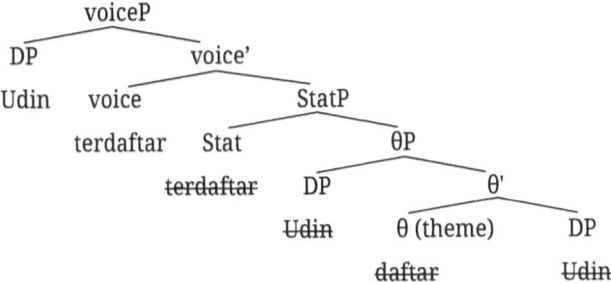

---

38 In the following no such detailed representation of head-merge will be given.
39 For convenience I will use the label Stat to comprise both result and state.

Equivalent to the unaccusative form, we can also derive undative (121) or unergative forms (122).

(121) Udin ber-istri.
      Udin GO.VOICE-wife
      'Udin is married.'

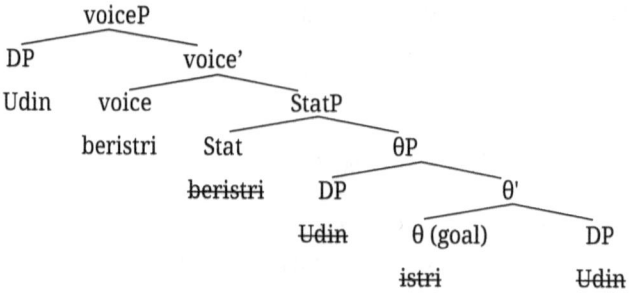

(122) Udin me-nangis.
      Udin CAUS.VOICE-cry
      'Udin cries.'

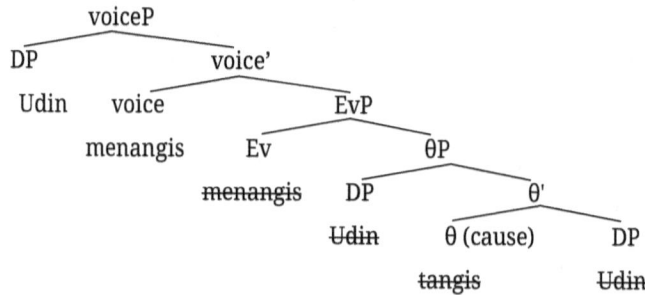

However, in structures with more than one argument, we need to assume more functional heads between θ and voice. As outlined in the first chapter, we need to duplicate our general structure (123):

(123)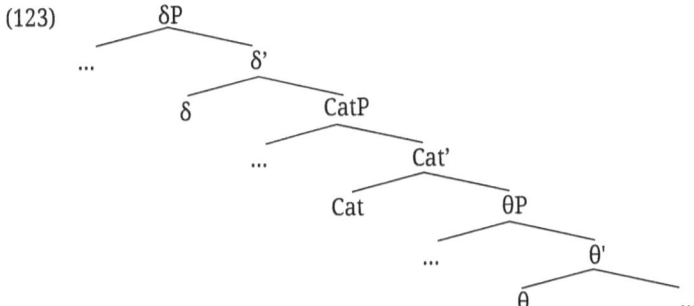

The first δ-head is Trans in the sense of Bowers (2002), which in Indonesian is filled with overt -*kan* (124), -*i* (125), or a null-affix (126), which selects either the THEME or the GOAL as the secondary pivot. The relevant constituent moves into the specifier of TransP. This can explain why the object is always closest to the verb (at least in active voice).

(124) Udin meng-ajar-kan   matematika   kepada Adit.
       Udin CAUSE.VOICE-teach-TH.TRANS   mathematics to   Adit
       'Udin teaches mathematics to Adit.'

(125) Udin meng-ajar-i   Adit matematika.
       Udin CAUS.VOICE-teach-GO.TRANS   Adit mathematics
       'Udin teaches Adit mathematics.'

(126) Udin me-mukul   Adit.
       Udin CAUS.VOICE-hit   Adit
       'Udin hit Adit.'

The CAUSE is merged in a second θP. The δ-head of the higher θP is voice, choosing either the semantic subject (active voice) or the semantic object (passive voice) to be the structural subject. For both the voice and the Trans-domain, we still have a Cat-layer, whose realization depends on the verb chosen. Since only the subject and the object can be given default case, the third constituent, if available, is both rightmost in the sentence and occurs with a case-assigning preposition, either *kepada/ke* for the GOAL, *oleh* for the CAUSE, or *Ø/dengan* for the THEME. The result is the following tree structures for transitive sentences with either a THEME-object (127) or a GOAL-object (128):

(127) Udin me-nidur-kan   anak-nya.
      Udin CAUS.VOICE-sleep-TH.TRANS child-3S.POSS
      'Udin put his child to sleep.'

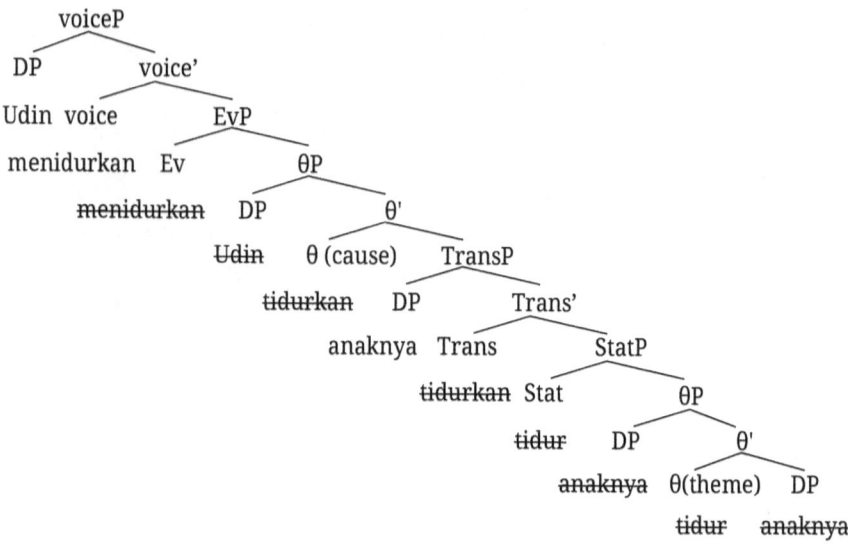

(128) Udin mem-bumbu-i   sop.
      Udin CAUS.VOICE-spice-GO.TRANS soup
      'Udin spiced the soup.'

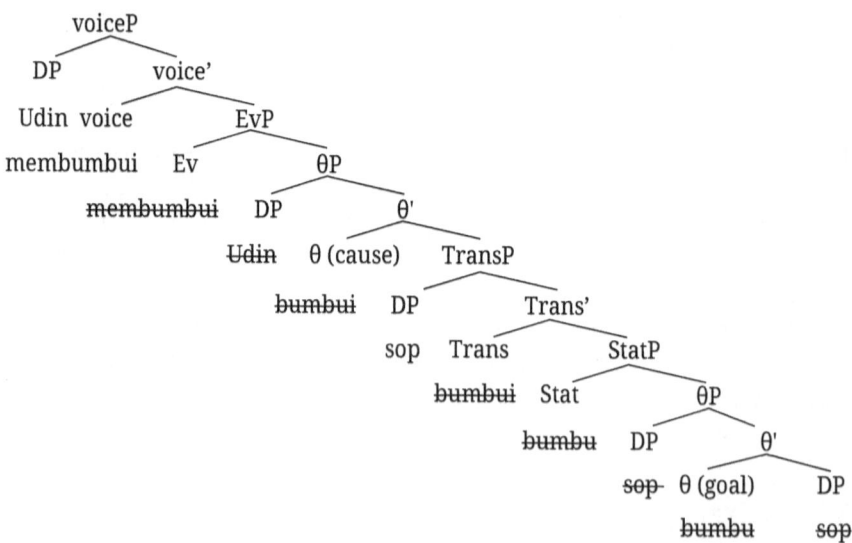

3.3 The D-layer

Before we continue with the higher functional heads T and C, we must consider the status of noun phrases, which become arguments of the predicates described above. With Loewen (2011), I assume that D is the uppermost projection of a noun phrase. This D is the 'locus of definiteness' (Carson 2000: 31; Loewen 2011: 18). However, with Loewen (2011), I assume that there is more to noun phrases than D, especially as I do not treat N as a lexical category but as a syntactic category based on derivation. Any discussion of the noun phrase in Indonesian must deal with the derivational nominal morphology -an, peN- and per-, classifiers (*orang, ekor, buah*), quantifiers and numerals, possessive constructions with -nya, punya or milik, the nominalizer or relativizer *yang* and the demonstratives *ini/itu*. Whereas classifiers, quantifiers, and numerals normally occur to the left, all other forms occur to the right.

3.3.1 Derivational morphology

Besides the sophisticated affix system related to voice, Indonesian shows a similarly complex system for nominal morphology, normally placed under derivational morphology (see amongst others Sneddon 1996). The following affixes are presented: *peN-, pe(r)-, -an,* and the circumfixes *peN-an, pe(r)-an,* and *ke-an*[40]. Here the latter will not be analyzed as circumfixes but divided into parts. Hence, this work only has to deal with three basic affixes: *per-, peN-,* and *-an*. In the verbal structures, we assigned three basic theta roles, from which it seems logical that each nominal affix also fits these categories.

The *peN-* prefix is normally identified as the actor prefix, which yields the actor of what the base describes (Sneddon 1996: 28). Thus, it fits the AGENT (CAUSE)-role[41].

(129) a. *menulis*   → *penulis*   (*yang menulis*)
         write   → writer   (the one who writes)
      b. *membohong* → *pembohong* (*yang membohong*)
         lie   → liar   (the one who lies)

---

[40] This form will be left aside in this work.
[41] Although the work makes reference to the notion theta-role/thematic role, this should be understood as a general semantic relation and not necessarily describe the relation of a predicate and its argument.

Pe(r)- correlates with the verbal *ber-* (Sneddon 1996: 28) and should therefore fit the GOAL role.

(130) a. *bekerja* → *pekerja* (*yang bekerja*)
 work → worker (the one who works/has work)
 b. *berenang* → *perenang* (*yang berenang*)
 swim → swimmer (the one who swims)

This AGENT and GOAL distinction can explain the examples where both *peN-* and *pe(r)-*forms are possible.

(131) a. *penatar* (the one who gives training) – *petatar* (the one who receives training)
 b. *penyuruh* (the one who gives a command) – *pesuruh* (the one who receives a command)

Whereas a. is the SOURCE, the CAUSE, the AGENT, i.e., the one who trains or gives orders, b. is the addressee, so the GOAL, and not the PATIENT as identified by Sneddon (1996: 29). It can even explain problematic cases like:

(132) *penyerta* (companion) – *peserta* (participant)

Whereas the companion actively accompanies somebody, the participant is the GOAL of a show, a course, etc.

If we assume the same threefold system as for verbal forms, the theta-role which remains for *-an* is the THEME. This fits perfectly well since *–an* marks the object of the action indicated (Sneddon 1996: 31).

(133) a. *lukisan* → *yang terlukis*[42]
 painting → what is painted
 b. *tulisan* → *yang tertulis.*
 writing → what is written

But, how can we account for them in a tree structure? All three forms should be understood as describing entities. In order to describe objects or entities, they

---

[42] A *di*-passive is also possible.

should have a Cat-head distinct from the verbal forms above. For simplicity, I will label this head N. The affix has to agree with an abstract theta-relation inside of θP. Although the root is assigned this relation, there is no argument for receiving a theta-role. Thus, the Spec-θP is (normally) not filled. The NP also has no specifier. The agentive peN- forms give a hint that we build up the argument structure first. Here it is possible to have an overt complement (134) as well:

(134) a. *pe-nulis*   *buku*
        CAUS.NOM-write book   book
        'book author'
 b. *pe-main*   *sepak bola*
        CAUS.NOM-play   football
        'football player'

For (135) and (136), an overt realization of one of the arguments is possible[43]. In this case, it can be either the THEME argument (135) or the CAUSE argument (136):

(135) *Lukisan Monalisa*
       painting Monalisa
       'The Monalisa painting.'

(136) *Lukisan da Vinci*
       painting da Vinci
       'Da Vinci's painting'

Thus, we have the following structure for a form like *lukisan*[44] (137) or *pekerja* (138):

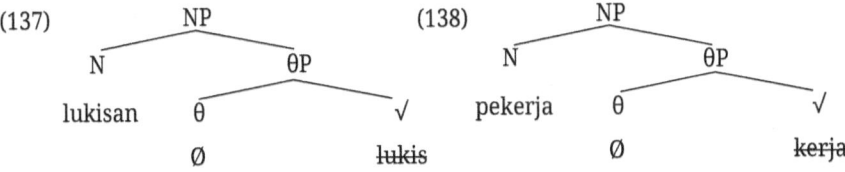

To summarize, the N-head with *peN-* with an uninterpretable CAUSE feature selects a CAUSE-marked θP and describes somebody/something that makes/causes what the

---

[43] It might be better to assume a transitive structure as underlying structure.
[44] *Sesuatu* and *orang* are only placeholders for the specifier position.

base represents, e.g., a *pelukis* is a painter, somebody who does the act of painting. The N-head *pe(r)-* selects the GOAL-marked θP making it somebody/something that has received what the root represents. Finally, *-an* is specified for an uninterpretable THEME feature that selects a THEME marked θP. *-an* describes an entity that is what the base represents.

However, we can even go a step further and combine the two prefixes, *peN-* and *pe(r)-*, with the suffix *-an*. As with transitive verbs, two thematic relations (not necessarily arguments) are selected; one is the THEME, and the other is either the GOAL or the CAUSE. Standard Indonesian grammars (see Sneddon 1996, Alwi et al. 2003, etc.) identify the difference between *per-an* forms and *peN-an* forms normally as one being a result and one a process. Therefore, these refer to abstract ideas and not to concrete entities, such as a certain person. Therefore the *-an* must be merged later than the *peN- /per-*. At a second look, we should even assume that the nominalization process like above is only realized for *-an* and that *peN- /per-* are realized in a voice layer in these cases. Let us consider the two forms *perkembangan* 'development' and *pengembangan* 'developing'. In the first case, *kembang* is merged into a GOAL-theta-head. The θP is merged with StatP and voiceP. If we stopped here, we would have *berkembang*[45]. Now we have to merge an abstract theta specified for THEME (see above) and finally an N-head making it an individual. In contrast to this structure, the embedded voiceP is specified for the cause-role and event in the second form. Therefore, we reach two different interpretations.

We should expect the same structure for bare nouns, yet without overt noun morphology, similar to verbs without overt voice-markers. I assume the THEME role (in some cases, we might be able to omit the θ-layer and merge the root directly into the N-head) as default. Hence, for a form like *guru* 'teacher', we have something like (139):

(139)
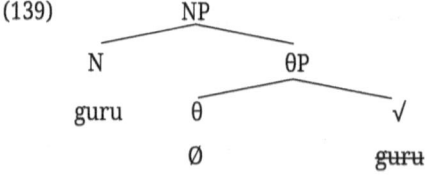

---

[45] Since we have late insertion, the form *berkembang* is only hypothetical here.

3.3.2 Modification by adjectives

Having dealt with overt noun morphology with affixes, we now proceed to consider modification by adjectives.

Indonesian allows constituents traditionally labeled "noun+adjective", like (140).

(140) *rumah besar*
      house big
      'big house'

This direct modification has to be differentiated from indirect modification with *yang* (Loewen 2011). Whereas we will deal with the *yang*-construction further below, this direct modification is treated as head adjunction[46] as proposed by Loewen (2011) for Indonesian and Davies and Dresser (2005) for Javanese and Madurese. Head Adjunction is seen like head-merge in head-movement (Travis 1984), but without movement (Loewen 2011: 16; see also Travis 1988; Ghomeshi 1997). The main advantage of this head adjunction analysis is that the result of the merging process is still a head. This analysis can explain why it is possible to merge these heads into a voice-head (141):

(141) *Udin be-kerja keras.*
      Udin GO.VOICE-work hard
      'Udin is hard-working.'

The identical pattern is identifiable for noun+noun constructions like (142):

(142) *Udin ber-bahasa Indonesia.*
      Udin GO.VOICE-language Indonesia
      'Udin speaks Indonesian.'

Since categories like nouns or adjectives cannot be taken for granted, an important question to resolve concerns what is being merged? On the left side, we have N since it is possible to have a noun with overt N-marking as the head (left branched) of the complex head (143). Therefore *sikap* and *bahasa* should be treated as N-heads, as well.

---

[46] Ideas on such an interpretation have been proposed amongst others by Stowell (1981), Sadler and Arnold (1994) and Baker (2003).

(143) Udin ber-pen-didik-an   tinggi.
      Udin GO.VOICE-CAUS.NOM-educate-TH.NOM High
      'Udin is highly educated.'

What about the modifier? The modifier can bear both overt voice- (144) and N-morphology (145).

(144) per-nikah-an   ter-daftar
      GO.NOM-marry-TH.NOM   TH.VOICE-register
      'registered marriage'

(145) menteri   pen-didik-an
      minister CAUS.NOM-educate-TH.NOM
      'education minister'

However, this head does not have to be overt, so it could be either N, marking an individual (146), or Stat(e) (147) or Ev(ent) (148).

(146) bahasa   Indonesia
      language Indonesia
      'Indonesian'

(147) sikap   baik
      attitude good
      'good attitude'

(148) orang   muntah
      human   vomit
      'vomiting person'

Often the status of the second word is not free of ambiguity since *bahasa Indonesia* could be either the language of Indonesia (Indonesia as an individual) or the Indonesian language (Indonesia as 'state'). Although there are two different underlying (here simplified) structures, namely (149) or (150), this is normally not relevant for the interpretation:

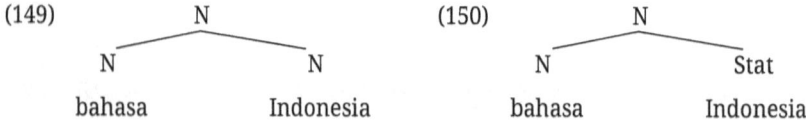

(149)   N
          ┌─────┴─────┐
          N   N
        bahasa   Indonesia

(150)   N
          ┌─────┴─────┐
          N   Stat
        bahasa   Indonesia

3.3.3 Classifiers

The next items in our hierarchy are classifiers. Indonesian has three main classificatory terms and some more minor ones, which only have a few members in their class. The major classifiers are *orang* (man), *ekor* (tail) and *buah* (fruit) (Kähler 1965: 68). *Orang* classifies human beings, *ekor* classifies animals, and *buah* is anything that is not placed explicitly in one of the minor categories. Minor categories are, amongst others, *butir* for grain, *helai* for something very thin, and *pucuk* for sprout (Kähler 1965: 69).

In prescriptive terms, every lexical item is categorized for its classifier; however, innovative usage is normal and comprehensible. In (151), the speaker compares her children with animals, e.g., due to a certain behaviour. In (152), the speaker complains about the size of the tomato by comparing it to a seed. In standard Indonesian, we would expect the classifiers *orang* (151) and *buah* (152), respectively:

(151) Dua   ekor   anak   ini   memang...
      two   CL.AN   child DEM   really
      'These two children are really...'

(152) Dua   biji   tomat   saja   20.000   Rupiah.
      two   CL.SEED   tomato only   20.000   Rupiah
      'These two small tomatoes for 20.000 Rupiah?'

Carson (2000: 1) states that the main function of classifiers in Malay[47] is to make nouns countable. However, these classifiers are no longer obligatory in contemporary Indonesian (Macdonald 1976). With Loewen (2011), I assume that the function of current classifiers is to provide information about shape, etc. Classifiers in Indonesian therefore have an ambivalent status. On the one hand, they are not strictly functional since they are not obligatory to make nouns countable, as in other languages; on the other hand, they have ceased to bear their original lexical meaning.

At first glance, classifier constructions look similar to the attributive forms described in the previous section. These attribute forms are a product of head adjunction, either N+N or N+Stat.

---

[47] The Malay of Malaysia and Indonesian go back to the same language, however have developed differently especially after independence of the two nation states (see also chapter 1).

In many cases, classifier constructions could even be literally translated identically to "normal" N+N or N+Stat forms, e.g., *orang guru* 'a teacher human/a teacherish human' or *buah pisang* 'banana fruit'. However, the forms are semantically empty in other cases since the literal meaning exists while having a different reading to the classifier, e.g., *ekor kuda*, which could either be 'horse' with the classifier reading or 'horsetail' with the literal reading. However, in both cases, the result is N. Whenever we are faced with two possible interpretations, there should be a structural difference between the two. *Ekor kuda* with the meaning 'horsetail' should result from head-adjoin, most likely N+N as in (153). Both *ekor* and *kuda* started as roots and subsequently merged with a functional head, N before. For classifier constructions, the classifier is not a complex N-head but the functional head N itself. The attributive form no longer needs a Cat-layer and can be merged as a root. We then just have a simple nominalization process (154).

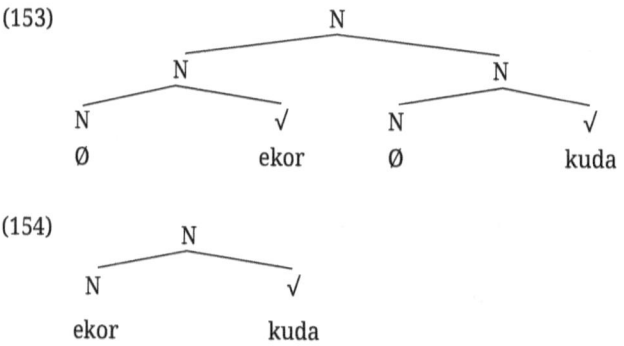

(153)

(154)

Classifier constructions should accordingly be seen as nouns. We will henceforth treat them as Ns. Having dealt with classifiers, we now turn our attention to numerals and quantifiers.

Numerals (155) and quantifiers (156) normally occur to the left.

(155) dua   orang   guru
      two   CL.HUM   teacher
      'two teachers'

(156) beberapa   ekor   kuda
      Some   CL.AN   horse
      'some horses'

Since both numerals and quantifiers can be used either predicatively (157–158) or modified by *yang* (159–160), I will treat them as irreducible elements, namely as roots.

(157) *Anak   kami   dua.*
      child 1P(EXCL).POSS   two
      'We have two children' (literally: 'Our children are two.')

(158) *Anak   kami   banyak.*
      child 1P(EXCL).POSS   many
      'We have many children.' (literally: 'Our children are many.')

(159) *Orang   yang   satu   ini*
      human   REL   one   DEM
      'This one particular person'

(160) *Orang   yang   banyak   ini*
      human   REL   many   DEM
      'These many people'

So far, we have merged our roots into heads, namely into θ. I see no reason to treat numerals or quantifiers differently. Let us consider the NP *dua ekor harimau* (two tigers). As mentioned above, *dua* is a root that is merged into θ and assigns a THEME role to its specifier, which is *ekor harimau* (a DP[48]). Now, the numeral itself is made a noun by head-moving to N. This results in the following structure (161):

(161)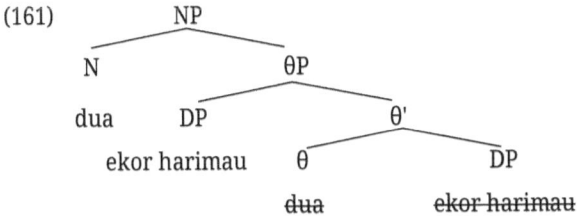

We could thus paraphrase *dua ekor harimau* with something like *the two which are tigers* or with an indefinite reading *a group of two which are tigers*.

---

48 Some null-D assumed

The same structure is available for quantifiers like *banyak* (many) (162):

(162)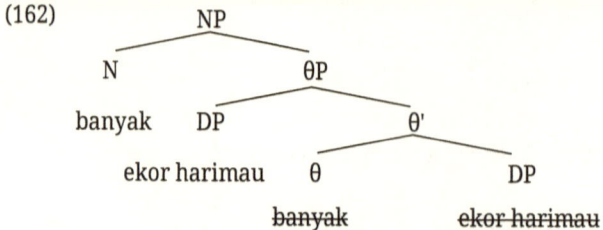

This structure could be paraphrased as *a multitude of tigers*.

Evidence for such a movement can be found in Javanese; a ligature *–ng* is required if the numeral occurs to the left (163).

(163) *telu-ng   macan* (Javanese)
three-LIG tiger
'three tigers'

This structure looks similar to the numeral construction in Indonesian. However, we even have an overt nominalizer, *-ng*, which is required only in such constructions. If the numeral is used as a predicate (164) or as a modifier in head-merge (165), then *-ng* is ungrammatical.

(164) *Anak-e   Udin telu/*telung.* (Javanese)
child-3S.POSS Udin three
'Udin has three children.'

(165) *Iki   buku telu/*telung.* (Javanese)
this book three
'These are three books.'

Before proceeding to the next group, we should pay some attention to a special numeral+classifier form used for the numeral one (*satu*). Instead of using the full numeral, it is phonetically reduced to *se-*, *seorang*, *seekor*, and *sebuah*. Besides its morphological peculiarity, this *se*-form also displays structural differences from other numeral+classifier constructions. Whereas *seorang guru* cannot be combined with *ini* (166), *dua orang guru* can be modified by this demonstrative (167).

(166) *Seorang guru ini selalu malas.
　　　Q　　　　teacher DEM always lazy
　　　Intended meaning: 'This one teacher is always lazy.'

(167) Dua orang guru ini selalu malas.
　　　two CL.HUM teacher DEM always lazy.
　　　'These two teachers are always lazy.'

That the ungrammaticality of (166) should be a structural and not a semantic problem is shown by the fact that the intended meaning can be expressed with a structure like (168):

(168) Guru yang satu ini selalu malas.
　　　teacher REL one DEM always lazy
　　　'This one teacher is always lazy.'

This example indicates that the se+classifier has grammaticalized and cannot be analyzed into its former morphemes anymore. It functions like the English indefinite article 'a, an' (Sneddon 1996: 135).

For *seekor harimau*, there are two possible structures, one with *se-* as root before grammaticalization (169) and the other with *seorang* as Q (D) after grammaticalization (170). In current Indonesian, both structures exist; however, there is an inclination towards (170).

(169)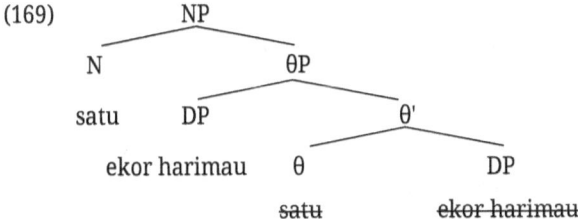

(170)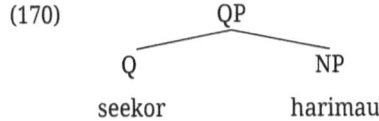

With its functional usage as Q, the *se*-classifier bears information about definiteness (here indefinite), so it is in complementary distribution to Ds like *ini/itu*.

3.3.4 yang

The next marker that we must deal with is *yang*. For this marker, amongst others, the following functions are attested: relativizer (171), the definite article (172) and nominalizer (173) (see van Gerth Wijk 1985; van Ophuijsen 1915; Mees 1969, Verhaar 1981, Kaswanti Purwo 1983; van Minde 2008). Often it is seen as a ligature between a noun and its attribute (Verhaar 1981):

(171) orang   yang   baru   datang
      CL.HUM REL   REC.ANT   come
      'the person that just came'

(172) mobil   yang   biru
      car   REL   blue
      'the blue car'

(173) yang   biru
      REL   blue
      'the blue one'

Although *yang* is often described as a relativizer both in descriptive and, more importantly, in prescriptive grammar, this usage has developed from the nominalizing function, which is identified as the original one (see Yap 2011). I will even go as far as to argue that the relativizer and the nominalizer function are structure-wise identical with *yang* as N.

As a first example, we can consider a clear nominalizing example (174).

(174) yang   biru
      NOM   blue
      'The blue one.'/'The one which is blue.'

Biru is a root that needs to be merged into a θ-head like any other root. Since the target is a noun, there is no argument. On top of the θP, we merge our N, namely *yang*, and receive an NP, *yang biru*, with the following structure (175):

(175)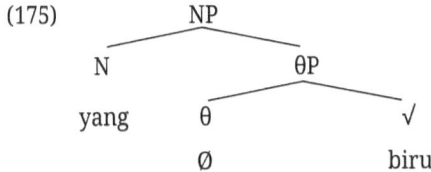

If the argument is not abstract but filled with an overt item, we have a construction like (176):

(176) mobil yang biru
     car   NOM blue
     'blue car'

The structure is identical to the structure above; however, both Spec-θP and Spec-NP are filled overtly with *mobil* (177).

(177)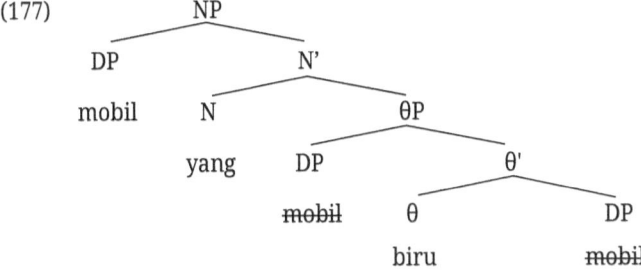

With this structure in mind, we can take a step further to a structure that is normally coined as a relative clause (178).

(178) orang yang baru datang
     human REL REC.ANT come
     'The person that just arrived.'

What makes this structure different from the structures before is that there is an overt T, here *baru*. So, we should talk about a clause. However, this is the only difference. The rest follows the procedure as in the previous examples. We should proceed step by step as follows:

Datang is merged into θ, takes *orang*[49] as its specifier, and assigns the theta-role. After that, Ev and voice are merged, here with a null realization. *Datang* moves via Ev to voice, and *orang* moves to Spec-voiceP. On top of that, T is merged with the overt *baru*. *Orang* becomes the subject and moves into Spec-TP. For a relative clause, we would expect our relative pronoun in C and the reference moving to Spec-CP. We repeat the same two steps, however, by using the nominalizer *yang*, which results in the following structure (179):

(179)

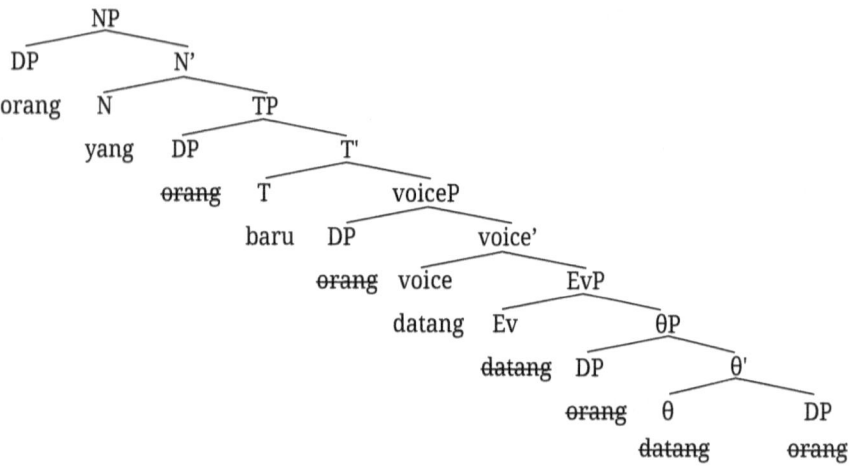

Other ligature forms are *ciptaan* (creation), *buatan* (made by), *milik* (possession) or *punya* (have) (see Loewen 2011: 80; Sneddon 1996: 146).

Thus, we have seen several 'nominalization' processes. Thanks to recursion, we can combine these processes, e.g., in *dua penulis yang sudah terkenal* (two writers who are famous already) (180).

---

[49] Note that *orang* here is the lexical root referring to the concept human and not the homophonous classifier.

(180)

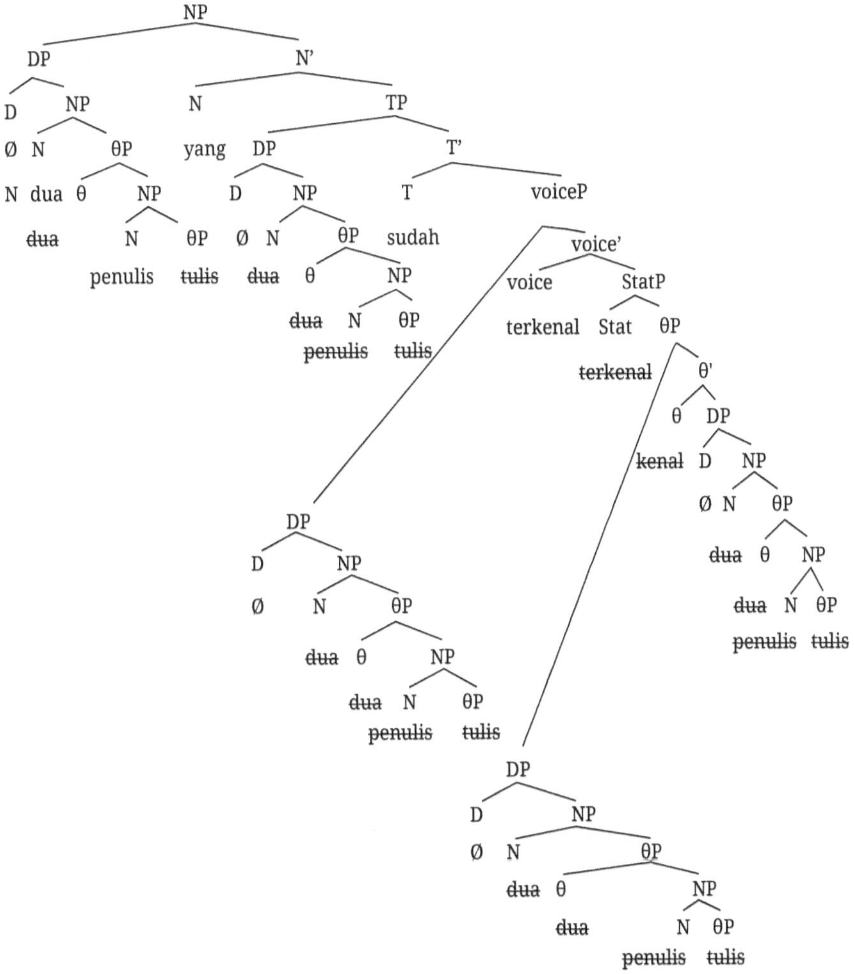

[tree diagram]

3.3.5 Zero-nominalizers

After dealing with overt nominalizers, the next construction of interest is bare forms that are interpreted as nouns, e.g., names like *Udin* or *Jakarta*.

Since we do not assume lexical nouns, *Udin* or *Jakarta* cannot be nouns per se; consequently, we must treat them as roots. We have said that roots merge into a theta-assigning head position. Since we have no overt argument, we take a placeholder item like *orang* (man) for *Udin* or *kota* (city) for *Jakarta*. Here, of course, we find a THEME relation. On top of it, we merge the N-head with a null-nominalizer, e.g., silent *yang*. The abstract argument can move into Spec-NP. So we arrive at a structure like *orang yang Udin* (a man who is Udinish) (181) or *kota yang Jakarta* (a city which is Jakarta) (182). At this stage, the forms are not specified for a definite or indefinite reading. This specification is done in the D-layer merged on top of it.

(181)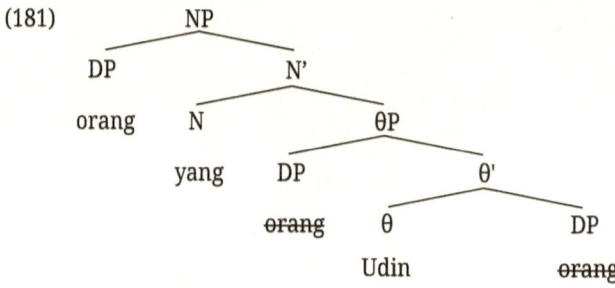

(182)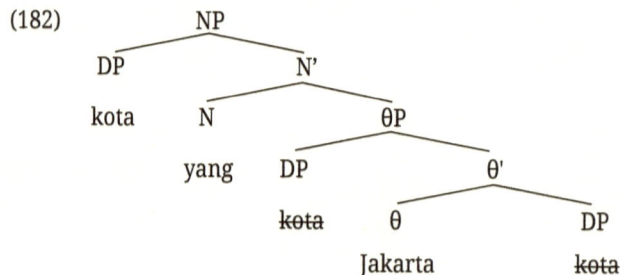

(183)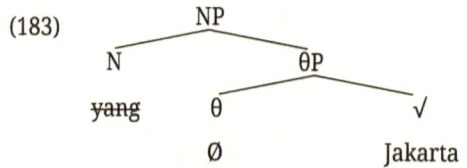

At spell-out, neither the *yang* nor the *orang* is realized. Since these forms are just placeholders, it is possible to take them as inherently null. No movement to Spec-NP is necessary in such cases, and we have a flatter structure (183). That there is some realization possible is shown by a structure like *kota Jakarta* (the city of Jakarta).

So I have shown different realizations of the N-head with either overt noun morphology like *-an*, *peN-* or *per-*, the nominalizer *yang*, and null-Ns either as silent Ns or inherent null-Ns.

However, as stated above, the highest functional head of nominal phrases is D, which will be the topic of the next sections.

3.3.6 -nya

The first form that has to be considered for D is the marker *-nya*. Originally, *-nya* is the enclitic form of the pronoun *dia/ia* for third person singular. However, Dardjowidjojo (1983: 36) offers at least six functions, namely as a third-person possessive pronoun (184), as a topic marker (185), as an object replacement (186), as a prepositional object (187), as a verb nominalizer (188) and as definiteness marker (189):

(184) *Koeswata dari Bandung dan istri-nya dari Cianjur.*
Koeswata from Bandung and wife-3s.POSS from Cianjur.
'Koeswata is from Bandung and his wife from Cianjur.' (Dardjowidjojo 1983: 36)

(185) *Rumah itu atap-nya bocor.* (Dardjowidjojo 1983: 36)
house DEM roof-3s.POSS leaking.
'Concerning the house, its roof is leaking.'

(186) *Dia mem-beli-nya[50] kemarin* (Dardjowidjojo 1983: 36)
3s CAUS.VOICE-buy-3s.POSS yesterday.
'She bought it yesterday.'

(187) *berikan ini kepada-nya.* (Dardjowidjojo 1983: 36)
give DEM to-3s.POSS
'Give it to him.'

(188) *Mem-beli-nya di mana?* (Dardjowidjojo 1983: 36)
CAUS.VOICE-buy-3s.POSS in which.
'Where was the buying?'

(189) *Tolong papan tulis-nya di-hapus.* (Dardjowidjojo 1983: 36)
help board write-3s.POSS PASS-erase.
'Please clean the blackboard!'

For our present purpose, only (184), (188), and (189) are of interest.

Although the first usage is seen as prototypical possessive marking, the possessive semantics are not always that clear. In (190) reference is not the statue in possession of General Sudirman but the statue representing General Sudirman. In (191), it is the writing done by Pramoedya Ananta Toer and not the writing in his possession.

---

[50] Tadmor (2007) argues for Arabic influence on that construction.

(190) *Jenderal Sudirman sangat penting bagi Indonesia. Patung-nya*
General Sudirman very important for Indonesia. statue-3s.POSS
ada di Jakarta.
be in Jakarta.
'General Sudirman was very important for Indonesia. His statue is in Jakarta.'

(191) *Pramoedya Ananta Toer penulis Indonesia. Tulisan-nya terkenal*
Pramoedya Ananta Toer writer Indonesia. writing-3s.POSS famous
di seluruh dunia.
in whole world
'Pramoedya Ananta Toer was an Indonesian writer. His work is known around the world.'

Since it is possible to have the "possessor" expressed overtly, the *-nya* constructions could be treated as a ligature, especially since the occurrence of *-nya* is not obligatory.

(192) *Anak Adit* vs. *Anaknya Adit* (Adit's child).

Like the voice-head that links a predicate to its subject, a ligature can be seen as a functional head connecting a noun with its attributes (see Verhaar 1981). In other words, the functional head voice (v) makes a constituent a verb, whereas the ligature makes it a noun. Hence, *-nya* would be a nominalizer. Therefore we can subsume functions (184) and (188) as nominalization[51].

We can even find the same semantic relations between thematic roles for nouns and attributes. Verhaar (1988) (see also (Foley 1976: 79–81) identifies three basic relations between nouns and attributes, which are possessive relation, agentive, and object relation. These are easily translatable into the three basic thematic roles: GOAL, CAUSE, and THEME.

Comparable to the examples above, (193) can either be the statue in possession of Udin, the statue that represents Udin, or the statue made by Udin (see also Foley 1976 and Verhaar (1988).

(193) *Patung-nya Udin*
statue-3s.POSS Udin

---

[51] Since syntactic categories are dependent on both the Cat-layer and the δ-layer, nominalisation can occur both in the N and the D-head.

In each case, *patung* is merged into the θ-head and Udin in the Spec-θP, where it is assigned a thematic role depending on the interpretation. Since *patung* has the referential status of an object, *patung* is merged with N, however, without overt morphology. Equivalent to voice, *-nya* attracts the theta-relation assigning head and assigns reference status and argument status (194). According to the threefold system introduced for syntactic categories, *-nya* as comparable to voice should occupy the δ-layer. The δ-head for a nominal expression is D. Therefore *-nya* is treated as D, which makes sense since *-nya*-forms are generally interpreted as definite. Therefore *-nya* itself bears the information on definiteness.

(194)

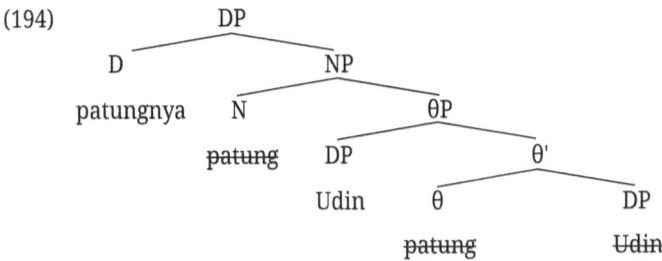

We have the equivalent process for Dardjowidjojo's verb nominalization (1983: 36). The only difference is that we merge a different Cat-layer, here a StatP (195) and no NP (194).

(195) *putih-nya   kuda*
      white-NYA   horse
      'The whiteness of the horse.'

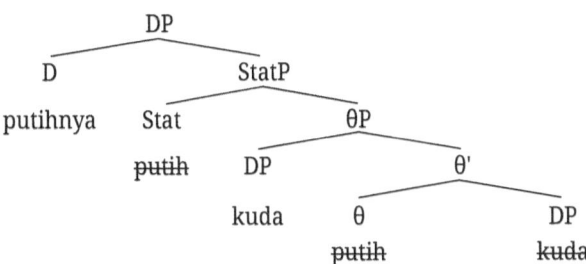

One important question that we have to address is the definiteness of *-nya*. *-nya* can only occur in definite nominal phrases. However, despite the empirical evidence that *-nya*-phrases are always interpreted as definite, *-nya*-phrases – at least in their ligature occurrence – are combinable with the demonstratives *itu* or *ini* (196).

(196) a. anak-nya   Adit itu
         child-3s.POSS   Adit DEM
     b. anaknya   Adit ini
         child-3s.POSS   Adit DEM

Since demonstratives should be seen as instances of D as well, we would expect them to occur in complementary distribution. However, similar to a split in the T and C-layer, several scholars have argued for a split DP (see Kariaeva 2004; Kirk 2007; Isac and Kirk 2008; Zamparelli 2000). In these accounts, the lower DP is concerned with definiteness, while the higher DP is concerned with pragmatic information (Isac and Kirk 2008: 140). Since the *ini/itu* in the examples above have either deictic, emphatic, or topic reading, it fits into the classification of the higher DP. *-nya*, however, is only concerned with definiteness and therefore is a realization of the lower DP. Therefore the co-occurrence of *-nya* and *ini/itu* is no problem for the D-analysis of *-nya*.

3.3.7 Demonstratives

The second candidate for D-categories comprises the demonstratives *ini* and *itu*.
    Ini/itu can be used substantively (197) or attributively (198) (Kaswanti Purwo 1984: 65).

(197) *Ini/itu*   rumah   saya.   (Kaswanti Purwo 1984: 65)
       this/that   house   1s
       'This/that is my house.'

(198) *rumah   ini*   (Kaswanti Purwo 1984: 65)
       house   this
       'this house'

Contemporary colloquial Indonesian allows a substantive and attributive reading in the same constituent (199).

(199) *Itu   tuh[52] enak   banget deh.*
       this   this   delicious very   EM.PAR
       'This is so delicious.'

---

[52] Shortened form of *itu*

The attributive *ini/itu* has three functions (see Dardjowidjojo 1983; Kaswanti Purwo 1984). It can either mark definiteness by deixis (200) or by discourse (201) or function as a topic marker (202).

(200) *rumah itu* ('that house over there')

(201) *rumah itu* ('the aforementioned house')

(202) *rumah itu* ('the house in topic position')

Since both *ini* and *itu* can be used substantively, we have to treat them as lexical roots (203), similar to *mahal* (204) or *biru* (205).

(203) *rumah ini* ('this house')

(204) *rumah mahal* ('expensive house')

(205) *rumah biru* ('blue house')

All three allow a nominalization with *yang*.

(206) *rumah yang ini*[53] ('this house')

(207) *rumah yang mahal* ('the expensive house')

(208) *rumah yang biru* ('the blue house')

According to the nominalization structure presented above, (206) should have the following structure (209):

(209)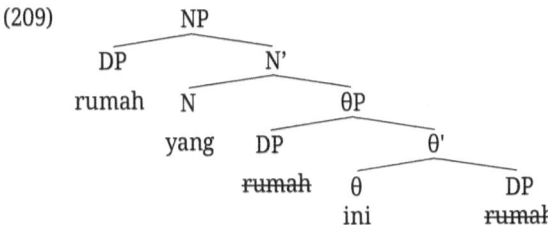

---

[53] This is only possible with a spatial reference but not with a discourse reference (see Kaswanti Purwo 1984).

So far, we have seen *ini/itu* as a lexical root, which is not a candidate for a functional category like D. However, a lexical root *ini/itu* is a perfect candidate for a grammaticalization process towards a D-category. Therefore, we have two instances of *ini/itu* in today's Indonesian, one as lexical root and one as functional head D.

In contrast to *-nya*, *ini/itu* are realizations of the external DP (see split-DP hypothesis in the *-nya* section), as its functional range reaches from deixis, through emphasis to a topic marking (210).

(210) guru-nya   Adit   itu
      teacher-3s.POSS Adit   DEM/TOP
      'Adit's teacher' (pointing at him)
      'Adit's teacher here' (and not the other one)
      'Adit's teacher' (the one we talked about)

This variability can explain the usage of *ini/itu* with pronouns like *aku* (1.Ps.Sg.) without imputing multiple personalities (211).

(211) Aku ini sangat lapar.
      1s   TOP very   hungry
      'I am very hungry.'

For bare nominals with a definite reading like in (212), a null-D must be assumed. Ultimately, it is not important whether it is a deleted *-nya* or an inherent null-D; of importance is that the D-head is syntactically available.

(212) Saya pergi ke dapur   untuk ambil minum.   (Dardjowidjojo 1983: 27)
      1s   go   to kitchen for   take   drink
      'I go to the kitchen to take a drink.'

3.4 The T-layer

If we assume the traditional layers of a clause, namely C, I/T, and V, we must focus on the T (INFL) layer next. Traditionally, this layer is connected with inflection and tense marking, both categories that cannot be expressed as overt verbal morphology in Indonesian (213–215):

(213) Saya makan nasi.
      1s   eat   rice
      'I eat rice.'

(214) *Udin   makan   nasi.*
      Udin   eat   rice
      'Udin eats rice.'

(215) *Hari ini/Kemarin/Besok   Udin   makan   nasi.*
      today/yesterday/tomorrow   Udin   eat   rice
      'Today Udin eats rice.'/'Yesterday Udin ate rice.'/'Tomorrow Udin will eat rice.'

However, this does not mean that Indonesian cannot express temporal relations. Indonesian avails itself of what Grangé (2011) calls TAM-markers, preverbal free morphemes. Grangé (2011: 43) identifies at least 14 of them.

3.4.1 Non-verbal vs. verbal TAM-markers

However, a closer look reveals that these TAM-markers are not as homogenous a group as might be expected since some forms can be embedded under negation (216) while other forms do not allow this (217). Additionally, certain combinations are possible (218), whereas the reversed order is ruled out (219). Further below, we will see more differences between these forms:

(216) *Udin   tidak   pernah   makan.*
      Udin   NEG   once   eat
      'Udin has never eaten.'

(217) **Udin   tidak   sudah   makan.*
      Udin   NEG   ANT   eat
      Intended: 'Udin has not eaten.'

(218) *Udin   sudah   pernah   makan.*
      Udin   ANT   once   eat
      'Udin has once eaten.'

(219) **Udin   pernah   sudah   makan.*
      Udin   once   ANT   eat

On the one hand, we find a non-verbal group (although of verbal origin) that is per se finite similar to English modals. On the other hand, verbal forms are similar to auxiliaries like *have, need,* or *be.*

The following evidence can be used to distinguish these two groups:

a) Occurrence in control clauses

Arka (2013: 27) pointed out that TAM markers in Indonesian are per se finite since it is impossible to embed them in a subordinated, non-finite control clause (220–221).

(220) Saya   men-yuruh   dia   *sedang/akan/sudah/telah/mau
       1s   CAUS.VOICE-command   3s   PROG/POST/ANT/ANT/IMMPOST
       makan. (Arka 2013: 27)
       eat

(221) Saya   ingin   *sedang/akan/sudah/telah/mau
       1s   wish   PROG/POST/ANT/ANT/IMMPOST
       makan. (adapted from Arka 2013: 27)
       eat

This observation, however, is only true for the non-verbal group. The auxiliaries can still be embedded in control clauses (222).

(222) Saya   ingin   bisa/harus/sering   makan.
       1s   wish   can/must/often   eat
       'I wish that I can/must/often eat.'

b) Negation

Similar evidence comes from negation. Whereas auxiliary verbs can be negated with *tidak* (223), this is not possible for non-verbal auxiliaries (224).

(223) tidak pernah   (NEG once → never)
       tidak harus   (NEG must → need not)
       tidak bisa   (NEG can → cannot)
       tidak akan[54]   (NEG POST → will not)

(224) *tidak sudah   (NEG ANT)
       *tidak telah   (NEG ANT)
       *tidak sedang   (NEG PROG)

---

[54] *Akan* provides mixed evidence since it can be negated by *tidak*, but cannot be embedded in a control clause (see above). We will deal with this problem further below.

c) Nominalisation

The third category of evidence is nominalization. Since no overt derivational morphology indicates such a process, we need to identify a nominal form by its syntactic behaviour. One possibility is the copula *adalah*, which is limited to nominal and clausal predicates but does not allow verbal complements.

(225) *gejala yang di-rasa-kan adalah sering buang air kecil*[55]
symptom REL PASS-feel-TH.TRANS COP often waste water small
'One symptom that is felt is the need to urinate frequently.'

(226) *prestasi klub ini adalah pernah ber-main di Divisi Satu*[56]
success club DEM COP once GO.VOICE-play in division one
'One success of this club was to play once in the first Division.'

(227) *Permasalahan lain-nya adalah masih banyak-nya dosen*
problem another-TOP COP CONT many-NOM lecturer
lulus-an sarjana yang meng-ajar di
graduate-TH.NOM bachelor REL CAUS.VOICE-teach in
Perguruan Tinggi.[57]
university
'Another problem is that many lecturers at universities only have a Bachelor's degree.'

(228) *salah satu-nya adalah sudah mengenal betul sepakbola Indonesia.*[58]
one-NOM COP ANT know right football Indonesia
'One of these is to really understand Indonesian football.'

Although sentences (225–228) look alike at first sight, they have different syntactic structures. When we try to insert a *bahwa* (that), a typical C-head, the operation turns out to be possible for (227) and (228) (see [231] and [232]) but not for [225] and [226] (see [229] and [230]).

---

[55] https://ekonomi.kompas.com/read/2015/06/21/111100123/Kenali.Berbagai.Jenis.Kista.Ovarium, last visited 23.04.2020
[56] https://id.wikipedia.org/wiki/Persim_Maros, last visited 23.04.2020
[57] http://harnas.co/2016/02/29/calon-dosen-wajib-ikuti-tes-urine, last visited 23.04.2020
[58] https://sport.detik.com/sepakbola/liga-indonesia/3219015/persela-sudah-kantongi-nama-nama-calon-pelatih-baru-mereka?device=desktop last visited 23.04.2020

(229) gejala   yang   di-rasa-kan   adalah bahwa sering buang
      symptom REL   PASS-feel-TH.TRANS COP   COMPL often   waste
      air   kecil
      water small
      'One symptom that is felt is the need to urinate frequently.'

(230) prestasi klub ini adalah bahwa pernah ber-main   di
      success   club DEM COP   COMPL once   GO.VOICE-play in
      Divisi   Satu
      division one
      'One success of this club was to play once in the first Indonesian Division.'

(231) Permasalahan lain-nya   adalah bahwa masih banyak-nya dosen
      problem   another-TOP   COP   COMPL CONT   many-NOM   lecturer
      lulus-an   sarjana   yang meng-ajar   di Perguruan Tinggi.
      graduate-TH.NOM   bachelor   REL   CAUS.VOICE-teach   in university
      'Another problem is that many lecturers at universities only have a Bachelor's degree.'

(232) salah satu-nya adalah bahwa sudah mengenal betul sepakbola
      one-NOM   COP   COMPL ANT   know   right football
      Indonesia.
      Indonesia
      'One of these is to really understand Indonesian football.'

As a result, in sentences (225) and (226), the predicate must be nominal; in (227) and (228), clausal. The implication is that the TAM markers in (225) and (226) are verbal, whereas those in (227) and (228) are non-verbal. This analysis makes sense if we consider the non-verbal group as per se finite. Thus, the finiteness blocks nominalization.

d) The capacity of being embedded
Grangé (2011) allows the markers to occur in the TAM clusters' first or second position. However, it turns out that certain markers can only occur in the first position. These are *sudah* (233), *masih* (234), *sedang*, *telah*[59] and *baru* (235), basically the non-verbal group.

---

59 *Sedang* and *telah* do not allow any clustering not even in first position.

(233) a. *Adit sudah pernah makan nasi.*
  Adit ANT once eat rice
  'Adit once ate rice.'
  b. **Adit pernah sudah makan nasi.*
  Adit once ANT eat rice

(234) a. *Adit masih harus be-kerja.*
  Adit CONT must GO.VOICE-work.
  'Adit still has to work.'
  b. **Adit harus masih makan*
  Adit must CONT GO.VOICE-work

(235) a. *Adit baru bisa datang.*
  Adit REC.ANT can come.
  Adit could just come.
  b. **Adit bisa baru datang.*
  Adit must CONT come

However, some speakers might accept sentences like (236) or (237).

(236) ?*Kamu harus sudah di sini jam lima.*
  2s must ANT in here hour five
  'You must be here by five o'clock.' (Sneddon 1996: 202)

(237) ?*Kami akan sudah selesai kalau anda kembali jam lima.*
  1P(EXCL) POST ANT finished if 2S(POL) come_back hour five
  'We will already be finished if you come back at five.' (Sneddon 1996: 203)

As we will see below, these TAM-markers are products of a grammaticalization process. Thus, *sudah* still has two 'entries' in the lexicon, one as functional T and one as root. In these cases, *sudah* has to be seen as the verbal remnant of the stative verb with the meaning 'done', 'finished'. This ambiguity may explain the controversial acceptability.

e) Constituency with other auxiliaries
Another indication of the two distinct categories is that they behave differently in embedding the negator *tidak*.[60]

---

[60] *Tidak* itself should be treated as auxiliary as well.

Consider the following sentences:

(238) *Saya sudah tidak makan.*
      1s   ANT   NEG   eat
      'I do not eat anymore.'

(239) *Saya pernah tidak lulus.*
      1s   once   NEG   pass
      'I once did not pass.'

(240) *Pelamar   harus tidak kawin.*
      applicant must   NEG   married.
      'The applicant has to be unmarried.'

Although they look identical at first sight, they are very different in their structure. Whereas in (241), the aspect and the negation marker form one constituent, in (242) and (243), they do not.

(241) *[[sudah tidak]makan]*

(242) *[pernah [tidak lulus]]*

(243) *[harus[tidak kawin]]*

Sentence (244) shows that in co-ordinated clauses, *sudah tidak* is replaced by *masih*, indicating that it has to be a complex marker. The *tidak* can't refer to both VPs.

(244) *Saya sudah tidak makan coklat,   tetapi dia masih*
      1s   ANT   NEG   eat   chocolate   but   3s   CONT
      me-lakukan-nya.
      CAUS.VOICE-do-3s
      'I do not eat chocolate anymore, but he still does.'
      '*I do not eat chocolate anymore, but he still does not.'

(245), on the other hand, shows that *sudah tidak*[61] as one constituent has scope over both VPs.

---

[61] *Sudah tidak* means 'not anymore'. The anterior *sudah* refers to the negation, so the negation has started before the reference time. Since it always presupposes that the negated deed has been

(245) *Saya sudah tidak makan cokelat   dan minum anggur.*
      1s   ANT NEG eat   chocolate and drink wine
      'I don't eat chocolate and don't drink wine anymore.'

(246) demonstrates that *pernah tidak* does not form a constituent as only the *pernah* refers to the two embedded VPs *tidak lulus* and *naik kelas*.

(246) *Saya pernah tidak lulus ujian dan naik   kelas.*
      1s   once NEG pass test and go_up class
      'Once I did not pass the test, and I reached the next level regardless.'
      '*Once, I did not pass the test and did not reach the next level.'

(247) shows the same structure.

(247) *Pelamar   harus tidak kawin   dan rajin.*
      applicant must NEG married and diligent
      'The applicant has to be unmarried and diligent.'
      '*The applicant has to be unmarried and not diligent.'

A similar phenomenon can be observed in the structure of (248).

(248) *Saya sudah mau   pulang.*
      1s   ANT IMMPOST go_home
      'I am already about to go home.'

Sudah mau has to be seen as one constituent. Although (249) and (250) are possible, the *mau* in (249) is the lexical verb 'want', whereas the *mau* in (250) is the immediate future marker.

(249) *Sudah-kah kamu mau pulang?*
      ANT-QUEST 2s   want go_home
      'Do you already want to go home?'

---

done before, we arrive at the translation 'not anymore', although it is not necessarily deductible from the forms used itself.

(250) Sudah mau[62]-kah   kamu pulang?
       ANT   IMMPOST-QUEST   2s   go_home
       'Are you about to go home?'

This clustered structure does not apply to all combinations, as we can see in the auxiliary fronting for yes-no-questions. Clustering is restricted to non-verbal markers (251, 252). Whether it is obligatory or optional depends on the example. This mixed evidence (see also 253) favours the idea of ongoing grammaticalization (see further below). Two auxiliary verbs cannot be clustered (254).

(251) a. Sudah   pernah-kah   kamu makan nasi?
          ANT   once-QUEST   2s   eat   rice
          'Have you ever eaten rice?'
      b. *Sudah-kah   kamu   pernah   makan nasi?
          ANT-QUEST   2s   once   eat   rice

(252) a. Masih   harus-kah   kamu   pergi?
          CONT   must-QUEST   2s   go
          'Do you still have to go?'
      b. Masih-kah   kamu   harus   pergi
          CONT-QUEST   2s   must   go

(253) a. Akan-kah   kamu bisa datang?
          POST-QUEST   2s   can   come
          'Will you be able to come?'
      b. ??Akan bisa-kah   kamu datang?
          POST   can-QUEST   2s   come

(254) a. Pernah-kah   kamu harus tahan kelas?
          once-QUEST   2s   must   hold   class
          'Have you ever had to repeat a class?'
      b. *Pernah   harus-kah   kamu   tahan kelas?
          once   must-QUEST   2s   hold   class

---

62 Clusters like *sudah mau* or *baru mau* might become one complex T-element. In Manado Malay, there is such a grammaticalized posterior marker *somo* which derived from *so* (*sudah*-perfect) and *mo* (*mau*-immediate future). *De somo kaweng.* He will marry soon.

f) Obligatory to have an overt subject

The last evidential property is the behaviour towards subjects. The finite T-markers always require an overt subject[63] (257–258), whereas the auxiliary verbs can have an expletive null-subject (256–257). Consequently, (255) and (256) should be seen as biclausal structures with a cleft-like *pernah / sering* without an overt subject (not even an expletive subject). For the finite T-markers, this clefting is not possible.

(255) *Pernah seorang laki-laki tidur di kamar dia.*
      once   Q   male   sleep in room   3s
      'It was once that a man slept in her room.'

(256) *Sering seorang laki-laki tidur di kamar dia.*
      often   Q   male   sleep in room   3s
      'It is often that a man sleeps in her room.'

(257) **Sudah seorang laki-laki tidur di kamar dia.*
      ANT   Q   male   sleep in room   3s

(258) **Akan seorang laki-laki tidur di kamar dia.*
      POST   Q   male   sleep in room   3s

This is why the auxiliary verbs are treated as raising verbs.

In summary, non-verbal TAM-markers can be distinguished from verbal TAM-markers based on the following characteristics (see Table 3):

Table 3: Verbal and non-verbal TAM-markers.

Non-verbal TAM-markers	Verbal TAM-markers
Cannot be negated	Can be negated
Cannot be nominalized	Can be nominalized
Cannot be embedded under another auxiliary	Can be embedded under another auxiliary
Can build auxiliary clusters	Cannot build auxiliary clusters
Cannot take clausal complements	Can take clausal complements
Require an overt subject	Allow an expletive null-subject.

Some TAM-markers like *akan* or *sudah* show mixed evidence. How can we account for this? The answer is ongoing grammaticalization.

---

[63] Subjectless sentences like '*sudah makan*' are results of inversion and deletion (see section on the C-layer).

3.4.2 TAM-markers and grammaticalization

Presumably, many (or all) of these markers have derived from stative verbs. The common marker *sudah*, for instance (originally adopted from Sanskrit [Tadmor 2007: 315]), can still be used as a stative verb with the meaning 'finished, done' (259) or as a perfective/anterior marker (260). Other more recent processes like *baru*[64] (from the adjective *new* [261] to the recent perfective aspect [262]), *mau*[65] (from the experiencer verb *want* [263] to the prospective aspect [264]), and *suka* (from the experiencer verb *like* [265] to the habitual aspect [266]) – to mention just a few – also show this trend.

(259)   Setelah   sudah,   kirimkan   lekas-lekas   baju   itu.   (KBBI 2008)
        after   finished   send-TH.TRANS   fast-fast   shirt   DEM
        'When you are done, send the shirt quickly.'

(260)   Udin   sudah   mem-beli   mobil.
        Udin   ANT   CAUS.VOICE-buy   car
        'Udin has bought a car.'

(261)   Ini   mobil   baru.
        DEM   car   new
        'This is a new car.'

(262)   Udin   baru   datang.
        Udin   REC.ANT   come
        'Udin just arrived.'

(263)   Udin   mau   minum   teh.
        Udin   want   drink   tea
        'Udin wants to drink tea.'

(264)   Udin   mau   muntah.
        Udin   IMMPOST   vomit
        'Udin is about to vomit.'

---

[64] The Vietnamese form *mới* can be used as "adjective" with the meaning 'new' or as recent perfective aspect. So it is very similar to the Indonesian *baru*. It therefore seems not to be an Indonesian peculiarity.

[65] The grammaticalization of *mau* correlates more or less the desire-future path proposed by Bybee et al. (1994: 254)

(265) *Udin suka minum teh.*
      Udin like   drink tea
      'Udin likes to drink tea.'

(266) *Kepala saya suka sakit.*
      head   1s   HAB   sick
      'I often have headaches.'

What is striking about the last three examples (262, 264, 266) is that they are still regarded as colloquial and non-standard, whereby the grammaticalization process is so recent that it has not (yet) been attained standardized status. There is evidence for a lexical verb stage for most (or all) auxiliary verbs (raising verbs). Therefore, we can assume a process with the forms starting as unaccusative verbs, which change to raising verbs that can only take clausal arguments towards finite non-verbal markers with a strict Extended Projection Principle (EPP). A question that presents itself is what happened in such a process syntactically.

Let us consider *mau* (*want* to immediate future). *Mau*[66] started as a lexical verb *want* (this, of course, is implemented in structure and not in a lexicon). Accordingly, *mau* is a two-place predicate assigning a theta-role to a THEME and an EXPERIENCER. The THEME argument can be nominal (267) or clausal (268).

(267) *Udin mau   mobil.*[67]
      Udin want car
      'Udin wants a car.'

(268) *Udin mau   beli mobil.*[68]
      Udin want buy   car
      'Udin wants to buy a car.'

In the course of time, *mau* has lost its volitional meaning and is reduced to a posterior aspect marker. Structure-wise, *mau* cannot assign the EXPERIENCER theta-role anymore. It has been reduced to a one-place-predicate.

We should, then, assume the following hypothetical intermediate structure:

---

[66] Note that the lexical *mau* is still available in today's Indonesian. However, there is the grammaticalized T-marker as well.
[67] Some Indonesians would even prefer overt transitive morphology: *Udin memaukan mobil.*
[68] Some Indonesians would even prefer overt transitive morphology: *Udin memaukan mobil.*

(269) Mau   Udin beli mobil.
      IMMPOST/want Udin buy   car

At the same time, Indonesian/Malay changed from a mainly verb-initial language to a strict SVO language and developed an EPP feature in T. From an optional fronting of the subject as the topic of the sentence, it became obligatory due to the EPP feature. Like the English modal *will*, it is reduced to a non-verbal form, which is per se finite and is base-generated in T. By now, it can no longer assign a theta-role but only takes a complement.

In the language spoken today, nearly all TAM-markers (at least those of Grangé's list) cannot take nominal complements (stative or unaccusative verbs); however, only some forms have lost their verbal status completely and are per se finite. Instead of dealing with clear cut-offs between the categories, we should treat them as constituting a continuum between stative verbs and non-verbal TAM-markers. This conceptualization allows us to include many more words in this continuum, like *sering* (270), *asyik* (271), or *cepat* (272), which are often grouped as adverbs in traditional grammar:

(270) Udin sering makan nasi.
      Udin often   eat   rice
      'Udin often eats rice.'

(271) Udin asyik be-kerja   di kebun.
      Udin busy   GO.VOICE-work   in garden
      'Udin is busy working in the garden.'

(272) Udin mudah men-cari   pekerjaan (Sneddon 1996: 208)
      Udin easy   CAUS-VOICE-search   work
      'Udin found work easily.'

Asyik still takes a nominal argument, namely *Udin*, and still has overt voice morphology since even (273) is possible with overt voice morphology (*ke-an*)

(273) Udin ke-asyik-an   be-kerja   di kebun.
      Udin PT.VOICE-busy-TH.NOM   GO.VOICE-work   in garden
      'Udin is busy working in the garden.'

Whereas *asyik* still takes *Udin* as its complement, *mudah* takes the whole verbal structure as its argument. It cannot be paraphrased as *Udin mudah* (Udin is easy) and *Udin mencari pekerjaan* (Udin looks for work).

Sering is even further in the process of grammaticalization since it cannot be used as a stative verb anymore.

(274) **Acara   ini   sering.*
       event   DEM   often

(275) *Acara   ini   sering   ter-jadi.*
       event   DEM   often   TH.VOICE-happen
       'This event happens often.'

One salient question arises that we need to address at this juncture: why should we not treat this extended group of TAM-markers as one of adverbs? There are at least two hints that argue against an adverbial reading. The first one comes from head movement.

As we have seen above, T+auxiliary build a constituent, but auxiliary+auxiliary do not. One way of explaining those data is by head-movement, namely V-to-T-movement respectively auxiliary raising. We find evidence for that kind of T-to-C-movement in focus constructions with *-lah*. Here is the evidence for our TAM-markers:

(276) *Sudah   pernah-lah   Udin   bekerja   di   universitas.*
       ANT   once-FOC   Udin   work   in   university
       'It was once that Udin worked at university.'

(277) **Sudah-lah   Udin   pernah   bekerja   di   universitas.*
       ANT-FOC   Udin   once   work   in   university

(278) *Pernah-lah   Udin   harus   bekerja   di   universitas.*
       once-FOC   Udin   must   work   in   university
       'It was once that Udin had to work at university.'

(279) **Pernah   harus-lah   Udin   bekerja   di   universitas.*
       once   must-FOC   Udin   work   in   university

The same holds for potential adverbs.

(280) *Masih   mudah-lah   Udin   mencari   pekerjaan.*
       CONT   easy-FOC   Udin   search   work
       'It is still easy for Udin to find work.'

(281) *Masih-lah Udin mudah mencari pekerjaan.
       CONT-FOC Udin easy   search   work

Since *masih* and *mudah* build a constituent, there should be head movement from *mudah* to T (*masih*). Head-movement, however, is not possible with phrases, so an adverb interpretation is precluded.

The second piece of evidence is of similar nature, namely negation. It is possible to either negate the auxiliary (potential adverb) or the embedded verb and thereby deriving different interpretations:

(282) Udin tidak pernah lulus ujian.
      Udin NEG once   pass exam
      'Udin never passed an/the exam.'

(283) Udin pernah tidak lulus ujian.
      Udin once   NEG   pass exam
      'Udin did not pass an exam once.'

(284) Udin tidak sering lulus ujian.
      Udin NEG   often pass exam
      'Udin does not pass the exam often.'

(285) Udin sering tidak lulus ujian.
      Udin often NEG   pass exam
      'It often happens that Udin does not pass the exam.'

Tidak, however, can only negate verbal structures (voiceP).

(286) Mobil itu tidak biru.
      car   DEM NEG   blue
      'The car is not blue.'

(287) *Udin mem-beli   mobil tidak biru.
       Udin CAUS.VOICE-buy   car   NEG   blue

(288) Udin mem-beli   mobil yang tidak biru.
      Udin CAUS.VOICE-buy   car   REL NEG   blue
      'Udin bought the car, which is not blue.'

Additionally, these negated forms show the identical behaviour when it comes to focalization. For (282) and (284), it is only possible to front the negation+auxiliary cluster (289),[69] whereas, for (283) and (285), it is only the auxiliary that may be fronted (290).

(289) a. *Tidak pernah-lah Udin lulus ujian.*
       NEG once-FOC Udin pass test
       'It has never been that Udin passed a test.'
   b. **Tidaklah Udin pernah lulus ujian.*

(290) a. *Pernah-lah Udin tidak lulus ujian.*
       once-FOC Udin NEG pass test
       'It was once that Udin didn't pass the test.'
   b. **Pernah tidaklah Udin lulus ujian.*

With an adverbial status of *pernah /sering* as an adjunct to either NegP or voiceP, such clustering would be least likely. Thus, these forms should be treated verbally as raising verbs.

How are those raising forms represented in a tree structure? Let us consider an example for each stage, namely a raising verb with voice-realization (*asyik* [291]), a raising verb with theta-marking (*mudah* [292]), a raising auxiliary without theta-marking (*sering* [293]), and a finite T-auxiliary (*masih* [294]).

(291) *Udin asyik be-kerja.*
       Udin busy GO.VOICE-work
       'Udin is busy working.'

(292) *Udin mudah be-kerja.*
       Udin easy GO.VOICE-work
       'Udin works easily.'

(293) *Udin sering be-kerja.*
       Udin often GO.VOICE-work
       'Udin works often.'

(294) *Udin masih be-kerja.*
       Udin CONT GO.VOICE-work
       'Udin is still working.'

---

69 The focalization behaviour is exemplified for the *pernah*-case. The *sering*-examples work identically.

In all four sentences, *kerja* merges into θ and assigns a GOAL role to its specifier, *Udin*. After that, it merges with Stat and voice, overtly realized with *ber-*, and the GOAL moves into Spec-voiceP, becoming the pivot and, therefore, the later subject. This part of the structure is equivalent at all four stages that will be discussed here (295):

(295)
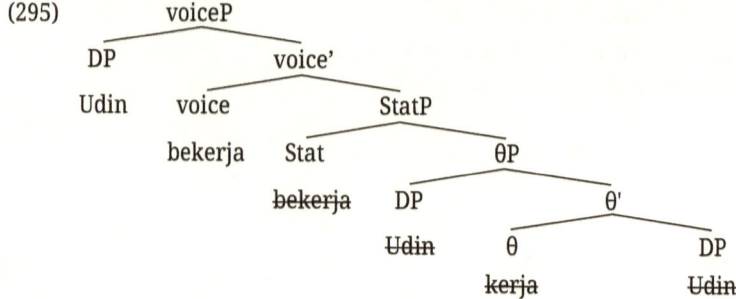

In the first case (296), *asyik* merges with a second θ-head and takes *Udin* as its argument. In order not to violate the theta-criterion, *Udin* is not internally merged (move), but, externally merged for a second time. Therefore, the lower *Udin* has PRO status and is not spelled out at PF. On top of that, we have Stat and voice, and *Udin* moves into Spec-voiceP.

(296)[70]
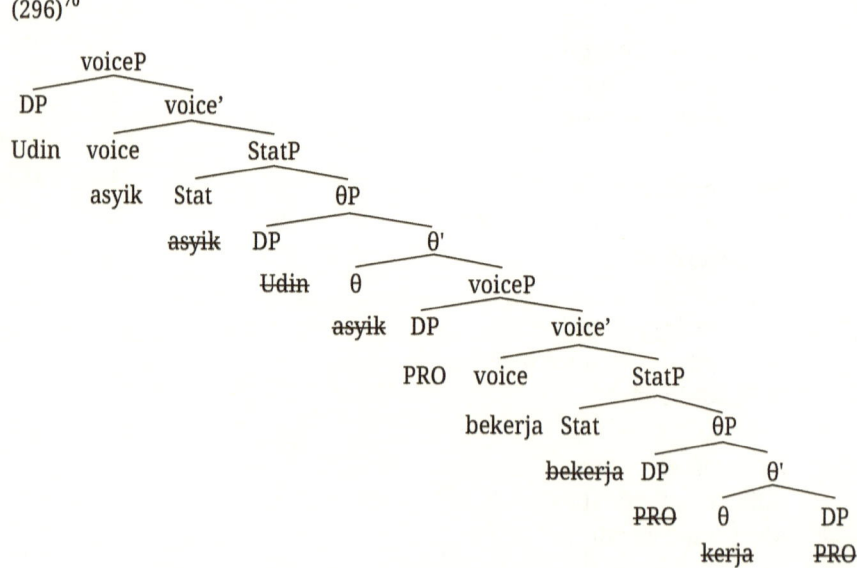

---

70 T and C-layer are left out in example (296) and (297).

In the second sentence (297), *mudah* is merged into θ, and the voiceP *Udin bekerja* is merged into its specifier. On top of that, we have both StatP and a pseudo-voiceP, attracting *mudah*, and *Udin* is extracted out of the inner Spec-voiceP and raised into the outer Spec-voiceP, thereby becoming the pivot of the clause. Since *mudah* does not assign a second theta-role to *Udin*, no PRO is required.

(297)

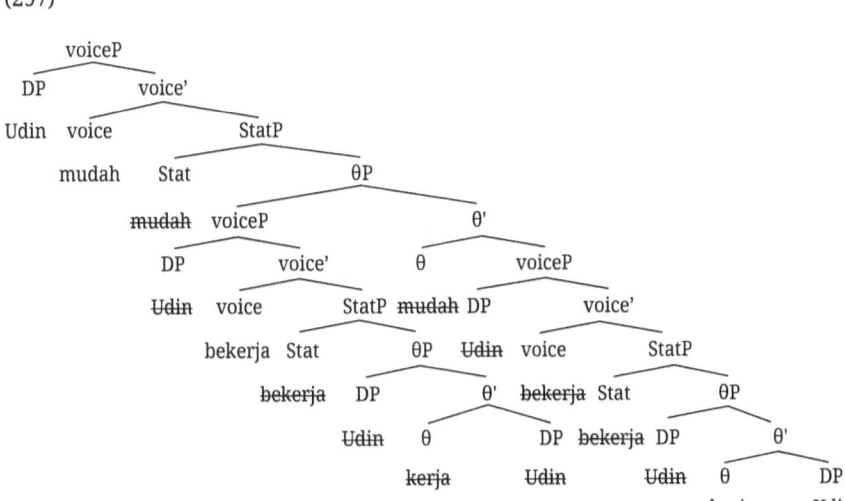

Here the stative verb loses both its theta-assigning capacity and the status of a stative. As a result, it can no longer be the main predicate of a construction. Therefore, in the third structure (298), *sering* does not have a θP and a StatP. As an outcome, only the pseudo-voice-head remains, which is relabeled with Aux. However, on top of Aux, we still have the T-layer.

(298)

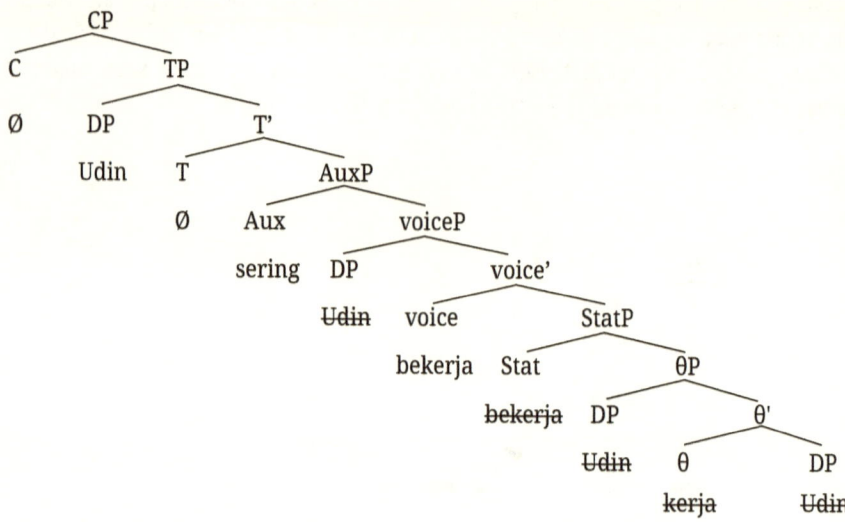

The last structure (299) no longer has an additional Aux-layer, but the head in question is merged directly into T. Thus, whereas Aux can be used both finitely and non-finitely, T is limited to a finite reading:

(299)

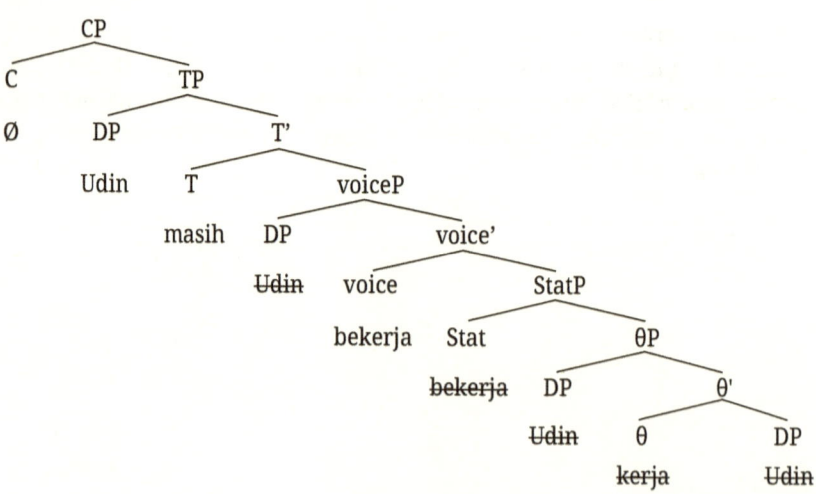

Besides the continuum of these four categories, a fifth category has to be dealt with, however, outside the process described above.

Similar to English adverbs, Indonesian raising verbs should be grouped in sentential (*sayangnya, biasanya, kayaknya, rupanya*) and verbal raising verbs (*pernah, harus, asysik, mudah*), embedding either a CP or a voiceP. Whereas the first group allows an overt T in the embedded phrase (300–303), for the second group, such examples are ungrammatical (304–310):

(300) **Sayangnya** *[Udin masih be-kerja].*
unfortunately Udin CONT GO.VOICE-work
'Unfortunately, Udin is still at work.'

(301) Udin **sayangnya** *[___masih be-kerja].*
Udin unfortunately CONT GO.VOICE-work
'Unfortunately, Udin is still at work.'

(302) Udin **biasanya** *[___masih ber-temu dengan mantan*
Udin normally CONT GO.VOICE-meet with ex
pacar-nya].
girlfried-3s.POSS
'Udin normally still meets his ex.'

(303) **Kayaknya** *[Udin sedang ber-libur di Bali].*
apparently Udin PROG GO.VOICE-holiday in Bali.
'Apparently, Udin is on holiday in Bali.'

(304) ??Saya **pernah** *[___masih be-kerja jam 8].*
1s once CONT GO.VOICE-work hour 8
Intended meaning: 'Once I still worked at 8 o'clock.'

(305) ??**Pernah** *[saya masih be-kerja jam 8].*
once 1s CONT GO.VOICE-work hour 8
Intended meaning: 'Once I still worked at 8 o'clock.'

(306) ??Saya **harus** *[___masih be-kerja jam 8].*
1s must CONT GO.VOICE-work hour 8

(307) ??**Harus** *[saya masih be-kerja jam 8].*
must 1s CONT GO.VOICE-work hour 8
Intended meaning: 'Once I still worked at 8 o'clock.'

(308) ?**Pernah** [Udin sudah pulang jam 12].
      once   Udin ANT come_home hour 12

(309) *Udin **asyik** [___masih be-kerja di sawah].
      Udin busy   CONT   GO.VOICE-work in rice_field

(310) *Udin **mudah** [___masih men-cari pe-kerja-an].
      Udin easy   CONT   CAUSE.VOICE-search GO.NOM-work-TH.NOM

These two groups fit the distinction between sentential and V-adverbs in English. Since we have talked about voiceP-embedding forms only so far, we should focus on the CP-embedding forms in the next lines.

Besides the difference in the constituent embedded, it looks like there is a second difference, namely in the inner structure of these forms. Whereas forms like *sering* (often), *pernah* (once), etc. are bare and should be treated as roots that are merged into head positions, *biasanya* (normally) or *kayaknya* (apparently) seem to be morphological complex consisting of the root *biasa/kayak* and the nominalizer *-nya*. It would be possible to say that *kayaknya* and *biasanya* are DPs with a null-N and an overt D, namely *-nya*. However, although we can identify the nominalizer *-nya*, the meaning cannot be necessarily deducted by composition but is rather opaque. If we consider sentence (311), the example is ambiguous. Its meaning could either be derived by composition (a) *rupa* (form) + *nya* (nominalizer/possessor) or has to be stored as one item (b).

(311) Udin beli mobil bekas. Rupanya masih bagus.
    a. Udin has bought a second-hand car, but it still looks good.
    b. Udin has bought a second-hand car. Evidently, it is still good/It is still good, though.

Therefore, the forms (*biasanya, kayaknya, rupanya, sayangnya*) have to be treated as one morpheme and consequently as roots.

Their structure, then, is identical to the raising structure above, with the exception that a CP is embedded. Let us consider sentence (312). The root *biasanya* is merged in the θ-head, and the CP *Udin bekerja* is assigned the theta-role. *Biasanya* moves via Stat to voice, and Udin, which occupies the Spec-CP position of the embedded clause, is extracted and moved to Spec-voiceP (raising). After that, *biasanya* is further head-moved to T, and *Udin* is A-moved in Spec-TP, where it is assigned subject status in the matrix clause.

(312) Udin biasanya be-kerja.
Udin normally GO.VOICE-kerja
'Normally, Udin works.'

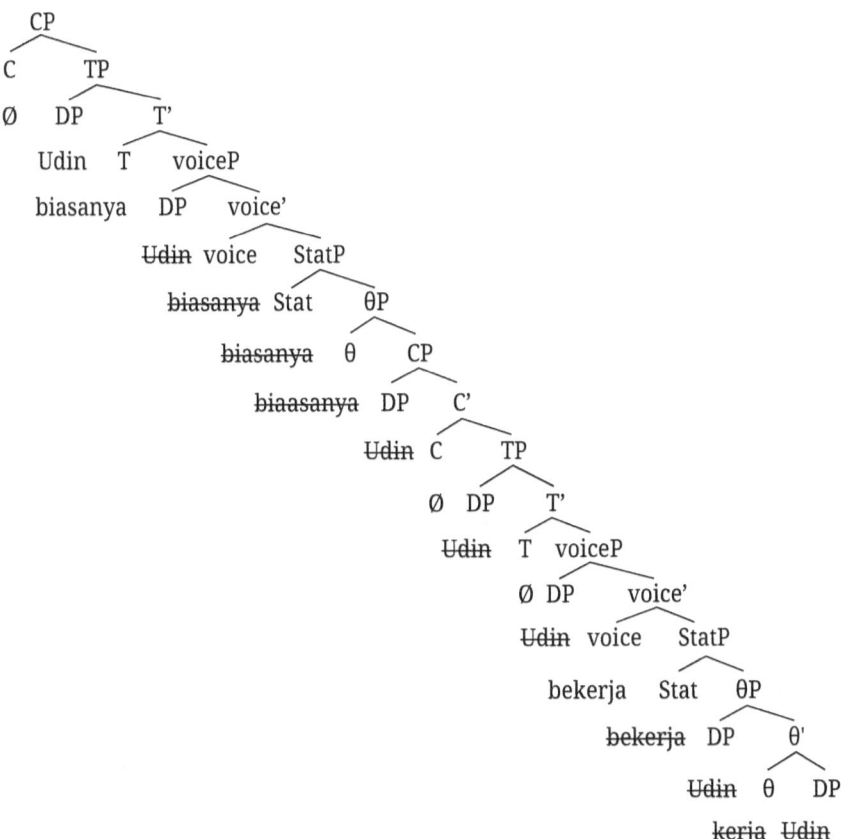

3.4.3 T as a category of relative tense

So far, I have labeled the non-verbal TAM-markers as T without justifying this. The goal of the next section is to supply the grounds for my labeling decisions:

At first sight, it is not very convincing to assume a T-head, given that Indonesian seems not to feature any overt tense marking. However, since any utterance must be related to the time axis, we need to assume that tense is somehow fixed in the derivation. A closer examination might indicate that there is at least some overt tense-marking. Based on Reichenbach's (1947) theory on tenses[71], Comrie (1985) argues for the distinction between absolute tense (the relationship between time of speech and time of event) and relative tense (relation between time of reference and time of event). Klein (1994: 3) replaces S, R, and E with the time of utterance (TU), the topic time (TT), and the time of the situation (TSit). For Klein (1994: 6), the two important relations are between TT and TU (tense) and TT and TSit (aspect). For tense, he (1994: 124) identifies three basic relationships:

TT before TU: past
TT after TU: future
TT includes TU: present

For aspect he (1994: 108) identifies four basic relationships:

TT incl TSit: imperfective
TT at TSit: perfective
TT after TSit: perfect
TT before TSit: prospective

Tense in the sense of Klein parallels Comrie's idea of absolute tense and aspect, as used by Klein, the idea of relative tense. I will use the terms absolute and relative tense instead of tense and aspect, as I follow Comrie (1976: 5) that "aspect is not concerned with relating the time of the situation to any other time-point, but rather with the internal temporal constituency of the one situation." In this regard, Klein's further terminology for aspect is not applicable in this work. I will subsume Klein's imperfective and perfective aspects as one relationship, namely simultaneous. For perfect, I use the label anterior and for prospective posterior. Often (absolute) tense is seen as the basic relationship, with relative tense (aspect) being the default (simultaneous/perfective). Although this may be a European overgeneralization, there is nothing to prevent us from exploring the possibility that relative tense rather than simple tense is the basic relation. And this is, indeed, precisely what Indonesian does. Indonesian TAM-markers do not indicate absolute tense, which is the relationship between TT and TU; Indonesian T indicates relative tense, namely the relation between TSit and TT.

Since relative tense is sometimes not separable from aspect[72], one might be inclined to call the relevant functional head aspect instead. However, suppose we assume the aspect feature to be the decisive feature. In that case, it is problematic

---

[71] According to Reichenbach (1947), tense is identified by the relationship of three points of time: the time of reference (R), the time of speech (S) and the time of event (E).
[72] Aspect in a broader sense not as narrowly used as by Klein as equivalent to relative tense.

that verbs with an aspectual feature like *pernah*[73] (Grangé (2013) argues for a semelfactive aspect) are not per se finite but allow, for instance, clausal complements.

(313) Pernah seorang laki-laki tidur di kamar dia.
      once   Q   male   sleep in room 3s
      'Once slept a man in her room.'

What unites the per se finite T-markers in Indonesian is their relative tense feature. Still, these forms have additional aspectual or even modal features. Nonetheless, these features are not relevant for the classification into verbal and non-verbal, which applies similarly to English modals. The classificatory difference between T-auxiliaries, such as *must* and verbal auxiliaries like *need*, lies in the inherent tense feature and not in their different modality.

The following section will introduce the most important T-auxiliaries of Indonesian.

Anteriority

Indonesian has three anterior forms, namely *telah*, *sudah* and *baru*.

(314) Waktu Adit tiba   di rumah, Udin sudah/telah/baru   pergi
      When Adit arrive in house, Udin ANT/ANT/REC.ANT   go
      'When Adit arrived at home, Udin had already gone.'

In all cases, Udin is not in the house at the moment of Adit's arrival because of his prior departure (anteriority).

Often it is argued that *telah* and *sudah* are identical, with *telah* being limited to the written register (Sneddon 1996: 197–198). The true picture, however, is somewhat more puzzling. *Telah* is a plain anterior marker with a strong perfective reading, therefore *telah* is normally limited to events (315) and not possible with statives (316).

(315) Udin telah pulang.
      Udin ANT   go_home
      'Udin has gone home.'

---

[73] Although *pernah* is normally related to events that happened in the past, it is not necessarily restricted to these. The cluster *tidak pernah* for instance, means "never have and never will".

(316) *Udin telah lapar.
Udin ANT hungry.
'Udin is hungry (already).'

Sudah, however, goes beyond that and has certain modality features implicating a certain expectation of the speaker, which cannot be found for *telah* (Grangé 2011), e.g., *sudah* can carry the information of emphasizing a certain point of achievement (317–319), perhaps counter to the expectation of the addressee. The event is not necessarily completed, with the result that *sudah* can also be used with non-eventive forms.

(317) Udin sudah me-mulai bab tiga.
Udin ANT CAUS.VOICE-start chapter three
'Udin has started chapter three.'

(318) Udin sudah di bis pulang.
Udin ANT in bus go_home.
'Udin is on the bus home.'

(319) Udin sudah lapar.
Udin ANT hungry.
'Udin is already hungry.'

Whereas sentence (320) can only be interpreted in the way that Udin is awake again, sentence (321) is ambiguous whether Udin is still asleep or has already finished sleeping.

(320) Udin telah tidur.
Udin ANT sleep
'Udin has slept.'

(321) Udin sudah tidur.
Udin ANT sleep
a. 'Udin has slept.' (He is awake now)
b. 'Udin is already asleep.' (He is still sleeping)

The third marker, *baru*, is limited to non-formal registers. This grammaticalized form (literally *baru* – new) states that an action or state has recently occurred (Sneddon 1996: 199). I will refer to this construction as recent anterior.

(322) *Saya baru makan.*
     1s   REC.ANT eat
     'I have just eaten.'

In its distributional features, *baru* is very similar to *sudah* but with a different emphasis.

Simultaneity

The most common Indonesian simultaneous markers are *masih* and *sedang*. Before we take a closer look at these two forms, it is necessary to highlight that simultaneity is the default interpretation. Whenever there is no indication to the contrary, either by an overt marker, context, or another decisive factor, a speaker will interpret a form as simultaneous. Hence, an inherent Null-T has a simultaneity feature.

The first important simultaneity T-auxiliary is *sedang*, normally marking progressive (Sneddon 1996: 199).

(323) *Saya sedang makan.*
     1s   PROG   eat
     'I am eating.'

It is not limited exclusively to a present reading (324), therefore must express relative tense (and aspect, of course).

(324) *Kemarin saya me-lihat Adit sedang makan.*
     Yesterday 1s   CAUS.VOICE-see Adit PROG eat
     'Yesterday, I saw Adit eating.'

The second important marker is the continuative marker, *masih*. It indicates that an action is still in progress (Sneddon 1996: 199), thereby marking somehow an imperfective aspect.

(325) *Saya masih makan.*
     1s   PROG   eat
     'I am still eating.'

While several other markers might fall into this group, the above two are sufficient for the purposes of this work.

Posteriority

Posterior forms are often wrongly identified as future forms. In this view, it is often maintained that *akan* indicates an action situated in the future (Sneddon 1996: 199).

(326) *Saya akan makan.*
1s POST eat
'I will eat.'

However, since *akan* is not limited to future usage (consider 327), a posterior reading is much more likely. In (328), it is impossible that Adit is asleep when Udin is home, which should be possible with a future reading. The only possible reading is posterior, meaning that Adit will wait for Udin to come home and then go to bed.

(327) *Tahun lalu Adit kata-kan bahwa dia akan pergi ke Amerika.*
year past Adit say-TH.TRANS that 3s POST go to America
'Last year, Adit said that he would go to America.'

(328) *Ketika Udin pulang ke rumah nanti, Adit akan tidur.*
When Udin come_home to house later Adit POST sleep
'When Udin comes home later, Adit will sleep/go to bed.'

As with the recent perfect, immediate posteriority arose via grammaticalization processes, in this case of the verb *mau* 'want'. Given that *mau* indicates a plan and readiness behind the wanting-expression, it could change from the *want/will* meaning to a pure *will*-meaning. With regard to (329), both aspects are still given, as the utterer both wants to go and is ready to go. However, claiming a theta-role in sentence (330) for the mau is not very convincing, as we would not expect volition in that kind of action. Hence we find the grammaticalized immediate posterior. This example is a prototypical usage of immediate posteriority.

(329) *Aku mau pulang.*
1s want go_home
'I want to go home.'

(330) *Aku mau muntah.*
1s IMMPOST vomit
'I am about to vomit.'

Interestingly, some of the TAM-markers described can combine, so constructions like *sudah akan, sudah mau, baru akan, baru mau,* and *masih akan* are common. In these constructions, a further grammaticalization process (understood as the loss of features) reduced the first constituent to their aspectual features, leading to complex markers with the tense feature of the second marker.

3.5 The C-layer

Traditionally the C-layer is concerned with concepts like topic and focus. Before we focus our attention more fully on these ideas with reference to the Indonesian language, it is necessary to sketch a general outline of Indonesian intonation since evidence for both topic and focus is inseparable from intonation patterns. I will start with a short overview of the most general intonation patterns and then examine the topic and focus on their relation specifically to the Indonesian language.

3.5.1 Indonesian intonation

That intonation plays a crucial role in Indonesian is a very old idea. The intonation of Indonesian has drawn the attention of scholars since Malay was chosen to become the language of an independent Indonesia[74]. In their works of the 1930s, the Indonesian scholars and writers Sutan Takdir Alihsjabana and Armijn Pane[75] (Indonesian scholars and writers in the 30s) had presented initial ideas on Indonesian intonation and prosody. They even argued for a syntactic dimension of intonation (for a detailed discussion, see Halim 1975). Halim (1975) himself connects Indonesian pitch patterns with the pragmatic roles, topic and comment, and focus. We require a general picture of Indonesian prosody before returning more fully to Halim's claim. For this purpose, we will commence at the word level before continuing to the clause level.

Word stress in Indonesian is a matter of ongoing debate. Pitch and duration are normally the crucial factors for stress. Unlike in other languages such as English or German, vowel length in Indonesian is not phonemic[76]. Consequently, lengthening can have no function relevant to the lexicon. Pane (1950) described the close rela-

---

[74] 28.10.1928 at the Youth Pledge (see chapter 1)
[75] Both belong to the publisher team of *Poedjangga Baroe*, one of the first journals to be published in Indonesia (Sneddon 2003a). This generation also had a huge impact on modern Indonesian literature (Sneddon 2003a).
[76] Although in German and English the vowels differ both in quality and quantity, the quantity is often seen as the more decisive factor (see Radford et al 2009).

tionship between pitch raising and lengthening in Indonesian. Both often go hand in hand. His idea is that the pitch accent results from lengthening in Indonesian and is a result of intensity in Dutch (Pane 1950: 63). These Indonesian lengthening and pitch accent effects, which result in prominence, are often not related to syllables but intonational phrases (Odé 1994). This pattern makes it hard to identify a word stress and leads to different analyses. I will follow the mainstream of research, assuming that primary stress normally falls on the penultimate syllable (see amongst others Macdonald 1976, Halim 1975, Lapoliwa 1981, Cohn 1989, van Zanten and van Heuven 2004) as, e.g., Laksman (1994) showed with words in isolation the pitch accent always lies on the penultimate syllable. Exceptions are found when the penultimate syllable appears to contain a schwa, a sound that is barred from taking stress, at least in formal Indonesian. In such cases, stress is preferably placed on the preceding syllable, or as a last resort, on the final syllable (Halim 1975: 62; Lapoliwa 1981: 129). This pitch accent may, of course, be different if embedded within larger constituents (Laksman 1994) or used to signal grammatical contrast (Halim 1975: 62). Otherwise, I assume default word stress as falling on the penultimate syllable.

After we set the word stress, a natural candidate for a pitch event, on the penultimate syllable, any prosodic event outside of this stress position, should be the result of mapping syntactic or pragmatic information onto phonology. Considering a standard Indonesian sentence like (331) or (332), we can easily identify high phrasal tones at the end of every intermediate phrase.

(331)

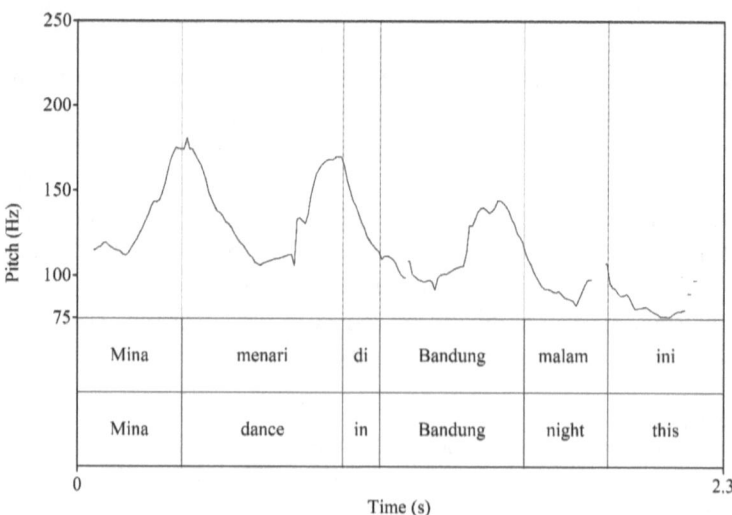

(332)

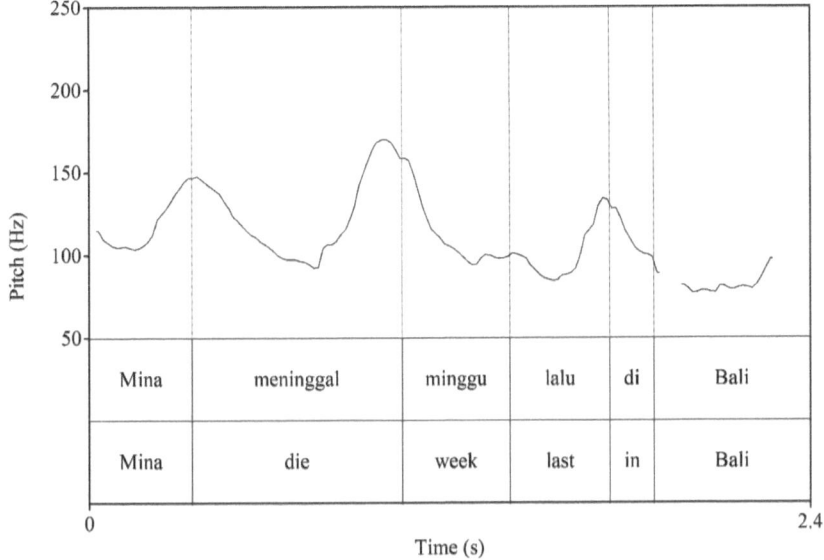

These phrasal tones generally correlate with syntax. There is a phrasal tone after the subject (*Lila/Mina*), the predicate (*menari/meninggal*) and the adjuncts (*di Bandung/malam ini/minggu lalu/di Bali*). Additionally, we find the low pitch accent normally on the penultimate syllable of an intermediate phrase. This pitch accent matches the default word stress on the penultimate syllable of a word.

Additional to this prosodic mapping of syntactic constituents, there is a pragmatic dimension of prosody in Indonesian, involving full intonation phrases. Here prosody is used to mark the topic and comment. Halim (1975) identifies four basic pitch patterns (333) for what he calls pause groups. This term could correspond with an intonation phrase.

(333) a. 233r
b. 211f[77]
c. 231f
d. 232f

---

[77] The numbers represent a pitch level with 1 being the lowest and 3 the highest pitch level. *f* represents a falling tone and *r* a rising tone.

These patterns are closely related to syntactic-pragmatic functions. (a) and (b) mark the topic. Whereas (a) is the focalized topic[78], (b) is a retracted (unfocused) topic. (c) and (d) are comments (d is used for focalized (fronted) comments). An unmarked pause group, e.g., if it is not embedded in a clause, will have the intonation pattern (c).

These pause groups lead to two different basic intonation patterns: topic-comment order (334) or comment-topic order (335). In general, the first is seen as the canonical word order and the second pattern as the inverted order. Whereas (334) is a neutral statement that Mina is hungry, in (335), the comment *mati* 'dead' is highlighted[79].

(334) 233r / 231f
      Mina / lapar
      Mina / hungry

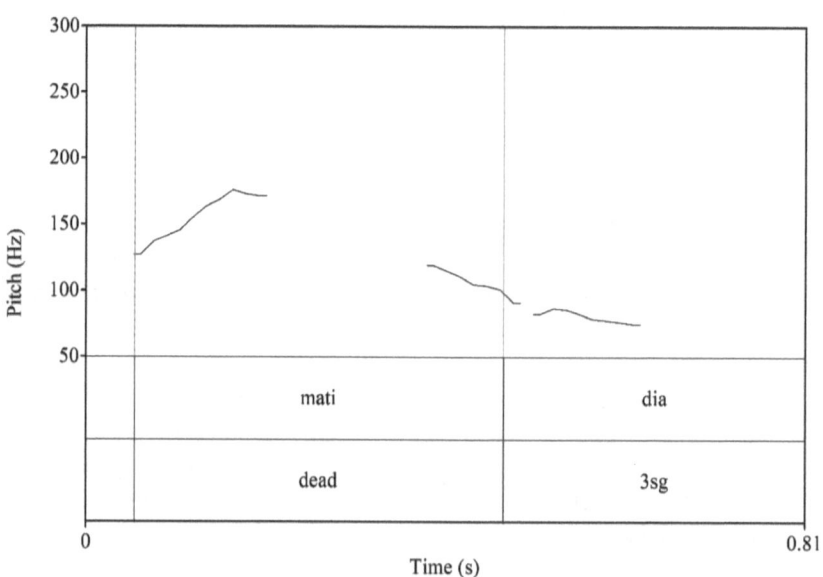

---

[78] These terms used by Halim might be a little bit misleading since the topic is at first position in canonical order. Therefore, (a) simply refers to the topic in its default position, whereas (b) is a topic that is preceded by a focalized element.
[79] For the recordings the sentences were given in isolation.

(335) 232f / 211f
       Mati / dia.
       dead / 3s

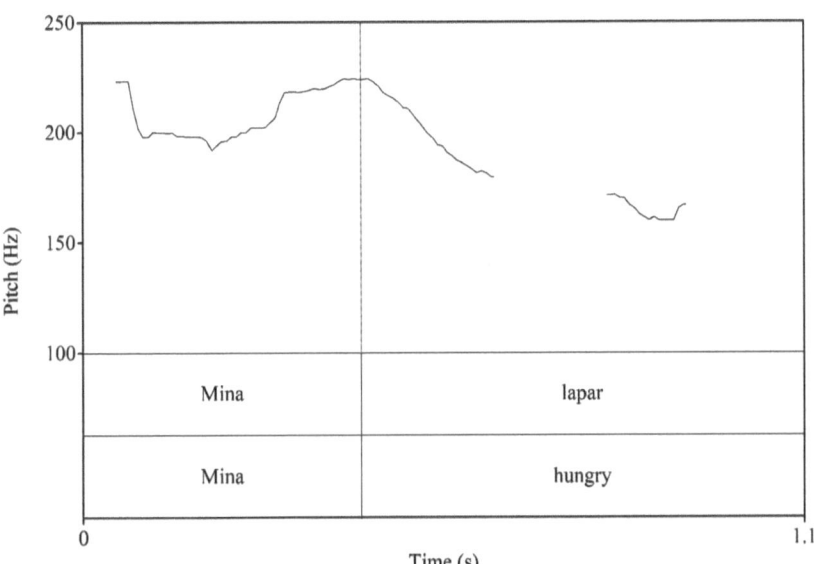

Furihata (2006) correlates topic and comment with subject and predicate. So (336) must be seen as the inversion of (335). This simplification makes intonation a reliable test for argument or predicate status in sentences with non-verbal predicates, which will be dealt with in the next chapter. However, this correlation is limited to clauses without topicalized adjuncts. As soon as the clause-initial position (topic) is filled by an element other than the subject, the picture changes, as there is an additional intonation phrase. Nevertheless, Furihata's simplification can provide important test results.

As soon as we have a fronted adjunct in the topic position (336), the break after that position is obligatory. It still follows Halim's general pattern for a topic. There is only a phrasal but no boundary tone between subject and predicate. Therefore it does not mark the boundary of an intonation phrase, and so a break is not possible.

(336)

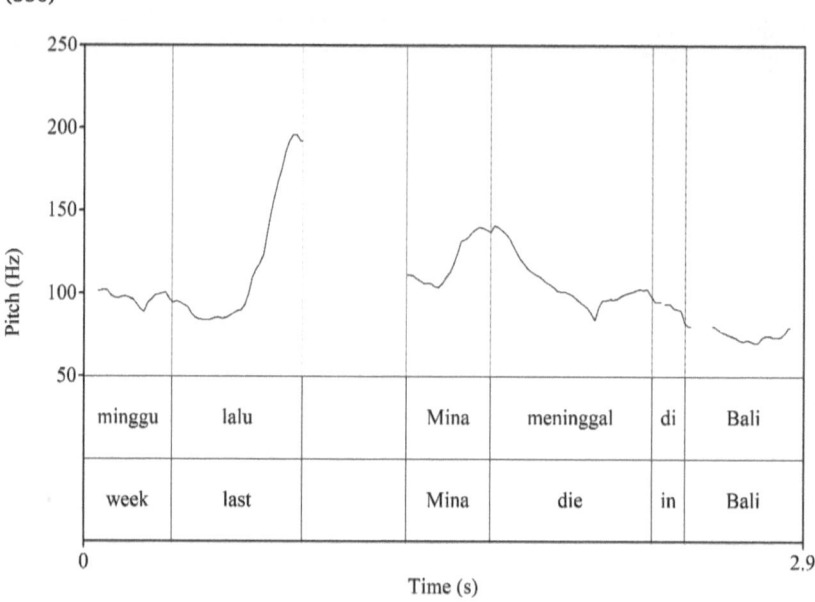

Since "it is a usual assumption that topicalized elements are parsed as separate I-phrases" (An 2007: 37), the break should be seen as a phonological cue to indicate a separate intonation phrase. A separate intonation phrase is only available for extra-clausal elements, so syntactically higher than C. Given that a break is available for both of Halim's standard prosodic patterns, the standard structure and the inverted structure should involve two iPs and therefore have a relation to the C-layer. Having dealt briefly with Indonesian prosody as an argument for a C-layer, I will address this layer's syntactic dimension in the next section.

3.5.2 Topic

The first pattern that needs to be accounted for is the "standard" pattern with topic-comment order. We have seen that the Spec-T position is a topical subject position. In a simple clause, the subject is also the topic, resulting in the typical intonation pattern described by Halim (1975), 233r. However, it is also possible to have a non-subject constituent, normally an adverbial or a prepositional phrase, in the clause-initial position. These adverbials can generally appear in a clause-initial (337) or a clause-final position (338).

(337) *Minggu lalu Mina meninggal.*
week past Mina die
'Last week, Mina died.'

(338) *Mina meninggal minggu lalu*
Mina die week past
'Mina died last week.'

These constituents should be seen as adjuncts to the voiceP that can be brought into a topic position, a clause-initial position at the surface. A first surmise might be that the structural subject in Spec-voiceP does not move to Spec-TP. Then this specifier position could be occupied by the topicalized adjunct. This, however, would lead to an unacceptable surface structure (339):

(339) **Minggu lalu sudah Mina meninggal.*
week last ANT Mina die

Therefore the adverbial must end up in a position higher than TP in the C-layer. This analysis is also in accordance with Chung's (2008) observation that the subject obligatorily moves to Spec-TP (Chung 2008). Since the moved constituent is a phrase, the position occupied must be a specifier position. Let us assume a TopP on top of TP. In this case, the topicalized adverbial, e.g., *minggu lalu*/last week, is moved into Spec-TopP.

In clauses where the subject is identical to the topic, the subject also moves to Spec-CP (Spec-TopP); however, this might or might not be mapped onto prosody (with a break).

3.5.3 Focus

Having thus dealt with the topic, we now need to account syntactically for the inversion. Likewise, with Top°, we need to assume a functional head that marks focus. This functional head must be peripheral since the subject obligatorily moves to Spec-TP (Chung 2008). Thus, the focus position should be a Foc-Head in the C-layer.

Indonesian makes available two different strategies for focusing: prosodically marked inversion (normally limited to colloquial Indonesian) and *-lah*-fronting.

(340) *Makan nasi / aku.*
eat rice 1s
'Eating rice is what I do.'

(341) *Makan nasi-lah aku*
 eat rice-FOC 1s
 'Eating rice is what I do.'

Generally, both strategies show the same distributional behaviour. Normally, the whole predicate and its arguments, which are not in the subject position, are fronted (342–345).

(342) *Men-cari-kan Adit buku / aku.*[80]
 CAUS.VOICE-search-TH.TRANS Adit book 1s
 'Looking for a book for Adit is what I do.'

(343) *Mem-bumbu-i sop itu dengan lada / aku.*
 CAUS.VOICE-spice-GO.TRANS soup DEM with pepper 1s
 'Seasoning the soup with pepper is what I do.'

(344) *Men-cari-kan Adit buku-lah aku.*
 CAUS.VOICE-search-TH.TRANS Adit book-FOC 1s
 'Looking for a book for Adit is what I do.'

(345) *Mem-bumbu-i sop itu dengan lada-lah aku.*
 CAUS.VOICE-spice-GO.TRANS soup DEM with pepper-FOC 1s
 'Seasoning the soup with pepper is what I do.'

In general, extraction of the verb is blocked, although it might occur (346) in spontaneous speech. However, these sentences are normally judged ungrammatical in a grammaticality judgment task.

(346) *?Makan(lah) / aku / nasi*
 eat(FOC) 1s rice

---

[80] These sentences may sound awkward to many native speakers since it is mixing registers. On the one hand, the inversion is limited to a colloquial register, but on the other hand, the affixation and the lexicon is in formal style. In order to not confuse the reader who is not familiar with Indonesian I stick to the formal variety in these examples. In a pure colloquial register the examples should be:
 Nyariin Adit buku/ gue.
 Bumbuin sop itu pake lada/ gue.

More complex predicates can be fronted, having either a T (347), an auxiliary (348), or even both (349).

(347) Sudah   makan   nasi(lah)   /   aku.
      ANT   eat   rice(FOC)   1s

(348) Pernah makan   nasi(lah)   /   aku.
      once   eat   rice(FOC)   1s

(349) Sudah   pernah makan   nasi(lah)   /   aku.
      ANT   once   eat   rice(FOC)   1s

Whereas for the bare inversion, a T-only (350) or Aux-only (351) fronting is not allowed, Aux-only fronting with -lah (352) is more common than Aux-voice cluster fronting (353). We find mixed evidence for T-only fronting with -lah (354–355).

(350) *Sudah   /   Adit   mem-baca   buku   itu.
       ANT   Adit   CAUS.VOICE-read   book   DEM

(351) ??Bisa   /   Adit   mem-baca   buku   itu.
       can   Adit   CAUS.VOICE-read   book   DEM

(352) Bisa-lah   Adit   mem-baca   buku   itu.
      can-FOC   Adit   CAUS.VOICE-read   book   DEM

(353) ??Bisa   mem-baca   buku   itu-lah   Adit
        can   CAUS.VOICE-read   book   DEM   Adit

(354) Masih-lah   saya   makan   nasi.
      CONT-FOC   1s   eat   rice
      'I am still eating rice.'

(355) *Sudah-lah   saya   makan   nasi.
       ANT-FOC   1s   eat   rice

If we assume every clause to have a T-layer (overt or non-overt), it seems that the T', that is the TP without the subject in Spec-TP, is moved (except for the Aux/T fronting in the *lah*-cases). However, such a movement has never been attested in a generative framework, nor will I argue for such a movement. Thus, the best guess should be remnant movement. The whole TP would be moved presumably into Spec-CP

(Spec-FocP), in which case the subject has been moved somewhere else before[81]. Thus, the subject would be moved from Spec-TP to what we can provisionally term (as) Spec-TopP before the remnant TP is moved to Spec-FocP.

(356)

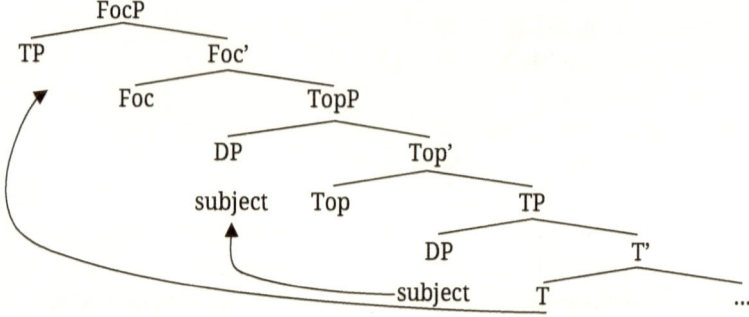

This concept of remnant movement bears an implication for the cartography of the split-CP. Since it is possible to have both an adjunct in topic position and the inverted structure with a fronted predicate, we need, as proposed by Rizzi (1997), a topic position below FocP as the landing position of the subject and TopP above FocP for the topicalized adjunct.

(357) Di   rumah / makan nasi / Adit.
       in   house   eat   rice   Adit

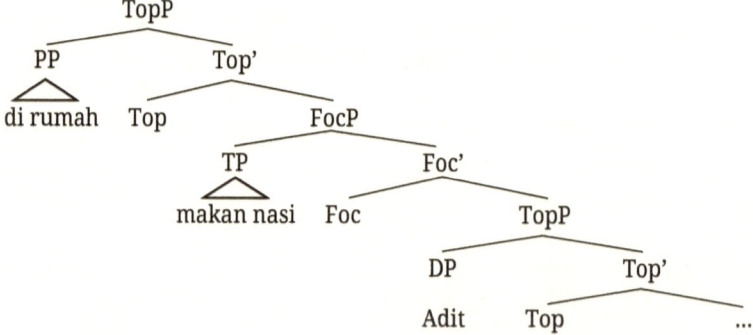

Although remnant movement works for most of the *-lah*-cases (with *-lah* as overt Foc-head), Aux- (and T-) only fronting with *-lah* cannot be easily explained. The only

---

[81] Such kind of remnant TP-movement has been proposed for Seediq (see Alridge 2002)

possibility to keep with the remnant-movement approach for these cases would be to assume the movement of the voiceP into a higher position (similar to the subject) before the remnant TP is moved. This kind of movement could be stipulated for theory internal requirements but lacks an empirical foundation.

Therefore, I will argue for a second strategy for the Aux and T-only cases, namely T-to-C-movement. Since Aux moves to T (see T-section), in both cases, T is fronted. Since we front the head only, head movement is our best supposition. Evidence for this movement can be provided from a diachronic perspective as well as from interrogative -*kah*, which behaves similarly to -*lah* in declarative clauses.

An inspection of data from Classical Malay reveals that at that stage, it was still possible to front the verb without its arguments (358) or simply highlight the verb (359):

(358) *Mem-bawa-lah   dia   kamus   yang   tiada   bersampaian.*[82]
       CAUS.VOICE-bring-LAH 3S   dictionary REL   NEG   attached
       'He brought a dictionary that belonged to nobody.'

(359) *Maka   sekalian rakyat pun   **mem-buanglah**   senjatanya*[83]
       so   all   people TOP   CAUS.VOICE-throw.away-LAH   weapon-3S.POSS
       'So, all people threw away their weapons.'

In Classical Malay, -*lah* was used to highlight the storyline (Cumming 1991). However, besides its role for information structure as a focus and foreground marker (Hopper 1983), there is also a temporal aspect to -*lah*. Since in Classical Malay, today's temporal markers (relative tense) were then still verbal, relative tense could only be expressed with subordination. However -*lah* could only be used in the main clause. Therefore -*lah* also indicated the simultaneity with the topic time (the main discourse). Additionally, -*lah*-forms should be treated as finite forms since embedding -*lah*-verbs was impossible.

Thus, -*lah* in Classical Malay could be seen as a T-category. Therefore, verb initial sentence order in Classical Malay was derived by V-to-T-movement comparable with what is proposed for present-day Tagalog (Aldridge 2002: 408).

With the change in word order, from mainly verb-initial in Classical Malay to SVO in today's Indonesian, -*lah* changed from a T-category to an emphasis and focus marker, thus realized in the C-layer.

---

[82] Von der Wall Letters RAH 67:4, taken from Malay Concordance Project: http://mcp.anu.edu.au/cgi-bin/tapis.pl, last vsited 28.04.2020

[83] Hikayat Nahkoda Asik, 40, taken from Malay Concordance Project: http://mcp.anu.edu.au/cgi-bin/tapis.pl, last vsited 29.04.2020

At the same time, Indonesian allows auxiliary inversion with the question marker *-kah* in yes/no questions. In the absence of an auxiliary, the question marker *apakah* is required:

(360) Bisa-kah Anda datang?
 can-INT 2SG come
 'Can you come?'

(361) Masih-kah Anda tidur?
 CONT-INT 2SG sleep
 Are you still sleeping?

(362) Apakah Anda makan daging?
 INT 2SG eat meat
 'Do you eat meat?'

There are two interesting things to these structures. First, it resembles the auxiliary inversion found in Germanic languages, e.g., English. Second, this structure is very formal. Therefore, it is possible that it has been brought into the language by language development and language prescription influenced by European grammars. Consequently, this auxiliary inversion should be an instance of T-to-C-movement, as we can find it in many European languages. In examples like (360, 361), *-kah* indicates interrogative and not necessarily focus. Therefore it should be realized in Force (a head lower in the C-layer than Foc, see Rizzi) and not in Foc. Consequently, if *-lah* is used in contrast to *-kah* as a declarative marker[84], it should also move to Force. Therefore we do not only have two different movement operations but even two different landing positions.

Therefore, we have two strategies when it comes to *-lah*-fronting: TP remnant movement to Spec-FocP and T-to-C-movement. Whereas the first one is similar to the bare inversion indicated by prosody, the head-movement account is motivated by historical data.

This short overview of the general structure of the Indonesian language should serve both as the foundation for further explanations in the coming chapters and some helpful background information for readers less familiar with the Indonesian language.

---

[84] *-lah* can also be used in imperatives.

4 Non-verbal predicates in English and Indonesian

After clarifying the theoretical background for the language description, this chapter contrasts non-verbal/non-eventive predicates in English and Indonesian. This contrast is a prerequisite for the competition pattern that will be dealt with in the fourth chapter.

As outlined in the first chapter, the term non-verbal predicates consists of two parts, non-verbal and predicate. The understanding of predicate is here the core of a proposition that describes some kind of situation and takes arguments as participants of this situation. Non-verbal refers to the word class of this predicate form of not being a verb. This structural explanation works completely fine for English; it is difficult to draw a line between an adjective and a verb class in Indonesian. Therefore, the predicate category is determined by a more semantic approach, the idea of being non-eventive. Since verbal forms in English are normally events (in the broadest sense), this semantic definition correlates to the syntactic category in English. Despite the shortcomings for the Indonesian case, the term non-verbal is used for both English and Indonesian forms.

In many languages, like in English, a non-verbal predicate requires the insertion of a copula.[85] Other languages like Indonesian do not necessarily make use of a copula. Therefore, the contrast between non-verbal predicates in English and Indonesian concerns itself ultimately with the distribution of copula(s).

4.1 Copular clauses

Since the idea of non-verbal predicates is inseparable from the concept of a copula, it is necessary and useful to have a brief overview of this topic in general. Copular constructions are a widely described field. Several often opposing approaches have been applied to these structures, and it lies beyond the scope of this work to give an exhaustive survey on the full spectrum of ideas concerning copular structures. My goal here is to present an outline and focus on those main aspects which pertain to the contrast of non-eventive predicates in English and Indonesian.

In general, it is assumed that copulas do not have any semantic (lexical) content (Pustet 2003: 8). They are consequently seen purely as function words; this view begs the question of what the function of a copula is?

---

[85] In certain constructions like small clauses the copula is not necessary.

Three syntactic functions are generally attested to copulas, namely (a) as a linker between subject and predicates, (b) as a hitching post to which verbal inflection can be attached, and (c) as predicators (Pustet 2003: 2). However, this definition does not mean that all copulas necessarily need these three characteristics. In particular, the functions (b) and (c) underlie cross-linguistic variation. In isolating languages like Vietnamese, where we have no overt tense morphology, the copula (here: *là*) cannot take any verbal inflection due to the general structure of the language. For (c), we even have to ask ourselves what is meant by the term 'predicator'. The definition proposed in formalistic approaches cannot be a basis since, in these cases, the lexical category (even if non-verbal) is seen as the (semantic) predicate. Hence, the concept must be based on the more traditional view of a predicate as the counterpart to the subject in a sentence. However, it is doubtful that they really form the predicate for non-verbal copulas (a category we will return to further below). (a) actually seems to be a universal description for copulas, although it remains unclear what kind of linking/relation is meant. As is often the case when dealing with language from a typological perspective, definitions have to remain at a very broad level. Lacking alternatives, I will use (a), despite its shortcomings, as the lowest common denominator to identify a copula category.

As we can see from these few lines, a copula category is far from being homogenous. Several attempts have been made to categorize and typologize copulas. The criteria underlying these categorizations, though, are often markedly divergent. There are at least two different traditions: First is the typological approach based on morphosyntactic criteria, which seeks to identify different copula strategies; the second is a semantic classification based on the status and the relation between NP1[86] (left of the copula) and NP2[87] (right of the copula). We will proceed with a synopsis of both ideas.

4.1.1 Typological classification

Although several typological classifications are available, I will present in exemplification only two classifications, namely one proposed by Curnow (2000) and one proposed by Stassen (2008). Curnow (2000) offers a classification of four copula strategies:

---

[86] Or DP1
[87] Alternatively DP2 or XP2

(i)   verbal copula construction
(ii) particle copula construction
(iii) "inflectional" copula construction
(iv) "zero" copula construction

The verbal copula behaves morphologically like a verb, i.e., bears inflection. The semantic predicate is considered the "copula complement", whereas the argument is treated as a "copula subject".

(363) *Der Junge ist mein Schüler.* (German)
      DET   boy   is   my   student.
      'The boy is my student.'

The particle copula is similar to the verbal copula; however, it does not behave morphologically like a verb. The Irish copula, for example, is not fully inflected but only shows a present/past distinction similar to other non-verbal complementizer particles (Carnie 1997: 61, see also Doherty 1996).

(364) *Is   dochtúir (é)   Seamus.* (Modern Irish)
       COP   doctor   (AGR) James
       'James is a doctor.' (Carnie 1997: 59)

In languages with an inflectional copula, the copula complement is inflected in the same (365) or at least a similar way as a verb (366).

(365) *ben doktor-um*[88] (Turkish)
       I   doctor-1s
       'I am a doctor.'

(366) *ben uyu-yor-um* (Turkish)
       I   sleep-IMPF-1s
       'I sleep. / I am sleeping.'

And finally, the zero copula strategy has no overt copula available.

---

[88] This can only be identified for the first and second person. For third person forms agreement is not overtly marked but remains zero.

(367) *Pnina tinoket* (Modern Hebrew)
　　　Pnina baby.F
　　　'Pnina is a baby.' (Falk 2004: 227)

Stassen (2008) argues for four categories as well:
a) verbal copula
b) pro-copula
c) particle copula
d) zero copula

Whereas the verbal and the zero copulae are similar to Curnow's classification, the particle group – although having the same label – might not be completely interchangeable with Curnow's particle copula. To understand the difference, we need to take a look at the class of the pro-copula, which is not available in Curnow's classification. Here a pronoun or demonstrative functions as the copula (Stassen, 2008), e.g., Hebrew.

(368) *Mose hu student.* (Modern Hebrew)
　　　Mose 3.S.M student
　　　'Moshe is a student.' (Li and Thompson 1977: 428)

The particle copula is the second group of non-verbal copulas, which are not pronominal but derived from several different forms such as conjunctions or focus markers. Since Curnow offers just one non-verbal copula category, Stassen's pro-copulas must be grouped within Curnow's particle copula. For Curnow, the particle copula is thus a larger category than for Stassen. Since the distinction between a pronominal non-verbal copula and a non-pronominal non-verbal copula is at no point decisive for the further discussion, I will retain the distinction between verbal and non-verbal copulas. Arguments for such a dichotomy are found in formalistic-syntactic approaches based on the position of base-generation, namely in V (verbal) in contrast to T (non-verbal).

　　For the verbal copula, it is generally assumed that it is base-generated in the v-layer or anything comparable like Pred (Bowers 1993, 2001), R (Den Dikken 2006), etc. Non-verbal copulas are base-generated in the T-layer, as argued for, inter alia languages, Scottish Gaelic (Adger and Ramchand 2003), Haitian (Degraff 1992), Modern Hebrew (Rothstein 2001), and Russian (Geist 2006). Hence, the T-copula subsumes both Curnow's particle copula (Scottish Gaelic would fit that group) and Stassen's pro-copula (Modern Hebrew and Russian could be placed there). If we take a step back to the function of a copula, we can combine both positions (V and T) with a function attested to copulas.

The V-layer is, in general, concerned with predication and argument structure, and the T-layer with temporal and aspectual marking. Then, these two layers can be easily related to two functions of the copula; the hitching post for tense-marking (T-layer) and as predicator (V-layer). Accordingly, verbal copulas can have all three functions that Pustet (2003) attests. Primarily they function as predicators (syntactic requirement) in the V-layer. Additionally, the copula can be the host of tense-marking, i.e., due to V-to-T-movement as it is attested for English. And last but not least, the verbal copula can function in general as a linker between subject and predicate. Non-verbal copulas, however, should not have a predicator function. They can be either the host of tense marking, i.e., in Russian or Gaelic, or alternatively only the linker between subject and predicate if tense is not marked overtly.

For the rest of this work, we retain the distinction between two copulas, one a verbal copula base-generated in the V-layer and the other a non-verbal copula base-generated in the T-layer.

This analysis leaves us with the categories inflectional and zero, for which we have to account. These two are somehow problematic; for both categories, it is not clear whether we have a copula construction or not. Curnow (2000) argues that a copula links two nominal phrases. In the Turkish example given for inflectional categories, however, *doktorum* can only be treated as NP if we deal with it semantically. Morphosyntactically, the suffix *–Vm*, here *–um*, marks agreement with the subject for the first person singular, which means that it syntactically behaves like a verb. Since I treat lexical items as roots, there is no reason to treat the predicate as a nominal phrase. However, since it bears the same inflection as prototypical verbal structures, I prefer to treat these as non-copula-constructions. In other words, there is no derivational process yielding a verb from a noun, but *doktor* simply started as a root. We only want to treat *doktor* as a noun because we know it prototypically as a noun. However, this tendency is based on our encyclopaedia and not on the lexicon. Therefore, the root is put into the verbal position with the inflection, and there is no need for a copula. To make the contrast explicit to languages where a copula is needed here, I will call the former construction a no-copula construction.

This leaves us with the zero-copula to account for. Here we have two options. Either we treat it as the null-realization of a copula, or we have a no-copula construction as in the 'inflectional copula' group. Here the inflection marking would thus be zero. It follows that for the categorical status, the "zero"-case is not relevant, as it is either a null representation of a verbal or a non-verbal copula or a no-copula construction with no overt inflectional morphology.

As a result, we have two copular categories, a verbal copula, and a non-verbal copula, and finally, a third construction that does not have a copula at all. We will see later on that Indonesian makes use of all three strategies.

4.1.2 Formalistic classification

Having dealt with the typological perspective on copulas, it is time to examine the second line of classification, a more formalistic perspective. Although it started in the area of semantics, I will focus mainly on the structural relevance here. As has already been pointed out, a function that can be attested to all copulas is the linking of subject and predicate. However, it is not a straightforward matter to identify subject and predicate (if indeed they always exist) in copula clauses. Especially in regard to nominal forms, in the following DPs, it is possible to determine more than one interpretation. One of the earliest observations in that direction was made by Donnellan (1966) and became known as the referential-attributive distinction. He observed that constituents like *John's girlfriend* must be treated attributively in (369) but referentially in (370).

(369) *John's girlfriend is Mary.*

(370) *John's girlfriend is crazy.*

One of the first classifications was made by Higgins (1979), who identified four types of copular clauses, namely predicationals (371), specificationals (372), identificationals (373), and equations (374).

(371) *John is the teacher.*

(372) *The author of "The Chronicles of Narnia" is C.S.Lewis.*

(373) *This is my brother*

(374) *Cicero is Tully.*

Although Higgins' fourfold system is no longer generally accepted, his pioneering work gave rise to a debate on classifying copular clauses. The two main questions under discussion are (i) how many types exist and, more importantly for us, (ii) how they differ (structurally).

    Although these classifications originated mainly on a semantic basis, they have immediate implications for structure. With the Principle of Compositionality, we assume that meaning depends on the words used and the structure in which they are embedded. If we assume a (slightly) different interpretation for (375) and (376), then we need two different structures since the words are the same.

(375) *Mary's boyfriend is John.*

(376) *John is Mary's boyfriend.*

The question that has been discussed in recent decades is where do we find the difference structurally.

There are at least three explanations that have been discussed in the literature:
a) Different verbs 'be'
b) Different 'predication' structure
c) Different constituents raised/moved

The first approach claims that there are two homophonous verbs 'be', namely the 'be of identity' and the 'be of predication'. Whereas the latter is a copula verb, semantically empty – it is not even assigning a theta-role – the former functions like a 'standard' transitive verb assigning a thematic role to both its subject and object (see Rothstein 2001: 237).

In the second approach, the difference is assumed in different "predication[89]" structures. In these approaches, the complement of the copula is structurally different. On the one hand, we have an asymmetric small clause (see Stowell 1978) with a fixed assignment of subject and predicate. On the other hand, we have a symmetric structure without assigning predicate status (see Heycock and Kroch 1998; Rothstein 2001; Lahousse 2009).

In the third approach, the difference is not in the predication structure, but operations applied in the derivation after it, namely internal merge. In these approaches (Moro 1997, Mikkelsen 2005, Den Dikken 2006, Adger and Ramchand 2003, Heggie 1989), either the subject or the predicate can be raised to higher positions, leading to different structures and consequently to different interpretations.

Since we have departed from the concept of lexicalism, the first approach cannot be fruitful in this framework. We do not assume that argument structure or something similar is stored in the lexicon but built up by the structure. Suppose the information is not stored in the lexicon and only structure matters. In that case, we cannot allow for two different homophonous verbs but only two different structures of "predication", which leads us back to the second approach. We accordingly only need to consider the possibility of different "predication" structures, and different constituents moved.

---

[89] The term predication is used as a place-holder, since only one of these structures is seen as predicative.

Preliminary to a focus more specifically on possible classifications, a remark on the identificational subgroup is in order: In general, the identificational subtype of Higgins' classification is either not explicitly dealt with or is subsumed under another type (see, e.g., Mikkelsen 2004). I will follow this trend and devote no further attention to this copula clause type.

If we assume Higgins' reduced classification in semantic terms (predicational, specificational, equation), three logical structural explanations present themselves:
(i) All forms have the same underlying 'predication' structure, and differences between categories (if they exist) can be explained by movement (377).
(ii) all three have different underlying structures, and movement is irrelevant (378).
(iii) Two together build a subgroup, so we are faced with two different underlying structures, and differences within a category (if they exist) are explained by movement.

For the last option, we once again have three possible groupings with either predicational/specificational (379), predicational/equation (380), or specificational/equation (381) as a subgroup. This leads us, in theory, to five possible explanations:

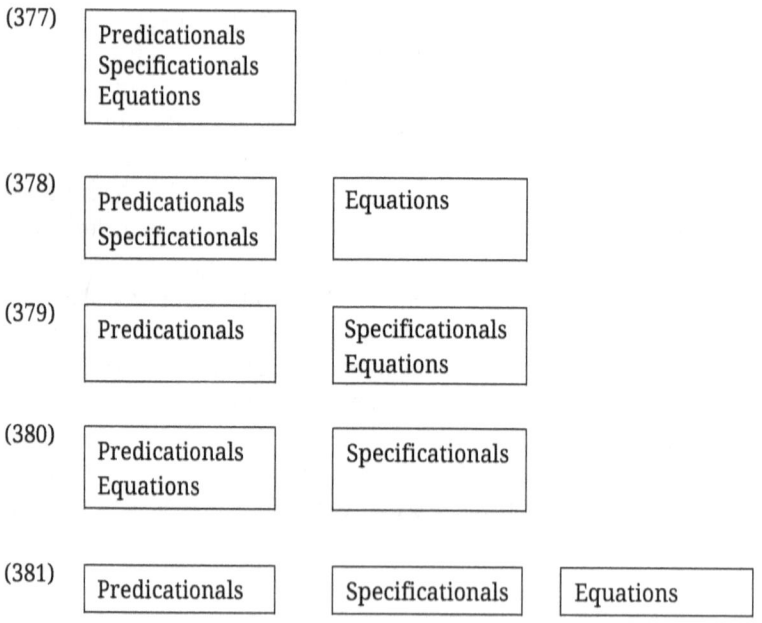

To my knowledge, nobody has seriously argued for options (380) or (381). I will therefore restrict my focus to the first three options only.

The most important example of a type-2 approach (378) is the idea of predicate raising as initially proposed by Moro (1997). In this approach (see, amongst others, Moro [1997] and Mikkelsen [2005]), predicational and specificational clauses are assigned the same underlying structure, an asymmetric small clause. The copula itself is considered a raising verb. The difference between predicational and specificational copular types lies in which constituent is raised. In predicational clauses, the small clause subject is raised to Spec-TP (IP) (382), whereas for specificational clauses, it is the small clause predicate that is raised to Spec-TP (IP) (383).[90]

(382)

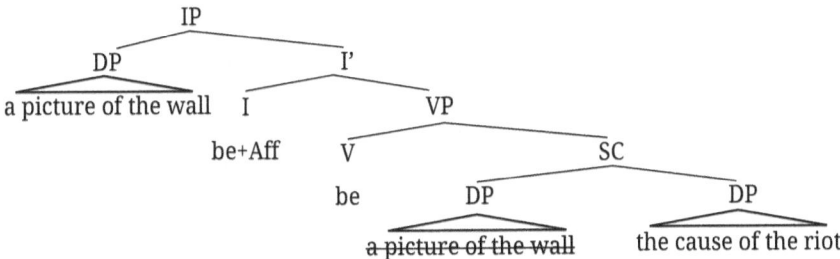

(383)

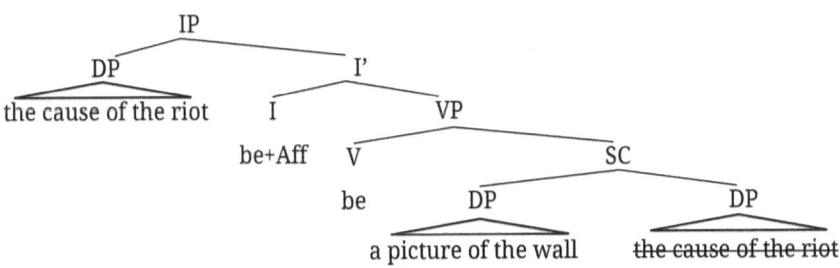

This leads to canonical word order for predicationals (384) and inverted word order for specificationals (385).

(384) *A picture of the wall was the cause of the riot.*

---

90 See Moro (1997: 35). I have adopted Moro's labels here, but changed the trace-representation in Moro's approach to a copy-delete approach according to the Copy-Theory-of Movement.

(385) *The cause of the riot was a picture of the wall.* (Moro 1997: 35)

This predicate raising has to be differentiated from predicate topicalization (see Heggie 1989), where the predicate moves into a position in the C-layer. As shown convincingly by Mikkelsen (2005), these structures can be attested, for example, in Danish but cannot explain specificational structures as originally proposed by Heggie. Predicate topicalization thus has to be treated as a different structure to predicate raising. Whereas this predicate raising approach accounts chiefly for the difference between predicational and specificational, it remains silent on the third group, the equations. However, most scholars who apply a predicate raising approach assume a different underlying structure for equations (e.g., Mikkelsen 2005, Adger and Ramchand 2003).

An exception is Den Dikken (2006), who goes even a step further, arguing for only one underlying predication structure, namely an asymmetric small clause. In contrast to Moro's small clause, Den Dikken's small clause is built with a functional head, which he labels R.[91] Based on this underlying structure, we can have either a canonical constituent order (movement of the complement of R) or a reversed constituent order (movement of Spec-RP). Whereas the predicational type always follows the canonical constituent order, equations and specificationals oscillate between canonical and inverted constituent order. This idea represents a Type-1 approach with the same underlying structure for all examples and movement as the decisive factor for different structures.

Linguists that favour a type-3 analysis normally do not argue against a small clause analysis for predicational clauses, though they reject the idea that specificationals are reversed predicationals. As a general rule, in these approaches, specificationals are grouped along with equations and not with predicationals. These two subgroups, predicationals vs. specificationals/equations, have different underlying structures for "predication". Whereas the asymmetric small clause is still accepted for the predicational group, the structure assumed for the second group varies among linguists.

Heycock and Kroch (1999) argue for some kind of a symmetric small clause (while not presented explicitly) to account for equatives. There is no difference between the two DPs in the small clause and, therefore, no subject and/or predicate assignment. The DP that is moved out of the small clause into higher positions becomes the subject. Since both DPs can become the subject, both constitu-

---

[91] The label R refers to a broader concept what den Dikken calls relator, which is not only available inside the small clause, but everywhere throughout the whole derivation. The copula would be an R as well.

ent orders are acceptable. Rothstein (2001) rejects the idea of a small clause for equations in general and has proposed a "transitive-like" structure for equations. Therefore, DP1 functions as the subject in Spec-IP, whereas DP2 is the complement of V.

4.1.3 Copular clauses and this work

In the light of the foregoing, where is the present work situated? Since this work only deals with English and Indonesian, its goal cannot and need not be to provide an explanation that works for all (or at least the majority of) the languages of the world. For this reason, my focus will naturally restrict itself to the two languages in question. Based on the English and Indonesian data, I will choose those structural representations which provide the fewest difficulties and stipulations. Let us start with the least uncontroversial part, the predicative structure.

One common denominator is the existence of predicationals as a group. For these predicationals, an asymmetric structure with an assigned subject and a predicate is assumed. Evidence for this asymmetry can be found in English bare small clauses (386), which are not possible in reversed order (387).

(386) *John considered James his best friend.*

(387) *John considered his best friend *(to be) James.*

The same asymmetry can be found for Indonesian as well:

(388) Saya   meng-anggap   Dewi   pacar-nya   Ridwan.
      1s   CAUS.VOICE-consider   Dewi   girlfriend-3s.POSS   Ridwan
      'I consider Dewi to be Ridwan's girlfriend.'

(389) *Saya   meng-anggap   pacar-nya   Ridwan   Dewi.
      1s   CAUS.VOICE-consider   girlfriend-3s.POSS   Ridwan   Dewi

A further test in Indonesian is the *merupakan/menjadi*-test. Both *merupakan* (stative) and *menjadi* (inchoative) are at least copular-like verbs (Sneddon et al. 2012: 246) if not even full copular verbs. Since they function syntactically as verbs, the DP1 can be easily identified as the subject and the DP2 as a predicate complement. As such, it is a straightforward matter to identify the subject and predicate for these clauses. *Merupakan* and *menjadi* can occur in typical predicational constructions, namely with an indefinite DP-complement (390) and a definite DP-complement with an attributive reading (391–392).

(390) Ridwan merupakan/menjadi se-orang guru.
      Ridwan be/become   one-CL.HUM teacher
      'Ridwan is/ becomes a teacher.'

(391) Jusuf Kalla merupakan/menjadi wakil presiden Indonesia.
      Jusuf Kalla be/become   vice president Indonesia
      'Jusuf Kalla is/ becomes the vice president of Indonesia.'

(392) Mina merupakan/menjadi istri-nya Ridwan.
      Mina be/become   wife-3s.POSS Ridwan
      'Mina is/becomes Ridwan's wife.'

For specificationals (393) and equations (394–395), the occurrence of *merupakan* or *menjadi* is ungrammatical.

(393) Wakil presiden Indonesia *merupakan/*menjadi Jusuf Kalla.
      vice president Indonesia be/become   Jusuf Kalla

(394) Gus Dur *merupakan/*menjadi Abdurrahman Wahid.[92]
      Gus Dur be/become   Abdurrahman Wahid.

(395) Abdurrahman Wahid *merupakan/*menjadi Gus Dur.
      Abdurrahman Wahid be/become   Gus Dur.

Thus, predicationals should have an underlying asymmetric structure.

The last two examples indicate that equations do not have an underlying predicative structure since *merupakan* and *menjadi* are ungrammatical in either order. Therefore, we need a second structure, one for equations, a view that has become widely accepted (see amongst others Mikkelsen 2005; Adger and Ramchand 2003; Heycock and Kroch 1998, Rothstein 2001, Carnie 1997). Next, we need to deal with the difficult questions:

---

92 Abdurrahman Wahid was the fourth president of Indonesia. He was often called Gus Dur.

(i) What about specificationals? Are they part of the equation or the predicational subgroup?
(ii) What do the underlying structures of "predication" look like?

For specificationals, there is mixed evidence concerning the status of the DP1. On the one hand, the DP1 has some kind of attributive reading (see Donnellan 1966) and a rather predicative status (see Mikkelsen's (2005) classification as <e,t>), while on the other hand, empirical arguments are inclining to the view that the DP1 is an argument, favouring an equation analysis over a reversed predication analysis. One argument concerns the insertion of relative clauses. Whereas it is not possible to add an appositive relative clause (396, 398), which would describe more the property than the entity, it is possible to insert a restrictive relative clause (397, 399), which refers to the entity.

(396) *The murderer, which is a horrible thing to be, is John. (Rothstein 2001: 257)

(397) The alleged murderer who was acquitted yesterday is John. (Rothstein 2001: 257)

(398) *Presiden   negara yang merupakan jabatan yang paling tinggi
      president   state   REL   be   office NOM SUP   high
      adalah   Jokowi.
      COP   Jokowi
      'The president of the state, which is the highest office, is Jokowi.'

(399) Presiden   negara yang lahir   di pulau Jawa adalah Jokowi.
      president state   REL   be.born   in island Java COP   Jokowi.
      'The president of the state who was born in Java is Joko Widodo.'

The second empirical argument is that a pronoun can be dependent on a discourse referent introduced by a definite description (Heycock 1991: 177 cited by Rothstein 2001: 257); here, 'he' refers to the murderer and not (yet) to John (400). Therefore 'the murderer' should be an argument.

(400) Now I realize that the murderer was John. He was wearing size 12 shoes and only John has feet that size. (Rothstein 2001: 257)

The third strand of empirical evidence is that definite forms lead to an agreement effect for plural when coordinated, whereas indefinite nominal phrases do not (Rothstein 2001: 257).

(401) *The Prime Minister and the Minister of Defence in the 1992 Labour government were (both) Yitzhak Rabin.* (Rothstein 2001: 257)

(402) *A teacher and educator is/*are John.* (Rothstein 2001: 257)

In (402), there is simply a reversed order of subject and predicate, whereas in (401), the DP1 has argument status. Based on this empirical evidence for English and Indonesian, I treat the DP1 as an argument and categorize specificationals as equations. However, as already mentioned above, this is by no means intended as a universal claim.

This leads us to the structural representation. Let us begin with the predicationals. For predicationals, I adopt the position that the copula takes an asymmetric small clause (SC) as the complement (see amongst others Moro 1997, Mikkelsen 2005, Adger and Ramchand 2003). One DP is assigned subject in this asymmetric small clause, and one DP is assigned predicate status. I follow Frank (2004) and Den Dikken (2006) and have a zero functional head in the small clause. This functional head is θ, as it would be for verbal predication.

(403)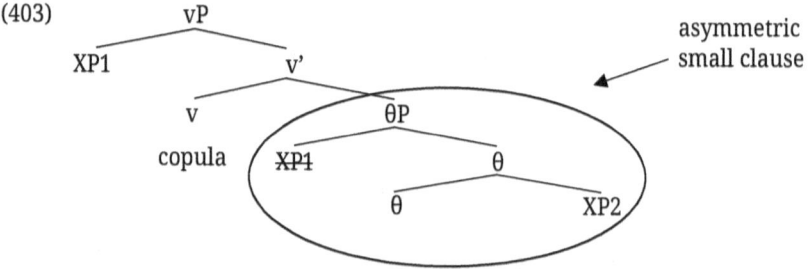

As the complement of theta (remember complements are not assigned a theta-role), the predicate-DP remains without a theta-role (see Geist 2006). Unlike an argument DP, the predicate-DP is not assigned a theta-role in the whole derivation and can therefore function as (part of) the predicate.

As Heycock (1994: 30) pointed out, a maximal projection should either be a predicate or an argument. Since neither of the DPs is the predicate, both must be arguments. Arguments, however, need the assignment of a theta-role (theta-criterion). However, the copula itself cannot assign any theta-role.

Therefore, both DPs have to receive their theta-roles from somewhere else in the derivation, in the best case, before the copula is base-generated. In equations, the two DPs have an identity relation. A sentence like (404) could be paraphrased with (405).

(404) *Cassius Clay is Muhammad Ali.*

(405) *Cassius Clay is identical to Muhammad Ali.*

Since we have two arguments, sentences (404) and (405) are birelational. Another group that is birelational are prepositions like *in, on,* or *at,* for which reason it should be possible to treat these structures similarly to prepositions with a null preposition. As with any structure with two arguments, we merge Stat and Trans, a structure identical to prepositions assigning a theta-role to the first argument. Due to its unsatisfied theta-feature, our Trans-head requires a second argument. Therefore, the second theta-head is merged, and in its specifier position, we merge the second argument. As the null-preposition cannot move into a Stat-head for the second time, nor does it have any semantic arguments for merging with Ev, the structure requires the help of a copula which is merged in Ev and v. From there, the derivation continues as with any other clause, namely with T and C. The following, then, should represent the predication structure for identity clauses:

(406)

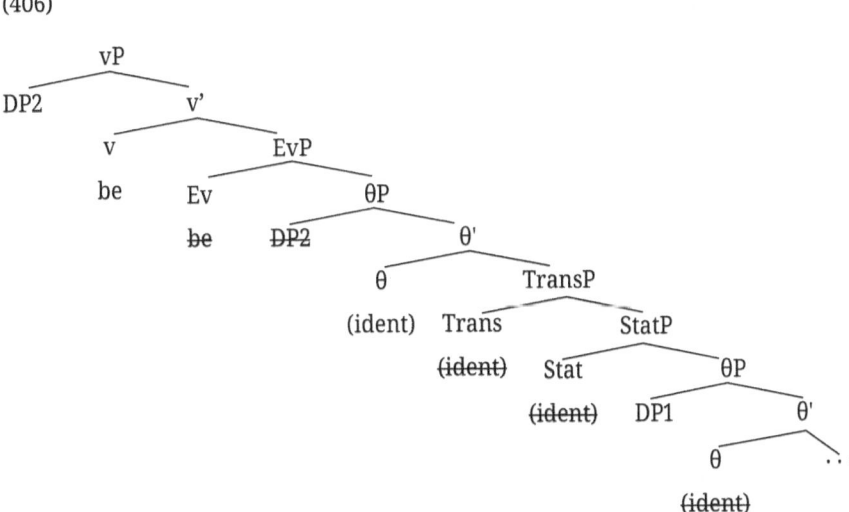

Since we are dealing with non-eventive predicates and not copula structures in general, only the predicational subgroup is relevant for our discussion. In general, the copular clauses dealt with in this work consist of a proper noun as DP1, hence as subject and an AP (407), PP (408), indefinite DP (409), or definite DP (410) predicate.

(407) *John is hungry.*

(408) *John is in New York.*

(409) *John is a teacher.*

(410) *John is the teacher.*

With the exception of (410), all examples are homogeneously grouped in the predicational subtype in the literature. For (410), an equation reading cannot be ruled out (see Rothstein 2001: 267), although the predicational reading is assumed as the default case.

The following sections will address these predicational clauses for both English and Indonesian non-verbal predicates.

4.2 Non-verbal predicates in English

Non-verbal predicates in English are easily translatable into copular structures of the predicational type (at least in its original classification) since, in general, the English copula *be* (in the predicational type) is required with non-verbal predicates, namely APs (411), PPs (412), and DPs (413, 414) (see also Mikkelsen 2005).

(411) *John is hungry.*

(412) *John is in New York.*

(413) *John is a teacher.*

(414) *John is the teacher.*

Recall that categories are not seen as simple lexical primitives in the present work but as results of different syntactic structures/functional heads. Hence, the main question is, what do PPs, DPs, and APs have in common that they need the occurrence of *be*? In other words, what characteristic is typical for a verb but not shared by the other categories?

This observation requires that, in order to deal with non-verbal structures properly, we first undertake a closer consideration of clauses with a verbal predicate. The second chapter outlines that syntactical categories are a threefold system of θP, CatP, and δP. Whereas θ assigns a certain thematic role, Cat assigns a certain semantic class, finally, δ determines the syntactic category. The lowest functional head is a theta-role-assigner; let us consider these two sentences.

(415) *The glass broke.*

(416) *I broke the glass.*

In (415), the functional head θ is merged with the root *break* and assigns the theta-role THEME to its specifier. Next, *break* is merged with the category-head Ev(ent), assigning event status. Subsequent to that, we merge the verb deriving head v (see Marantz 1997, comparable to Harley's (1995) Event, Bowers' (1993) Pred, or Kratzer's (1996) voice). The v-head has an uninterpretable event-feature that has to be checked by Ev. *The glass* moves to Spec-vP and becomes the pivot of the clause. The structural subject position is assigned in T, so *the glass* A-moves to Spec-TP (EPP). T selects the vP with its referential argument predicate. As a result, for (415), we have the following structure (417):

(417)

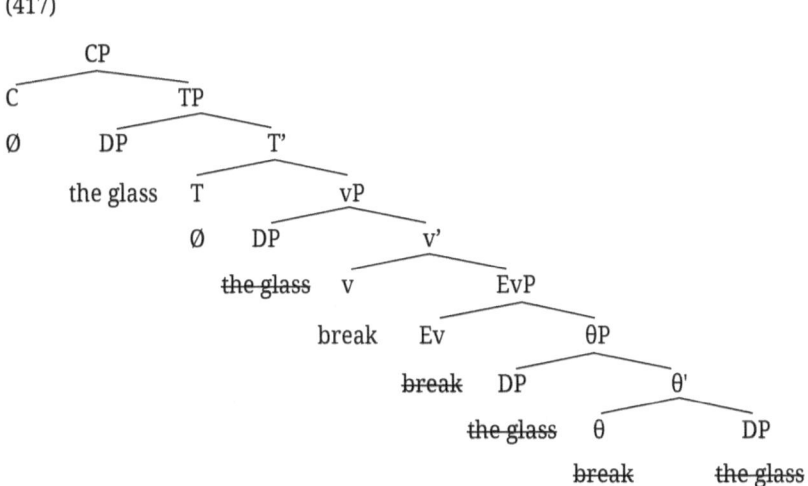

In the transitive case (416), the whole argument structure consists of two smaller parts, a causation (an event) and a result (a state). Therefore, the threefold system has to be doubled. We first merge *break* with a THEME-assigning head, and *the glass* is merged into Spec-θP, where it is assigned the THEME role. Since *the glass to be broken* is the result, hence a state, we merge the Cat-head, Stat. After that, we merge Trans (see Bowers 2002), which can only select a StatP, and move *the glass* into Spec-Trans, thereby making it the structural object (secondary pivot). Since Trans has two uTheta-features, one satisfied by the theta-feature of glass, the second uninterpretable feature must be checked via reverse agree by the second θP. Consequently, we need to merge our second theta-role assigner, θ, now assigning the cause-role to

'T', which is merged into the second Spec-θP. The θ-head specified for CAUSE bears an uninterpretable event feature and thus can only be selected by Ev. On top of that, we need the v-layer to make it verbal. 'T' is merged into Spec-vP, becoming the pivot. On top of that, we merge the TP with 'T', moving to Spec-TP, becoming the subject of the clause. Since T bears an uninterpretable v-feature, the vP is selected for merge. Finally, we merge the CP with a Null-C.

(418)

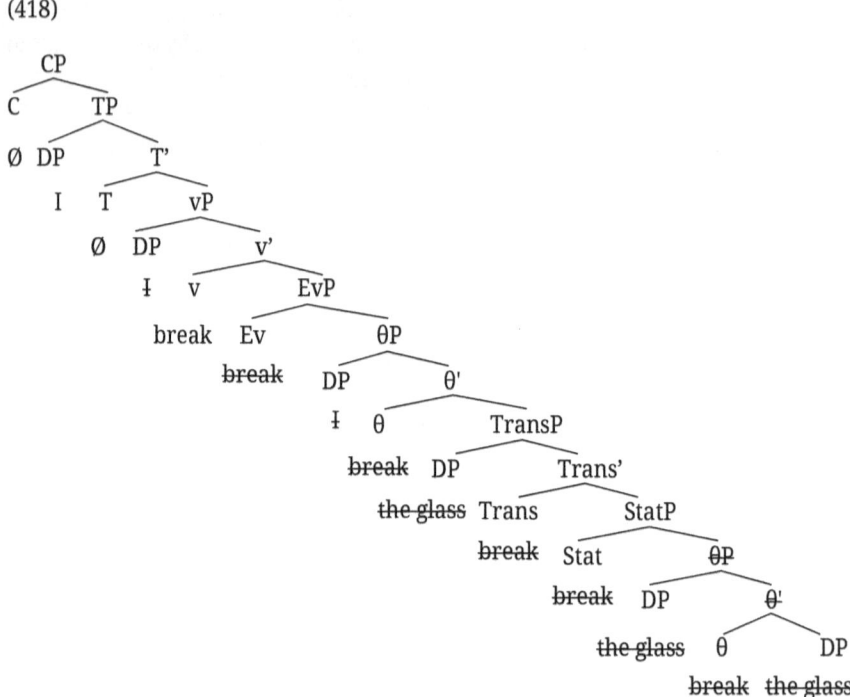

To summarize, the two main characteristics of a verbal predicate are the Ev and, consequently, the v-head with an uninterpretable event feature.

Are all verbal structures eventive then? When it comes to verb classification, scholars tend toward a stative vs. non-stative distinction (amongst others, Lakoff 1965, Vendler 1967, Dowty 1979). Although it might be tempting to see statives as non-eventives, I will show that stative verbs also bear the event-head. If we consider Dowty's stative group (Dowty 1979: 66), there are three possible categories of stative verbs: intransitive forms like *exist*, *stink* and *burn*; transitive verbs like *love*, *know*, *believe*, and two-place phrasal verbs (often locatives) like *sit (on)*, *stand (on)*, *lie(on)*. One test applied to stative verbs is the inability to build progressive forms. This test, however, only holds for the transitive group (419). For both the intransitive candidates (420) and the two-place prepositional verbs (419), we can indeed build a progressive.

(419) *James is sitting on the chair.*

(420) *The fire is burning.*

(421) **John is knowing the answer.*

Consequently, both the intransitive group as well as the locative group should involve an Event-head. Even from a semantic perspective, it makes sense to see forms like *burn* or *stink* as events, as we conceptualize them as such since physical or chemical reactions are at work. For locatives, the absence of movement seems to take us into the state concept. However, as many parents know from experience, sitting (quietly) sometimes needs the fullest concentration and effort for small children. It is possible to treat these cases semantically as events as well. We need to keep in mind that different languages can treat concepts differently. As seen in the previous chapter, Indonesian treats the concept 'laugh' as an externally caused action and not necessarily something done intentionally. Therefore 'laugh' in Indonesian is an unaccusative verb, whereas Germanic languages tend toward an unergative verb. The same is true for roots like *stink* (Indonesian: *bau*). In Germanic languages, it is arbitrarily connected to a concept as actively pouring out some bad odour, thus denoting an event. In Indonesian, it is normally marked with the prefix *ber-*, which marks an undative stative. It, therefore, must be connected to a concept like having a bad smell attached to someone. Consequently, it is a speculative and inadvisable project to group such concepts in some kind of metalanguage since grammar shapes our concepts, and concepts shape our grammar. To sum up, intransitive forms like *stink* and *burn* and two-place phrasal verbs like *sit (on)* have an Ev-head.

We are now left with the group of transitive stative verbs like *know, love,* and *see* as potential candidates for non-eventive verbs. Here, the decisive factor is transitivity. All transitive forms are somehow eventive, which can be explained based on the derivation. As outlined in the first chapter, a transitive form consists of a doubled argument structure comprising both Trans and v. Whereas Trans can only select Stat, v must select Ev. In Trans, there is an uninterpretable feature asking for a second argument. The second argument could be an AGENT, an INSTRUMENT, a CAUSE, or an EXPERIENCER. If we consider Reinhart's (2003) theta-feature system of c(ausation) and m(ental state), the second argument must have either a +m or a +c feature, thus fitting the non-[-clusters] or proto- CAUSE. If we turn it around, the only role that is ruled out explicitly is the proto-THEME. Accordingly, Trans has an uninterpretable feature with the specification [-THEME] or + [non-[-clusters]] and is thus selected by a theta-head with [-THEME]. This theta-head has an uninterpretable event feature and can only be selected by an Ev-head, which bears an event feature. The selection of Ev, then, is a syntactical requirement due to the status of the higher θ-head. It follows that transitive structures are always eventive, independent of their semantic conceptualization.

To state my position in brief, all lexical verbs bear an eventive feature, and consequently non-verbal structures are non-eventive.

Our overview of verbal structures completed, we may now return to non-verbal predicates. All these non-verbal predicates require a copula, normally *be*, from which fact two major questions arise: Why do we need the copula, and where in our structure is the copula placed?

In general, I adopt the position taken by Moro (1997), who treats the copula *be* as a raising verb that takes an asymmetric small clause (SC) (first proposed by Stowell [1978]) as its argument. Whereas the predicate-XP stays in situ, the subject DP is raised to spec-vP. This analysis has been widely adopted by, amongst others, Mikkelsen (2005). Adger and Ramchand (2003) adopt Bowers' (1993) Pred as a more neutral category than V.

However, since the copula is not a theta-assigner but a mediator of predication (see Den Dikken 2006), we need two different functional heads, one assigning a theta-role (at least if we assume that a theta-role is assigned) and one making the whole structure a predicate[93] (or should we say a verbal structure?). We have the θP for theta-assignment, EvP and the vP for the verbal feature. My θP is an asymmetric small clause in the sense of Frank (2004) and Den Dikken (2006) with a zero functional head. On top of that, I have Ev with some kind of pseudo-eventive status as a syntactic and not as a semantic requirement[94] and consequently a v (comparable to Pred) which makes it a verbal structure. Since there is no overt head in θ°, the copula must be inserted in Ev. In this way, we arrive at an analogous structure for both verbal (422[95]) and non-verbal predicates (423).

---

93 This is a structural problem only. Semantically of course, the adjective, preposition etc. can take over the predicate function.
94 The pseudo-event feature should be motivated similar to the event feature in transitive structures namely based on structural arguments. This will be dealt with in more detail in the adjective section.
95 Here, theta could take a complement XP as well, e.g. TransP.

(422)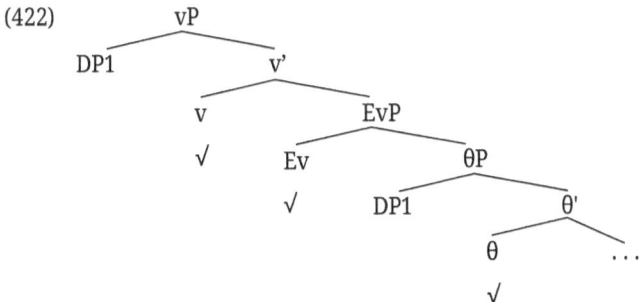

(423)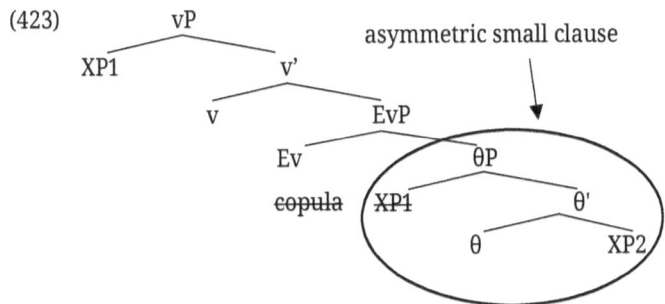

Having covered in outline the general structure, I now turn to the question that remains: Why can adjectival, nominal and prepositional predicates not move into v and become the structural main predicate of a clause on their own, or to put it differently, why do they have to be realized as the complement of the small clause and not be merged into theta themselves? I have argued that both verbal and non-verbal predicates have v-heads. However, for verbal structures, the v-head is filled with the "verb" itself, whereas for non-verbal predicates, it is filled with the copula. In the former case, the root merges and moves via θ to v, while in the latter case, movement to v is blocked. In the next section, I will go through these three different groups.

4.2.1 DPs

Let us take the most obvious case, namely nominal predicates, as our point of departure. Whereas verbs are traditionally categorized as events, nouns are categorized as entities (individuals, objects). Besides the object-denoting head for a standard nominal phrase, we need a D-layer, so the form is an argument and not a predicate. We need two functional heads, Cat(egory) and δ. In the beginning, our potential noun is just a root. This root is head-merged into the category head that is called N, making it a noun, an object, an individual, something that has the property of what the root denotes. Therefore, a book is an object with the property of being a book, and a woman is someone with the characteristics of being a woman.

On top of that, we need the referential functional head, D. This could be any entity with those characteristics, a book (indefinite) (424), or alternatively, a certain entity with those characteristics, the book (definite) (425).

What about "nominalized verbs" like *the fall* or verbalized nouns like *demonize*? Although *the fall* refers to an event (of somebody falling), it is not a predicate but an argument for another predicate. Since we have split this into two heads, we can obtain our structure just by merging the right heads. The root is merged with the θ-head and moves to an Ev-head, making it an event and giving us the impression of being a verb. However, after the EvP is merged with D and not with v, it becomes an argument and no predicate. Hence, it should have the following structure:

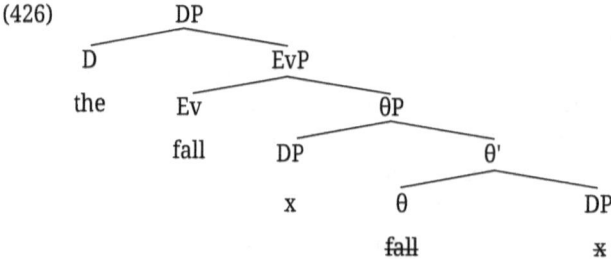

For *demonize*, we have a similar picture. First, we merge the root *demon* with the theta-head and assign the theta-role to its specifier. On top of θ, we need the structure of a transitive verb with StatP and TransP and a second domain with θP, EvP, and finally a vP.

(427)

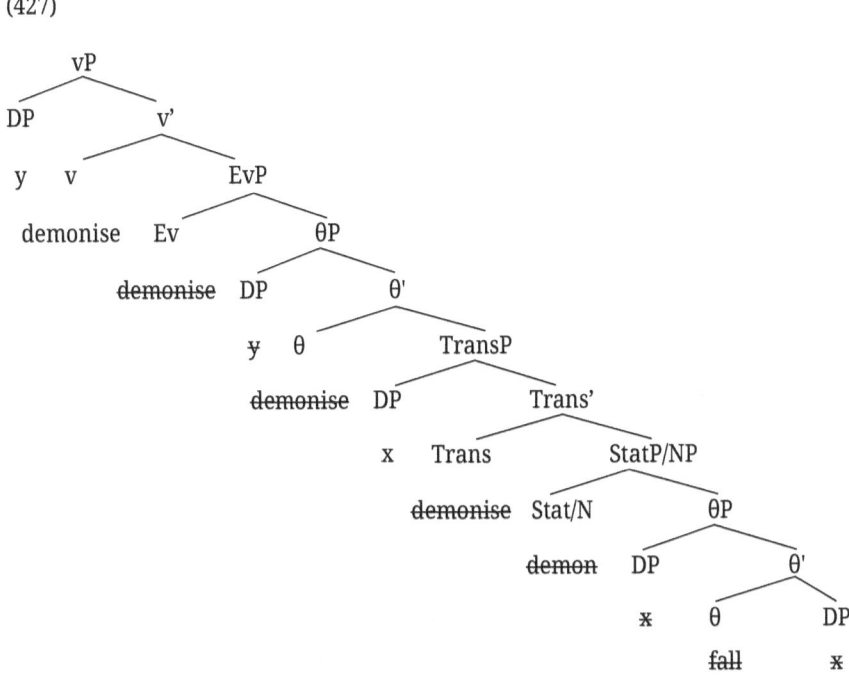

It is perceivable that *demon* merges either with an NP or a StatP. We would get an individual reading in the first case and, in the second case, an attributive reading. Whereas the former would capture the actual incarnation of a demon, the latter refers to a demon-like character.

Here, we have seen traditionally termed derivational processes as instances of head-movement. Whereas Cat still allows further derivational processes, δ blocks these processes. While it is possible to 'verbalize' a noun like a *demon* to *demonize*, it is not possible for forms like *a demon* to undergo further derivational processes by head movement. This makes particular sense since, normally, the merging of D does not involve head movement. Since *demon* in '*a demon*' is not moved to D, only the determiner *a* forms the highest head. Due to Relativized Minimality (Rizzi 1990), only the highest head is available for further movement here D. Therefore, *a demon* cannot undergo any subsequent head movement. Thus, further derivational processes are not possible.

(428)

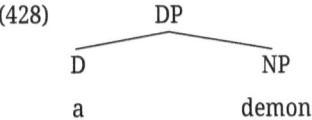

Whenever we want to make a DP a predicate, we need the help of another overt functional head, here a verbal form (429).

(429) *John makes Great Britain a democracy.*

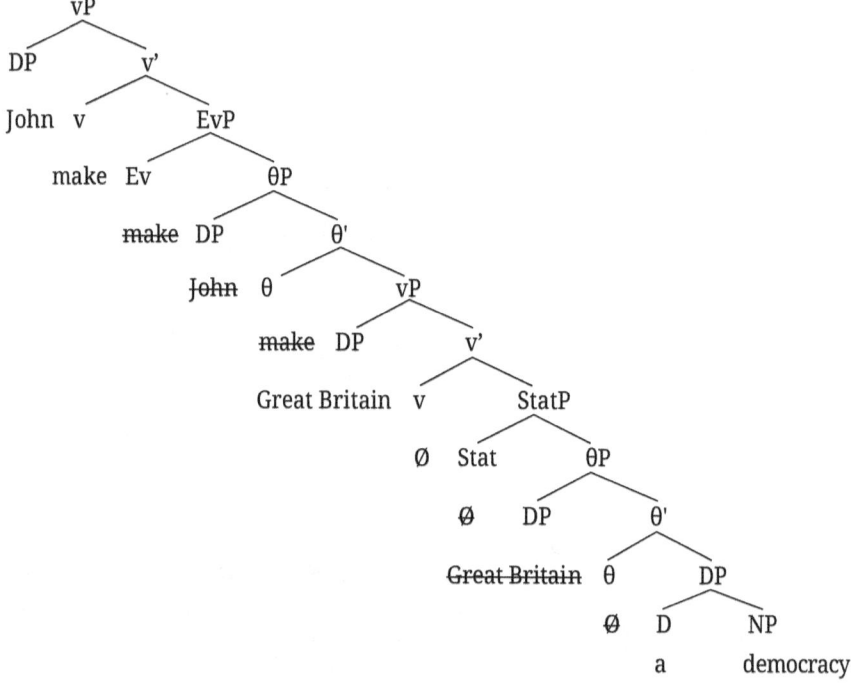

It is possible to argue that 'make' is something comparable to the copula 'be'. Since with a DP, no further head movement is possible, a copula is required. Then, we could subsume that the copula is required when a form can no longer be verbalized. Let us consider the copula *be* and deal with an example with the semantic predicate KING(john).

This form could be either stative (430) or eventive (431). If we allow a transitive form with a second argument, we get (431).

(430) *John is a king.*

(431) **John kings.*

(432) **William kings John.*

Although (431) and (432) are ruled out by prescriptive grammar and not attested in the data, we can still force an interpretation for these sentences. Interestingly, we can predict this meaning to a certain extent. (431) should have a meaning similar to John reigns as a king. It is not possible to get a stative reading. (432) can either be interpreted that William reigns over John or the other way around that William makes John the king or something like William treats John like a king. However, all these interpretations have important properties in common. William is understood as the causer and John as the undergoer, a proto- THEME, and therefore *king* as a transitive form, which must be eventive. How do we derive these interpretations?

We shall start with the last example (432), in which *king* starts like any item as a root and is merged to θ, where it assigns a theta-role to an argument in its specifier, here John. Since the form is transitive, *king* assigns the theta-role (proto-)THEME[96] to John. Since, in turn, the θ-head specified for THEME is rather underspecified concerning its selectional properties, it can merge with N, making it an individual, with Stat(e) and even Ev(ent). On top of the Cat-head, we merge Trans. Since Trans is specified for u[-Event], it can only select an NP or a StatP. The event-reading is thus ruled out since the derivation would crash. Now the path we are taking is fixed by the functional heads we are working with. TransP requires a [-THEME]-theta-assigner (in Spec-θP, we merge the second argument William). θ, specified for [-THEME], requires Ev. Finally, Ev requires v. As a result, we have two possible structures, one with the reading of William makes John the king (here John has actually the position of a king) (433). In the second reading, William treats John like a king (here, John is not, in reality, a king) (434). For the interpretation "William reigns over John," we would expect (434) too, though with a different specification for θ.

---

96 For the interpretation *William reigns over John*, we would have something like a GOAL-role (something like *William causes John to have a king*), which is still part of the proto-THEME.

(433)
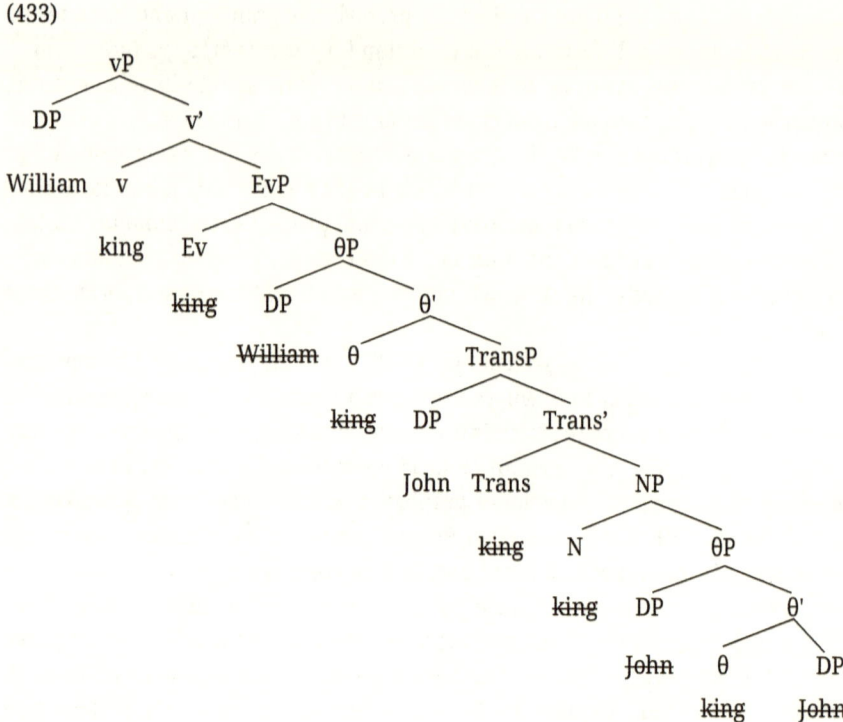

(434)
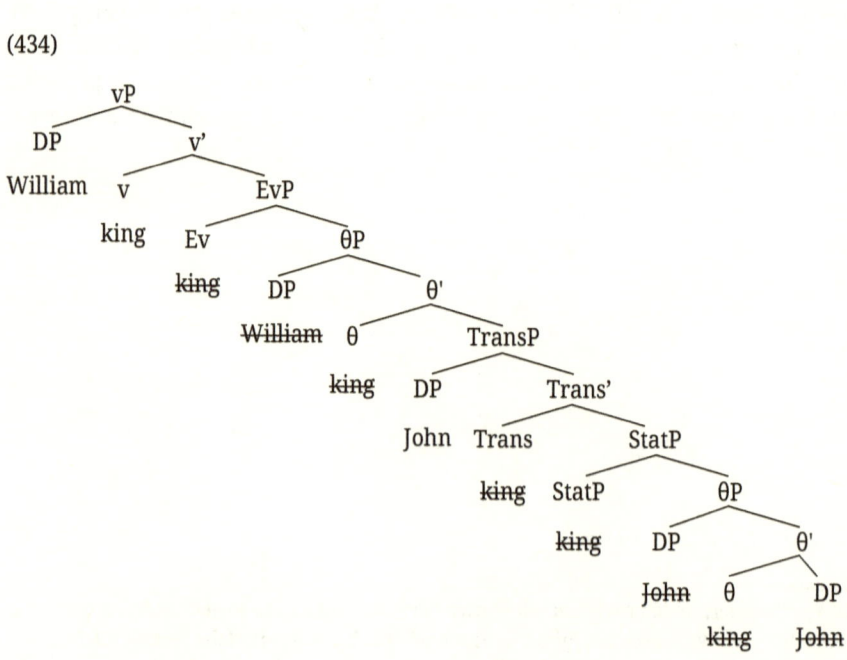

In (431), *king* is merged with the theta-head specified for CAUSE/AGENT.[97] Due to the selectional properties of the CAUSE/AGENT-assigning theta-role, it is merged with EvP and consequently with the vP. Therefore, it is the main predicate of the clause, which is merged with T. To merge it with T, it has to be a vP. To be a vP, it had to be merged beforehand with an EvP, resulting in the eventive reading for (435) as obligatory, so with the meaning of 'John reigns as king'.

(435)

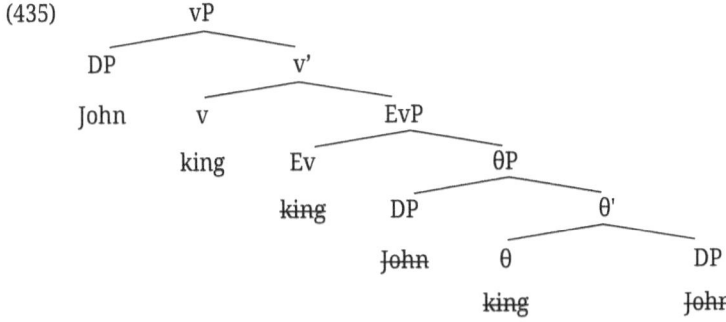

Now let us bring our focus back to the actual sentence in question (430), 'John is a king' with the copula *be*. Why do we need this copula?

First, we follow the same procedure as with (431) and merge 'king' with the theta-assigning head THEME. Since our aim is an individual reading, *king* has to be merged with N. Therefore, the argument in θP is at best abstract, more likely, there is just an abstract THEME-relation without any real argument. The merging of N is the crucial point of the derivation. N cannot be merged with v due to a selectional mismatch and the missing event feature. N can be merged either with Trans, leading to a transitive structure like that in (432), or with D to make it a reference, as in our present example. The D-head, however, cannot be merged with T since it lacks the v-feature. Hence, the DP cannot become the structural predicate of the clause. The outcome is that we need a pseudo-predicate, the copula.

First, we build our small clause, the θP. Since our DP, *the king* is a phrase, it cannot be merged into the head position but into the complement position of θ. The Null-θ-head assigns John a THEME role in Spec-θP. θ is merged into Ev to get the structurally required event feature. At this point, our copula is born. From now on, the structure stands as eventive. The EvP can be selected by v and the vP by T. The copula even head-moves to T, checks the v-feature, inherits the tense features, and is the "hitching post" for the tense inflection.

---

[97] It would be possible that the root *king* is merged with a THEME theta-head. This possibility though is left aside so as not to further complicate the case.

(436)

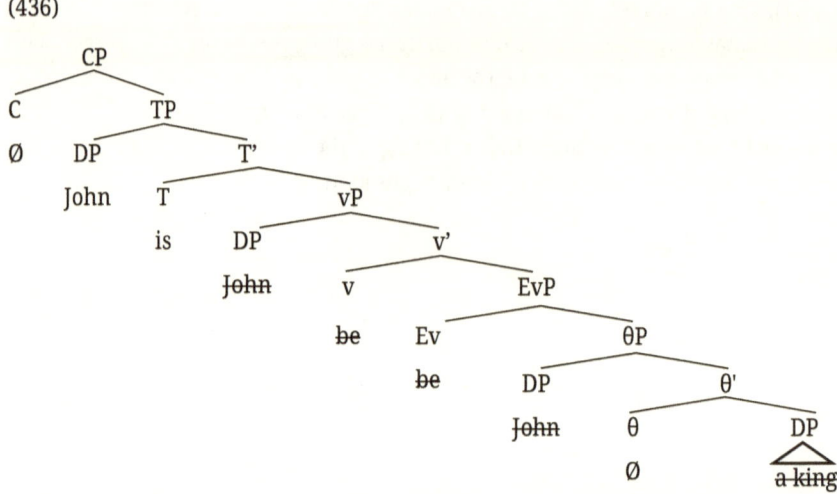

The initial reason for the copula usage is the lacking of an event feature in N. Without an event feature, it cannot merge with v but has to do so with D. The DP cannot merge with T, so the copula compensates for the missing event-feature (Ev) and consequently the verbal status (v).

4.2.2 Adjectives

Having dealt with DPs, we now need to examine adjectives (APs). Adjectives can occur in two functions, either as predicates with the help of a copula or as modifiers of NPs. Before we come to the more relevant case for this work, the predicate case, we shall first deal with the modifying function.

We need two functional heads for every syntactic category, assuming an identical structure with verbs and nouns, namely Cat and δ. In general, adjectives are seen as something denoting a property or a state. The latter especially provides a contrast to the eventive character of verbs. For this reason, I label the CatP identifying adjectives as StatP. Overt realizations of the Stat-head in English are suffixes such as *-ish*, *-y*, or *-ful*. Mirroring the structure of verbs with the v-layer and nouns with a D-layer, we need a second functional head on top of Stat. In the same fashion as D (if it is definite) denotes one unique entity selected from all individuals sharing a certain characteristic, e.g., one certain king among all kings, namely *the* king, the δ -head for adjectives should denote a certain state. Candidates for this category are forms like *too*, *quite*, or *so* and even comparative markers like *-er* or *more* (see Zwarts 1992). Besides delimiting the stative, they assign a certain referential argument to the whole constituent. With Croft (1991), I hold adjectives to represent modification so that the referential argument is modification, in consequence of which the δ-head for adjectives is labeled Mod. Hence, for a "standard adjective" like *free*, we have the following structure (note that the θ-layer is left aside for the moment, to be dealt with further below).

(437)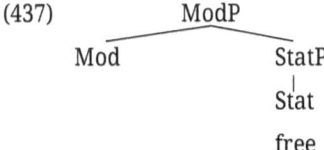

We may return at this juncture to AP-predicates and with that to the important question of adjectives and theta-assignment.

Baker (2003) proposed that adjectives, unlike verbs, cannot assign thematic roles. Their subjects are realized externally as specifiers of PredP headed by the copula that always assigns a THEME role. This is in two ways problematic. On the one hand, Den Dikken (2006) rejects the idea that copulas assign a theta-role, while on the other, Meltzer-Asscher (2012) – although she agrees on the externality of the subject – argues convincingly against the idea of all arguments of adjectives having assigned a THEME-role (even assigned externally), but that the whole range of roles[98] is assigned:

(438)   *broken, written*   → theme
        boring, confusing → subject matter
        confused   → experiencer
        protective   → cause (Meltzer-Asscher 2012: 157–158)

In the following, I will propose a reconciliation of these two approaches. I follow Meltzer-Asscher (2012) in that adjectives can assign a thematic relation, applying the whole range available, but cannot become the main predicate of a clause.

Although adjectives can assign different theta roles, intuition still inclines to follow Baker (2003) in that at least all copula+adjective structures have a THEME-marking.

---

98 I follow the categorization of (Meltzer-Asscher 2011, 2012), though nothing hinges on a certain label or category.

The suggestion here is that whenever we deal with adjectival predicates, there are two theta-relations, one assigned by the adjective itself and the other one assigned in the small clause. Let us consider example (439).

(439)　*I become protective.*

Protective is categorized by Meltzer-Asscher (2012) as assigning a CAUSE or something similar but not a THEME. However, the copula-verb assigns a THEME -role[99] since its argument is the undergoer of the action, and normally there is an external causer for the process. In the same line of reasoning, it would be possible to argue that the copular verb *be* (in the small clause) assigns a theta-role, namely THEME (440).

(440)　*The father is protective.*

With reference to the above, how does *the father* end up with two theta-roles, and how is it reconcilable with the theta-criterion?

To answer this question, the concept of theta-role has to be looked at in more detail. A thematic role is a role assigned to a certain argument by the predicate. Theta-roles are not only relevant for the interpretation but often have a syntactic dimension as well. Like in the Indonesian example, a CAUSE-role does not only contribute to the interpretation but also the selective properties of the verb. Thus, a theta-role requires a semantic and syntactic dimension. Nevertheless, as proposed for Indonesian nominal morphology, these thematic relations are possible without an argument. Still, we have both the semantic dimension and its relevance to meaning and the selective features for certain nominal morphology. The only difference is that there is no argument that is assigned this thematic role. Thus, the thematic relation remains abstract in the sense that no argument is assigned a thematic role. For our example here, the first one is a thematic relation without an argument and the second one is a thematic role with an argument.

Let us go back to the example *protective*. The root *protect* is merged into the theta-head specified for CAUSE. However, no argument is assigned the CAUSE role, and the specifier remains empty. Yet *protect* still bears the CAUSE-feature, and the thematic relation is perceivable. After that, *protect* is merged into Stat, takes the –*ive*[100]-suffix, and becomes a state. The Mod-head is subsequently merged, becom-

---

99 This is a simplification. As we saw above, the thematic role is assigned inside the small clause and not by the copula itself.
100 With the suffix -*ive* there is a special form of Stat-head that can select a θP specified for CAUSE.

ing a modifier and thereby a combination of Stat and Mod, namely an adjective. Although there is this interpretable CAUSE feature, there is no specifier, no argument that has been assigned the thematic role since it has no predicate status. This can explain the unclear status. On the one hand, adjectives bear information on thematic relations; on the other, they do not assign this thematic role to an argument.

From this, it can be proposed that the argument for the adjective internal thematic relation (no argument available) is abstract with all possibilities of theta-roles. However, the external role assigned in the small clause is always a THEME role assigned to an overt argument.

Before we go into some detail about the copula structure, a brief digression is called for to look into the question of why the copula is needed in the first place. After merging the Stat-head, the root has been merged and moved into θ and Stat. Why is it not possible to merge a v-layer on top of Stat? The previous section has given the answer; namely, due to the lack of an event feature in Stat, we have a selectional mismatch. Since we cannot merge v, we have to merge Mod instead. Therefore, we have a selectional mismatch with T, and the 'adjective' cannot become the main predicate without any help. Hence, a sentence like (441) is ungrammatical.

(441) *The father protectives.[101]

Therefore the copula/small clause kicks in. The ModP is merged with a θ-head. Since it is a phrase, it cannot merge into the head position but is merged as its complement. In Spec-θP, we merge the later subject. We have an asymmetric small clause. The small clause (θP) is merged with Ev and v, the copula, and the later subject is moved into vP. Given that the copula has an abstract event feature (syntactic requirement) in Ev, it fits the selectional properties of T. We can therefore merge T, and the subject is moved into Spec-TP. The derivation is completed by merging the C-layer, normally null-C. For a sentence like (442), we end up with the following structure:

---

101 This sentence is actually ungrammatical and not only unusual since it would require both a Stat and an Ev-head at the same time, which is not possible, since these two are in complementary distribution.

(442) *The father is protective*

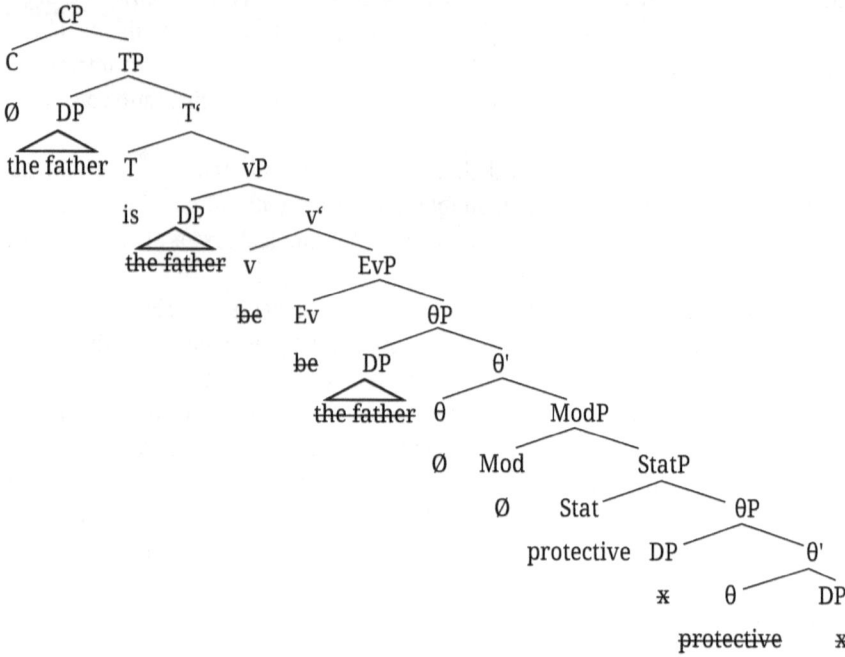

To summarize, then, in the ModP itself, the first (abstract) thematic relation is assigned, namely CAUSE, whereas the second role is assigned in the small clause, θP. Therefore, adjectives can bear whatever range of thematic relations is assumed, although the subject is always assigned a THEME role in the small clause and is therefore always external.

These two theta-heads also provide a good argument for the pseudo-event feature of the copula. At first sight, it sounds strange that a copula like *be*, which normally denotes stative propositions, should bear a pseudo-eventive feature. However, the same issue arose with certain stative verbs like *know* or *own*. These were the only cases where verbs did not have a semantic dimension of being events. However, a syntactic dimension argues for the eventive character, namely the transitivity. Since the internal argument structure always has a StatP, the external structure cannot reduplicate this StatP again. Therefore, the Cat-head for the external argument (CAUSE) has to be Ev. Although the adjective structure is different from the transitive structure, it still resembles two important features. First, the adjective structure has two instances of the three-head θP, CatP, and δP. Second, the first CatP has to be StatP. This is exactly the environment where the second CatP has to be Ev for derivational reasons. Therefore, the copula has to have this pseudo-event feature. Since eventive (semantic dimension) and verbal (syntactic dimension) go hand in hand in English, it is not surprising that the Ev-layer can be motivated by the semantic dimension, the syntactic dimension, or, in most cases, by both dimensions.

So much for the adjectival case, which allows us to proceed with the next group, namely prepositions.

4.2.3 Prepositions

The last non-verbal predicate we have to deal with is the preposition phrase. The major difference in regard to the two previous categories is that prepositions are birelational (see Hale and Keyser 2002: 8) and, therefore, normally treated as two-place-predicates. However, prepositions cannot end up in v. The question is what happens in the derivation. Let us start at the bottom. As with any other structure, we start with a theta-assigning head and merge the root that is to become the preposition into the theta-head. Similar to other two-place-predicates, i.e., transitive structures, the θP is merged with Stat and Trans. Trans has an uninterpretable theta feature that must be checked by a second θ-head. Unlike transitive forms, however, comparable to telic unaccusatives like *go (to)*, the second theta-role assigned is not CAUSE/AGENT but THEME. Hence, there is no uninterpretable event feature in the second θ-head, which would make the merge of Ev necessary for the derivation. Semantically, prepositions describe relations (states) and not events, so the second Cat-head merged should be Stat. However, similarly to the impossibility of merging a head into an Ev-head twice,[102] merging the preposition a second time into a Stat-head is also not possible. Therefore the preposition structure ends at the higher θP assigning the THEME. To continue with the derivation, we have to use a form similar to the light verb *make* for causing an event, namely the copula *be*. As we have seen above, the copula *be* comprises a Cat-head, Ev (syntactically not semantically motivated), and the δ-head, v, making it a verbal structure. Both a Cat-layer and δ-layer are missing for the preposition structure cut off after the second θP. Therefore, the copula is an absolute fit to compensate for the impossibility of merging a Stat-head for a second time and "saving" the derivation by providing a pseudo-event feature.

---

102 Transitive forms always comprise an event and state (He killed him – caused him to be dead), different to causative structure with a light verb which can denote two events (He made him sing).

Let us now have a look at a copular structure with a PP-predicate, as in (443):

(443) *John is in Chicago.*

The preposition *in* is merged into the θ-head and assigns the LOCATION role to its specifier, *Chicago*. Next, we merge the structure for a transitive structure Stat and Trans, in this case, specified with an uninterpretable THEME feature. This feature requires the merging of a second theta-position, namely the THEME. Accordingly, we merge our second theta-head, which is still filled by the preposition. This is comparable to the small clause structures for nouns and adjectives. In the specifier position of the external theta-position, *John* is merged. We continue with our standard derivation for verbal structures and merge Ev and v. The preposition, though, cannot move to the Cat-head as it lacks an Event-feature. We, then, need the help of the copula, which is inserted in Ev, and v. *John* moves into Spec-vP. The vP is merged with T, and *John* becomes the subject in Spec-TP. We complete our derivation with a null-C, yielding the following structure:

(444)

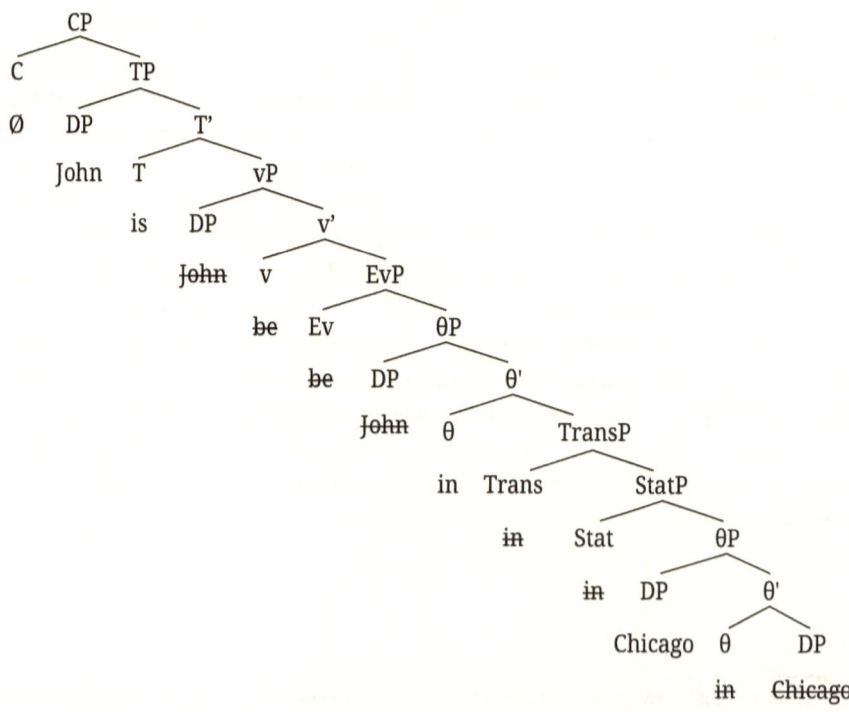

4.2.4 Conclusion

All non-verbal forms cannot become the main predicate of a clause since their category head (either Stat or N) lacks an event feature. For this reason, another δ-head has to be merged, namely, Mod, D, or Trans. ModPs, DPs, and TransPs are selectional mismatches for the merge with T and consequently cannot become the main predicate. Hence, there is a need for a pseudo-predicate, the copula. The non-verbal predicate is merged in the complement position of a θ-head (small clause). The copula is base-generated in Ev and v, the head that is merged with the small clause. This obtains the following general structure for all non-verbal predicates:

(445)
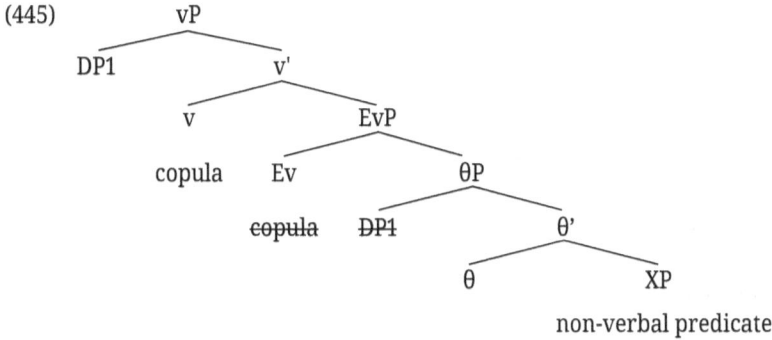

4.3 Non-eventive predicates in Indonesian

For English, we have seen that the copula *be* is only available for non-verbal (non-eventive) predicates. Non-verbal predicates are distinguished along the lines of lexical categories between nominal, adjectival, and preposition phrase predicates. If we assume similar semantic explanations for these categories, these three groups can also be identified in Indonesian. Structure-wise, the picture is quite different from the English categories, as we will clarify further below.

In contrast to the case in English, non-eventive predicates in Indonesian do not behave homogeneously copula-wise. On the one hand, none of these sentences needs an overt copula; if a copula is available, it is usually optional (Sneddon 1996: 237, Musgrave 2001: 223). On the other hand, the distribution of the copulas is different in that 'adjectives' do not allow an overt copula (446),[103] 'nominal' predicates

---

[103] In rare cases, *adalah* is acceptable with adjectival predicates for some speakers.

(447) allow *adalah* but not *ada*, while PPs (at least those in location) (448) allow *ada* but not *adalah*. In some cases, *adalah* is available with PPs as well.

(446) Udin (*adalah/*ada) lapar.[104]
 Udin COP/COP hungry.
 'Udin is hungry.'

(447) Udin (*adalah/*ada) guru-nya Siska.
 Udin COP/COP teacher-3S.POSS Siska
 'Udin is Siska's teacher.'

(448) Udin (*adalah/*ada) di sini.
 Udin COP/COP in here.
 'Udin is here.'

Nevertheless, with regard to what we would categorize traditionally as nouns, the picture is more complex. We can identify at least these three groups of nominal phrases: bare nouns, nouns with classifiers, and definite noun phrases (better DPs).

Whereas the occurrence of *adalah* for bare nouns is at least odd (449), it is completely grammatical with classifiers (450) or definite DPs (451).

(449) Udin (??adalah) guru.
 Udin COP teacher

(450) Udin (adalah) se-orang guru.
 Udin COP one-CL.HUM teacher
 'Udin is a teacher.'

(451) Udin (adalah) guru-nya Siska.
 Udin COP teacher-3S.POSS Siska
 'Udin is Siska's teacher.'

Besides *adalah*, two more forms are often considered copulas, namely *ialah* and *merupakan*. *Ialah* normally occurs in equations (452) (cf. Mustaffa 2018: 27).

---

104 Although Tadmor (2007) identified a tendency for *adalah* with adjectival complements in Malay, he accounts for this phenomenon via language contact with English, so it should still be treated as ungrammatical.

(452) *Abdurrahman Wahid   ialah   Gus Dur.*
      Abdurrahman Wahid   COP   Gus Dur
      'Abdurrahman Wahid is Gus Dur.'

Since it is derived from the pronoun *ia* plus the emphasis marker *-lah*, it is similar to Russian *eto*-constructions (see Geist 2008), which are not available in predicational structures. This holds true for the Indonesian language as well. Although it is possible to have *ialah* in a construction with definite DP as XP2 (453), a construction which could be interpreted either as predicational or equative, it is not possible with an indefinite DP (454).[105] On these grounds, it should be treated as a copula applicable to equations only. Since equations fall outside the scope of this work, *ialah* will be left aside for the remainder of this work.

(453) *Udin   ialah   guru-nya   Ridwan.*
      Udin   COP   teacher-3s   Ridwan
      'Udin is Ridwan's teacher.'

(454) **Udin   ialah   se-orang   guru.*
      Udin   COP   one-CL.HUM   teacher
      Intended: 'Udin is a teacher.'

The second form, *merupakan*, by contrast, can only be used in predicational constructions[106] (455) but is ungrammatical in equations (456):

(455) *Udin   merupakan   guru   SD.*
      Udin   COP   teacher   primary school.
      'Udin is a primary school teacher.'

(456) **Abdurrahman Wahid   merupakan   Gus Dur*
      Abdurrahman Wahid   COP   Gus Dur
      Intended: Abdurrahman Wahid is Gus Dur.

This should fit the context of the present work. However, there is another issue with *merupakan*, which makes it irrelevant for our case. *Merupakan* was derived originally from a transitive verb form with *rupa* (shape) as its root (cf. Moeljadi et al.

---

[105] Apparently this structure is available in Malay spoken in Malaysia.
[106] *Merupakan* is only possible with nominal predicates and ruled out with adjectival or prepositional predicates.

2016: 444). Although the form has fossilized to a certain extent (e.g., passivation is not possible), it remains unclear how much of the transitive status, and therefore of an *eventive* form, persists at this transitional stage. For this reason, *merupakan* does not necessarily meet the criterion non-eventive, so it is not considered relevant for this work. This work will limit its focus to *adalah* throughout the rest of this work and leave both *ialah* and *merupakan* out of consideration.

As an equivalent to the predicational copula clauses in English, non-eventive predicates are represented with three different structures in Indonesian, which are the no-copula-type, the *ada*-type, and the *adalah*-type. In the following, this work will account for all three types. For this discussion, it must be kept in mind that both *ada* and *adalah* are optional.

4.3.1 Adjectival predicates

It is an ongoing debate whether a distinction between adjectives and verbs is useful for a language like Indonesian. Although it is often doubted that Indonesian has such a distinction, the standard grammar for Indonesian (*Tata Bahasa Baku*[107]) maintains it.

Besides certain semantic criteria which say nothing about syntactic categories, the only morpho-syntactic criteria brought into the field is the possibility of building (periphrastic) comparative and superlative constructions (cf. Alwi et al. 2003). However, as Himmelmann (2008) points out, if the distinction is based on one feature alone, it should be seen as an ontological class (here, gradable concepts) and not as a linguistic one. It does not correlate with the adjective class since there are adjectives (*dead, ready*) that are not gradable and non-adjectives that are gradable (457).

(457) *Where would you find more beauty than in this place?* (Himmelmann 2008: 255)

The same holds true for the Indonesian case. On the one hand, we have concepts that are semantically classified as adjectives that are not gradable (*mati* – dead, *siap* – ready); on the other hand, prototypical verbs (even with agentive voice morphology) can be modified by the comparative marker *lebih* (458–459).

---

[107] See Alwi et al. 2003

4.3 Non-eventive predicates in Indonesian

(458) Udin lebih men-dukung Jokowi daripada lawan-nya.
Udin more CAUS.VOICE-support Jokowi than opponent-3S.POSS
'Udin supports Jokowi more than his opponent.'

(459) Dia lebih minum daripada makan.
3S more drink than eat
'It looks more like drinking and not like eating. (She is more drinking than eating).'

Comparative marking, then, is not a suitable candidate for defining an adjective group.

Another candidate on a morphological basis would be something that has been labeled as voice-markers in chapter 3, namely *ter-*, *meN-*, *ber-*, *di-*. If we perceive the distinction between eventive and stative on the one hand and/or agentive and non-agentive on the other, then *ter-* and *ber-* should prototypically mark adjectives and *meN-* and *di-* verbs. Although we can find exceptions like *berdoa* (pray), normally understood to be agentive, or *membahayakan* (dangerous), normally seen as an "adjective", we could argue, especially for the second one, that *meN-* is not productive here, but that it is a fossilized form.

There is no doubt that a difference exists between the various voice-markers (if there were no difference, why should we have distinct morphemes?). Nevertheless, such marking is not category assigning. The most important factors available to identify a syntactic category are distributional factors. Hence, any constituents that can substitute for each other should be seen as one group. However, there is no difference detectable in the distribution between "verbal" and "adjectival" forms. Both "adjectives" (461) and "verbs" (460) are negated with the negator *tidak*, whereas DPs (462) are negated with *bukan*.

(460) Udin tidak makan.
Udin NEG eat
'Udin does not eat.'

(461) Udin tidak lapar.
Udin NEG hungry.
'Udin is not hungry.'

(462) Udin bukan se-orang guru yang baik.
Udin NEG one-CL.HUM teacher NOM good
'Udin is not a good teacher.'

If they are used as noun-modifiers the ligature *yang* can occur (463–464).

(463) *Anjing yang lapar tidak boleh di-ganggu.*
dog NEG hungry NEG allow PASS-disturb
'Hungry dogs should not be disturbed.'

(464) *Anjing yang meng-gonggong tidak boleh di-ganggu.*
dog NOM CAUS.VOICE-bark NEG allow PASS-disturb
'Barking dogs should not be disturbed.'

However, both forms can be built without ligature *yang* (465–466).

(465) *Anjing lapar tidak boleh di-ganggu.*
dog hungry NEG allow PASS-disturb
'Hungry dogs should not be disturbed.'

(466) *Anjing meng-gonggong tidak boleh di-ganggu.*
dog CAUS.VOICE-bark NEG allow PASS-disturb
'Barking dogs should not be disturbed.'

Even in their distributional behaviour concerning voice morphology, it is impossible to draw a line between verbs and adjectives. The four roots *mati* (dead), *tidur* (sleep), *jatuh* (fall), and *sakit* (sick) can be used in their bare form (467–470) as roots for a *me-kan* (causative) form (471–474) or as *ke-an*-form (some kind of passive voice) (475–478).

(467) *Adit mati.*
Adit dead
'Adit is dead.'

(468) *Adit tidur.*
Adit sleep
'Adit sleeps/is asleep.'

(469) *Adit jatuh.*
Adit fall
'Adit falls/fell.'

(470) *Adit sakit.*
 Adit Sick
 'Adit is sick.'

(471) *Udin me-mati-kan Adit.*
 Udin CAUS.VOICE-dead-TH.TRANS Adit
 'Udin killed Adit.'

(472) *Udin me-nidur-kan Adit.*
 Udin CAUS.VOICE-sleep- TH.TRANS Adit
 'Udin put Adit to sleep.'

(473) *Udin men-jatuh-kan Adit.*
 Udin CAUS.VOICE-fall- TH.TRANS Adit
 'Udin made Adit fall.'

(474) *Udin me-nyakit-kan Adit.*
 Udin CAUS.VOICE-sick- TH.TRANS Adit
 'Udin hurt Adit.'

(475) *Adit ke-mati-an anak-nya*
 Adit PT.VOICE-dead-TH.NOM child-3POSS
 'Adit suffers from the death of his child.'

(476) *Adit ke-tidur-an.*
 Adit PT.VOICE-sleep- TH.NOM
 'Adit has fallen asleep.'

(477) *Adit ke-jatuh-an ranting*
 Adit PT.VOICE-fall- TH.NOM twig
 'A fallen twig hit Adit.'

(478) *Adit ke-sakit-an.*
 Adit PT.VOICE-sick- TH.NOM
 'Adit has pain.'

Unlike v in English, then, Indonesian voice does not bear an uninterpretable event feature. This means that in Indonesian, we have the same functional head, voice, that can be specified for unaccusative-resultative voice *ter-* (480), undative-stative voice *ber-* (482), agentive-eventive voice *meN-* (479), passive-eventive voice *di*[108]- or a zero-voice marker (481). Consequently, voice can select StatP as well. We thus have the same structure for what we could call adjectival predicates if applying English categories and verbal predicates. Let us consider the following sentences:

(479) Udin   me-nangis.
       Udin   CAUS.VOICE-cry
       'Udin cries.'

(480) Udin   ter-senyum.
       Udin   TH.VOICE-smile
       'Udin smiles.'

(481) Udin   lapar.
       Udin   hungry
       'Udin is hungry.'

(482) Udin   ber-senang.
       Udin   GO.VOICE-happy
       'Udin is happy.'

The root is merged into the θ-head and takes its only argument, *Udin*, in its specifier and assigns the AGENT-role (*menangis*), the THEME-role (*tersenyum, lapar*), or the GOAL-role (*bersenang*). After that, it is merged with either Stat (for *ber*, *ter*, and Ø) or Ev (*meN*) and voice, and the sole argument moves into spec-voiceP. Voice can be realized as *meN-*, *ter-*, zero, or *ber-*. Next, we merge T, make the whole structure a predication and assign subject status to Udin in Spec-TP. Finally, we merge a Null-C.

---

[108] Since the *di*-passive forms necessarily derived from a transitive form, they are left aside in the following discussion.

(483)

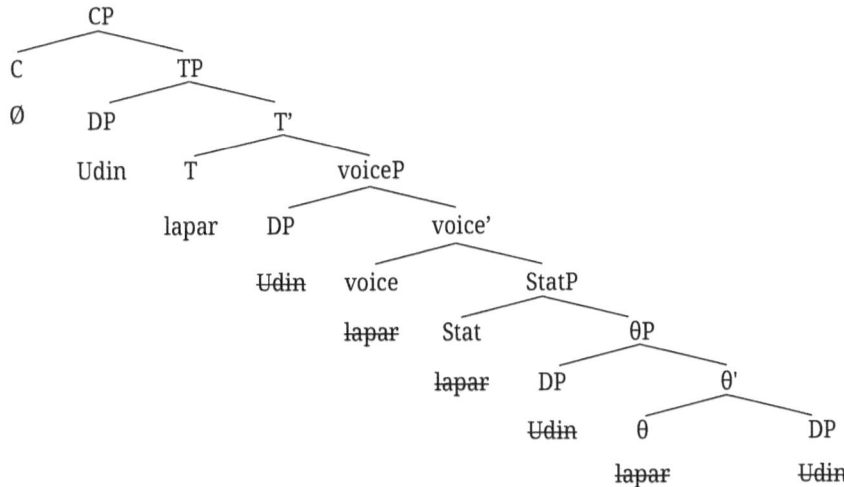

(484)

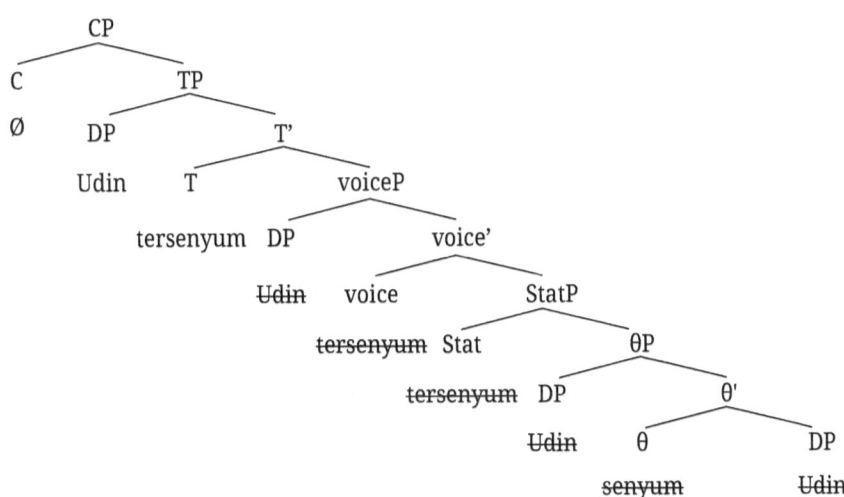

(485)

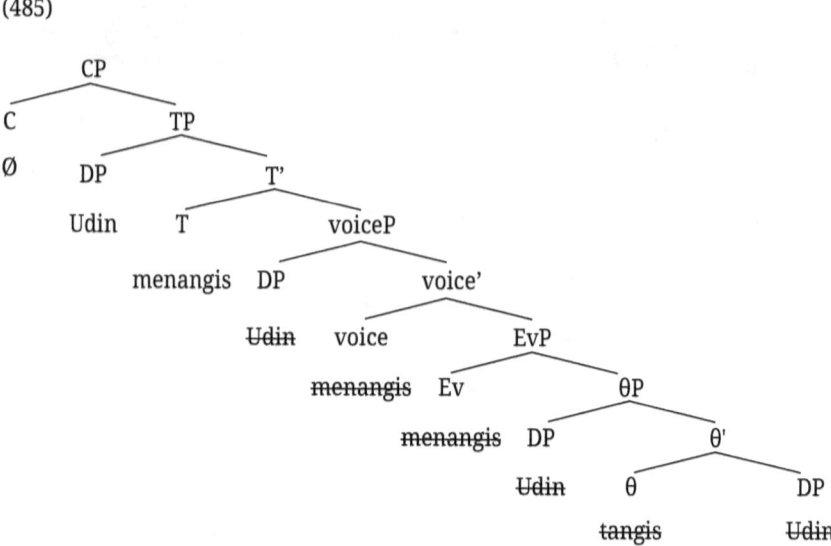

(486)

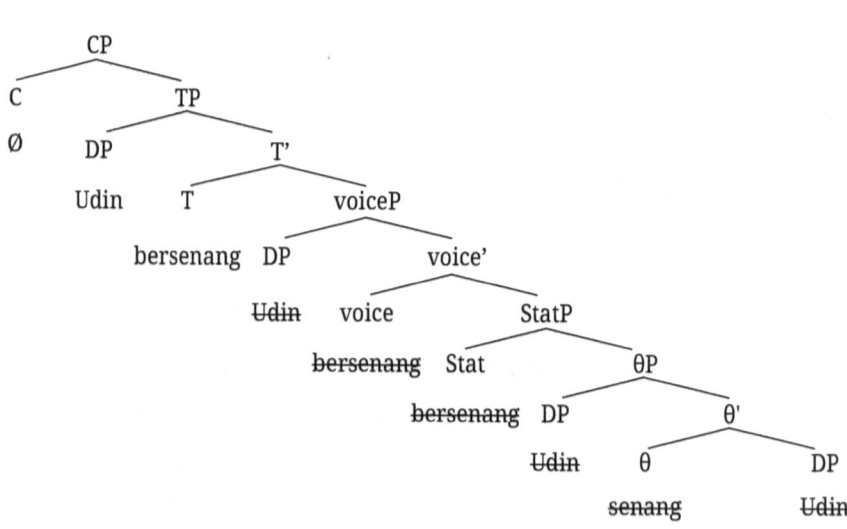

In concise terms, Indonesian has no distinct category for adjectives (at least not structure-wise). Potential adjectives must be treated as verbs, as they occupy the voice-head position. As a consequence, there is no position available for a copula. Although this structure is identical to the derivation with a "verbal" predicate in Indonesian, in the present context, we call it no-copula-structure to contrast it with English sentences, where we would expect a copula.

4.3.2 Nominal predicates

At the beginning of this subchapter, we saw that *adalah* could occur only with nominal predicates. However, we cannot treat all nominal structures, or what is traditionally understood as nominal, in the same way. There are at least three distinct structures, namely bare nominals, nominals with classifiers, and determined noun phrases. Interestingly, these three groups do not always show the same behaviour, e.g., for negation.

In general, verbal forms are negated with *tidak* whereas nominal forms are negated with *bukan*.

(487) *Udin bukan/*tidak guru-nya Siska.*
Udin NEG teacher-3S.POSS Siska
'Udin is not Siska's teacher.'

(488) *Udin *bukan/tidak tidur*
Udin NEG sleep
'Udin does not sleep.'

This correlates in general to the distribution of *adalah*, possible with nominal forms but blocked with verbal forms. For bare nominals, however, the case is puzzling. On the one hand, *adalah* is blocked for cases with a strongly attributive reading (490, 491, 494),[109] while on the other hand, these forms can be negated with *bukan* (489, 492). However, sometimes a negation with *tidak* is also possible (493).

(489) *Cincin bukan emas.*
ring NEG gold
'The ring is not made of gold.'

(490) *Cincin itu *adalah emas.*
ring DEM COP gold

(491) *Siska *adalah perempuan.*
Siska COP woman/female
'Siska is a woman.'

(492) *Adit bukan perempuan.*
Adit NEG woman/female
'Adit is not a woman.'

---

[109] These examples are adapted from Pustet (2003: 122–123).

(493) Dia tidak pe-marah (Sneddon 1996: 49)
      3s   NEG   CAUS.NOM-angry
      'He is not someone with anger issues.'

(494) Dia *adalah pe-marah
      3s   COP   CAUS.NOM-angry
      'He is someone with anger issues.'

To distinguish between these two groups,[110] *bukan/adalah* vs. *tidak/non-adalah*, it is helpful to draw the line between heads and phrases, by which the *tidak/non-adalah* group is limited to heads, whereas *bukan/adalah* refers to phrases. Structurally, bare nominals can be both, either heads or phrases. All bare forms start as roots that can merge with heads. One possible analysis is that the root, e.g., *anak* (child), merges with a θ-assigner and assigns a theta-role, following which it is merged with Stat and after that with voice, either with a null-voice if it has been assigned a THEME-role, or with overt *ber-* if it has been assigned a GOAL role. Accordingly, we arrive at the following two structures:

(495) *Udin masih anak.* (Udin is still a child/like a child).

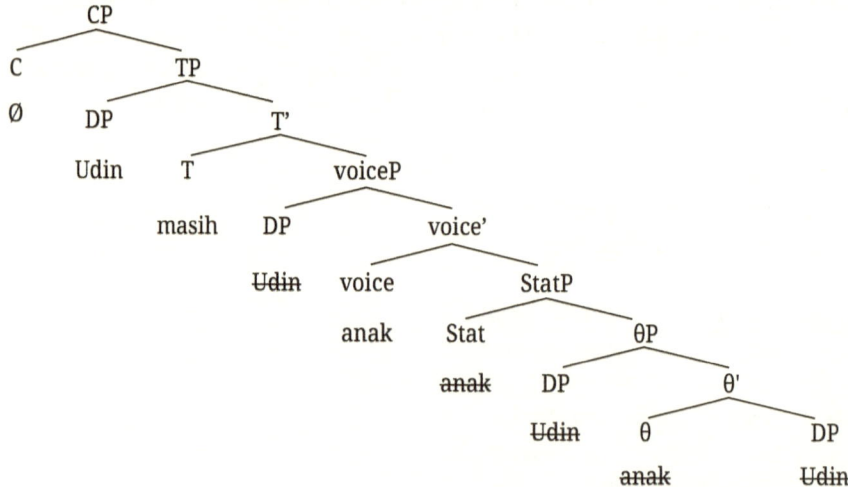

---

110 Bare nominals cannot always be categorized along the lines of this distinction. A phenomenon that will be addressed further below.

(496) *Udin sudah beranak.* (Udin has children already.)

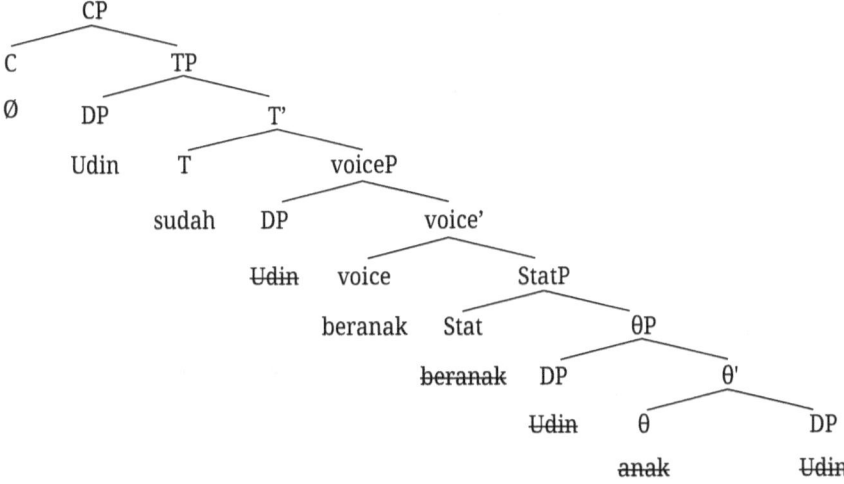

In this case, then, they follow the no-copula type, similar to the 'adjectival' predicates, and the use of *adalah* is blocked.

In sentences like (497), it is necessary to merge an N-head, which is later moved into voice, since the root *didik* has overt noun morphology *pe-an*.

(497) Udin   ber-pen-didik-an.
      Udin   GO.VOICE-CAUS.NOM-educate-TH.NOM
      'Udin is educated.'

In the light of this, the sentence above (*Udin masih anak*) could have an N-layer between θ and voice instead of Stat. The difference in interpretation is that the N-layer favours an individual reading, whereas the Stat-head favours a property reading; the sentence is ambiguous, meaning either *'Udin is childish/like a child'* or *'Udin is a child'*. For the second interpretation, we need an N-layer to get the individual reading, while for the first interpretation, a Stat-head is required. The highest head (Stat or N) head moves to voice in either case. Therefore, in both cases, they are of the no-copula-type.

However, *anak* could also be a referent, which requires a Null-Q/D, similar to English (whatever label is preferred). In such a case, *anak* is treated as DP, as a phrase, and the derivation follows the *adalah*-type, which is to be described below. Hence, depending on the underlying structure of the noun, here *anak*, either the no-copula or the *adalah*-strategy is chosen.

As the no copula structure has been described in the previous section on adjectical predicates, attention goes now to the *adalah*-strategy, where the nominal phrases have to be analyzed as DPs. (I will discuss the classifier forms further below, which can be analyzed as non-DPs).

Since we have already covered DP structures in detail in the previous chapter, this chapter will refrain from repetition. We could determine that DP structures are structure-wise comparable to English structures, having an N-layer[111] and a D-layer on top of that. As with English, the Indonesian N-head does not move into D, from which it follows that definite nominal expressions must be treated as phrases, namely as DPs. Due to the chain uniformity condition (Chomsky 1995: 253), a phrase cannot be moved into a head position, here voice. Additionally, since the D-head is not a theta-assigner, the head itself cannot move into voice. This means that a DP, which constitutes the semantic predicate, cannot form a syntactic predicate without the help of a copula, just as in English.

Unlike bare nominals, then, DPs are generated (moved) neither into the voice-head nor in a θ-head. This leads to the question of where they are generated. In the general structure offered in chapter 2, one position has not yet been filled in the derivation, namely the complement of θP. Since this is a non-head position, it is suitable for complex predicates. Hence, the copular-complement is merged into the complement of θ and the later subject into Spec-θP. θ itself is inherently null.

Examining other copula-like structures like *menjadi* (become) reveals that the complement position is a suitable candidate. *Jadi* (to become, to happen) can be used as unaccusative (498), unergative (499), or transitive, either active (500) or passive (501).

(498) *Ini ter-jadi.*
DEM TH.VOICE-happen
'This happened.'

(499) *Adit men-jadi dokter.*
Adit CAUS.VOICE-happen doctor
'Adit becomes a doctor.'

(500) *Tuhan men-jadi-kan Musa hamba-Nya.*
God CAUS.VOICE-happen-TH.TRANS Moses servant-3S.POSS
'God made Moses his servant.'

---

111 Sometimes an Ev- or Stat-head are possible.

(501) Musa di-jadi-kan   hamba-Nya.
      Moses pass-happen-TH.TRANS   servant-3S.POSS
      'Moses was made God's servant.'

In sentence (498), *ini* has been assigned the THEME role, according to what we have said so far, in Spec-θP. In (499), Adit is both the THEME and the AGENT. Thus, if we assume the theta-criterion, we need a PRO. Otherwise, Adit would appear in both positions. That *dokter* cannot be the THEME is obvious if we consider (500) and (501), where *Musa* is the THEME as it is assigned object function by *-kan* and subsequently moved to Spec-voiceP in (501). In sum, *dokter* and *hambanya* cannot be THEMES. If we give the matter some thought, it remains difficult to identify any thematic role. Furthermore, neither topicalization (502) nor passivation (503) is possible.

(502) *Hamba-Nya   di-jadi-kan   Musa oleh Tuhan.
      servant-3S.POSS   PASS-happen-TH.TRANS   Moses by   God

(503) *Hamba-Nya   Tuhan men-jadi-kan   Musa.
      servant-3S.POSS   God   CAUS.VOICE-happen- TH.TRANS Moses

Thus, following Geist (2006: 6), these complements are not part of the argument structure. The only position that is not assigned a thematic role is the complement of θP. This makes perfect sense because *dokter* and *hambanya* somehow complete *jadi* without being part of the argument structure. This fits the distinction made by Alwi et al. (2003: 322) between *pelengkap* (complement) and *obyek* (object).

Hence, for non-bare structures, we have the following basic structure. This structure is identical to the English structure with an asymmetric small clause:

(504)
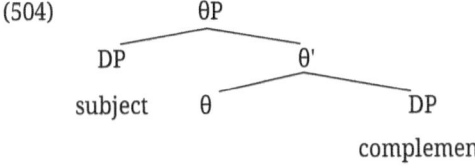

The constituent which is assigned the THEME role is moved via Spec-voiceP to Spec-TP to become the subject of the clause. The null-Theta-head moves via Ev to voice and T. The complement stays in its original position. This leads to the following structure:

(505) Udin guru-nya   Siska.
      Udin teacher-3S.POSS   Siska
      'Udin is Siska's teacher.'

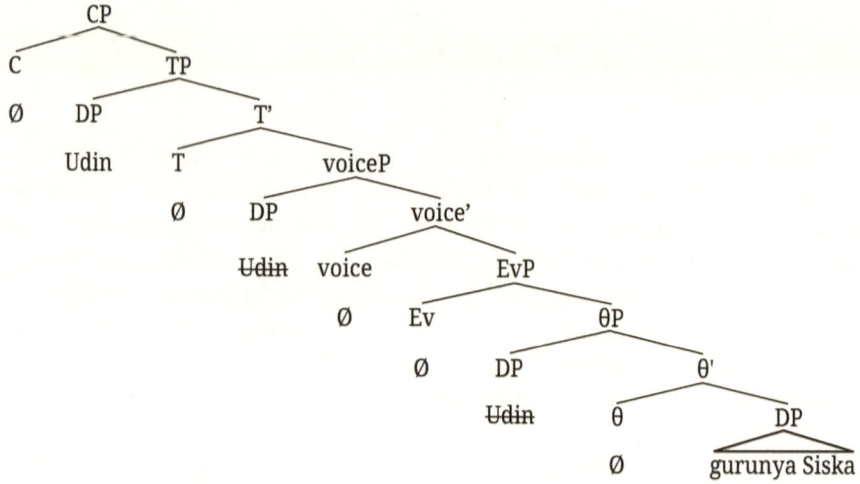

So far, the underlying structure looks identical to the English type. However, the copula *adalah* is not verbal and behaves differently than *ada*. This will be discussed in more depth in section 4.3.4, comparing *ada* and *adalah*. Another important difference is the possibility of the copula being zero. However, in all cases, a verbal layer has to be identified (cf. Moeljadi et al. 2016, Mustaffa 2018) independently from the question of whether the copula – if available – occupies this verbal position.

4.3.3 Indefinite nominal phrases with classifiers/numerals

After dealing with bare nominal and definite noun phrases, we now have to draw our attention to indefinite nominal phrases. It makes sense to group definite and indefinite noun phrases as two parts of one category for English. In general, it is claimed that in English, definite nouns are noun phrases merged with a definite article or determiner, and indefinite forms are noun phrases merged with an article or quantifiers (Q). However, D and Q are normally in complementary distribution.[112] Thus a phrase can either have a D or Q. Therefore, D and Q are seen as subgroups of the same category.

In Indonesian, noun phrases are much more puzzling. Similar to EvP and vP, we need two functional heads for nominal phrases, namely N (Cat), to assign the semantic category (being an individual) and D (δ) to assign the semantic function (an argument, a reference). Whereas D refers to a certain referent in the outside world,

---

[112] At least in English, cross-linguistically there is evidence that Q and D may co-occur.

Q describes a quantification of these individuals. N-heads are either the nominalizer *yang*, overt noun morphology like *-an, peN-, per-*, etc., or as always in Indonesian, a null-N. D is either *ini/itu, -nya*, or a null D. Determiners in Indonesian follow the noun.

But what about Q? All candidates for a Q category, namely quantifiers like *banyak* (many), *beberapa* (several), *semua* (all), or numerals, normally precede the noun.

(506) banyak orang
 many human
 'many people'

(507) beberapa guru
 several teacher
 'several teachers'

(508) semua binatang
 all animal
 'all animals'

(509) dua orang guru
 two CL.HUM teacher
 'two teachers'

Since quantifiers can also occur with classifiers, they should occupy the same position as numerals.

(510) Di dalam suatu lapangan be-rumput ter-dapat
 inside one field GO.VOICE-grass TH.VOICE- get
 beberapa ekor kuda.[113]
 several CL.AN horse
 'On a grassy field, there were several horses.'

Therefore, we can group quantifiers and numerals together. However, should we categorize them as Q? Both quantifiers and numerals can function as predicates on their own.

(511) Anak kami masih dua.
 child 1P(EXCL).POSS CONT two
 'We still have two children.'

---

[113] https://brainly.co.id/tugas/10638932, accessed on 12.06.2019

(512) Anak kami   baru   satu.
      child 1P(EXCL).POSS REC.ANT one
      'We have just one child.'

(513) Barang kami   baru   sedikit.
      stuff 1P(EXCL).POSS REC.ANT little
      'We just have a few things.'

(514) Pertanyaan kami   sudah banyak.
      question   1P(EXCL).POSS ANT   many
      'We have many questions already.'

Numerals and quantifiers can even take voice morphology.

(515) Indonesia ber-satu.
      Indonesia GO.VOICE-one
      'Indonesia is united.'

(516) Indonesia me-nyatu.
      Indonesia CAUS.VOICE-one
      'Indonesian becomes one.'

(517) Kami lagi ber-dua.
      1P   PROG GO.VOICE-two
      'Currently, we two are together.'

(518) massa yang mulai mem-banyak.[114]
      crowd REL begin CAUS.VOICE-many
      'the crowd that started to grow'

However, with a bare numeral/quantifier, the occurrence of *adalah* is ungrammatical.

(519) ??Anak kami   adalah satu.
      child 1P(EXCL) COP   one

(520) ??Barang kami   adalah sedikit.
      child   1P(EXCL) COP   little

---

[114] Example taken form the KBBI (Kamus Besar Bahasa Indonesia), the official dictionary of Indonesian (https://kbbi.kemdikbud.go.id/entri/membanyak)

4.3 Non-eventive predicates in Indonesian — 179

(521) ??*Pertanyaan kami adalah banyak.*
question 1P(EXCL) COP many

Quantifiers and numerals should consequently be seen as roots, which can merge into θ. They assign a θ-role to its sole argument in Spec-θP, which moves via Stat into Spec-voiceP. So, it works according to the no-copula-type.

(522) *Anak kami baru satu.*
child 1P(EXCL).POSS REC.ANT one
'We have just one child.'

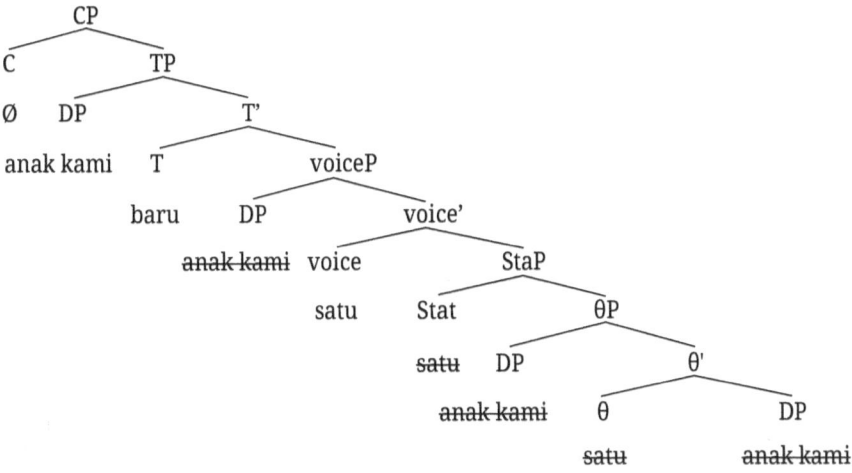

What happens if we have a noun phrase modified by a quantifier/numeral, so something like (523–524)?

(523) *Anak kami dua orang.*
child 1P(EXCL).POSS two CL.HUM
'We have two children.'

(524) *Udin se-orang guru.*
Udin one- CL.HUM teacher
'Udin is a teacher.'

The first possible analysis is based on the findings in the previous sentences. The quantifier/numeral is the root that is merged into the θ-head. Since the later subject is assigned the theta-role, it is merged into Spec-θP and therefore assigned the thematic role, whereas the classifier+noun-constituent is the complement, a position that is not assigned any function. The numeral becomes the main predicate in this interpretation and moves via Stat and voice to T. Here, the only argument is *anak kami* or *Udin*, which becomes the subject by moving to Spec-TP via voiceP. Accordingly, these sentences do not need a copula. One could even say that the numeral/quantifier functions as a copula.

(525)

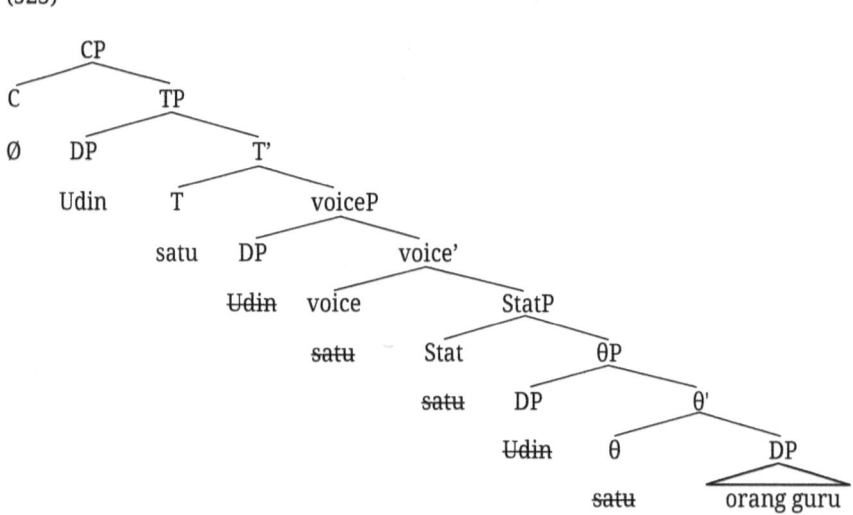

A second possible analysis is an analysis parallel to DPs. In this case, the numeral is merged into the functional head Q. It can no longer become the main predicate, and a null-copula is required. The whole QP is merged into the sentence like the *adalah*-type for DPs before.

Whereas this analysis is unlikelier for numerals like *dua* or *tiga*, cliticization of *satu* to *se-* makes the original root opaque and allows a reanalysis as a functional head more easily. Therefore, the structure (526) in particular should allow either a no-copula-type or an *adalah*-type analysis.

(526) *Udin seorang guru.*
 Udin a teacher
 'Udin is a teacher.'

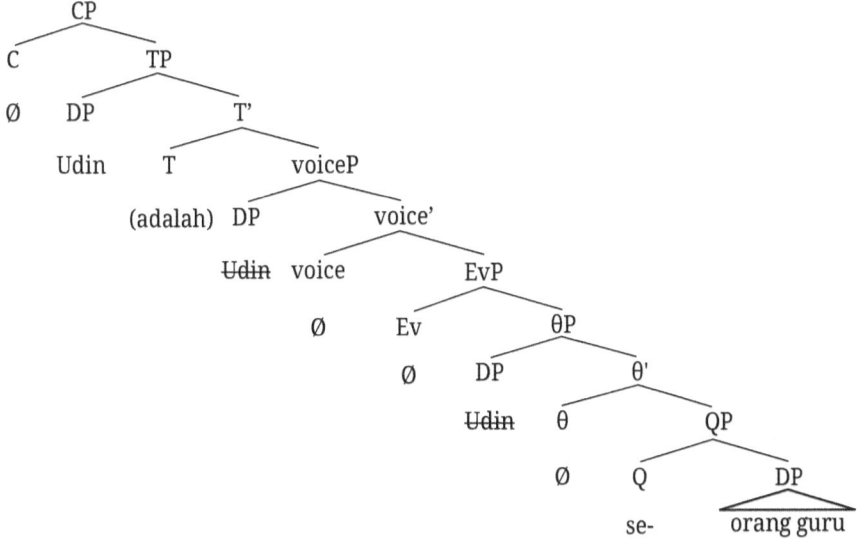

4.3.4 PP-predicates

In contrast to 'adjectival' predicates, preposition phrases allow a copula, normally *ada* (528) (not obligatory since it can be omitted [527]). The second copula *adalah* is ungrammatical (at least in most cases). Nevertheless, *ada* is not obligatory and can be omitted (527). In contrast to *adalah*, the copula *ada* is a verbal copula since it can take the voice-marker *ber-* (529), even without changing the meaning. More details on the differences between *adalah* and *ada* follow further below.

(527)   *Adit di Jakarta.*
       Adit in Jakarta
       'Adit is in Jakarta.'

(528)   *Adit ada di Jakarta.*
       Adit COP in Jakarta
       'Adit is in Jakarta.'

(529)   *Adit ber-ada di Jakarta.*
       Adit GO.VOICE-COP in Jakarta
       'Adit is in Jakarta.'

This section deals with the *ada*-less case (527) and the *ada* case (528). In general, there are two possible analyses. First, the *ada*-less case is simply the *ada*-structure with elided *ada* or the underlying predication structure for the *ada*-case, and the *ada*-less case is different.

Let us consider the *ada* scenario first before looking at the *ada*-less cases. With *ada* being a verbal copula, the *ada*-structure is identical to the English structure. The preposition *di* assigns both thematic roles and moves as high as the θ-head of the external argument. Then, however, the copula *ada* takes over and realizes both the Ev- and the voice-head.

(530)

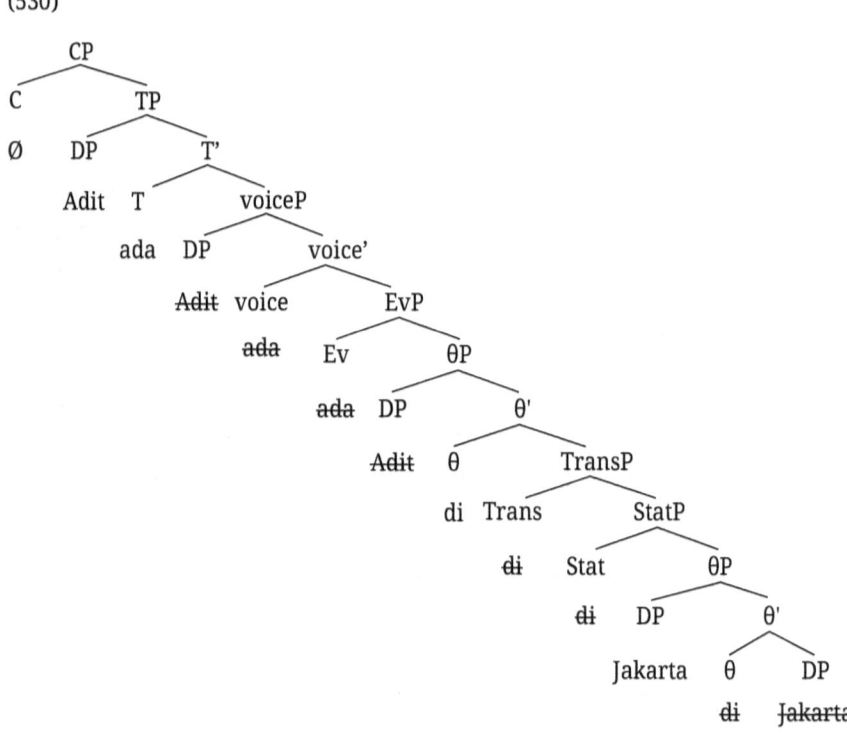

This structure also resembles the Indonesian *adalah*-structure. The difference lies in the realization of the copula (both position and substance), which will be discussed further below.

Having established a structure for the *ada*-cases, it is now time to look at the *ada*-less cases. As stated above, there are two possibilities. Either *ada* is elided, or the underlying predication structure is different from the *ada*-case.

In the second scenario, another element has to take over the predicate function. The only candidate would be the preposition, here *di*. Like transitive forms, *di* moves from the lower θ through Stat and Trans up to the second θ, Ev, and voice.

4.3 Non-eventive predicates in Indonesian

Although Indonesian voice can select a StatP, the second Cat-layer must be an EvP since Stat-head doubling is forbidden.

(531)

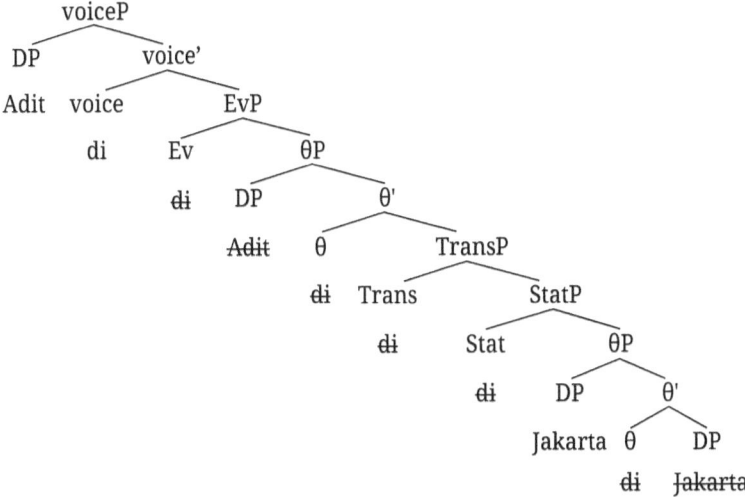

The second analysis is a copula+preposition construction without overt *ada*. A prescriptive perspective also proposes this analysis (see Alwi et al. 2003). In this case, the structure is identical to the *ada*-scenario, however, *ada* would be set on null-spell out.

(532)

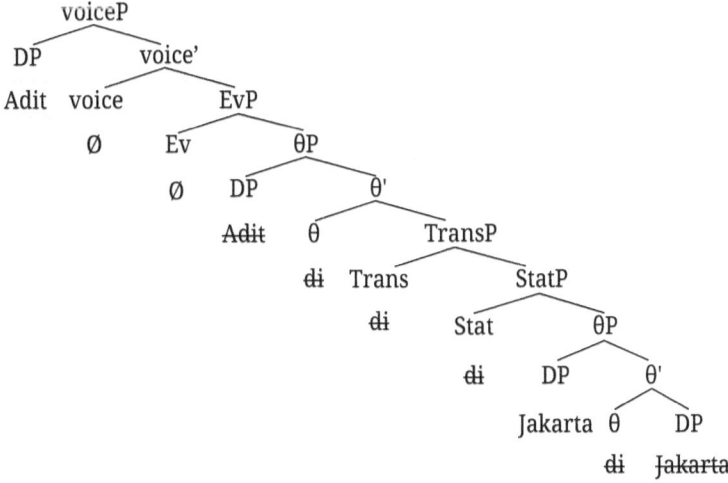

Although it is impossible to rule out the first analysis completely, there is more evidence for the null-*ada* analysis. One argument, which resists the first analysis, is the non-eventive reading of *di*. This leads to a system-internal problem since *di* would have to go through the Stat-head twice, which should be precluded. Unlike the English language, the Event head has no syntactic prerequisite for the realization of the voice layer. In other words, stative forms are not precluded from becoming the main predicate themselves. Thus, the event-head should be semantically motivated by *di*, which is not the case.

The second argument is the impossibility of *di* to function as an answer to a yes-no question. In a yes-no-question with overt *ada*, *ada* can be the fragment answer given (533). In an *ada*-less case, the answer must be *iya*(yes) (534).

(533) Ada di dalam rumah-kah   Udin? – ada/tidak
       be   in inside house-QUEST Udin   be/NEG
       'Is Udin at home? – yes/no'

(534) Di dalam rumah-kah   Udin? – iya/tidak
       in inside house-QUEST Udin   yes/NEG
       'Is Udin at home? – Yes or no'

Thus, *di* has ceased to qualify as a full "verbal" form, therefore, the requirement of the null-*ada* is very likely.

The only arguments in favour of a verbal *di*-reading come from a potential grammaticalization process (more details in the section on the origin of *ada*). This, however, should not have a (strong) impact on today's analysis. Accordingly, this work treats the null-*ada* analysis as the standard analysis.

In conclusion, for PP-predicates with overt *ada*, we have a structure comparable to English. Similar to the English clause, the PP (TransP) is merged into the complement position of the small clause (θP^{115}), and the later subject is introduced in Spec-θP. The copula *ada* is merged in Ev and then moved to the voice-head (English v). The later subject is moved to Spec-voiceP, so becoming the pivot. Thereafter, we have a verbal structure, and there is no problem with merging T checking the verbal features and for the pivot moving into Spec-TP to become the subject. Finally, we merge the C-layer, and the derivation is complete. For (535), we thus have the following structure:

---

[115] The preposition is still merged into this theta-position. However, comparable to other non-eventive structures, I still assume a small-clause structure.

(535) *Udin masih ada di Jakarta.*
    Udin CONT be in Jakarta
    'Udin is still in Jakarta.'

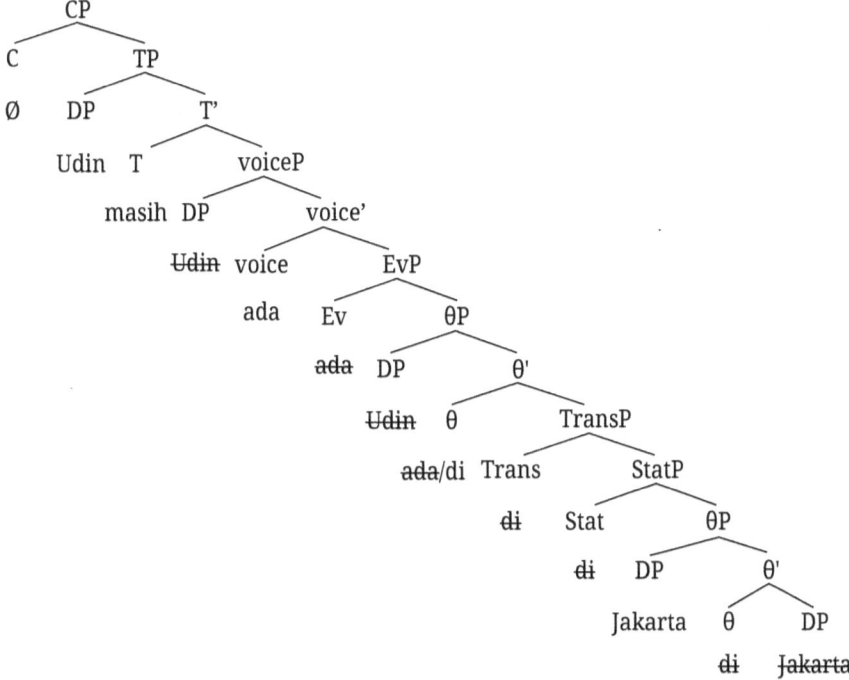

If the copula is not realized overtly, we expect an identical structure with null-*ada*.

4.4 Ada vs. adalah (vs. be)

Based on the predicate structure, the *adalah*-type and the *ada*-type are not that different. Both types apply a small clause structure to merge the non-eventive predicate and the copula structure. In both cases, the semantic predicate does not end up in voice and thus, does not become the syntactic main predicate of the clause. With that, their structure resembles the copula structure in English.

Nevertheless, the two copulas differ quite strongly. These differences can be presented on the line of their position, optionality, and origin.

4.4.1 Position

The first major difference is the verbality of *ada* and *adalah*. Whereas *ada* is clearly verbal, *adalah* has to be analyzed as a non-verbal element (cf. Musgrave 2001: 223, Mustaffa 2018: 28–29, Hopper 1972: 130). This difference can be shown by its morphosyntactic behaviour:

a. Overt verbal morphology

Ada can take overt voice morphology, namely, *ber-* (536) or *meng-kan* (537), whereas *adalah* cannot take such affixes (538, 539).

(536) Udin   ber-ada   di Jakarta.
      Udin   GO.VOICE-ada   in Jakarta
      'Udin is in Jakarta.'

(537) Udin   meng-ada-kan   pesta.
      Udin   CAUS.VOICE-ada-TH.TRANS   party
      'Udin throws a party.'

(538) *Udin ber-adalah   guru.
       Udin GO.VOICE-adalah   teacher

(539) *Udin meng-adalah-kan   guru.
       Udin CAUS.VOICE-adalah-TH.TRANS   teacher

b. Negation

Unlike *ada* (540), *adalah* cannot be embedded below a negation auxiliary like *tidak/bukan* (541).

(540) Adit   tidak   ada   di   Jakarta.
      Adit   NEG   COP   in   Jakarta
      'Adit is not in Jakarta.'

(541) *Adit tidak   adalah   guru-nya   Udin.
       Adit NEG   COP   teacher-3S.POSS   Udin

Furthermore, *adalah* cannot be embedded into a *bukan*-phrase (542). A *bukan*-phrase can, however, be embedded below *adalah* (543).

(542) *Udin bukan adalah se-orang guru.
       Udin COP   COP   one-CL.HUM teacher

(543) Bahasa   Indonesia adalah bukan bahasa   yang
      language Indonesia COP   COP   language REL
      pe-nampil   subyek.
      CAUS.NOM-show   subject
      'Indonesian is not a subject-prominent language.' (Sneddon 1996: 238)

Since *bukan* should be grouped among the auxiliaries (higher than voice but below T), *adalah* must be higher than Aux.

c. T-auxiliaries

Additionally, *adalah*, unlike *ada* (544), cannot be embedded below a T-auxiliary such as *masih*[116] (545).

(544) Adit masih ada di Jakarta.
      Adit CONT COP in Jakarta
      'Adit is still in Jakarta.'

(545) *Adit masih adalah guru-nya   Udin.
       Adit CONT COP   teacher-3s.POSS Udin

Adalah is even in complementary distribution with T. Normally, the only T available for non-bare complements is *masih* (546). However, *adalah* and *masih* cannot co-occur (548).

(546) Adit masih guru-nya   Siska.
      Adit CONT teacher-3s.POSS Siska
      'Adit is still Siska's teacher.'

(547) Adit adalah guru-nya   Siska.
      Adit COP   teacher-3s.POSS Siska
      'Adit is Siska's teacher.'

(548) a. *Adit adalah masih guru-nya   Siska.
          Adit COP   CONT teacher-3s.POSS Siska

---

[116] In very rare cases a combination of *masih adalah* is possible for some speakers.

b. *Adit masih adalah guru-nya   Siska.
   Adit CONT COP teacher-3S.POSS Siska

Accordingly, *adalah* cannot occur below any other auxiliary like *sering* (often) (550), which are realized lower than T (549). *Ada*, on the other side, can be embedded under these auxiliaries (551).

(549) Adit sudah sering makan nasi
     Adit ANT often eat rice
     'Adit has often eaten rice.'

(550) *Adit sering adalah guru-nya   Siska.
      Adit often COP teacher-3S.POSS Siska

(551) Dia sering ada di Jakarta.
      3S often COP in Jakarta
      'He/she is often in Jakarta.'

d. Control verbs

Finally, *adalah* cannot be embedded below control verbs like *ingin* (want) (552), which is grammatical with *ada*.

(552) *Adit ingin adalah se-orang   dokter.
      Adit want COP one-CL.HUM doctor
      Intended: 'Adit wants to be a doctor.'

(553) Adit ingin (ber)ada   di Jakarta.
      Adit want GO.VOICE-COP in Jakarta
      'Adit wants to be in Jakarta.'

Whereas *ada* behaves like a verb, *adalah* does not behave verbally at any point. Consequently, *ada* – similar to English *be* – has to be realized in the voice layer; *adalah*, however, cannot be inserted there. Thus, *adalah* has to be realized higher than the voice layer.

The most promising candidate is T. As we have seen, *adalah* is in complementary distribution with T-auxiliaries like *masih*. In conformity with the concept of complementary distribution, *adalah* should then be base-generated in T. Besides this structural argument, there is also an interpretative argument for *adalah* in T. We saw in chapter 3 that the Indonesian T is relative tense and not absolute tense.

All *adalah*-occurrences describe the default case, simultaneous with no aspectual specification. However, it is not sensitive to future (554), present (555), and past (556). This is a good reason to assume that *adalah* itself is the bearer of the relative tense information in these cases:

(554) *Sukarno adalah presiden pertama Indonesia.*
Sukarno COP president first Indonesia
'Sukarno was Indonesia's first president.'

(555) *Jokowi adalah presiden Indonesia.*
Jokowi COP president Indonesia
'Jokowi is the president of Indonesia.'

(556) *Tahun depan Jokowi adalah presiden Indonesia.*
year front Jokowi COP president Indonesia.
'Next year, Jokowi will be the president of Indonesia.'

For *ada*, it has been established that it has to be realized inside the voice layer due to its verbality. For the English copula *be*, it was stated that it is realized in Ev and v. If *ada* is identical to the English verbal copula, it should occur in Ev and voice. The main argument for the English case is that it is semantically vacuous; however, can the same be said about Indonesian *ada*.

So far, we have only had a look at location PPs, but the English copula *be* can also be combined with source PPs (557) and benefactor PPs (558).

(557) *John is from Ireland.*

(558) *This book is for John.*

In Indonesian, the use of *ada* in the environment of source-PPs is ungrammatical.

(559) **Udin ada dari Singapura.*
Udin COP from Singapura

In these cases, the overt verb form *berasal* (to have the origin) is possible. If a source-PP is selected by *berasal*, then the location-PP should be selected by *ada*. According to this observation, *ada* should still bear some semantic content.

Taking a look at the case of the benefactor PP, *ada* is possible; however, it leads to a two predicate reading in the sense that This book exists and exists for *Udin*.

(560) *Buku ini ada untuk Udin.*
 book this be for Udin
 'This book exists, and it exists for Udin.'

As we will see later, *ada* is part of a grammaticalization process of the verb *ada* (to exist) to a copular verb. However, this process is still ongoing, so it is not easy to decide whether *ada* still bears semantic content or not.

As long as *ada* bears at least little semantic content, it is possible to consider *ada* as a theta-assigner and therefore being inserted in θ. With no semantic content left, it cannot function as theta-assigner any longer, at which point it would then be inserted in Ev like the semantically empty copula be. This question, however, cannot be answered satisfactorily as *ada* is in a state of flux, changing from a lexical verb to a copula.

4.4.2 Optionality

Although both *adalah* and *ada* are optional, there is also an important difference in their optionality. Although *adalah* should be realized in the T-position due to the complementary distribution with both T-elements and elements moving to T like auxiliaries, it cannot undergo any movement operations, unlike other T-elements. T-auxiliaries can undergo focalization in inverted structures with (561) or without overt *-lah* (562). In the former case, this focalization requires a particular prosodic contour, namely 232f / 211f (cf. Halim 1981: 91). With overt *-lah*, these T-auxiliaries can even be fronted on their own (563).

(561) *Masih guru-nya Siska-lah Adit.*
 CONT teacher-3S.POSS Siska-FOC Adit
 'Being Siska's teacher is what Adit is.'

(562) *Masih guru-nya Siska Adit.*
 CONT teacher-3S.POSS Siska Adit
 'Being Siska's teacher is what Adit is.'

(563) *Masih-lah Adit guru-nya Siska.*
 CONT-FOC Adit teacher-3S.POSS Siska
 'Being Siska's teacher is what Adit is.'

None of these movement operations is available with *adalah* (564–567).

(564) *Adalah guru-nya   Siska Adit.
       COP   teacher-3S.POSS   Siska Adit

(565) *Adalah-kah   Adit. guru-nya   Siska
       COP-QUEST   Adit   teacher-3S.POSS   Siska

(566) Masih   guru-nya   Siska   Adit.
      CONT   teacher-3S.POSS   Siska   Adit
      'Is it still being Siska's teacher what Adit is?'

(567) Masih-kah   guru-nya   Siska   Adit.
      CONT-QUEST   teacher-3S.POSS   Siska   Adit
      'Is Adit STILL Siska's teacher?'

Hence, although *masih* and *adalah* should occupy the same position because combining them is impossible, they manifest differences in their syntactic behaviour. Whereas *masih* can be subject to a syntactical operation as movement (here T-to-C), *adalah* is not available for this movement. This leads to the assumption that *adalah* is not the phonological realization of a certain feature bundle but the realization of an operation separated from syntax, most likely at PF. For this reason, *adalah* should not be treated as syntactical but as PF-operation, similar to do-support or affix-hopping (see Chomsky 1957) in the English language. Thus, even in their substance *ada* and *adalah* are different. This also perfectly matches the observation that whenever an *ada*-less clause is possible, it can also have the same sentence with *ada*. In contrast, the use of *adalah* is sometimes ruled out, even if we have a complex nominal phrase. Thus, *ada* has to be the default case, which can be omitted in certain circumstances. In contrast, however, no-*adalah* is the default, and *adalah* is optional or even required in certain environments.

Thus, as a consequence *ada* and *adalah* do not only differ in their substance but also in their optionality. How can we explain these differences? Since there is no structural difference between *adalah* and no-*adalah*-cases and *ada* and no-*ada* cases, the only difference has to be at PF, whether *ada(lah)* is overt or not?

Processes at the PF-interface
Since *ada* is the more 'normal' case, it should be addressed first. There is no indication that *ada* behaves differently than any other vocabulary item. Therefore, it is inserted during the process of vocabulary insertion. The syntactic feature bundle is matched with the respective vocabulary item, here *ada*. Vocabulary insertion in Indonesian is always subject to the efficiency tendency discussed in chapter 3.

Thus, whenever the realization of *ada* is inefficient, it can be set on null-spell out. This process, however, is not specific to *ada* but occurs with many functional items, like Ts, voice-morphology, or complementizers, as shown in chapter 3.

The question for *adalah* is whether we can apply the same process to it. Is it part of vocabulary insertion, which is subject to the efficiency tendency? As seen before, *adalah* is not sensitive to movement; in other words, it can only be realized in T. *Adalah*-realization in C is ruled out completely. This ruling out is much stronger and absolute than the non-occurrence of *ada*. As said before, in any environment where *ada* is omitted, it could have been realized as well. The sentence might be inefficient but definitely not ungrammatical. Thus, the *adalah* case is different. As a consequence, *adalah*-insertion has to be seen as an operation different from vocabulary insertion (see Halle and Marantz 1994). Thus, it is not the phonological realization of a functional head. With no *adalah* as default and *adalah* not being sensitive to syntactic operations like movement, *adalah*-insertion must be seen as a post-syntactic operation.

To understand the nature of this post-syntactic operation, it is important to address when and why *adalah* occurs. The following can only deal with certain aspects. For a more detailed discussion, see Besier (2021).

Descriptive and prescriptive Indonesian grammars (see Sneddon 1996, Alwi et al. 2003, and Sneddon et al. 2012) assign two important characteristics to the copula *adalah*. Firstly, *adalah* is seen as optional, and secondly, more likely to occur with long constituents, e.g., to break heavy DPs. Sneddon (1996: 237) calls this "smoothening" of the clause. Hence, we could say *adalah* is added for the convenience of the speaker, to utter the expression in an easier way, and as a facilitator to the parser of the addressee. In other words, *adalah* is added when it is seen as required mapping syntax into PF to make it more understandable; in short, an "anti-ambiguity device" (Eid 1983). Since Indonesian has very little overt morphology, the hearer is often heavily dependent on phonological and prosodic cues to correctly interpret the sentence. The primary function of an overt copula, here *adalah*, is to mark both the subject (Spec-TP) and the predicate (complement of T) phonologically. In this way, it functions as an overt break or link (copula) between these two parts (Hopper 1972: 130). Lindblom (1990) presented the H&H-theory (Hyper-Hypo), stating that we use Hypospeech, that is, less accurately articulated speech when speaking with people we know, and conversely, Hyperspeech, highly accurately articulated speech, in the case of talking to foreigners, or in noisy conditions and so on. The same reasons that drive Hyper and Hypo-speech are relevant for the occurrence of *adalah* since *adalah* should be seen as part of Hyperspeech. Whenever an utterance given in its environment, including context, participants, etc., is not unproblematic without *adalah*, *adalah* has to be added. This, of course, is not possible to formulate with a rule or even a set of rules since context and participants are impossible to control. However, there are certain tendencies for the occurrence of *adalah*.

Although it is hard to say when *adalah* has to occur, it is far easier to identify certain rules to rule out the grammaticality of *adalah*, that is, contexts in which *adalah* is blocked.

As mentioned at the beginning of the chapter, the main function of a copula is to link subject and predicate. Quite the reverse is true for *adalah*. *Adalah* is not required to link subject and predicate (in the broader sense as the counterpart to the subject) but to separate subject and predicate. As we have seen above, the subject is in Spec-TP, and the predicate is voice (as phase-head), which can move to T. In linear order, the subject is to the left of T and the predicate to the right. This means that whenever we have an overt T, *adalah* is blocked, and it makes perfect sense since we have already seen that T is the place of *adalah*-support. To be more concrete, whenever we have an overt form of T, an occurrence of *adalah* is ungrammatical (568):

(568) *Udin masih adalah guru-nya Siska.
 Udin CONT COP teacher-3S.POSS Siska

The same is true for raising auxiliaries like *sering* (569) or *pernah* (570) and negators (571) like *bukan* since these auxiliaries head-move into T.

(569) *Udin sering adalah guru-nya Siska.
 Udin often COP teacher-3S.POSS Siska

(570) *Udin pernah adalah guru-nya Siska.
 Udin once COP teacher-3S.POSS Siska

(571) *Udin bukan adalah guru-nya Siska.
 Udin NEG COP teacher-3S.POSS Siska

Adverbs like *juga* (too) (572) do not rule out *adalah*, given that they do not move to T, though *adalah* is very unlikely to occur.

(572) Udin juga #adalah guru-nya Siska.
 Udin too COP teacher-3S.POSS Siska
 'Udin is Siska's teacher, too.'

In a neutral sentence, the subject is the topic of the clause. The topic can be marked either with intonation alone (a break) or with the overt topic-marker *ini/itu* (573), which is derived from a deictic expression. What is advantageous about these topic markers is that they stand at the right edge of the topic. In a copula structure with the subject in topic position, these mark off the boundary of the subject. When the copular clause consists only of subject and predicate, they mark the boundary between subject and predicate perfectly, with *adalah* becoming superfluous and, in most cases, omitted.

(573) *Joko Widodo   itu   #adalah presiden   Indonesia.*
      Joko Widodo   TOP   COP   president Indonesia
      'Concerning Joko Widodo, he is Indonesia's president.'

A second strategy of information structure is the focalization of the predicate. This is affected by TP-remnant movement to Spec-FocP. The subject is moved to the lower Spec-TopP first, and the remnant TP (the predicate) is moved to Spec-FocP. Therefore the whole predicate, including complements, is fronted, leading to an inverted structure of predicate and subject. This alone has not solved the problem of *adalah* since we encounter the same problem in another guise; we still do not know where the predicate ends. However, there are two strategies to avoid *adalah*. In Standard Indonesian, overt *-kah* in questions and *-lah* in declaratives are overt realizations of C, here Foc. They are realized as enclitics to the predicate, so the right edge is marked, and no *adalah* is used.

(574) *Makan   nasi-lah   Adit.*
      eat   rice-FOC   Adit
      'Rice eating is what Adit does.'

In colloquial Indonesian, this inversion is marked with a completely different pitch pattern, described in Halim (1975) as (575) in contrast to (576) to a topic-comment structure.

(575) 232f   / 211f
      Makan nasi / *Adit*
      eat   rice   Adit

(576) 233r   /   231f
      Adit / *makan nasi.*
      Adit   eat   rice

Since this colloquial form is mainly reduced to spoken language, no problem for the prosodic mapping is given, as intonation gives strong enough cues.

Another aspect of *adalah* is that it does not normally occur in colloquial Indonesian. While it is possible to prescribe or forbid certain structures in a standard variety, it is harder to influence a non-standard variety. In theory, colloquial Indonesian should be in the same need for an anti-ambiguity device as the standardized variety. Since *adalah* is not of high occurrence in colloquial Indonesian, alternative strategies should be available. One such strategy lies in the rich inventory of so-called emotive particles at the right edge of the topicalized or the focalized element. Besides marking the topic or focus, these convey an attitude of the speaker towards the situation. (The particle *kok* used in the example below indicates that the information dealt with in the utterance is contrary to the expectation of the addressee.). They can occur either at the end of a clause (577) or stand between topicalized subject and predicate (578) or focalized predicate and subject (579), respectively. Any other position is not possible (580–581).

(577) *Nyokap gua udah masak kok.*
mother 1s ANT cook EM.PAR
'My mother has already cooked (contrary to what you have thought).'

(578) *Nyokap gua kok udah masak.*
mother 1s EM.PAR ANT cook

(579) *Udah masak. kok nyokap gua.*
ANT cook EM.PAR mother 1s

(580) **Nyokap kok gua udah masak.*
mother EM.PAR 1s ANT cook

(581) **Nyokap gua udah kok masak.*
mother 1s ANT EM.PAR cook

As they mark the boundary between subject and predicate, emotive particles provide a cue that renders *adalah* unnecessary.

These forms have been radically marked as non-standard and therefore ruled out of Standard Indonesian. Consequently, Standard Indonesian had to evolve another strategy, so the usage of *adalah* became more widespread.

A second strategy resorts to intonation. Although colloquial Indonesian can occur in a written register, it is mainly used in spoken language; therefore, intonation is always available. Since intonation can convey important cues, the occurrence of *adalah* is less likely. Even when colloquial Indonesian is used in a written form (e.g., text message), sentences are generally shorter compared to Standard

Indonesian. Shorter sentences are less likely to be ambiguous, and *adalah* is less likely to occur.

Having now touched on the idea of spoken and written language, this is an opportune juncture to deal with this factor in more detail. *Adalah* occurs in written language more often than in spoken language, owing to the fact that written language lacks any prosodic cues. Therefore, an overt boundary between subject and predicate is a helpful decoding tool.

If we consider the following string of words (582), it is highly ambiguous:

(582) *Gurunya Lila Mina Surawati.*

(583) *Gurunya Lila Mina / Surawati.* Lila Mina's teacher is Surawati.

(584) *Gurunya Lila / Mina Surawati.* Lila's teacher is Mina Surawati.

(585) *Gurunya / Lila Mina Surawati.* Her teacher is Lila Mina Surawati.

Whereas spoken language will avoid ambiguity by inserting a break at the right point, written language has no opportunity to make use of prosodic cues. If the context is unknown to the participants, or if one tries to preclude unnecessary ambiguity, an *adalah* in the right position can easily solve the problem.

(586) *Guru-nya   Lila   Mina   adalah   Surawati.*
       teacher-3s.POSS Lila   Mina   COP   Surawati
       'Lila Mina's teacher is Surawati.'

(587) *Guru-nya   Lila   adalah Mina   Surawati.*
       teacher-3s.POSS Lila   COP   Mina   Surawati
       'Lila's teacher is Mina Surawati.'

(588) *Guru-nya   adalah Lila   Mina   Surawati.*
       teacher-3s.POSS COP   Lila   Mina   Surawati
       'Her teacher is Lila Mina Surawati.'

Besides intonation, a second strategy is available in spoken language, which is not used in written language, namely direct address. It is seen as polite to address one's interlocutor directly.[117] It is more polite to say something like (589) instead of just (590):

(589) *Selamat   pagi,   bu.*
       Good   morning,   mam.

(590) *Selamat   pagi.*
       Good   Morning.

This mode of addressing is expressed with a shortened form of an appropriate kinship term, e.g. *(ba)pak* (father), *(i)bu* (mother), or *(ka)kak* (older sibling), or the shortened form of the name, e.g., *Sis(ka), (U)din* or *(Ye)ris(ca)*. However, such forms of address can occur not only at the end but also in the middle of an utterance. Comparable to emotive particles, they can only be placed in a certain position: at the end of the clause (591) or following the topic. In (592), the subject is the topic, so address-insertion is possible. In (593), the adverbial *'kemarin'* (yesterday) is the topic so that we can have the address form after *'kemarin'*, but not after the subject.

(591) *Saya   mem-beli   buku   itu,   bu.*
       1s   CAUS.VOICE -buy   book   DEM   mam
       'I bought the book, mam.'

(592) *Saya,   bu,   mem-beli   buku   itu,*
       1s   mam   CAUS.VOICE-buy   book   DEM
       'I bought the book, mam.'

(593) *Kemarin,   bu,   saya   *bu,   mem-beli   buku   itu.*
       Yesterday   mam   1s   mam   CAUS.VOICE-buy   book   DEM
       'Yesterday, I bought the book, mam.'

In summary, these forms can only occur after an intonation phrase, where a pause can be inserted (Nespor and Vogel 1986). As a positive side effect, they can mark the boundary between subject and predicate if the subject has been moved to the topic position. The occurrence of this type of address form marks the right edge of the topicalized subject constituent and makes *adalah* less likely, though not impossible.

The last factor that is important for the usage of *adalah* is the length of the constituents, namely subject and predicate. As Sneddon (1996) pointed out, *adalah*

---

[117] This is relevant for both colloquial as well as for standard Indonesian.

is very likely for long subjects or predicates, or as he calls them, heavy DPs. How can we explain this?

In chapter 3, we saw that Indonesian normally has a high phrasal tone between different intermediate phrases.

(594)

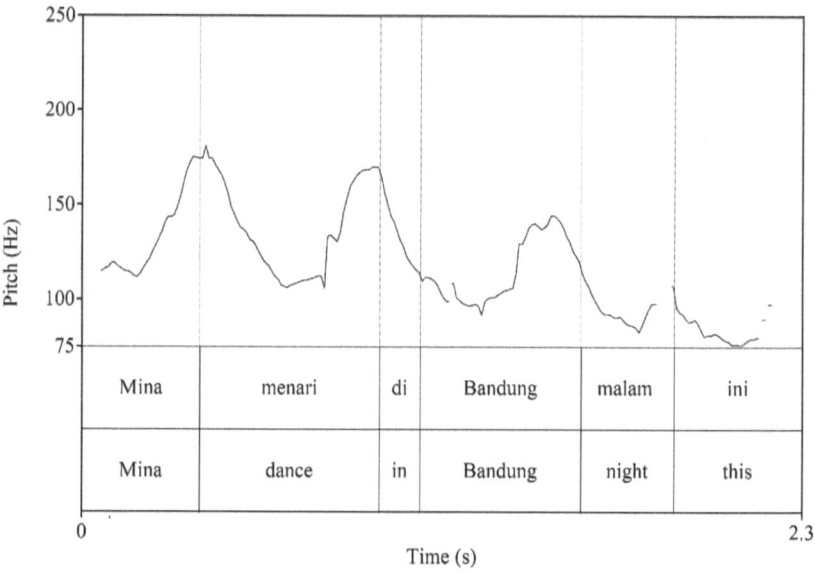

At the edge of an intonation phrase, we also find a high boundary tone. The only difference between the end of an intermediate phrase and the end of an intonation phrase is that a break is only possible after an intonation phrase. Since such a break would be a very weak intonational cue, *adalah* is inserted, thereby building its own intermediate phrase allowing both a break before and after *adalah* (see 605) as an additional cue.

(595)

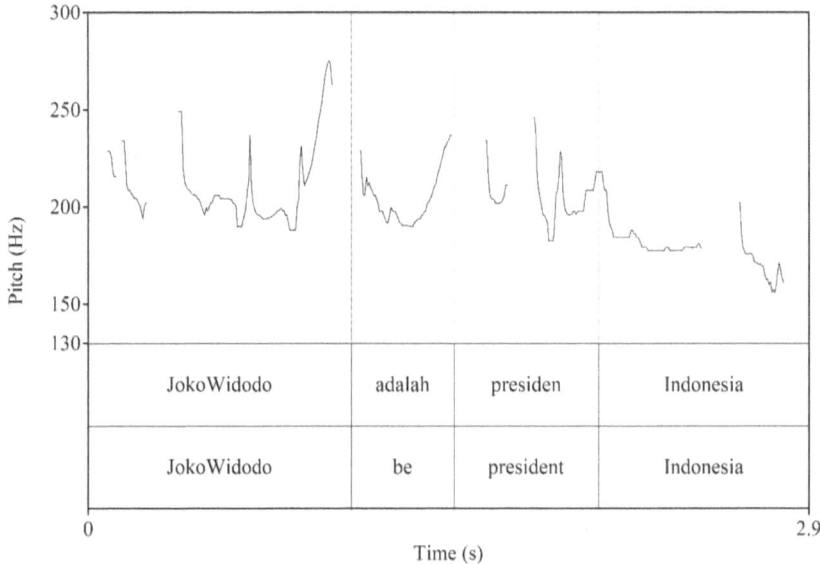

Besides this general disambiguating aspect, there is also a smoothening effect when we have an asymmetry between subject and predicate when either the subject (596) or the predicate (597) is very short. Both sentences have been judged as very awkward if *adalah* is omitted.

(596) Susilo Bambang Yudhoyono *(adalah) jendral.
      Susilo Bambang Yudhoyono COP   general.
      'Susilo Bambang Yudhoyono is/was a general.'

(597) Sukarno *(adalah) presiden Indonesia yang pertama.
      Sukarno COP   president Indonesia REL   first
      'Sukarno was the first president of Indonesia.'

Here, a break between subject and predicate or, more accurately, between topic and comment would be easily possible; however, due to the brevity of either the first or the second part, a long break as a clear cue is very odd for which reason *adalah* is inserted to smoothen this sentence and to avoid such an odd break.

In addition to these utterance internal factors, there are utterance external factors relevant to the realization of *adalah*. These factors are the participants involved, context, and register. For these factors, it is much harder to identify certain tendencies since the use of *adalah* depends on the personal preferences of the speaker as well. Therefore, the next section will present some possible considerations without claiming anything near exhaustive reasoning.

Suppose one of the participants is not very proficient in the Indonesian language. In that case, it is likely that the more proficient speaker will choose the overt realization of *adalah* more often than in a conversation with a more proficient speaker. Additionally, people normally tend towards a more standardized (textbook) version when speaking to non-native speakers to mirror the language instructed in a language school. This leads automatically to higher usage of *adalah*, even in contexts where it would not be necessary for discourse between native speakers.

In some contexts, speakers apply a more formal register to underscore their education or authority. The ability to use standard Indonesian, especially close to the version prescribed by the language department, is not as widespread as one might expect. Thus, using this variety is marked and can have an impact on the listener. While not everyone is successful in using this variety, if a speaker deliberately uses a more formal register, she will automatically tend towards more frequent usage of *adalah*.

In other contexts, avoiding ambiguity and misunderstanding takes a very high priority, e.g., in law courts, politics, or public talk, especially as concerns sensitive topics. In such situations, higher usage of *adalah* again should be expected.

The goal of the examples given is merely to illustrate the general idea. What should be obvious, since these utterance-external factors are close to impossible to control, is that getting grammaticality judgments for the usage of *adalah* is likewise close to impossible.

To sum up: *Adalah* is only a tool to provide further cues to help the parser map the correct structure. Since *adalah* is only a phonological convenience, it is at no point obligatory; hence, in theory, every sentence could be uttered without *adalah*. However, because some circumstances would be so problematic for the parser, *adalah* is required by nearly all speakers. In these cases, *adalah* may give the appearance of a syntactic requirement, although it is, in fact, still a PF matter.

4.4.3 Origin

Although *ada* and *adalah* are derived from the same verb *ada*, their position and syntactic behaviour are quite different. How can we come up with two different copulas? The explanation given here is that they are the product of two different and independent language change processes.

Ada

The grammaticalization process relevant for *ada* as a copular verb is related to the preposition phrase following it. It is a grammaticalization process from a serial verb construction to a copula+preposition construction as it has been attested cross-linguistically by, amongst others, König and Kortmann (1991) and Lord (1973). Let us first deal with the preposition part before dealing with *ada* itself.

Taking a look at a prototypical isolating language, Vietnamese, we can see that a clear distinction between prepositions and verbs is impossible to draw. Considering the following examples (598–601) without any overt verbal morphology, we cannot decide whether *cho* or *đến* should be treated as a preposition or verb.

(598) *Hôm qua   Phường   đến   Hà Nội.* (Vietnamese)
      yesterday Phường   arrive   Hanoi.
      'Yesterday Phường arrived in Hanoi.'

(599) *Phường   cho   tôi   chiếc   đồng hồ.* (Vietnamese)
      Phường   give   1s   CL   watch.
      'Phường gives me a watch.'

(600) *Phường   đi   đến   Hà Nội.* (Vietnamese)
      Phường   go   arrive   Hanoi
      'Phường goes to Hanoi.'

(601) *Phường   mua   một   cái   ti vi   cho   tôi.* (Vietnamese)
      Phường   buy   one   CL   television   for   1s
      'Phường buys a television for me.'

(600) and (601) are normally grouped as serial verb constructions (SVC). Although different authors have grouped a wide range of constructions as SVCs, this section will focus on structures like the Vietnamese example (600) above, which are labeled as agent-sharing directional SVCs by Haspelmath (2015). This group corresponds to telic unaccusative verbs that take a PP-complement in English. It has the following characteristics.

a) Both verbs can be used independently as the main predicate of a clause.
   As observed in the Vietnamese example, *đến* (arrive) can be used as the main predicate of a clause, see (598); thus, the second verb of the serial construction arguably has a verbal status of some kind.
b) Both verbs share the same focused argument (the argument that ends up in Spec-voiceP/vP). If we consider the sentence (600), the verb *đến* has two arguments, namely *Hà Nội* and *Phường*. *Phường* is moved into Spec-voiceP. *đi*,

however, has only one argument, namely *Phường*, which automatically has to become the argument for Spec-voiceP. For both verbs, then, *Phường* is the pivot in Spec-voiceP.

c) The embedded predicate is a two-place predicate.
d) The internal theta-role of the embedded two place-predicate is proto-GOAL.
e) The second theta-role assigned is proto-THEME.
f) The second verb phrase is merged as the complement of the higher base-generated verb.

If we translate these structures into English using a preposition, we obtain a complement status for the constituent in question.

(602) Phuong goes <u>to Hanoi</u>.

These examples can be found in Indonesian as well, e.g. *masuk*.

(603) Udin   pergi   masuk   kelas.
       Udin   go   enter   classroom
       'Udin goes to his classroom.'

(604) Udin   pergi.
       Udin   go
       'Udin goes.'

(605) Udin   masuk   kelas.
       Udin   enter   classroom
       'Udin enters the classroom.'

Masuk is a two-place predicate that assigns the GOAL and the THEME role to its arguments. The external argument of *pergi* and *masuk* is *Udin*, so it is shared. The question is, how can we represent such a structure in a tree?

Since it is possible to treat both verbs as predicates independent of each other, we need two different argument structures. The first one is *masuk* (enter), and the second one is *pergi* (go). Whereas *masuk* is a two-place-predicate with *kelas* as GOAL and Udin as either AGENT or THEME (we will deal with it further below), *pergi* is a one-place-predicate. Let us treat its argument as a THEME argument.

All arguments are base-generated in Spec-θP. Therefore, for *masuk*, we need two different θPs, one for *kelas* and one for *Udin*. Therefore, we need some kind of two-place-predicate structure. We have two theta assigners, two Cat-heads (either Stat(e) or Ev(ent) and two δ-heads (Trans and voice). This voiceP is the complement of the *pergi*-θP. *Pergi* is an intransitive structure and only needs one θ-layer, one

Cat-layer, here Ev, and one δ-layer, here voice. We now have two verbal structures with a voiceP, one transitive and one intransitive. The transitive voiceP is the complement of the intransitive form. (Remember, the complement is assigned neither a theta-role nor any other function). The following structure represents the above:

(606)

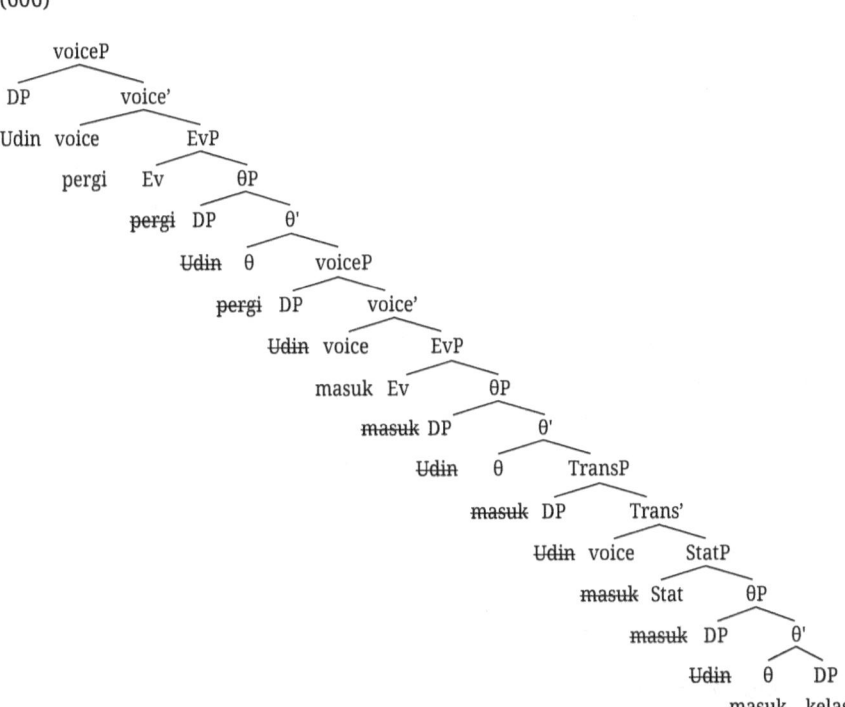

This structure is the departure point of our grammaticalization process. To understand this process, it is necessary first to have a look at features. Before considering the combination *pergi masuk*, we need to take a step back and pick up with the fully passivizable transitive form *pergi memasuki*. In a passivizable transitive structure, the Trans-Head must be specified for uCAUSE asking for a CAUSE. This uninterpretable feature is checked via reverse agree by the higher θP introducing the AGENT/ CAUSE. At the same time, this +CAUSE -Trans-Head assigns object status to its specifier. Movement is triggered with an uninterpretable THEME or GOAL feature, leading to a *-kan* (THEME) or *-i* (GOAL)-realization at PF. Hence, for a structure like *memasuki*, *masuk* is merged into θ with the specification [GOAL]. Therefore, *kelas* is assigned the GOAL role in Spec-θP. Following that, we merge the Stat-head, as the embedded part always describes a state in a transitive structure. Next, we merge the Trans-head with the following features [uCAUSE,uGOAL, OBJECT], corresponding to the suffix -*i* at vocabulary insertion. The uGOAL feature is checked by *kelas,* which moves to Spec-TransP to receive the object status. The uCAUSE is satisfied via reverse agree by the higher θ-head, which is specified for CAUSE, assigning the CAUSE-role to its specifier, here Udin. The theta-assigner specified for CAUSE is always selected by an event-head, which is then selected by voice specified for CAUSE, thus *meN-*. Udin as the CAUSE is moved into Spec-voiceP and becomes the pivot of the clause. We thus end up with the form of *memasuki*. It is at this point that the grammaticalization process starts.

Due to phonological reduction, both the overt voice-marking and the Trans-marking is set on null-spell out. Instead of *memasuki* one uses *masuk*. This reduction makes way for reanalysis. The Trans-head does not bear a uCAUSE-feature, but this feature is reduced to an abstract default theta-feature. For this reason, the higher θ-head cannot be specified for CAUSE anymore; otherwise, there would be a mismatch. Hence, the CAUSE role is ruled out. To compensate for this, the default θ-head specified for THEME is merged, so *masuk* assigns the roles THEME and GOAL to its two arguments. Additionally, without overt voice-marking, the eventive character of *meN-* (in Ev) is lost. As a default, the form is reanalyzed as Stat(e), as a result of which the former "verbal" form no longer refers to an event, e.g., in (607), *masuk* does not refer to an event of entering a building. As such, we are not talking about all the students who enter the school building but about all students who are registered at a school; therefore, it refers not to an event but a state.

(607) *Peraturan ini   berlaku bagi siswa-siswi yang sedang*
      rule   DEM count   for students   REL   PROG
      masuk sekolah.
      masuk   school
      'This rule holds for all registered students.'

This leads to an interesting situation for our serial verb construction. The shared argument is marked for the THEME-role by both verbs, which should be impossible theta-role stacking. At the same time, since *masuk* no longer has an event feature, it is possible to interpret the former two-event construction as one event construction similar to transitive structures, which are built by an event and a state. Therefore, the first theta-role is assigned by *masuk* and the second one by *pergi*.

Since *kelas* loses its object status, it is no longer moved to Spec-TransP. From here on, Trans does not have an uninterpretable CAUSE feature but an uninterpretable THEME feature. Now *masuk* attains a status comparable to a preposition. This results in the following structure:

(608)

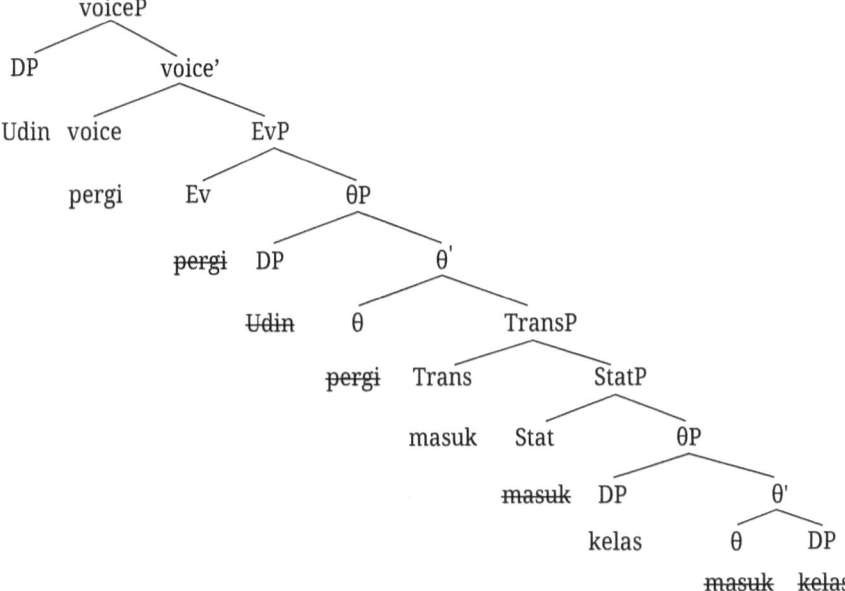

In the course of grammaticalization, *masuk* can even lose its lexical status completely[118] and is reduced to case-marking. Now, *masuk* is no longer a root merged into θ. The higher verb is merged to the lower θ and moves via Stat and to the higher θ and Ev and v, respectively. The former unaccusative one-place-predicate verb has become a telic two-place predicate. *Masuk* has been reanalyzed as case-marking necessary at PF to mark the GOAL-marked argument, here, *kelas*. Therefore, the surface realization of (609) would still be *Udin pergi masuk kelas*.

---

118 In today's Indonesian there is evidence for *masuk* with lexical status and *masuk* without such lexical status. For now grammaticalization is still on its way and the path described here is somewhat hypothetical, although there is evidence from other forms that we might end there.

(609)

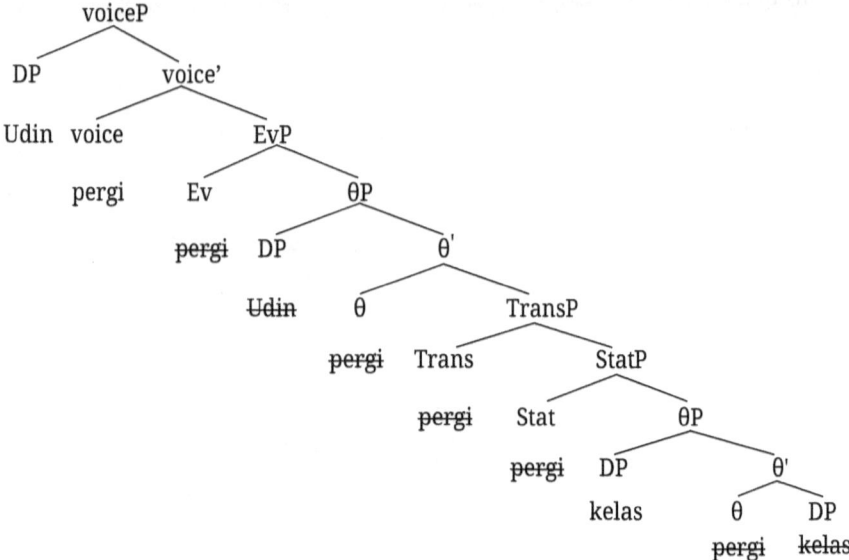

It is even possible that we lose the overt realization of the preposition completely, as is attested for so-called Hood German (610) in contrast to Standard German (611):

(610) Isch geh Schule
I go school.
'I go to school.'

(611) Ich gehe zur Schule.
I go to school.
'I go to school.'

In summary, in this grammaticalization process, a transitive verb has been reanalyzed first as a lexical preposition, then as PF-operation to mark case, and finally is omitted completely.

When we talk about grammaticalization processes, we need to keep in mind that we always talk within the frame of continua. For many forms or even all forms, it is hard to decide which category/stage they belong to. There are inconsistencies between speakers or even in the speech of one individual.

In the following, a few examples are represented for the Indonesian verb-to-preposition continuum.

In (612), the embedded verb form still has obligatory voice-marking, *meN-*. As a single form, it can even be passivized (613), so the sentence should be analyzed as SVC with two fully lexical verbs.

(612) *Pesawat ini terbang me-nuju Jakarta.*
airplane DEM fly CAUS.VOICE-head_to Jakarta
'The airplane heads to Jakarta.'

(613) *Jakarta di-tuju.*
Jakarta PASS-head_to.
'Jakarta is the destination of the plane.'

In other forms, voice- and/or trans-marking is possible, though normally omitted:

(614) *Udin jalan lewat/me-lewat-i pasar.*
Udin walk pass/CAUS.VOICE-pass-GO.TRANS market
'Udin passed the market.'

For forms with omitted voice morphology, it is possible to find forms that can have an eventive (before reanalysis) and a non-eventive (after reanalysis) reading. (615) could refer either to the event of entering the office through the door or to the situation in that *Udin* is at work. The same is true for (616), which could refer either to the event of leaving the house or the state of being outside.

(615) *Hari ini Udin masuk kantor.*
today Udin enter office
'Today Udin enters his office/is in his office.'

(616) *Udin sedang keluar rumah.*
today PROG go.out house
'Today Udin enters his office/is in his office.'

With the second meaning, it is semantically not dissimilar to forms such as (512) or (513), prototypical prepositions in Indonesian.

(617) *Udin ke Jakarta.*
Udin to Jakarta
'Udin goes to Jakarta.'

(618) *Udin dari Jakarta.*
       Udin from Jakarta
       'Udin is from Jakarta.'

However, adding a full verb (615, 616) would change the meaning (619, 620). In (617) and (618), a full verb could be inserted without changing the meaning (621, 622).

(619) *Hari ini Udin pergi masuk kantor.*
       today   Udin go   enter office.
       'Today, Udin went to the office.' (Udin is still on his way, not there yet)

(620) *Udin sedang pergi keluar   rumah.*
       Udin PROG   go   go.out   house.
       'Udin is leaving home.'

(621) *Udin pergi ke kamar.*
       Udin go   to room
       'Udin goes to his room.'

(622) *Udin ber-asal   dari Jakarta.*
       Udin GO.VOICE-origin from Jakarta
       'Udin comes from Jakarta.'

In this sense, then, (617) and (618) are elliptic structures (see Alwi et al. 2003), whereas (615) and (616) are not. Here *masuk* and *keluar* are still the main predicates. This leads to two competing structures with an elliptic verb plus a preposition, a verbal structure without a preposition, or an intermediate status between these two. In a continuum, of course, certain tendencies are available while no clear-cut boundaries are possible.

How does this relate to *ada*? PPs occurring in *ada*-contexts show the same continuum as we have seen for directional verb phrases before. For all *ada*-contexts (623), it is possible to have the same sentence without *ada* (624).

(623) a. *Udin ada dengan Siska.*
          Udin be   with   Siska
          'Udin is with Siska.'
      b. *Buku ini   ada untuk Siska*
          book DEM   be   for   Siska
          'This book is for Siska.'

c. *Udin ada di Jakarta.*
    Udin be in Jakarta.
    'Udin is in Jakarta.'

(624) a. *Udin lagi dengan Siska.*
    Udin PROG with Siska
    'Udin is with Siska.'
  b. *Buku ini untuk Siska.*
    book DEM for Siska
    'This book is for Siska.'
  c. *Udin di Jakarta.*
    Udin in Jakarta
    'Udin is in Jakarta.'

Although the pattern looks identical for all sentences, there is nevertheless a difference in interpretation. Whereas for *ada untuk* (623b), there is a strong two-predicate reading (*This book exists and is for Siska*) similar to *pergi masuk* (go inside) in the previous section, the *ada di* (623c) is identical to the bare *di* (624c) similar to *pergi ke* (go to) before. *ada dengan* (623a) lies somewhere between these two extremes on this continuum. We may then assume the same grammaticalization process for *ada di* as *pergi masuk*.

At the starting point, *ada* should be an unaccusative verb assigning the THEME and *di* a transitive form with a CAUSE and a GOAL argument. Whereas the existential form *ada* (625) fits the criterion of THEME- assignment perfectly, a transitive *di*-form is purely hypothetical, though not impossible. Nevertheless, we can agree that the first theta-role assigned by *di* is definitely something like a GOAL/LOCATION.

(625) *Tuhan ada.*
    God exist
    'God exists.'

According to the process described above, the transitive *di*-form loses its causation. The external argument is assigned a THEME role. Finally, the form is reduced to a preposition, and the external theta-role is assigned by the higher verb, in this case, *ada*. If grammaticalization had continued, *di* would first be reanalyzed as PF-operation marking the GOAL-argument and later on dropped completely. Therefore, we should have a two-place-predicate derived from the existential verb *ada*. This is obviously not the case for Indonesian since (626) is ungrammatical. However, Javanese, Indonesia's most important regional language, shows exactly this outcome.[119]

(626) *Udin ada Jakarta.
　　　Udin be Jakarta

In the higher register,[120] Krama, the form *wonten* can be used as an intransitive existential verb (627), as transitive form 'be_at' (628), and even as a locational preposition (629).[121]

(627) *Gusti wonten.* (Javanese)
　　　God exist
　　　'God exists.'

(628) *Udin wonten Surabaya.* (Javanese)
　　　Udin be.at Surabaya
　　　'Udin is in Surabaya'

(629) *Udin dhahar wonten griya-nipun.* (Javanese)
　　　Udin eat be.at house-3SG
　　　'Udin eats at home.'

What, then, happened in the Indonesian case? Why did we not end up with a form like *wonten*? The answer given here lies in a counter-rotating language change process, namely from a lexical verb to a copula. The existential verb *ada*, similar to English *be*, lost more and more of its semantical content and, with that, more importantly, the possibility of assigning a thematic role. Syntactically *ada* is reduced to the abstract Ev-head and the voice-head, those two heads that are occupied by the English copula.

If we combine these two processes *di* from a transitive form to preposition and *ada* from lexical verb to the copula verb, we end up with the structure that we expect (copula+preposition). The preposition *di* is merged in the first theta-position assigns the GOAL-role to its specifier, here Jakarta. It moves to Stat and Trans. The internal role, however, is no longer moved into Spec-TransP. A second theta-head has to be merged on account of an unsatisfied theta-feature. Here we can either merge the preposition *di* or the lexical verb *ada*. As long as *ada* has semantic

---

[119] Hood German allows a similar constructions: *Isch bin Uni.* (I am at the university)
[120] Javanese has different language registers/level which has to be chosen depending on the counterpart in a conversation.
[121] The last case could be analyzed as serial verb construction as well.

content, it should occupy the theta-position and perhaps even shift *di* in the direction of a PF-analysis. However, as soon as *ada* loses its semantic content, it cannot be merged into the theta-head but only in the event-head and voice-head on top of it (copular status). Then the preposition should move into the second θP. Hence, we end up with a copula (voice+Ev), a small clause (higher theta-head), and a preposition (Trans-structure) (TransP, StatP, θP), comparable to the English structure.

(630)

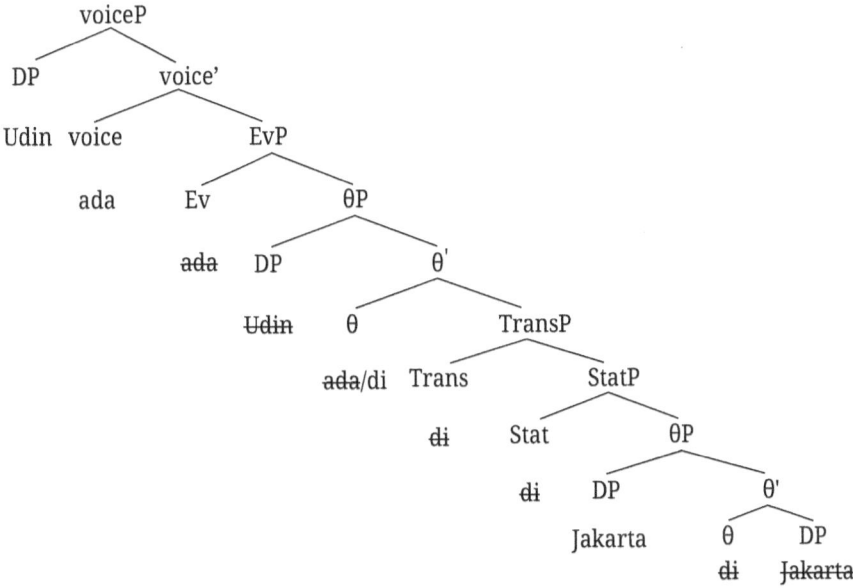

With *ada* being a product of ongoing language change, the question of semantic content is hard to answer. Depending on the stage of the process, *ada* should or should not have semantic content.

Adalah

Having dealt with a potential origin of *ada*, it is now time to turn to *adalah*. The Indonesian copula *adalah* must be seen as a relatively recent development in the Indonesian/Malay language. There are at least three indications:

1) Concerning copulas, Indonesian is the exception among the Austronesian languages. In her study on copular structures, Pustet (2003) categorizes many languages worldwide, of which about 20 Austronesian languages are included. Among

these Austronesian languages, Indonesian is the only language with a copula. The copula, then, cannot be seen as prototypical Austronesian.

2) *adalah* can be separated into *ada* (existential verb) and *-lah* (emphasis marker). Both morphemes are still available and productive in today's Indonesian. However, the copula *adalah* is not the productive usage of *ada+lah* but must be treated as one morpheme (Hopper 1972: 130). In a sentence like (631), *adalah* is the combination of *ada+lah*, whereas in (632), the copula is not such a combination.

(631)   *Maka   ada-lah   se-buah   rumah   Yahudi*   (Mohd. Yusof Md. Nor. 1989)[122]
        so   exist-EMPH   one-CL   house   Jew
        'So, there was a Jewish house.'

(632)   *Sukarno   adalah   presiden   Indonesia   yang   pertama.*
        Sukarno   COP   president   Indonesia   REL   first
        'Sukarno was the first president of Indonesia.'

3) Looking at older Malay texts, we find mixed evidence for *adalah*, though seldom for *adalah* as a copula. In older Malay texts, *adalah* is common as an emphatic existential verb, exemplified in (633).

(633)   *Maka   ada-lah   seorang   raja   di dalam   negeri Badagra*
        So   exist-EMPH   CL.HUM   king   inside   state Badagra
        nama-nya
        name-3S.POSS
        'So, there was a king in the state named Badagra.' (Mohd. Yusof Md. Nor. 1989)

Besides this, *adalah* could be used as a set phrase in a narrative, comparable to the German:

"*Es begab sich. . . .*"

(634)   *Maka   ada-lah   raja   itu   telah   wafat.*   (Mohd. Yusof Md. Nor. 1989)
        so   exist-EMPH   king   DEM   ANT   die
        'So it came that the king has died.'

---

[122] All examples of Classical Malay have been found in the corpus "*Korpus Teks Melayu Lama*" (http://sbmb.dbp.gov.my/korpusklasik/Researchers/Search.aspx)

However, we even find evidence for sentences with something at least proximate to copular usage:

(635) Adalah   hamba   orang yang kaya   (Mohd. Yusof Md. Nor. 1989)
      Adalah   servant (1s) man   NOM   Rich
      'I am a rich man.'

(636) Adalah rupa-nya   seperti kepala babi lagi ber-duri.
      COP   form-NOM   like   head   pig   PROG GO.VOICE-thorn
      'Its form was like a pig with thorns.' (Mohd. Yusof Md. Nor. 1989)

To conclude on these indications, we should treat *adalah* as a result of a grammaticalization process. In the following, I will outline certain ideas and possible outcomes, with the caveat that, as is often the case with historical linguistics, much of it must be based on assumptions.

In order to understand a possible grammaticalization process, we need first to understand the original morphemes of *adalah*. If we split *adalah* into its two morphemes, we obtain *ada* and *lah*. *Ada* is a 'lexical' verb that can mean both 'to exist' (637) and 'to be around' (638).

(637) Orang tua   masih ada?[123]
      man   old   CONT   exist
      'Are your parents still alive?'

(638) Bapak-mu   ada,   nggak?
      father-2s.POSS   be.around   NEG
      'Is your father around?' (Yes-No-Question)

-lah is a focus marker for predicates (639). *-lah* attracts the predicate to move into C and leads to an inverted structure.

(639) Lapar-lah   Adit.
      hungry-FOC   Adit
      'Adit is HUNGRY.'

However, *-lah* itself has changed in the process of time. In Classical Malay, *-lah* was used to highlight the storyline (Cumming 1991). Aside from its role for information

---

[123] A common question asked when meeting somebody for the first time.

structure as a focus and foreground marker (Hopper 1983), there is also a temporal aspect to -*lah*. Since in Classical Malay today's temporal markers (relative tense) were still verbal, relative tense could only be expressed with subordination. However, -*lah* could only be used in the main clause, thereby also indicating the simultaneity with the time of reference (the main discourse). Thus, -*lah* can be seen as a T-category. Additionally -*lah*-forms should be treated as finite forms since embedding of -*lah*-verbs was not possible.

At that time, Malay still had an unmarked verb-initial order (see Cumming 1991). With time the T-category with today's markers *sudah, masih,* etc. underwent increasing grammaticalization. These markers lost their verbal features and grammaticalized from voice to Aux to T.[124] With the new T-category, -*lah* lost its tense and aspect features and was reanalyzed solely as a focus marker. It was thus reanalyzed into C, leading to today's usage.

To summarize, -*lah* attracted and continues to attract the predicate into a clause-initial position; formerly into T, currently into C. This movement operation is important to understand the grammaticalization of *adalah*.

Since *ada* was (is) a full verb, nothing hindered *ada* from undergoing -*lah*-marking, and consequently movement to a clause-initial position, at one time T, and nowadays C.

(640) *Ada-lah   rumah orang Yahudi.*
      exist-EMPH house man   Jew
      'There is a Jewish house.'

On top of the fronted predicate in T, a topicalized element could be merged into Spec-CP.

(641) *Adit   makan-lah nasi.*
      Adit   eat-FOC   rice
      'Concerning Adit, he ATE rice.'

Frequent use of topics identical to the subject in Spec-VoiceP led to a reanalysis of the topic in Spec-CP as a topical subject in Spec-TP, such as the case in today's Indonesian. The constantly filled Spec-TP led to an EPP-feature reanalysis on T. Thus, Malay changed from a VOS language to an SVO language (see also Cumming 1991).

However, with the emergence of a new T-category of relative tense, -*lah* lost its productivity for T. At the same time, *ada* was desemanticized, losing its meaning 'to

---

[124] See chapter 2

be present'. Consequently, it was decategorialized and no longer has verbal status. Hence, *adalah* was reanalyzed as one morpheme, chiefly bearing only its relative tense feature (simultaneity). Therefore the whole form has been stranded in T.

Although this process was driven by many language-internal factors, such as the emergence of a T-category and the change from a verb-initial to an SVO language, influences, such as contact with European languages (Portuguese, English, Dutch, and German via colonization or missionary activity) as well as standardization by intellectuals educated in European languages from the 1920s on have also played a crucial role in the shift towards a more frequent use of a copula (cf. Hopper 1972: 130).

As described in the previous section, *ada* and *adalah* underwent different grammaticalization paths. Although both are derived from the existential verb *ada*, which still exists additionally to the copulas *ada* and *adalah*, the processes are unique. Whereas *ada* grammaticalized into a copular verb conditioned by the grammaticalization process from serial verbs to prepositions, *adalah* is derived from a former T-marking process with -*lah*. These different grammaticalization processes can also explain the difference in position (v vs. T) and, consequently, their syntactic behaviour (verbal vs. non-verbal).

4.5 Conclusion

For predicational copular structures, English and Indonesian contrast in three major points:
1. The category of the non-verbal (non-eventive) predicate
2. The number of copulas
3. The copula type

4.5.1 The category of non-eventive predicate

English subsumes adjectives, nouns, and prepositions as non-verbal. Whereas the verbal category requires an Ev-head with an eventive feature, non-verbal categories have either a Stat-head (adjectives and prepositions) or an N-head (nouns). Since the English v-head has an uninterpretable event feature, only EvP can be merged with v. Since T can only select v, non-verbal predicates cannot become the main predicate of the clause since, due to their non-eventive character, movement to v is not possible. Therefore, they require a different δ-head for their category, namely Mod for adjectives, D, respectively Q, for nouns, and Trans (with an uninterpretable THEME-feature) for prepositions. On top of that, we need the help of an extra theta-assigner (small clause) and, more importantly, the copula with a pseudo-event feature forming both the Ev- and the v-head. T can select the v-head, and the derivation can be successful.

In contrast, the voice-head is not sensitive to an eventive feature in the Indonesian language but can also select StatPs. The voice-head is rather specified for certain theta-role/Cat-head combinations, which lead to different realizations of the voice-morpheme at PF. Thus adjectives (if such a category exists at all) and verbs are subsumed as one syntactic category in Indonesian, such that semantic adjectives, moved into Stat, can become the main predicate of a clause by moving into voice and consequently to T if T is not overtly filled. In these cases, no copula can be used; therefore, it is labeled the no-copula type.

Hence, in this case, the English sentence (642) must have a copula, whereas the Indonesian equivalent (643) must not have a copula:

(642) *John is hungry.*

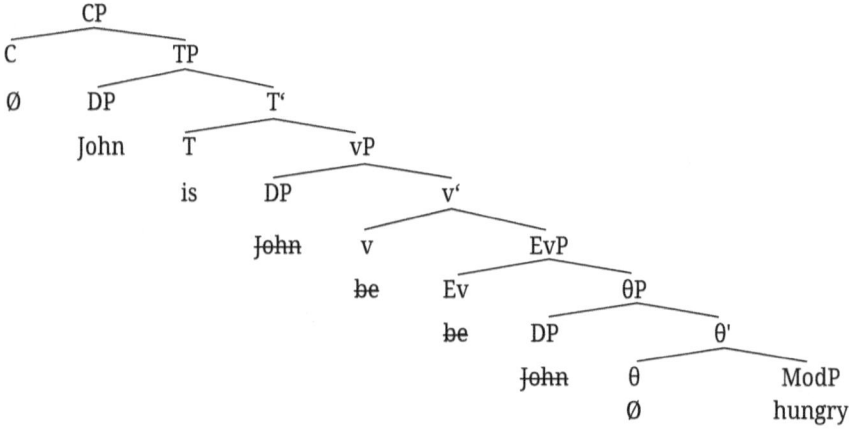

(643) *Yahya lapar*
     John hungry
     'John is hungry.'

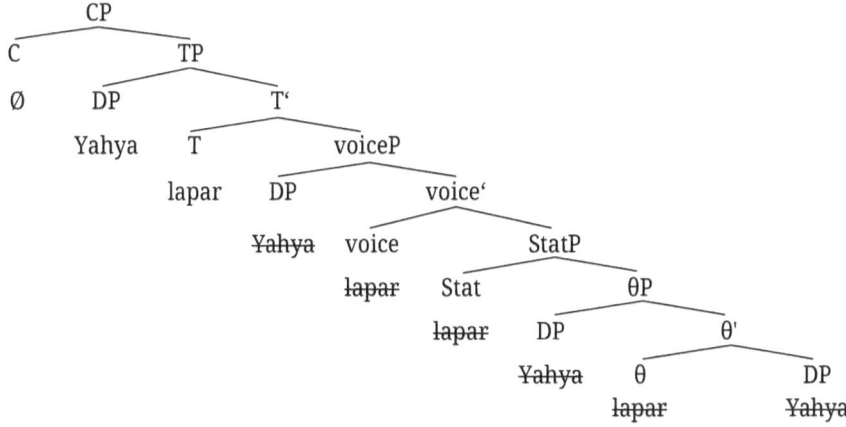

For nominal phrases and preposition phrases, the non-verbality is also attested for Indonesian since they merge with distinct δ-heads from voice, namely D/Q and Trans. However, for both QPs and PPs, there are two competing structures, one equivalent to the English structure as a non-verbal category and one as a member of the verbal category.

Since prepositions have been derived diachronically from verbs, a preposition analysis or a predicate analysis is possible depending on the speaker and the form in question. Whereas the English sentence (644) only allows the preposition analysis (646), the Indonesian equivalent (645) can be analyzed as copula structure (here a null-*ada*) with prepositional structure (647) or as no-copula-structure with voiceP (648).

(644) *John is in Japan.*

(645) *Yahya di Jepang.*
      John in Japan
      'John is in Japan.'

(646)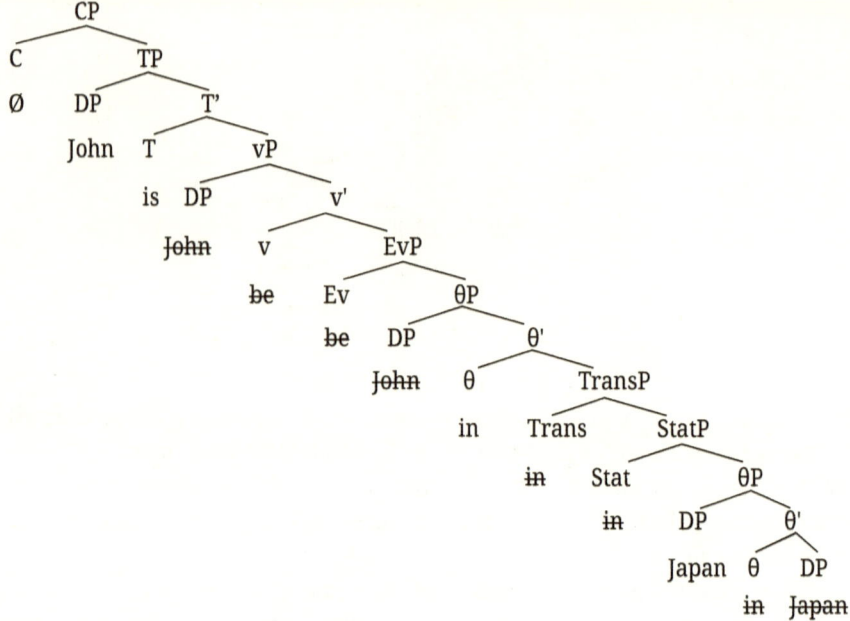

(647)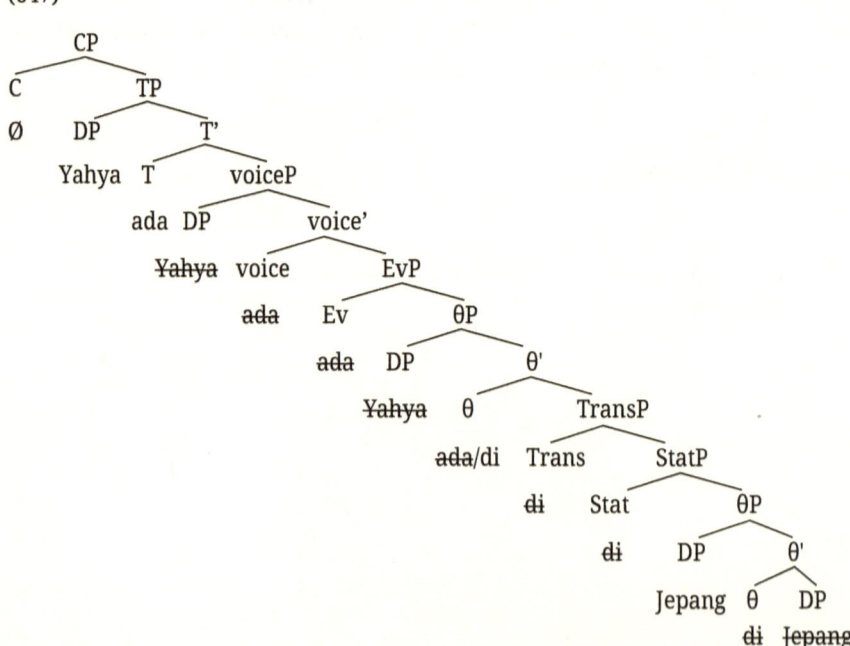

(648)

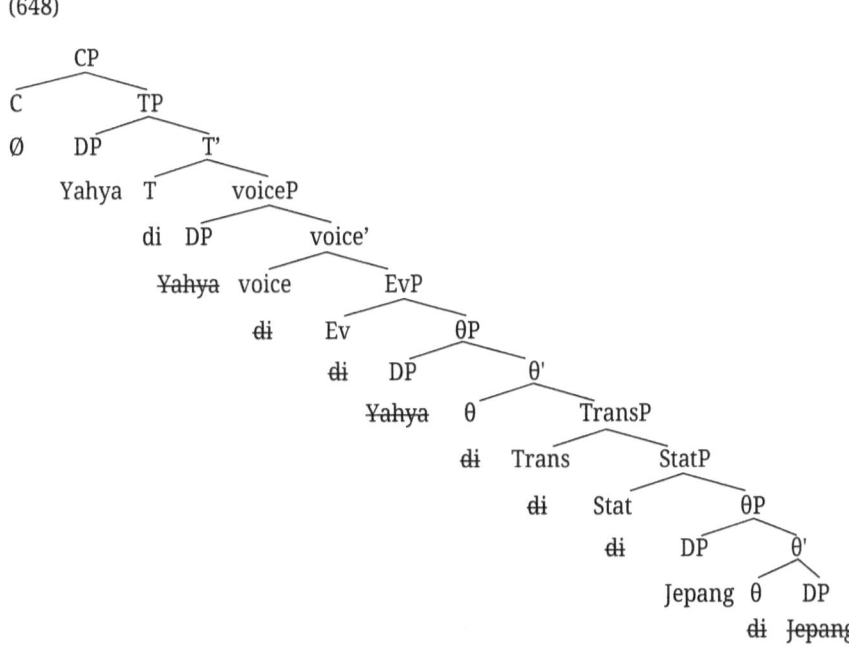

Indonesian quantifiers and numerals can be interpreted either as functional head Q or as roots merged into θ and voice, comparable to semantic adjectives. In the first case, they mark a non-verbal category, while in the second, they can become the main predicate of a clause, and no copula is required. Whereas the English sentence (649) must have a copula (651), the Indonesian equivalent (650) can be with (652) or without copula (653), both at spell-out and in the underlying structure.

(649) *John is a teacher.*

(650) Yahya (adalah) seorang guru.
John COP one-CL.HUM teacher
'John is a teacher.'

(651)

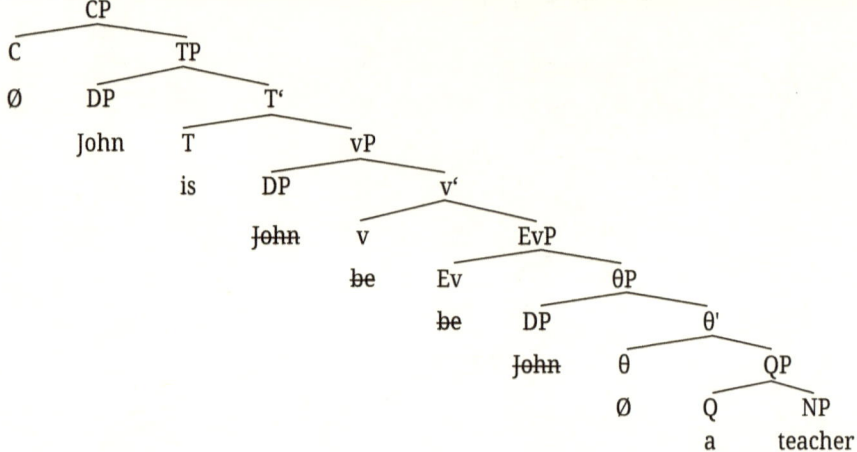

(652)

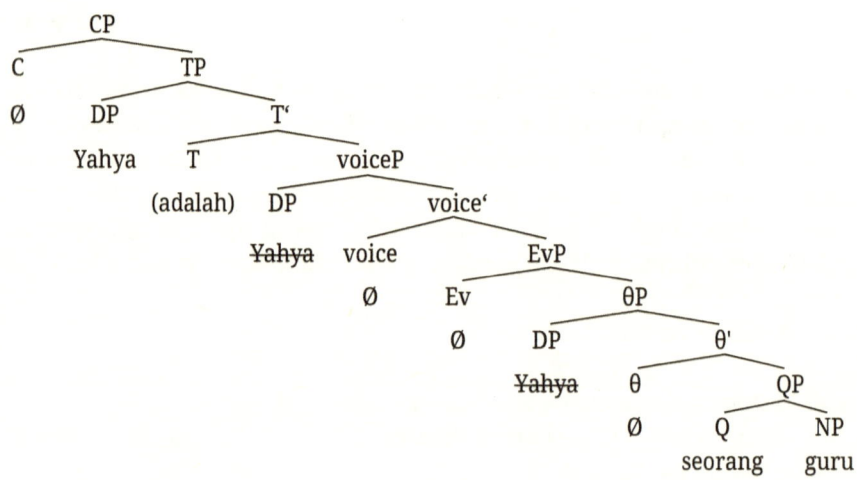

(653)

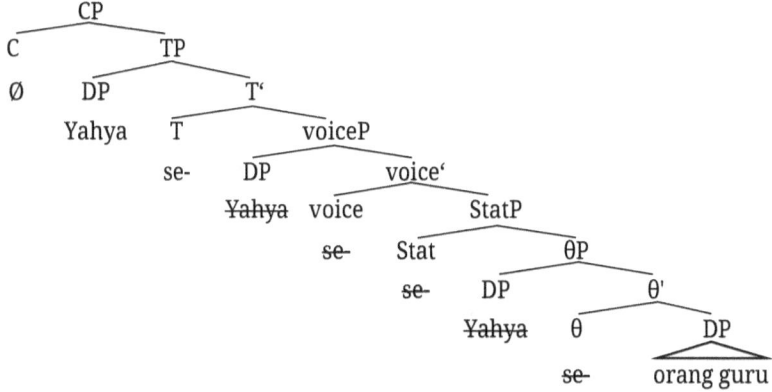

Ds in Indonesian and English are comparable functional heads (except for the branching direction). Therefore, with a DP-predicate, both languages make use of a copular structure, which is identical concerning the heads required. However, the two copulas inserted are of different types. For the sake of completeness, the relevant structures are represented:

(654) *John is Mary's teacher.*

(655) Yahya adalah guru-nya   Siska
       John   COP   teacher-3S.POSS Siska
       'John is Siska's teacher.'

(656)

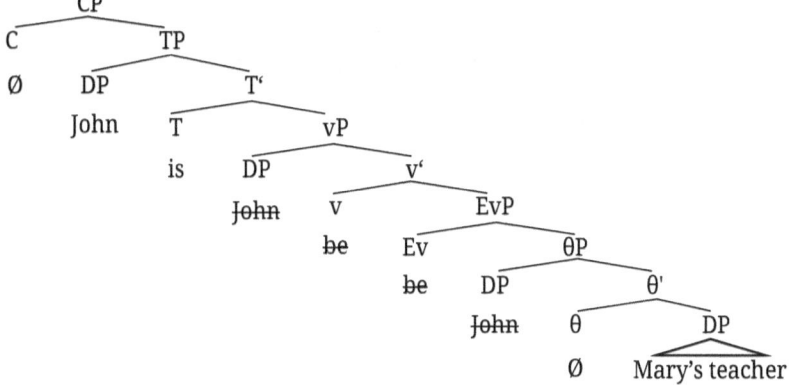

(657)

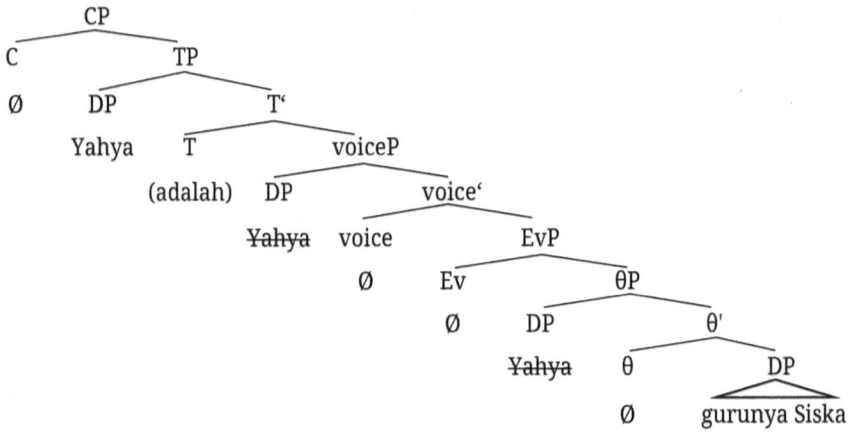

4.5.2 The number of copulas

In English, the same copula is used for all kinds of non-eventive predicates, namely, *be*.

(658) *John is hungry.*

(659) *John is in Japan.*

(660) *John is a teacher.*

(661) *John is Mary's teacher.*

In Indonesian, there are two copulas: One is *ada*, which is used with PP predicates, and the other is *adalah* which is used with DP/QP-predicates:[125]

(662) Yahya ada/*adalah di Jepang
      John COP   in Japan
      'John is in Japan.'

---

125 Both copulas are not obligatory.

(663) Yahya *ada/adalah se-orang guru.
 John COP one-CL.HUM teacher
 'John is a teacher.'

(664) Yahya *ada/adalah guru-nya Maria.
 John COP teacher-3S.POSS Mary
 'John is Mary's teacher.'

From the preceding, it can be seen that Indonesian has not just two distinct copulas, but indeed two distinct copulas of different types.

4.5.3 The copula type

Cross-linguistically two copula types can be identified; the verbal copula base generated in the V-layer and the non-verbal copula base generated in the T-layer.

The English copula *be* belongs to the verbal type. Since it is semantically empty, it does not assign a theta-role. Consequently, it is merged/inserted in the v-head and not the θ-head. The Indonesian copula *ada* is also a verbal copula comparable in structure with the English copula *be*. Depending on the degree of grammaticalization attested to *ada*, it is either base-generated in voice comparable to *be*, or in θ if it is ascribed some semantic content and the capacity to assign a theta-role. The second Indonesian copula is non-verbal; therefore, it is inserted in T. However, *adalah* is not a product of normal vocabulary insertion, by reason of certain features in T, but a product of an additional phonological operation, *adalah*-support. *Adalah* is only required if it makes the utterance smoother or easier to understand for the addressee. Although both Indonesian copulas are optional, the optionality of each is premised on different processes. On the one hand, *ada* can be set on null-spell-out at PF, while on the other, there is no necessity for *adalah*-support, so the T-position remains phonologically null. In the first case, we have a null-*ada*, and in the second case, it is inherently null.

As a concluding remark, we can keep for the record that *ada* is comparable to the English *be* (except as regards optionality). In contrast, *adalah* differs in its category (non-verbal), its substance (PF-operation), and its position of insertion (T).

These major differences should naturally lead to difficulties for Indonesian learners of English.

5 The empirical study

Anyone who had the chance to teach English in Indonesia will have recognized that many of her students struggled with the correct use of the English copula *be*. However, not only students but even teachers may have difficulties with the correct use, as we can see in the example given by Marcellino (2015: 64):

(665)   A: *Guys, say, she is going to happy, John.*
        B: *John is going to happy.*
        A: *Bill.*
        B: *Bill is going to happy.*

Although this example was meant to present a typical teaching pattern between the teacher (A) and the student (B), it reveals the struggle with the use of *be* (here, omission of *be* in the environment of an adjectival predicate). Although it is easy to make this general observation of problems using the copula *be*, the goal of this chapter and this work, in general, is to identify which difficulties are caused by L1 competition. Considering the contrast between copula constructions in English and Indonesian, as pointed out in the previous chapter, it is not surprising that there are difficulties. Nevertheless, the interesting question is where exactly the difficulties are or, in other words, if there are certain error patterns observable that can be explained by the contrast described in the previous chapter? Are and, if yes, when are these difficulties caused by the structural difference between English and Indonesian non-verbal predicates? These questions shall be answered to a certain degree in this chapter.

5.1 Theoretical background

Although many factors can cause error patterns, this work focuses on the influence of the L1 Indonesian when learning English non-verbal predicates. Therefore, it is important to clarify how this interaction is understood from a theoretical perspective before continuing with the test design.

As outlined in the first chapter, this work adopts the Grammar Competition (GC)/ Multiple Grammars (MG) approach (see Roeper 1999, Yang 2003, Roeper and Amaral 2014).

In this framework (see Roeper 1999, Yang 2003, Roeper and Amaral 2014), optionality is explained by having (at least) two competing rules. Although it has been proposed for L1 settings (see Roeper's 1999 Universal Bilingualism), here we are more interested in its implications and applications for Second Language Acquisition (amongst others Roeper 2016, Amaral and Roeper 2014, Rankin 2014, Bauke 2018, 2020a, 2020b). Assuming Sprouse's and Schwartz's (1996) Full Transfer/Full Access Hypothesis, the L1 is seen as the initial state of L2 acquisition, which means that all rules of the L1 are copied. During the acquisition process, rules for the L2 are added without deleting any of the L1 rules. Since the L1 rules are not deleted, they can be applied in an L2 context, even if the L2 rule has been acquired. Transfer is then understood as applying an L1 rule for an L2 example. Two scenarios can cause this. The speaker just follows the default, the L1 rule, as the L2 has not yet been acquired or 'the speaker is unable to temporarily block the use of a productive rule from Lx.' (Amaral and Roeper 2014: 36). Whereas in the first scenario, the L2 speaker should make the same errors constantly (with (almost) no exception), in the second scenario, the errors should occur, however not all the time.

In this work, we will not explicitly deal with rules but rather with the outcome of applying rules, namely structures. Since we deal with a grammatical judgment experiment, we should expect the participants to assign a structure to each utterance (White, 2003: 153). Depending on which structure (L1 or L2) is assigned to the sentence, he/she will judge the sentence as grammatical or not. When, then, should we expect an effect?

As presented in the first chapter, competition of the L1 in L2 acquisition should be visible if three conditions are fulfilled.
a) The L2 speaker deviates from the L1 speaker.
b) There is a structural difference between L1 and L2
c) The deviation of the L2 speaker imitates their L1 structure

In a grammaticality judgment task, the method used here a) means that the L2 speakers come to a different judgment concerning the grammaticality than the (hypothetical) L1 speaker. c) requires that the item imitates L1 Indonesian structure and b) that L1 structure and L2 structure are actually different.

Let us take a look at this scenario in more detail: Let us assume an abstract pair of languages, L_A as L1 and L_B as L2. For each sentence, we have a surface and a deep structure. Surface structure (S) deals with linear order but also with vocabulary insertion, a process separated from syntax (see Distributed Morphology). Deep structure (Struc) is the underlying syntactical structure based on a tacit grammar of either L_A or L_B. In the test here, S is given, and the participant can either apply $Struc_A$ or $Struc_B$. We now have to specify the test item further. Exemplary, we will assume an ungrammatical target sentence (this scenario will be sufficient for the test); thus, the sentence is of type $S_B{}^*$. In the test, we would expect the participant to either apply $Struc_A$ (the native/L1 structure) or $Struc_B$ (the target/L2 structure), which leads to two possibilities:

a) Participant applies Struc$_A$
b) Participant applies Struc$_B$

In the second scenario, the participant should come to the result that the sentence is ungrammatical since the target item was S$_B$*. Here, the result would be identical to the native judgment. Thus, condition a) would not be fulfilled, ergo no competition.

For the first scenario, there are two possibilities since there are two potential relationships between S$_B$* and S$_A$.
c) S$_B$* matches S$_A$.
d) S$_B$* does not match S$_A$.

In the case of d), the participant should come up with an ungrammaticality judgment since even with applying Struc$_A$, the surface structure would not be identical to the target item S$_B$*. Once again, we would have no deviation from the L1 speaker and hence no competition. In the unlikely case that the L2 speaker comes up with a positive grammaticality judgment, it still should not be seen as competition since the sentence does not imitate the L1. Thus, any other reason must be the reason for this deviation.

For the c) scenario (the participant applies Struc$_A$), we would expect them to judge S$_B$* grammatical, which then would be a case of competition. Only in this scenario all conditions for competitions are fulfilled:
a) The L2 judgment, here positive, is different from the L1 judgment, here negative.
b) Struc$_A$ and Struc$_B$ are different.
c) S$_B$* imitates Struc$_A$.

This scenario is even possible if the learner has already acquired the underlying structure of the target language. They are just not able to block the structure of language A at that moment (Amaral and Roeper 2014: 36).

That concept leads to another important argument against the competition in the case of d). Based on the mismatch in linear order for d), it is unlikely that the structure of language A has to be blocked. There is no reason that Struc$_A$ is triggered as it could not represent S$_B$* in that case. If that structure cannot be triggered, it should not be blocked. Nevertheless, if StrucA and StrucB are applied, it should lead to the same judgment anyway. Thus, no deviation could be seen.

This means that in order to find competition, all three conditions have to be fulfilled. First, the linear order of the target sentence must match the linear order of the equivalent in the native language (imitation of L1). Otherwise, the native structure cannot be triggered or would not lead to a positive grammaticality judgment. Second, the linear order of the target sentence must not match the structure of the target language (ungrammatical sentence) (structural difference between L1 and L2). Otherwise, the result will be identical irrespectively of what structure is applied. There will be no effect visible, even if we have transfer. Thus, the third condition is not met: the L2 judgment does not deviate from the L1 judgment.

5.2 The test

5.2.1 The idea

Based on the theoretical deliberations before, L1 competition should only be available where we find structural differences, here between English and Indonesian concerning non-verbal/non-eventive predicates. Thus, the findings of the previous chapter should be the starting point.

We saw two major differences between English and Indonesian in the previous chapter. Firstly, while English applies the same strategy for all kinds of non-verbal predicates, namely the use of the copula *be*, Indonesian uses one of three strategies, depending on the category of the non-eventive predicate. The three strategies are the no-copula-strategy for adjectival predicates, the *ada*-strategy for prepositional predicates, and the *adalah*-strategy for nominal predicates. Only in the latter strategies a copula is possible. As a consequence, the English copula strategy shows a similar predication structure compared to the Indonesian *ada*- and *adalah*-strategy. However, the no-copula structure applies a different type of predication structure with the non-eventive element being the syntactic predicate. Hence, competition should be expected where the no-copula strategy is available, mainly with adjectival predicates. Thus, the first factor that has to be considered is the category of the non-verbal predicate.

Secondly, there is a difference in the copula type between English *be* and Indonesian *adalah*. They differ in their category (verbal vs. non-verbal), their substance (syntax vs. PF-operation), and their position of insertion (Ev/v vs. T). One consequence is that *adalah* is in complementary distribution with auxiliaries, especially with T-auxiliaries such as *sudah* and *masih,* since both the copula *adalah* and the T-auxiliaries occupy the same position, namely T. Based on their meaning, these T-auxiliaries correspond to English adverbs like *already* or *still*. Hence, forms like *sudah* are often translated with *already* despite their categorical differences. There is even evidence outside of Second Language Acquisition that these Indonesian auxiliaries are connected to English adverbs, in this case, anecdotal evidence from two bilingual children of German and Indonesian. In German, the categorical status of *schon* (*already*) and *noch* (*still*) is identical to the categorical status of their English counterparts. Those are adverbs. These bilingual children used a single *schon* as a fragment answer to a question. This reflects the Indonesian use of *sudah* while a single *schon* is ungrammatical in German as would be *already* in English. The only way to explain this single *schon* is by transfer from Indonesian to German. Hence, even for these children, there is/was a connection between *sudah* and *schon* (*already*). Since these children were between 2–3 years at that time, it cannot be the result of any teaching or translation effect.

Based on participant observation (a method introduced and pioneered by Malinowski (1922) for social anthropology), it is possible to identify a tendency[126] that the copula *be* is more often omitted if an adverb is placed between the subject and the predicate. Consequently, sentences such as (666) with an adverb should be more likely to be judged grammatical by Indonesian learners of English than sentences such as (667). Of course, in Standard English, both sentences are ungrammatical.[127]

(666) **John still a teacher.*

(667) **John a teacher.*

As hypothesized above, the omission might be the consequence of the competition of the T-realization of certain adverbs/auxiliaries and the copula. If this is true, there should be differences among English adverbs depending on the categorical status of their Indonesian counterparts. Thus, the second factor considered here is the influence of adverbs/adverb categories.

In summary, when we have L1 competition, we should expect two major effects: an effect caused by certain adverbs due to the different nature of the copula in English and Indonesian and an effect based on the category of the non-eventive predicate.

Therefore, the experiment was created to test for error patterns along the lines of these potential effects. Only if we found a deviation of the L2 speaker in this area, would we have evidence for competition. Hence, the experiment was divided into two tests[128] concerning the two major differences as outlined above.

1) Influence of adverbs[129]
2) Influence of lexical categories of the predicate

---

[126] For now this is just a subjective observation and not objective numbers.
[127] In this work only main clauses are considered. In main clauses these sentences are ungrammatical. In a small clause (664) would be grammatical
[128] A third test was developed and tested concerning copular clause types (predicational, equation, specificational). However, this test is not considered in this work.
[129] Caveat: The term adverb is chosen based on the description of English. The Indonesian counterparts do not have to be adverbs.

5.2.2 Purpose of the study

As outlined above, this study targets L1 competition for L2 acquisition, hence error patterns that are based on structural differences between the L1 (Indonesian) and the L2 (English). Based on the idea of competition, these error patterns should be the result of having two competing grammars that can be applied for a construction. Grammars are understood as abstract sets of rules stored in our brains. According to Roeper (1999: 4), grammar equals Chomsky's (1986) concept of internalized (I-)language (Chomsky 1986: 21–24). This Chomskian (1986) distinction between the internalized language (I-language) and externalized language (E-language) is vital to understanding the purpose but also the limitations of this study. Where I-language is understood as competence (knowledge) (Chomsky 1986: 24), E-language more concerns the utterances produced normally as an outcome of the internalized grammar (Chomsky 1986, see also Araki 2017: 20); nevertheless, other processes may interfere here.

As the structural differences should be stored as competing internalized systems (competing grammars), this study only focuses on competition on the competence level and not on the performance level. Thus, the goal is to find error patterns based on grammar competition (competence) and avoid any other performance factors as good as possible. One method that has been widely used to get to the competence level (Arthur 1980: 182) is a grammaticality judgment task, which will be the topic of the next section.

5.2.3 The test design

The test consisted of a grammaticality judgment task with 87/60[130] English sentences. Out of these, about one third was test items:
1) 36 test items and 51 filler sentences, so three pages with 29 sentences each
2) 24 test items and 36 filler sentences, so two pages with 30 sentences each

The participant's task was to read the sentence and mark it as either grammatical or ungrammatical. All instructions were given in Indonesian to avoid any priming effect using the English copula *be*. Thus, the participants had to choose *benar* (right) or *salah* (wrong).

---

[130] Note that the copula type (predicational etc.) test (30 items) was combined with the category test (adjectives etc.). Therefore the second test consisted of 90 items, however only 60 are relevant for this work.

In general, Grammaticality Judgment Tasks (GJTs) are a standardized design where speakers are asked to make a judgment on the grammaticality of an utterance (see Leow 1996). Based on Chomsky (1965: 11), Tremblay (2005: 133) argues for a distinction between grammaticality and acceptability. Whereas grammaticality is only based on a judgment of an internal grammar, acceptability can also include judgment based on prescriptive language norms or register violations. Thus, grammaticality is included in the larger concept of acceptability. GJTs then do not test grammaticality but acceptability. However, since the test items given in the GJT at hand do not underlie any particular prescriptive grammar norm nor any register effect, the expectation is that the judgments are still based on grammaticality. Therefore, this work uses this concept being aware of the possibility that acceptability might be based on other factors.

Normally, the methodology of GJTs is common in elicitation processes. Thus, the test subject is a native speaker. The advantage/goal of this method is to test for grammar competence, the tacit underlying knowledge. This idea goes back to Chomsky's (1986) distinction between an internalized and externalized language. As mentioned above, grammatical judgment tasks normally address a speaker's competence, so their internalized grammar. This idea has been extended to SLA research; thus, GJTs were given to L2 speakers. As Gutierrez (2013: 425) points out, this methodology has been commonly used in SLA for decades. In general, it was claimed that GJTs in SLA also target competence and not performance (Arthur 1980: 182). In more recent contributions (see Ellis 1991, 2004, 2005, Gutierrez 2013, Vafaee, Suzuku, and Kachisnke 2017), it has been discussed whether the participants would apply implicit or explicit knowledge in the tasks. In contrast to tacit implicit knowledge, "explicit knowledge is potentially verbalizable" (Ellis 2004: 239). Krashen (1981: 1–2) draws the distinction between being acquired (implicit) and being learned (explicit). These two types of knowledge are generally seen as dichotomous (Krashen 1981, Ellis 2004). Therefore, this distinction is important for the validity of GJTs.

Whereas GJTs that include a reparation task (item has to be corrected or a mistake has to be identified) must exploit explicit knowledge, for GJTs without such a task, the question remains which kind of knowledge is required (Gutierrez 2013: 426). Ellis (2005: 152) proposes that several criteria provide a tendency for which knowledge is applied. Amongst others, he suggests (i) degree of awareness, (ii) time available, (iii) the focus of attention, and (iv) systematicity.

	implicit	explicit
(i) degree of awareness	feel	rule
(ii) time available	timed	untimed
(iii) focus of attention	meaning	form
(iv) systematicity	consistent responses	variable responses

Two criteria have been tested by Gutierrez (2013), namely time (timed vs. untimed) and task stimulus (grammatical vs. ungrammatical sentence). He (2013: 440–441) concludes that for judging grammatical sentences, generally implicit knowledge is applied, and for ungrammatical sentences, explicit knowledge; in untimed GJTs, the participants apply explicit and in timed GJTs implicit knowledge. Vafaee, Suzuki, and Kachisnke (2017) even say that all GJTs target explicit knowledge.

This research employs an untimed GJT with ungrammatical sentences only that refer to a construction that is semantically empty and hence only refers to form. All these ingredients should lean towards applying explicit knowledge. Although the participants have used explicit knowledge in one way or another, the following paragraph discusses the possibility that, in this particular case, the test can still measure implicit knowledge. That is based on the following factors of the test design:
1. All test items are ungrammatical.
2. The result of interest are the items that have been judged grammatical.
3. There is no explicit rule that could explain the contrast we see.
4. The instructions given.

Although ungrammatical test items have been connected with explicit knowledge, this mainly holds for judging ungrammatical items as ungrammatical. In many cases, this judgment can be based on one explicit rule that has been learned. In our case, with sentences with omitted copula, the explicit knowledge of the required copula likely leads to the right judgment of ungrammaticality. However, this research is interested in those items where the wrong choice has been made: an ungrammatical test item has been accepted as correct. Since there is no reason to assume false explicit knowledge, in these cases of interest, the explicit knowledge must not have been sufficient to identify the missing copula and thus the ungrammaticality. Ellis (2004: 255–256) pointed out that in the absence of relevant explicit knowledge, the participant can either rely on implicit knowledge or guess. As (potential) guessers will be excluded from the sample by implementing a threshold of correct answers (see further below), the danger of guessing can be reduced. Thus, it is likely that the participants lacking any alternative had to rely on their implicit knowledge. With taking the error pattern into account, only "grammatical" items are considered, which according to Ellis (1991, 2004) and Gutierrez (2013), should lean towards implicit knowledge. The second argument is the way of contrasting item groups and not contrasting speaker groups. The item groups are based on different underlying constructions in Indonesian. In English, however, these groups are quite homogenous. The only explicit rule that is required in all cases is that a copula is required with non-verbal predicates. However, this rule is relevant for all test items. Hence, there is no reason why explicit knowledge should provide such an effect. Finally, although the test was untimed, in the instruction given before the test, the participants were animated to judge based on intuition and to answer quickly. This might be a weak indication, but it still favors the idea that implicit knowledge has been used. As a result, it is impossible and not necessary to rule out the possibility that explicit knowledge has been applied. For the test items where the correct ungrammatical judgment has been chosen, it is even likelier that this has been based on explicit rules. However, for the items that were wrongly judged ungrammatical, it is likelier that implicit knowledge has been applied and that these error patterns represent the L2 I-language at this particular stage in acquisition.

A second criterion concerning the validity of the data is potential performance errors. In general, the GJT does a reliable job reducing potential performance errors in contrast to (most) production tasks. In this case, the omission of a copula could easily be just a case of sloppiness in any production task. Another risk of a production task is that the experiment gets too complex or the instructions are misunderstood. A GJT, in contrast, has very simple instructions. Giving the participants a choice between inserting a copula or not (e.g., a cloze test) could easily prime them. Despite these advantages, GJTs are not free from performance factors (Tremblay 2005: 134; see also Gass 1994, White 2003). Yet, performance errors should not play an important role in this test design. By comparing item groups and not speaker groups, all potential external factors should not lead to an effect; as such an effect should be the same throughout the whole test. If, e.g., a participant had concentration issues, this should not have an effect on particular items only but all items in the test. Thus, the only danger would be test-internal factors that influence performance. Since all test items were of comparable length, complexity, and grammaticality (all ungrammatical), no performance effect should be caused by these factors. One potential performance effect lies in the imbalance between grammatical and ungrammatical items. As Ellis (1991: 164) pointed out, participants normally tend to bring grammatical and ungrammatical sentences in balance. Since 50% of the filler items were grammatical and 50% grammatical, with all test items being ungrammatical, there were more ungrammatical items than grammatical ones. Thus, there is the possibility that the position of an item in the test could have led to a different judgment to balance out the proportion of grammatical and ungrammatical sentences. With four items for each group, such an effect should not be available for all items. Thus, it should be possible to consider this factor as a free variable in the statistical model. Once again, performance effects cannot be excluded completely, but the test design reduced potential distortions. The balance effect, which is the hardest to control, should be taken care of in the statistical analysis.

For these reasons, the grammaticality judgment test best served this study's purpose. Despite all potential shortcomings, the results should give us some insights into the L2 grammar of the participants. More information on the test design will be given in the next section.

Test items
What might be uncommon is that all test items were ungrammatical English sentences. In all these items, the copula *be* in its third-person singular simple present form (*is*)[131] was omitted. Although this might sound like a strange approach, there are three good reasons to proceed like this. First, offering the participants sentences with the copula *be* could have easily primed them. Hence, there is a good chance that the results changed after the first occurrence of *be*. To avoid such a priming effect, the copula was omitted in all cases.

Second, as pointed out by Ellis (2004, 2005) and Gutierrez (2013) results of grammatical and ungrammatical items are different. With having only ungrammatical test items, this factor has been taken out of the calculation.

The third argument for this unorthodox implementation comes from the concept of the grammaticality judgment task itself. A disadvantage of a grammaticality judgment task is that we do not get information on the reason for a certain judgment (at least if no reparation task is given). Especially when it comes to a negative judgment, it is impossible to identify why the sentence was judged ungrammatical. In a grammaticality judgment task, it is possible that participants derived the choice for (un)grammaticality for the "wrong" reasons. Thus, the judgement does not have to based on the structure the researcher intended (Ellis 2004: 257). This issue occurs mainly with sentences that are judged ungrammatical. Whereas a positive judgment is only possible if all aspects of the utterance are judged grammatical, a negative judgment could come from any feature of the item, not necessarily the one targeted. With only ungrammatical items, this problem should not be too severe. Since all items are ungrammatical, competition from L1 should lead to a false positive judgment and never to a false negative judgment. Therefore, the only danger is that effects may remain unattested in this format since other aspects of the items lead to negative judgments. False effects, however, should be ruled out. Ergo, if there is an effect, it should be related to the tested pattern.

Control group
One concept of empirical data is to compare the data to some kind of default setting. Hence, to make any statement about a significant effect, two environments have to be compared. One possibility would be to have a control group. This could be a group of native speakers (see, e.g., Bauke 2020a, b) or two different groups of non-native speakers (e.g., second language learners and foreign language learners, see, e.g., Rothman 2008). The advantage of comparing two groups would be that

---

[131] For certain sentences, the past forms would be likelier. This does not matter since the copula was omitted anyway.

a significant difference leads in the direction of L1 influence, at least if this is the only factor different. However, this is often only a desired situation. Whenever two groups are involved, one must ensure that these two groups are comparable in all learner-specific factors like proficiency, age, etc. Too much diversity could easily distort the results.

The empirical design used here opts for a different approach. Instead of comparing two groups, the target environments are compared to a control or default environment. Thus, the contrast goes along the line of grammatical constructions and not speaker groups. This design goes back to the three conditions relevant to competition:

a) Deviation from L1 speakers:
Since all target items are undoubtedly ungrammatical and very basic sentences, this work abstains from a native control group. The only advantage of a native control group would be to identify any processing or sloppiness effects (if there are any). However, even then, nothing guarantees that these effects should be comparable strong for both the target and the hypothetical control group. Individual factors like motivation, concentration, etc., could easily distort the results. If, for example, the target group was more concentrated, sloppiness errors should be less relevant. Thus, using a native control group does not outweigh its disadvantages.

b) Structural Difference
The second condition for competition is that we find structural differences between English and Indonesian. Thus, the target items are items where there is such a structural difference, and the control items are the items where there is no such difference. The major advantage of this strategy is that only competition effects are targeted. Only if the results of the target items are significantly different from the control items, the condition of competition is met. Another important advantage of comparing structures and not groups is that the individual factors of the participants are not relevant. Whether a participant was highly motivated does not matter since they used the same motivation for target and control items. The same holds true for any individual factor of the participants.

c) Imitation of L1
The third condition was that the target items should imitate the L1 structure. By comparing structures, there is also the possibility of having control items that are ungrammatical in English but do not imitate the L1 structure. Thus, there is a second option for control items.

With these deliberations in mind, the two tests will be presented in more detail.

Test 1: Influence of adverbs

The first part tested for the influence of adverbs on the omission of the copula. Here, two factors were considered, the categorical status of the Indonesian counterpart of the English adverbs and their position in linear order. As presented in chapter 3, Indonesian does not have an adverb category comparable to the one we find in English. Many assumed equivalents[132] are grouped as auxiliaries, somewhere in the continuum between a per se finite T-auxiliary, raising auxiliaries with only little lexical content, and raising verbs with lexical content. Raising verbs in Indonesian can be grouped into two categories: voiceP-embedding verbs roughly corresponding to verb adverbs in English and CP-embedding verbs roughly corresponding to sentential adverbs. For all categories, four test items were provided. Additionally, there were four items with the negation *not*. Although the Indonesian equivalent *bukan* is a raising auxiliary, the adverb status of *not* in English is not uncontroversial. Consequently, it is treated as an independent category. As a control group, four test items without an adverb were added. In all the cases mentioned above, the adverbs were positioned between subject and predicate, from now on referred to as 'second'. To test for a position effect of the adverbs, for certain categories (two items for T, two items for raising auxiliaries, and four items for CP-embedding-raising verbs), there were additional test items where the adverb was placed either clause-initially or clause-finally from now on labeled as 'non-second'. These non-second items do not imitate Indonesian structure and are thus some kind of control group. In summary, we have the following 32 items[133] in Table 4:

Table 4: Test items of the first test.

Adverb	position	number of items	category of the Indonesian translation
still	second	2	T
already	second	2	T
already	non-second	2	T
often	second	2	raising auxiliary
often	non-second	2	raising auxiliary
once	second	2	raising auxiliary
not	second	4	raising auxiliary
verb adverbs	second	4	voiceP-embedding raising verb
sentential adverbs	second	4	CP-embedding raising verb
sentential adverbs	non-second	4	CP-embedding raising verb
no adverb	–	4	–

---

132 Theses vocabulary items in question are related to the same or at least a very similar concept.
133 Additionally one item with *still, already, often* and *once* and an adjectival predicate was inserted. These however will be left out in the further analysis.

For all 32 test items, the subject was a proper noun. The names were equally distributed into male and female names, as well as into Indonesian and English names. The predicate consisted of a DP, 50% definite, and 50% indefinite since the competition between an auxiliary and the copula is only given in Indonesian for the non-verbal copula *adalah*, generated in T, which can occur with DP or CP predicates/complements only.

Test 2
In the second test, the test items were categorized according to the lexical category of the predicate, namely AP,[134] PP, definite DP, and indefinite DP. Additionally, there were CP-complements with either an overt or a null complementizer. These sentences, however, will not play any role in the further analysis. For each category, four items were provided. As in the first test, the subject consisted of a proper noun with an identical distribution for male/female and Indonesian/English names.

Demographics and placement test
At the beginning of the test, the participants were asked to give some personal information concerning their gender, the languages they have learned, and the languages they speak at home. All instructions were given in Indonesian.

At the end of the test, the students were asked to participate in a placement test[135] in order to control the factor of proficiency. The placement test consisted of 40 multiple choice questions with four answer options each. Although initially planned to take a closer look at how these factors (proficiency, languages spoken at home, e.g.) influence the results, this enterprise had to be given up due to the small valid sample (see next section). Thus, no statements can be made concerning the influence of these factors.

5.2.4 Test sample

The data was collected in March 2018 at one Indonesian high school (grade 11) and two private universities/colleges (undergraduate students) in Bandar Lampung, the capital of Lampung province, at the southern tip of Sumatra. Besides pragmatism, one important factor made Bandar Lampung a suitable option for this research.

---

[134] For an easier understanding, I will consequently use the traditional labels, if we do not talk about structure. The underlying structure, however, does not involve the labels A and P (see previous chapters).
[135] Thanks to Nicholas Hurford for his help with picking the right placement test.

Lampung (at least in the urban centers of Bandar Lampung) is one of the few regions where Indonesian has become the language of daily interaction. This is mainly based on migration. In two waves, the government brought people from the densely populated areas of Java (and Bali) to Lampung. The first wave started under the Dutch administration at the beginning of the 20th century. The second wave was caused by the transmigration program[136] in the Suharto era (Suyanto 2017: 373). These transmigrants became increasingly successful based on their higher education and the pressure to succeed without having the larger family around them. Soon the original Lampungnese population was outnumbered. Today close to 65% of the population are of Javanese origin (Badan Pusat Statistik 2010). Language-wise the transmigrants in general and the Javanese majority of those, in particular, kept their own regional languages but did not learn Lampungnese, at least not to a great extent. Even though Lampungnese is taught at school and is compulsory for all students, this language is seldom spoken by non-Lampungnese. Consequently, over time the language of daily interaction changed either to Indonesian as the language in common or to the language of the majority, Javanese. In the census of 2010 (Badan Pusat Statistik 2010), 55% of the population of the Lampung province indicated that they use Javanese as their language for daily conversation,[137] 23 % Indonesian, and less than 15 % Lampungnese. Although not explicitly indicated in the census, there should be regional differences among certain areas of Lampung province. Since Indonesian is more widely spoken in urban compared to rural areas (Suyanto 2017: 368), the quota of people with Indonesian as their language for daily interaction should be higher in the capital Bandar Lampung than the average for the whole province as specified above. In Java, the situation differs. In West Java, people use Sundanese, even if they are not ethnical Sundanese; in Central and Eastern Java, they use Javanese in daily conversation (at least the lower register). In these areas, the percentage of people using Indonesian at home is below 5% (Badan Pusat Statistik 2010). The second important factor language-wise for Bandar Lampung is the local proximity to Jakarta. As a result, the Indonesian spoken in Lampung is influenced by the Jakarta region. Since the colloquial Indonesian spoken in Jakarta is the one that is promoted on television, it could be identified as 'standard colloquial Indonesian'. The colloquial Indonesian spoken in Lampung is very similar to this clandestine standard and not strongly influenced by the local language, e.g., Lampungnese, compared to other areas with, e.g., a strong Malay influence, for instance, in Northern and Central Sumatra.

---

[136] Political program to move people from the highly densely populated areas in Java to the less-populated areas on the outer islands
[137] This is only possible with a Javanese counterpart. In interethnic conversation people will use Indonesian.

The data was collected in randomly picked classes. One student could participate in only one test. The distribution of test 1 and test 2 was done randomly as well.

131 students took part in the first test and 87 in the second. For the first test, 71 were female, 60 were male, 72 were university students, and 59 were students of a high school. For the second test, 57 were female, 30 were male, 48 were students of a university, and 39 were high school students.

To ensure that the results are reliable and not distorted by guessers, it is necessary to filter the sample. The goal is to exclude the results from students who were either not motivated or not capable of doing the test in an acceptable manner, e.g., guessing. Therefore two criteria were chosen, the placement test score and the test items score.

a) Placement test

At the end of the experiment, the participants were asked to take part in a placement test. That test consisted of 40 questions with four options but only one correct answer. To reach a score that is significantly different from guessing, the students must have scored a minimum of 16 (p-value = 0.04229) if we assume a threshold of p = 0.05. Since placement tests are normally designed in such a way that difficulty increases during the test, we should expect that the participants score highest on the first page. As the first page had 16 questions, the participants must have scored more than 8 to have a significantly different result from guessers (p-value = 0.03715). Any result of a participant who did score neither eight or more on the first page nor 16 or more in the whole test has been labeled 'non-valid' and was eliminated from the sample, as there was the possibility that the participant did not fill out the test seriously, but guessed or answered randomly. Of course, this might have excluded results from students who answered seriously with very low proficiency.

b) Test results

In the second step, the test results were considered. The first test had 87 items (test items + filler sentences) with only two options and one correct answer. That means that the students were not allowed to have more than 33 errors to be significantly better than guessing (p-value = 0.03142). The second test consisted of 90 items[138] (test items+filler sentences) with two options each. Hence, the participants must not have made more than 35 mistakes to have a significantly better result compared to guessing (p-value = 0.0446).

---

[138] The thirty items not considered in this work are included here.

As a consequence, all results with more than 33/35 errors in the test were declared 'not valid' and removed from the sample. Once again, with this method, non-guessers with a very low proficiency were also excluded. However, since there is no way to differentiate between guessers and non-guessers with a very low proficiency, this price had to be paid.

After applying these two criteria to the original sample, we arrive at the following valid sample:

For the first test, only seven valid samples were left. Three participants were male, four female, five high school students, and two university students; six used only Indonesian at home, and one additionally Sundanese. Although this study targets only at L1 Indonesian competition, the Sundanese speaker is left in the sample. As Sundanese is similar to Indonesian when it comes to adverbs/auxiliaries, no structural difference should be expected here. Thus, no major effects from Sundanese are expected.

In the second test, 19 results were valid; 7 were female, and 12 were male. Only one result came from a university student, 18 results were from high school students. Concerning the language used at home, we obtain the following distribution (see Figure 2):

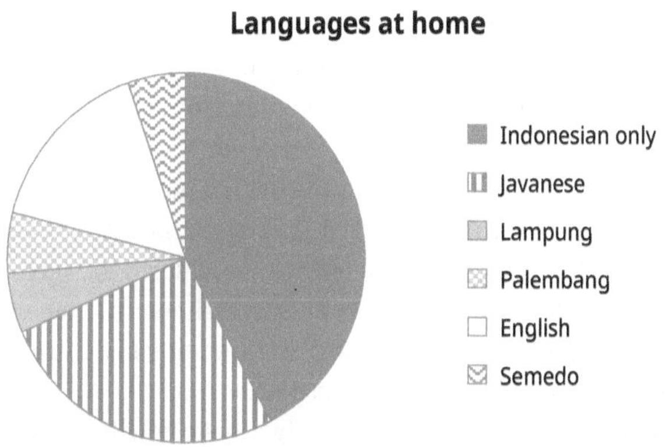

Languages at home

- Indonesian only
- Javanese
- Lampung
- Palembang
- English
- Semedo

Figure 2: Languages spoken at home in the sample of the case study.

Surprisingly, three students said that they used English in their daily environment, especially since their placement result was not significantly better than that of other participants. Therefore, it is not very likely that they had significantly more or regular native input. Since there is no local Indonesian English variety as in other countries of South-East Asia, e.g., Malaysia (Manglish) or Singapore (Singlish), the English they speak/practice at home should be identical to the one they would use at school/university. Consequently, the English spoken at home should not have an influence on the test result, and these three students are grouped in the 'Indonesian'-group. Since Indonesian is copula-wise different to (most of the) Austronesian languages – Pustet (2003) did not attest to another Austronesian language with a copula) – a regional language might have an effect. Therefore, the sample is reduced to the 'Indonesian-only'-group to avoid any other competition. Thus, the relevant sample only consists of 11 participants. This reduction was unnecessary for the first sample since Indonesian and Sundanese (the only language mentioned) are comparable when it comes to auxiliaries.

Comparing the original number of samples with the number of valid samples, the number of non-valid samples outweighs the number of valid samples drastically. Not even a tenth of the samples are valid in the first test. How can we explain this outcome? Before digging into the valid data, it is first necessary to contemplate possible factors for this result. Although English is compulsory from the first until the last day in school and even in university, the proficiency levels of Indonesian students are highly diverse. Some students leave school without knowing how to introduce themselves in English; others speak the language fluently. One important factor here is the quality of the English lessons. In general, the quality of education depends on the school. Therefore, it is common in Indonesia that schools are ranked. The two universities have a lower ranking than the high school, which has a comparably high ranking for Bandar Lampung. The second factor is the discrepancy between urban and rural areas. As I heard after having conducted the test, many students of the two universities came from rural areas. Since more remote areas have less access to good education, this can explain why the overall proficiency was that low. Additionally, many students were first-semester students who did not join university right after finishing high school. Since the test was conducted in March and the school year ends in July, some participants were at least eight months out of formal English instructions and most likely without English input/practice during that time. For this reason, they were no longer used to English.

Another factor is motivation. Although there was no obligation to join the experiment, Indonesian social norms do not allow the students not to participate. It would be both disrespectful to the foreign guest and the teacher conducting the class. For them, it was important to do the test to follow the cultural codex but not to score a significant or good result. It is also possible that some of them were motivated only by the placement test as they were promised to receive their results[139] as an incentive for their participation. The actual items, however, were not given full attention.

---

[139] The students had to memorize their participant number to identify their test result on an anonymous list that was send to them after the test.

The second component of these few valid data is test internal factors. It is possible that the test was too long, causing frustration and frustration leading to guessing. It is also possible that the test was too complicated for a certain proficiency level. As a result, the students were overwhelmed by the task and could not answer properly. It is also possible that the instructions were misleading. As initially expected that the task was too easy, the participants were instructed to follow their intuition. However, it seems that for many of them, it would have been worthwhile to spend some more thought on the sentences before answering them.

These factors can explain the huge number of non-valid data. Nevertheless, the small valid sample provides interesting results that will be discussed in the remainder of this chapter.

5.3 Results and discussion

The general idea behind these tests is the concept of grammar competition. Here, there are two competing rules/representations for a certain construction. Whenever the L1 structure is applied, it should be considered competition. This, however, is only visible if the linear order of the L1 construction and the L2 construction differ. Only in the case where the ungrammatical English sentences match the linear order of the L1 counterpart competition should be identifiable. In all other cases, there should be no difference to the expected judgment by a native speaker.

As indicated above, the first test aims at two different factors concerning adverbs, (i) the category of the adverb and (ii) the position of the adverb:

5.3.1 Adverb category

The adverb category might affect copula omission because Indonesian and English forms match at the surface structure but differ in their deep structure. There are at least four different categorical types (see also chapter 3) in Indonesian for what in English are adverbs, namely T-auxiliaries, raising auxiliaries, voiceP embedding raising verbs, and CP embedding raising verbs.

a) T-auxiliaries
Similar to English modals, these forms are per se finite and base-generated in T. However, they express relative tense. The most important forms are *sudah* (anterior), *sedang* (simultaneous), *masih* (continuative), and *akan* (posterior). They are represented in the following general structure:

(668)

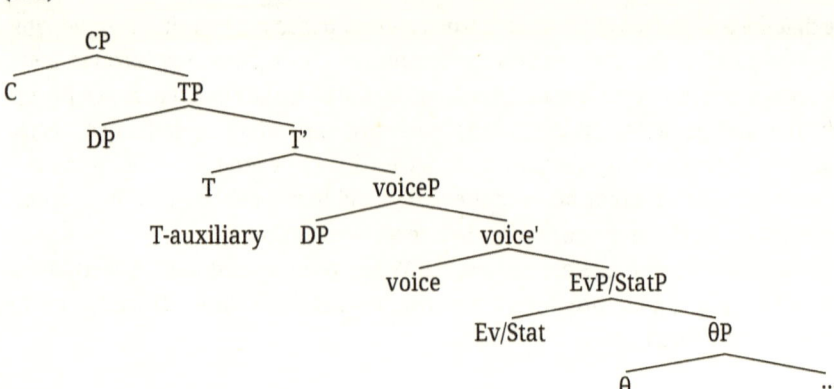

b) Raising auxiliaries
These forms are not per se finite but can be embedded below a T-auxiliary:

(669) *Udin sudah pernah pergi ke Jakarta.*
Udin ANT once go to Jakarta.
'Udin has once gone to Jakarta.'

Normally, they do not assign a theta-role but take a voiceP as a complement without assigning a theta-role. Important members of this group are *pernah* (once), *sering* (often), *harus* (must), and *bisa* (can). In the absence of an overt T, auxiliaries are head-moved into T. We arrive at the following structure:

(670)

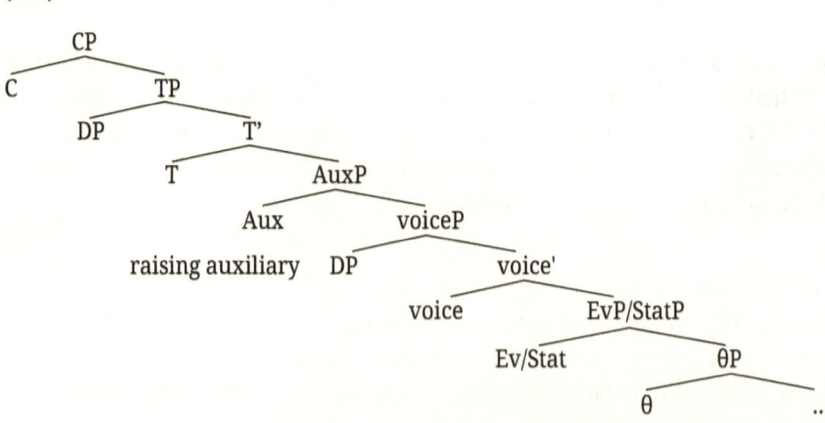

c) voiceP-embedding raising verbs

It is hard to identify a clear boundary between voiceP embedding raising verbs and raising auxiliaries since these two categories must be perceived as a continuum of the same process of language change. In theory, the difference is that raising verbs are verbal and assign a theta-role to the voiceP. Additionally, they have more lexical content than the auxiliary verbs in b).

This category is an open class, so it is hard to identify the most important members. Examples are forms such as *mudah* (easy) (671) or *cepat* (quick) (672) if they modify voicePs.

(671) Udin   mudah   men-cari   pe-kerja-an.
       Udin   easy   CAUS.VOICE-search   GO.NOM-work-TH.NOM
       'Udin can easily find some work.'

(672) Udin   cepat   pulang.
       Udin   quick   go.home
       'Udin went home quickly.'

Their usage is comparable to verb adverbs in English although the structure (head vs. phrase) is completely different. In the same way as for raising auxiliaries, if T is not filled overtly, voice-P embedding raising verbs move to T. This is represented in the following general structure:

(673)
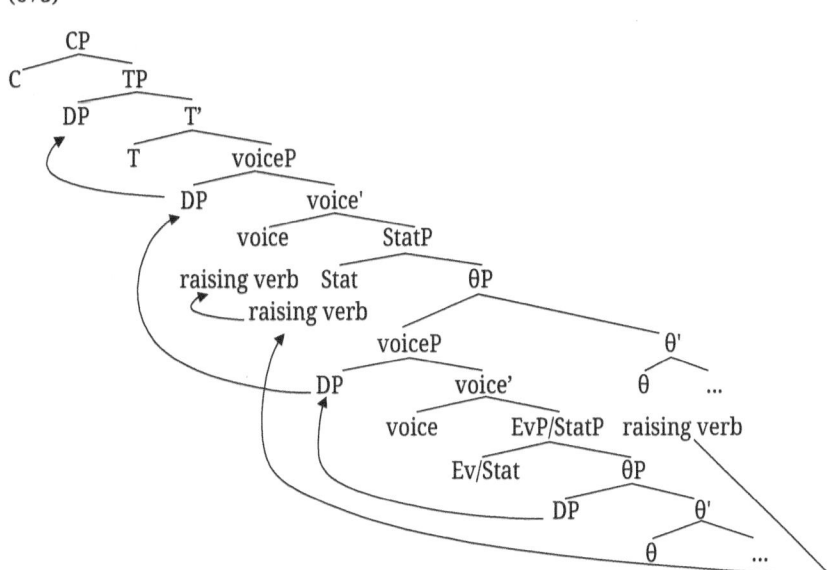

d) CP-embedding raising verbs

The last group, which is, in contrast to the three categories mentioned before, not part of the grammaticalization continuum, is CP-embedding raising verbs. As the name says, these forms differ from c) in such a way that they embed complete CPs. While it is not possible to embed a finite form under c) (674), it is, in contrast, possible to embed a finite form under d) (675).

(674) *Udin   mudah   masih   men-cari   pe-kerja-an.
        Udin   easy   CONT   CAUS.VOICE-search   GO.NOM-work-TH.NOM
        'Udin can still find work easily.'

(675) Udin   sepertinya   masih   men-cari   pe-kerja-an.
        Udin   apparently   CONT   CAUS.VOICE-search   GO.NOM-work-TH.NOM
        'Udin apparently still looks for work.'

The subject of the matrix clause is extracted from Spec-CP of the embedded clause and raised to Spec-voiceP and finally moved to Spec-CP of the matrix clause, which leads to the following structure:

(676)

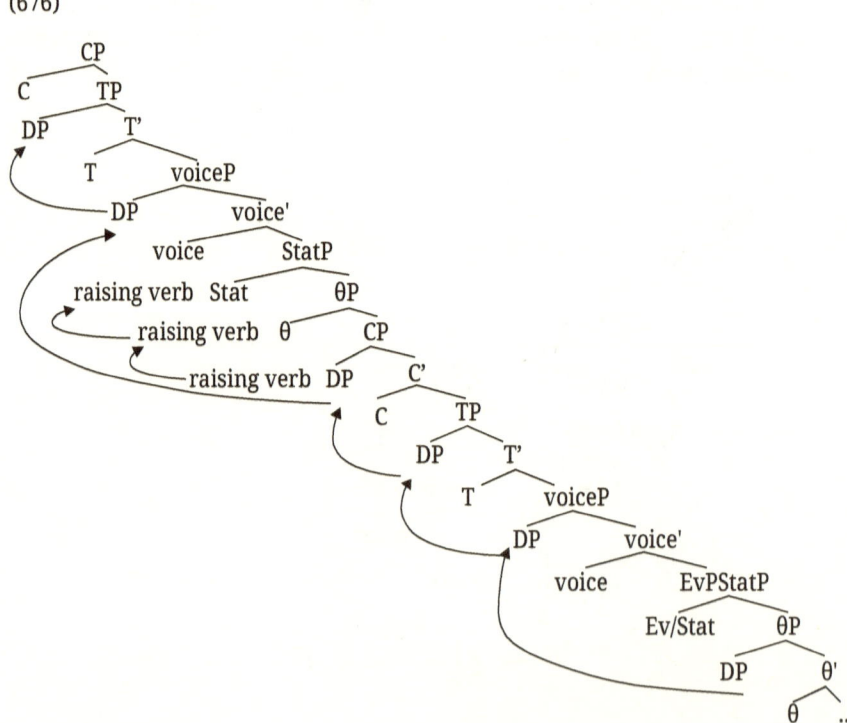

Based on this structure, an important difference emerges concerning the distribution of the copula *adalah*. In sentences with CP-embedding raising verbs, there are two T-layers, one in the embedded clause and one in the matrix clause. The embedded T cannot be filled by the raising verb. The copula *adalah*, however, if necessary, would be realized in the embedded clause. Consequently, *adalah* and CP-embedding raising verbs can co-occur:

(677) *Udin   sepertinya   adalah   guru-nya   Siska*
      Udin   apparently   COP   teacher-3S.POSS   Siska
      'Udin is apparently Siska's teacher.'

In contrast, sentences with T-auxiliaries, raising auxiliaries, and voiceP-embedding raising verbs are generally monoclausal and have only one T-layer. The T-head is occupied by the auxiliary, either via base-generation (T-auxiliary) or via movement (raising auxiliaries, voiceP-embedding raising verbs). As a consequence, all these forms are in complementary distribution with *adalah*.

(678) **Udin   masih   adalah   guru-nya   Siska*
      Udin   CONT   COP   teacher-3S.POSS   Siska
      Intended meaning: 'Udin is still Siska's teacher.'

(679) **Udin   sering   adalah   guru-nya   Siska*
      Udin   often   COP   teacher-3S.POSS   Siska
      Intended meaning: 'Udin is often Siska's teacher.'

(680) **Udin   mudah   adalah   guru-nya   Siska*
      Udin   easy   COP   teacher-3S.POSS   Siska
      Intended meaning: 'Udin is easily Siska's teacher.'

If this competition for the T-position interferes with English,
a) the error rate for sentences with T-auxiliaries, raising auxiliaries, and voice P-embedding raising verbs should be higher compared to the error rate of sentences with CP-embedding raising verbs,
b) the error rate for sentences with T-auxiliaries, raising auxiliaries, and voice P-embedding raising verbs should be higher in contrast to sentences without adverbs,
c) there should be no error rate difference for sentences with CP-embedding raising verbs compared to sentences without adverbs.

Before testing the hypotheses, it is necessary to take a look at the results in general. In the test, there are five adverb categories and the default category with no adverb. These categories provide the following results (see Table 5–10). The error rate is the number of participants that judged the ungrammatical test item as grammatical. Data is provided in an absolute number of positive judgments and as percentages. Categories proceed in alphabetical order.

Table 5: Error rates for the CP-embedding raising auxiliaries category.

Test item	Positive judgments	Error rate in %
Whitney definitely a friendly person with humour.	1	14.285714
Bintang certainly a faithful friend to everybody.	0	0
Kiki normally the first to finish an exam.	0	0
Jackson probably the most annoying person here.	2	28.571429

Table 6: Error rates for the negation category.

Test item	Positive judgments	Error rate in %
Jason not the first person to cry.	1	14.285714
Tara not a true friend for me.	1	14.285714
Taufan not the winner of the election.	0	0
Bella not a nice person to talk to.	1	14.285714

Table 7: Error rates for the no adverb category.

Test item	Positive judgments	Error rate in %
Akik the father of two boys and a girl.	1	14.285714
Ronny a good math teacher and a nice man.	0	0
Daisy the most beautiful person in this room.	0	0
Ratu a mother of two children.	0	0

Table 8: Error rate for the raising auxiliaries category.

Test item	Positive judgments	Error rate in %
Jeffrey often the loudest person in class.	1	14.285714
Lori once a good math teacher in my school.	2	28.571429
Indah often a great help to me.	3	42.857143
Bambang once the boyfriend of my sister.	0	0

Table 9: Error rate for the T-auxiliary category.

Test item	Positive judgments	Error rate in %
Bulan already a clever child for her age.	2	28.571429
Harto still the most powerful man in Indonesia.	2	28.571429
Abbey still an important part of this family.	3	42.857143
Donald already the worst president of the USA.	2	28.571429

Table 10: Error rate for the VP-embedding raising auxiliaries category.

Test item	Positive judgments	Error rate in %
Britney quickly a very angry woman	1	14.285714
Tulus easily the fastest boy in his class.	1	14.285714
Peter willingly the one to clean up the house.	2	28.571429
Cantik accidentally a mother of a girl.	4	57.142857

As a summary, in Figure 3 are the error rates according to the categories set before:

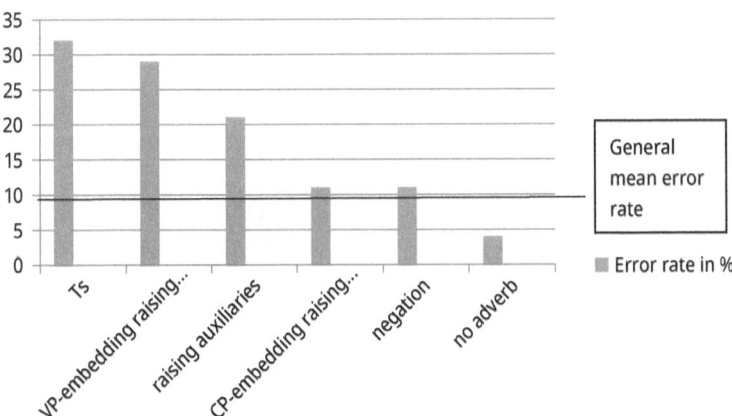

Figure 3: Error rates according to adverbial categories in %.

The general idea of the hypotheses is that three groups should provide (more) competition than the other two groups in contrast to the intercept "no adverb". For these three groups (T, VP-embedding raising verbs, raising auxiliary), the Indonesian counterpart would end up in T (T-adverbs). The mean error rate for all these test items is 17.857%. The mean error rate for the T-adverbs is always higher than the general mean, whereas it is lower for the other groups. This matches the general idea of the hypotheses; however, for (more) valid results, it is necessary to test the hypotheses. To do that, the data is modeled in generalized linear mixed models. The fixed variable here is the adverb category. The free variables are the test item and the participants. The no adverb category is seen as intercept.

The results of the linear mixed model with the adverb category as a fixed variable are as follows (see Table 11):

Table 11: Results of the linear mixed model with the adverb category as fixed variable with no adverb category as intercept.

	Estimate	Std. Error	z value	Pr(>|z|)
(Intercept)	−3.330	1.027	−3.242	0.00119**
raising auxiliary	2.010	1.119	1.796	0.07251
Neg	1.181	1.188	0.994	0.32036
CP-embedding raising verbs	1.254	1.149	1.091	0.27522
T-auxiliary	2.570	1.098	2.340	0.01928*
VP embedding raising verbs	2.398	1.103	2.174	0.02969*

Assuming a threshold of 0.05, the adverbs that match VP-embedding raising verbs and T-auxiliaries in Indonesian show a significant difference to the intercept, test items with no adverb. No such difference is identifiable for the categories negation, CP-embedding raising verbs and raising auxiliaries.

These results match most of the expectations of hypotheses b) and c). The only expectation not met is that raising auxiliaries did not show a significant difference. This is most likely based on the rather small sample and the high variation inside the raising auxiliary group. In the end, with 0.07, the value still remains below the higher threshold of 0.1. Although not necessarily providing a significant result, this finding does not provide a general argument against the general claim of hypotheses b) and c). Whereas adverbs, which correlates in Indonesian end up in T and show significantly higher results than test items without adverbs. Adverbs, which correlates do not end up in T, do not show such an effect. Thus based on this data, both hypotheses b) and c) remain plausible.

Since the model above only contrasted each category to the intercept, no adverb at all, the model has to be adapted to take a closer look at hypothesis a). In this model, the three categories of T-auxiliaries, VP-embedding raising verbs, and raising auxiliaries are lumped together in one category of adverbs, which correlates end up in T, from now a T-adverb. In the new linear mixed model, there are only four categories, namely no adverb, negation, sentence adverb (Indonesian correlates are CP-embedding raising verbs), and T-adverbs.

Having the T-adverbs as intercept, the model provides the following results (see Table 12):

Table 12: Results of the linear mixed model with the adverb category as fixed variable with no adverb category as intercept.

	Estimate	Std. Error	z value	Pr(>|z|)
(Intercept)	−0.9913	0.2692	−3.682	0.000231***
No adverb	−2.3372	1.0485	−2.229	0.025801*
Negation	−1.1567	0.6608	−1.751	0.080023
Sentence adverb	−1.0837	0.5875	−1.844	0.065113

Once again, the model shows the hypothesized differences between the T-adverbs and the no adverb category with a value below the threshold of 0.05. The difference to negation and sentence adverbs undermatches the more general threshold of 0.1. Thus, based on this data, hypothesis a) remains plausible.

Since all three expectations are met, the results favour the idea of a T-effect: English adverbs that correspond to Indonesian auxiliaries that are either base-generated in T (*already, still*) or move to T (*often, once,* V-adverbs), so T-adverbs, demonstrate an effect on the omission of the copula. Copular constructions (with omitted copula *be*) with such an adverb are significantly more often judged grammatical by Indonesian learners of English in comparison to copular constructions without adverbs and to copular constructions with sentence adverbs (their Indonesian counterparts do not end up in T, at least not in the relevant clause).

According to this sample, (681) and (682) are likelier to be judged as grammatical by Indonesian learners of English than (683) and (684).

(681) *John already a good teacher.*

(682) *John often a good teacher.*

(683) *John a good teacher.*

(684) *John normally a good teacher.*

How can we explain this T-effect? There are two important differences between the English and the Indonesian structure for these constructions: the category of the 'adverb' and the status of the copula.

Let us start with the categorical status of the adverbs. In English, all the forms in question can be grouped as adverbs, a non-verbal category. Like all other non-verbal categories in English, adverbs cannot become the syntactic main predicate of a clause. Therefore, they must have a different Cat-head and, consequently, a different δ-head. Category-wise, they can be grouped as statives since many adverbs have a corresponding adjective. However, the Mod-head merged on top must be specified differently. Since it is not the goal of this work to discuss the difference between adverbs and adjectives, for simplicity, the δ-head for adverbs is labeled Adv. Adverbs, then, if merged in the tree, must be treated as phrases. Merging adverbs requires adjunction, which is a stretching of the maximal projection. In contrast to the specifier position, for adjuncts, we do not have any selectional features satisfied (see Adger's adjoin [2003: 89]). While V-adverbs merge as a sister of vP (685), sentential adverbs merge as sisters of CP (686):

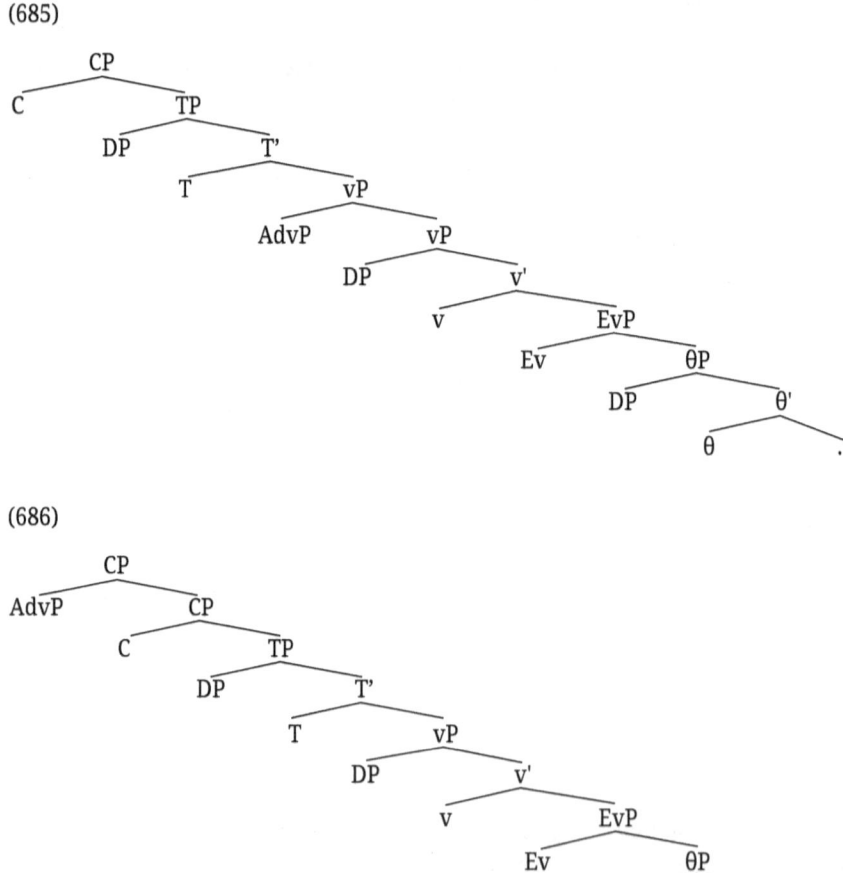

For the Indonesian counterparts, we saw that they are all realized as heads (either in a verbal structure, Aux, or T). Thus, they are inserted with merge (feature checking) and not with adjoin. As a consequence, the Indonesian forms have head status while the English forms as adjuncts have phrase status. Since the Indonesian forms are either base-generated in T (T-auxiliaries) or a projection below T (Aux for raising auxiliaries and θ/Stat/voice for raising verbs) and move to T (only if no overt T is available), they end up in T. In contrast, the English adverbs are adjuncts merged as sisters of vP (or CP).

The second important difference is the copula itself. While English has a copular verb that starts in the V-realm (687) and can move to T (if finite) (688) and even to C (in questions) (689), the Indonesian copula is not verbal but generated in T.

(687) *John will be hungry.*

(688) *John is hungry.*

(689) *Is John hungry?*

Additionally, *adalah* insertion is not part of vocabulary insertion but is based on another phonological process, namely *adalah*-support. In the Indonesian case, T-auxiliaries and raising auxiliaries/verbs (at least in their finite form) compete with the copula *adalah* for the same position in the tree. As a result, the Indonesian copula cannot co-occur with those (690–691).

(690) **Udin   masih   adalah   se-orang   guru.*
       Udin   CONT   COP   one-CL.HUM   teacher

(691) **Udin   pernah   adalah   se-orang   guru.*
       Udin   once   COP   one-CL.HUM   Teacher

In English, however, adverbs and copula occupy two completely different positions. The occurrence of an adverb does not influence the obligatoriness of the copular verb *be* (692–693).

(692) *John is still a teacher.*

(693) *John was once a teacher.*

What happens with the T-effect? Let us consider the following ungrammatical English sentence (S_{ENG}*):

(694) *Harto still the most powerful man in Indonesia.

If we apply the English structure (Struc_ENG), *still* is an adjunct of the vP. Therefore the sentence lacks a verbal form. Since English does not allow a null-copula, the sentence is ungrammatical.

(695)

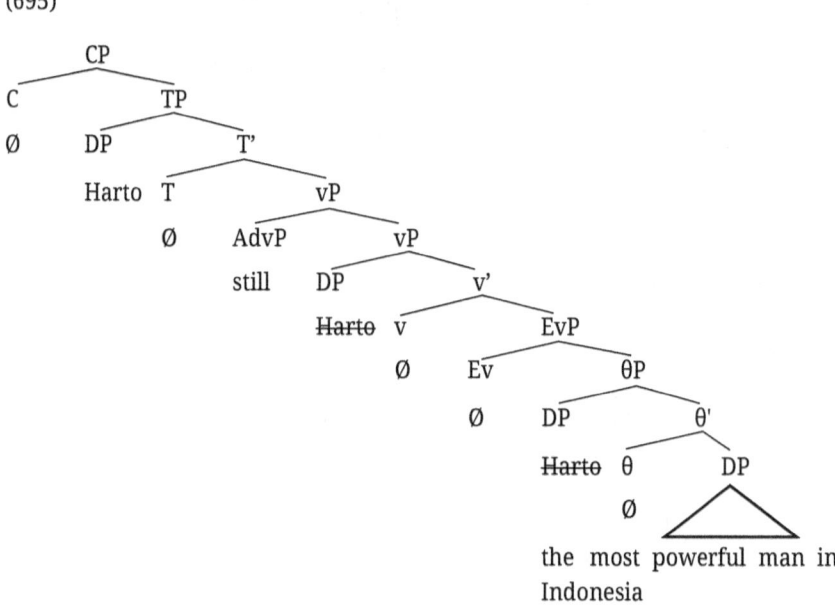

This is how we would expect a native to judge. However, what happens with an Indonesian learner of English? For him, Struc_ENG and his Indonesian structure (Struc_IND) are available.

If we consider the Indonesian counterpart (S_IND), *still* is most likely translated with *masih*, which, however, is not an adverb but a T-auxiliary. A possible Indonesian translation for the whole sentence, then, would be (696):

(696) Harto masih orang yang paling ber-kuasa   di Indonesia.
       Harto CONT   man   REL   SUP   GO.VOICE-power in Indonesia

Since we have an overt T (*masih*) in this sentence the occurrence of the non-verbal copula *adalah* is not possible (697).

(697) *Harto adalah masih orang yang paling ber-kuasa*
Harto COP CONT man REL SUP GO.VOICE-power
di Indonesia.
in Indonesia

For S_{IND}, we should have the following structure ($Struc_{IND}$):

(698)
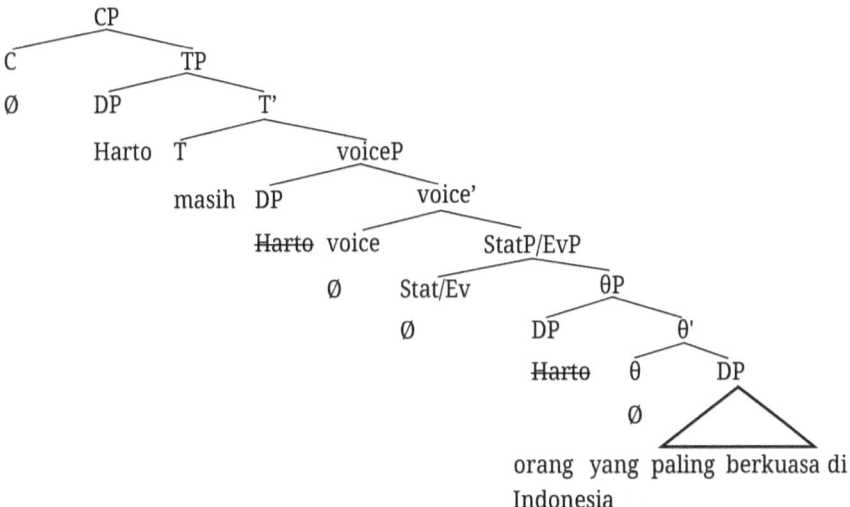

If this $Struc_{IND}$ is applied to the English sentence above (Indonesian structure but English vocabulary items), *still* is analyzed as T. At the same time, θ, Ev/Stat, and voice remain inherently null (all unproblematic for the Indonesian structure). With T being overtly filled, the copula cannot be inserted in T. Based on $Struc_{IND}$, a copula-less structure is desired. Consequently, the sentence with omitted copula is judged grammatical.

In a sentence without an adverb, e.g., *Daisy the most beautiful person in this room*, both voice and T are empty in the Indonesian structure.

(699)

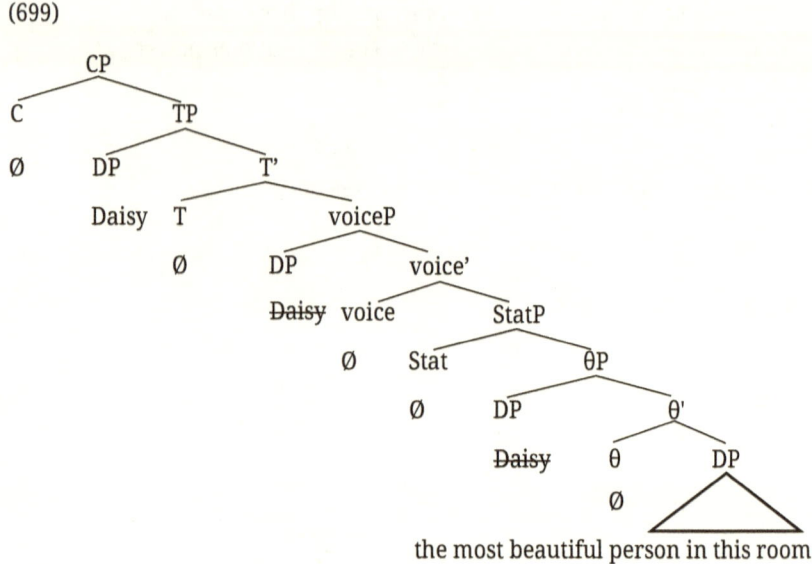

This is a structural requirement for *adalah*-support to be an option. In this case, the copula cannot be generally ruled out on a structural basis, as it was in the case of *still*. The question is, then, whether *adalah*-support (copula-support) is triggered or not? At least two reasons indicate that copula-support should be used when the $Struc_{IND}$ is applied to the test items[140] in question. First, the predicate is long and heavy, and second, there is an asymmetry between a quite short subject and a heavy predicate. Both favour the use of *adalah* to smoothen (Sneddon 1996: 237) the sentence (see chapter 4). Hence, it is likely that if $Struc_{IND}$ is applied to $S_{ENG}*$, still the missing copula is identified. In more general terms, the structure without an adverb is less likely to be judged grammatical compared to sentences with a T-adverb since there is no structural blocking effect by an alleged overt T.

For the contrast between sentence adverbs and T-adverbs, the picture is similar. While the overt T blocks the realization of a copula, there is no such blocking effect for sentence adverbs. English sentence adverbs correspond more or less to Indonesian CP-embedding raising verbs. In contrast to the T-adverb structure, sentences with CP-embedding raising verbs are biclausal. The CP-embedding raising verb is

---

140 (i) *Daisy the most beautiful person in this room.*
    (ii) *Ronny a good math teacher and a nice man.*
    (iii) *Ratu a mother of two children.*
    (iv) *Akik the father of two boys and a girl.*

realized in the matrix clause, while the non-eventive predicate is realized in the embedded clause. If a copula is realized, it is realized inside the embedded clause.

(700)

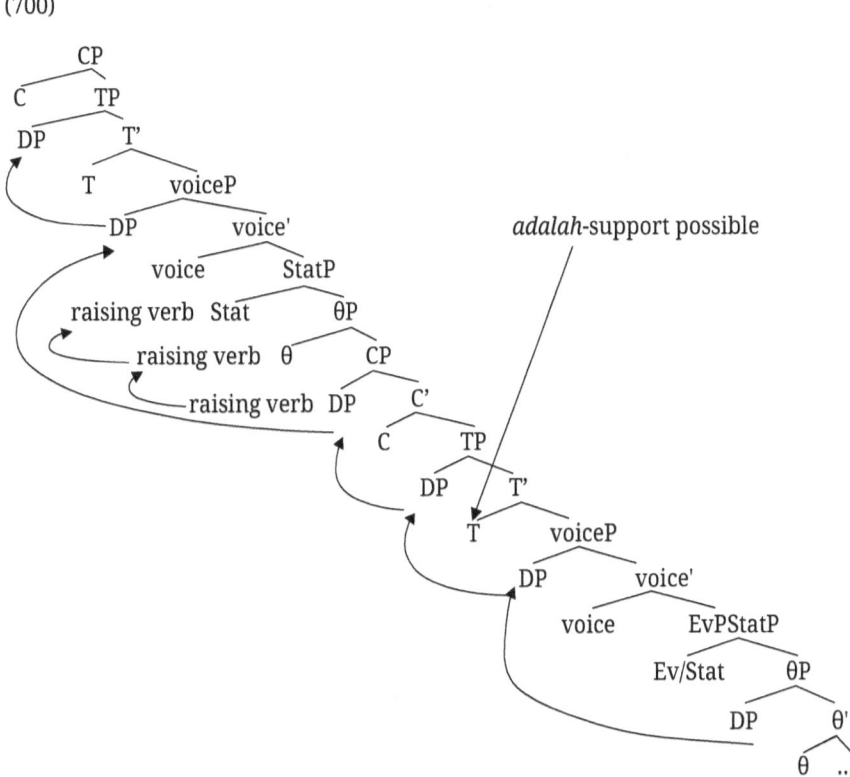

In this clause, both voice and T remain null, which, as we saw before, is a prerequisite for the insertion of *adalah*. With the long and heavy predicate and the short subject in the test items,[141] there are two indications for *adalah*-support if the Indonesian structure is applied. Thus similar to the no-adverb-cases in the previous section, even with applying Struc$_{IND,}$ it is not unlikely that the sentence is judged ungrammatical because of the missing copula.

However, there is one exception to this T-effect, namely negation. Although negation is expressed by raising auxiliaries/verbs in Indonesian (*bukan/tidak*), there

---

141 (i) Whitney definitely a friendly person with humour.
  (ii) Jackson probably the most annoying person here.
  (iii) Bintang certainly a faithful friend to everybody.
  (iv) Kiki normally the first to finish an exam.

is no visible effect in negated English copular clauses with the omitted copula. The mean error rate for *not*-items is identical to the error rate of items with a sentence adverb. Why is the T-effect not available for negation? At least three indications: one structural, one psycholinguistic, and one didactical. The structural indication concerns the status of negation. Leaving the debate aside whether *not* is the head or the specifier of the Neg-phrase (see, for example, Ernst 1992), there is consensus that negation projects a phrase on its own. Therefore the structural status is quite different from adverbs such as *already*, *still*, etc. As a consequence of the Neg-head, affix hopping is not possible, and do-support is required whenever there is no overt auxiliary or copula. Hence, there is no case where a bare *not* is grammatical (701) while it is acceptable for *already/still* (702).

(701)   *Democracy not works.

(702)   Democracy still works.

The second factor is saliency. Negation is an important and salient structure in any language, which is used very frequently. High frequency, in turn, should lead to more proficiency. The third factor is closely related to both factors mentioned before. Since negation is very salient and 'extravagant' (do-support), it is taught regularly and extensively. Adverbs, however, are often below the radar of the curriculum. They are hard to be pressed into a certain grammar lesson. Additionally, they do not seem to be difficult. As a consequence, they are often not paid too much attention to in class. These three indications can explain the absence of an effect for *not*-cases.

5.3.2 Adverb position

After seeing that the competition for a structural position in deep structure plays a crucial role, it is now time to consider surface structure, linear order. While in Indonesian, T-adverbs can occur only in a preverbal position in linear order, labeled as 'second', English adverbs can also occur in the post-subject (second) position, but also clause-initially or clause-finally, so 'non-second'.

In general, the Indonesian non-verbal copula *adalah* is required to 'smoothen' (Sneddon 1996: 237) and disambiguate clauses with nominal predicates. Based on its PF character, *adalah* is not sensitive to syntactic operations and can occur only between subject and predicate, the position we labeled 'second' in linear order. Since the insertion of *adalah*-support highly depends on a variety of intralinguistic and extralinguistic factors, *adalah*-support is hard to predict. However, one factor that reduces the probability of *adalah*-support is an overt element in linear order between subject and predicate.

(703) *Udin juga ??adalah anggota partai demokrat.*
 Udin too COP member democratic party
 'Udin is a member of the democratic party, too.'

Since *juga* is not realized in T, *adalah*-support is not ruled out but not likely. Only for T-auxiliaries, raising auxiliaries, and voiceP-embedding raising verbs that end up in T, there is a structural competition between the copula *adalah* and the auxiliaries/raising verbs for the T-position. In this case, *adalah*-support is ruled out. One question that has to be tested is whether there is a pure linear order effect. To be more precise: Do all test items with any adverb in the second position provide a higher error rate than sentences without an adverb or an adverb in a non-second position? Or, is this effect limited to the structural position of T, which we find with auxiliaries and voiceP-embedding raising verbs?

The second question is whether the position in linear order is relevant at all. In general, T-auxiliaries, auxiliaries, and voiceP-embedding raising verbs can occur only in a second position. In certain environments, raising auxiliaries can occur clause-initially. All these examples, however, are marked.

(704) *Sering Udin anak yang paling rajin di kelas.*
 often Udin child REL SUP diligent in class
 'Often, Udin is the most diligent child in his class.'

In these cases, *adalah*-support is still ungrammatical:

(705) **Sering adalah Udin anak yang paling rajin di kelas.*
 often COP Udin child REL SUP diligent in class
 Intended: 'Often Udin is the most diligent child in his class.'

(706) **Sering Udin adalah anak yang paling rajin di kelas.*
 often Udin COP child REL SUP diligent in class
 Intended: 'Often Udin is the most diligent child in his class.'

Suppose linear order is relevant for the grammaticality judgment. In that case, we should expect that the T-effect is only available with the 'correct' linear order, so only with the T-adverb in the second position. As outlined above, the correct linear word order (imitation of L1) should be a prerequisite for competition.

This leaves us with two possibilities. There is an actual linear order effect, or the linear order is only a requirement for the T-effect:

In the first scenario, we should hypothesize the following outcome:
a) Sentences with adverbs in the second position have a higher error rate than sentences without an adverb.
b) Sentences with adverbs in a non-second position have no higher error rate than sentences without an adverb.

In the second scenario, there should be two important differences. On the one hand, we should find the outcome matching the first scenario but only for T-adverbs and not for sentence adverbs (a-b). On the other hand, the T-effect described in the previous section should only be available for adverbs in the second position but not in a non-second position (a and c):
a) Sentences with a T-adverb in the second position have a higher error rate than sentences without an adverb.
b) Sentences with a sentence adverb in the second position do not have a higher error rate than sentences without an adverb.
c) Sentences with a T-adverb in a non-second position do not have a higher error rate than sentences without an adverb.

Before testing for significance, it is necessary to describe the general data and clarify the groups that will be compared. There were eight test items where the adverb was not placed in the second position but either clause-initial or clause-final. Four items had sentence adverbs (here categorized as CP-embedding raising verbs according to their Indonesian counterparts), two the adverb *already* (here T), and two the adverb *often* (here raising auxiliary). For each item, we find the following error rates (see Table 13–15):

Table 13: Error rates for CP-embedding raising verbs in a non-second position.

Test item	Positive judgments	Error rate in %
Definitely Angie a good mother for her twins	1	14.285714
Definitely Gary a good husband and loving father.	2	28.571429
Certainly Gusti the best player in this team.	0	0
Normally Ratna the teacher in this class.	1	14.285714

Table 14: Error rates for Ts in a non-second position.

Test item	Positive judgments	Error rate in %
Nicky the best player of her team already.	1	14.285714
Davie a good teacher of biology already.	1	14.285714

Table 15: Error rates for raising auxiliaries in anon-second position.

Test item	Positive judgments	Error rate in %
Often Vera the first in the classroom.	1	14.285714
Often Darma a very nice and friendly person.	0	0

Now it is time to turn to the two scenarios. Three categories are important for the first scenario: 'non-second', 'second', and 'no adverb'. The 'non-second' category comprises all test items with an adverb in either clause-initial or clause-final position regardless of the adverb category, here including *already* (T-auxiliary), *often* (raising auxiliary), and sentence adverbs. The 'second' category consists of all test items with an adverb at the second position regardless of the category of the adverb. T-adverbs and sentence adverbs are grouped together. However, to keep these two categories at comparable sizes, only the adverbs that occur in a second and non-second position are considered. Hence, the set is reduced to two instances each of *often* and *already* and four instances of sentence adverbs. Here are the relevant items and their mean error rate (see Table 16–17):

Table 16: Error rate in a non-second position.

Test item	Positive judgments	Error rate in %
Nicky the best player of her team already.	1	14.285714
Davie a good teacher of biology already.	1	14.285714
Often Vera the first in the classroom.	1	14.285714
Often Darma a very nice and friendly person.	0	0
Definitely Angie a good mother for her twins	1	14.285714
Definitely Gary a good husband and loving father.	2	28.571429
Certainly Gusti the best player in this team.	0	0
Normally Ratna the teacher in this class.	1	14.285714

Table 17: Error rate in a second position.

Test item	Positive judgments	Error rate in %
Jeffrey often the loudest person in class.	1	14.285714
Indah often a great help to me.	3	42.857143
Bulan already a clever child for her age.	2	28.571429
Donald already the worst president of the USA.	2	28.571429
Whitney definitely a friendly person with humour.	1	14.285714
Bintang certainly a faithful friend to everybody.	0	0
Kiki normally the first to finish an exam.	0	0
Jackson probably the most annoying person here.	2	28.571429

The last category is the test items without any adverbs (Table 18).

Table 18: Error rate for test items without an adverb.

Test item	Positive judgments	Error rate in %
Akik the father of two boys and a girl	1	14.285714
Ronny a good math teacher and a nice man.	0	0
Daisy the most beautiful person in this room.	0	0
Ratu a mother of two children.	0	0

For these three categories, the following means can be detected (see Figure 4):

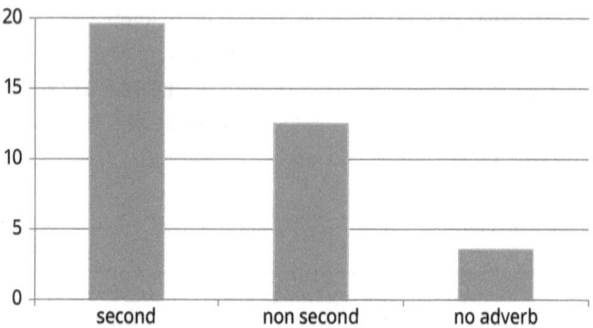

Figure 4: Error rates for the test items with adverbs in different positions in %.

Once again, the data is modeled in a generalized mixed model, taking the position categories (second, non-second, and no adverb) as fixed variables. The participant and the test item are free variables. If the control group (no adverb) is chosen as intercept, the model (see Table 19) shows the following contrasts:

Table 19: Results of the linear mixed model with the adverb position as a fixed variable with no adverb category as intercept.

	Estimate	Std. Error	z value	Pr(>|z|)
(Intercept)	−3.475	1.056	−3.292	0.000995***
Non-second	1.361	1.104	1.234	0.217368
Second	1.911	1.065	1.794	0.072845

Since both adverbs in second and non-second positions show no significant difference (value above 0.05), the data here does not provide strong evidence for a general second effect. The value for the second position still underscores the threshold of

0.1. This, however, is only a very slight indication and most likely due to the T-adverbs inside this group, as will be shown in the following section. Consequently, the first scenario is not very likely and will be dismissed.

We now turn to the second possible scenario in which the linear order is only a trigger for the T-adverb effect, described in 4.3.1. Here, the groups 'second' and 'non-second' are split into sentence adverbs and T-adverbs,[142] which leads to five categories: T-adverbs second (Table 20), T-adverbs non-second (Table 21), sentence adverbs second (Table 22), sentence adverbs non-second (Table 23), and no adverb (Table 24). Here are these five categories with the mean error rates:

Table 20: Error rates for T-adverbs in the second position.

Test item	Positive judgments	Error rate in %
Jeffrey often the loudest person in class.	1	14.285714
Indah often a great help to me.	3	42.857143
Bulan already a clever child for her age.	2	28.571429
Donald already the worst president of the USA.	2	28.571429

Table 21: Error rates for T-adverbs in a non-second position.

Test item	Positive judgments	Error rate in %
Nicky the best player of her team already.	1	14.285714
Davie a good teacher of biology already.	1	14.285714
Often Vera the first in the classroom.	1	14.285714
Often Darma a very nice and friendly person.	0	0

Table 22: Error rates for sentence adverbs in the second position.

Test item	Positive judgments	Error rate in %
Whitney definitely a friendly person with humour.	1	14.285714
Bintang certainly a faithful friend to everybody.	0	0
Kiki normally the first to finish an exam.	0	0
Jackson probably the most annoying person here.	2	28.571429

---

[142] Once again, only the T-adverbs that occur sentence-final and sentence-initial in the test are considered.

Table 23: Error rates for sentence adverbs in a non-second position.

Test item	Positive judgments	Error rate in %
Definitely Angie a good mother for her twins	1	14.285714
Definitely Gary a good husband and loving father.	2	28.571429
Certainly Gusti the best player in this team.	0	0
Normally Ratna the teacher in this class.	1	14.285714

Table 24: Error rates for items with no adverb.

Test item	Positive judgments	Error rate in %
Akik the father of two boys and a girl	1	14.285714
Ronny a good math teacher and a nice man.	0	0
Daisy the most beautiful person in this room.	0	0
Ratu a mother of two children.	0	0

For these groups, the means are as shown in Figure 5:

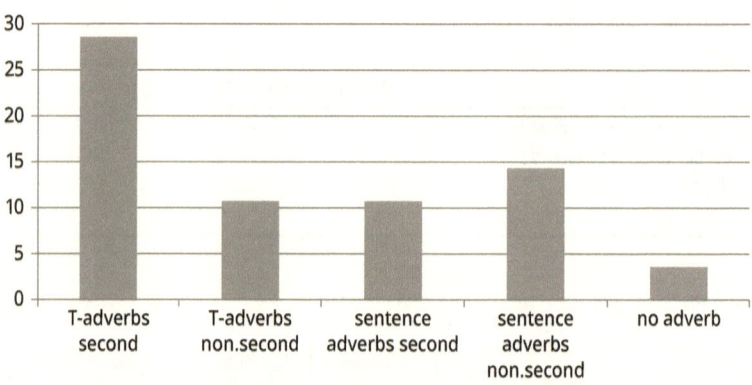

Figure 5: Error rates for the test items with different adverb categories in %.

Considering these categories as fixed variable for a generalized mixed model (Table 25) leads to the following outcome (The no-adverb-category remains the intercept):

Table 25: Results of the linear mixed model with the adverb category and position as fixed variables with no adverb category as intercept.

	Estimate	Std. Error	z value	Pr(>|z|)
(Intercept)	−3.496	1.061	−3.294	0.000989***
sentence adverb non second	1.495	1.193	1.253	0.210121
sentence adverb second	1.284	1.146	1.121	0.262469
T adverb non second	1.251	1.186	1.055	0.291586
T adverb second	2.490	1.107	2.251	0.024414*

The only contrast that shows a significant result is the T-adverb at the second position. All other categories show no significant result. This matches perfectly the outcome of the second scenario. Whereas T-adverbs at the second position show an effect, T-adverbs at a non-second position and sentence adverbs at a second position do not provide a significant contrast.

Taking the T-adverb in the second position as the intercept (Table 26) provides an interesting contrast as well:

Table 26: Results of the linear mixed model with the adverb category as fixed variable with T-adverb in the second position as intercept.

	Estimate	Std. Error	z value	Pr(>|z|)
(Intercept)	−1.0058	0.5084	−1.978	0.0479*
no adverb	−2.4904	1.1066	−2.251	0.0244*
sentence adverb second	−1.2065	0.6939	−1.739	0.0821
sentence adverb non second	−0.9956	0.7673	−1.298	0.1944
T adverb non second	−1.2393	0.7594	−1.632	0.1027

Whereas the only contrast below the threshold 0.05 is with the no adverb category, the contrast with category sentence adverb in the second position is still below the more general threshold of 0.1. That is the same range as the contrast of a general second category to the no adverb category in the first scenario. That is another indication that the general contrast is only available due to the T-adverbs and not a general second effect. This leads to the conclusion that with the data available, we have a position effect as a trigger for the T-effect and not a general second effect

How can we account for this observation? As the first scenario was not supported by the data available, a pure linear effect is not likely. The sheer presence of an adverb in the post-subject/pre-predicate position is not sufficient for competition. There is significant competition only if the structural competition for the T-position (see T-effect) is given. Similar to the explanation above, the null-voice and null-T position for non-T-adverb structures provides a potential copula position. With this position available, the overt omission of the copula is a PF matter. Even when the Indonesian structure is triggered, there is a chance that the omitted copula is seen as "problematic". Since indications for *adalah*-support (long predicate and asymmetry between subject and predicate) are given, it is more likely that even the Indonesian structure would require an overt copula. With T-adverbs, the T-position (potential position of *adalah*-support) is filled, and the copula is ruled out. Therefore, the omitted copula is more likely accepted.

However, as we saw in the second scenario, linear order is still required for the T-effect. There is a significant effect only for T-adverbs realized in the second position. If the T-adverb is realized in a non-second position, there is no error rate difference to test items without an adverb. How can we explain this observation?

English adverbs (at least those that correspond to the T-adverbs that we talk about) are realized as adjuncts of the vP. Since adjuncts are adjoined, both branching directions are accessible (at least for some of them). As a consequence, in linear order, they can end up between T (if filled overtly) and v (707) or clause-final (708). If in (707), T is not filled overtly or omitted on purpose (as it was done in the test items), the adverb ends up in the second position (709).

(707) *John is already a clever child.*

(709) **John already a clever child.*

(709) **John already a clever child.*

Additionally, movement to Spec-CP for topicalization is possible. This would lead to a clause-initial position (710).

(710) *Often John is the last person to finish the exam.*

For Indonesian auxiliaries, however, we have a different picture. There is the possibility of fronting T-auxiliaries. However, this is part of focalization (movement to Spec-FocP). Here the whole predicate is fronted along with the overt Ts, which leads to an inverted structure (711). T-only fronting – which would match the linear order of an English clause with a clause-initial adverb – is ungrammatical (712).

(711) Masih   se-orang   guru   Udin.
      CONT   one-CL.HUM teacher Udin
      'Udin is still a teacher.'

(712) *Masih   Udin   se-orang   guru
      CONT   Udin   one-CL.HUM   Teacher

Since the auxiliary is generated in the T-head, there is no 'branching-freedom' as we have for the adjoined adverbs in English. Hence, it cannot occur in a clause-final position.

For raising auxiliaries, we have a similar but still slightly different picture. On the one hand, as they are base-generated in the Aux-head position, they cannot occur sentence-final (similar to the T-auxiliaries). On the other hand, they can end up in a clause-initial position (713), due to T-to-C-movement or as a remnant of a raising verb with an expletive null-subject.

(713) Sering   Udin   orang   yang   paling   rajin   di   kelas.
       often   Udin   human   REL   SUP   diligent   in   class
       'Udin is often the most diligent person in the class.'

Although sentence (713) is grammatical, it is not very common. Since raising auxiliaries are part of a continuum, it is possible that this structure is no longer grammatical for many speakers. Moreover, even for those speakers, who would accept it, the sentence would be marked. In conclusion, we can say that Indonesian auxiliaries cannot occur clause-finally at all and clause-initially only under certain circumstances. However, these structures are either highly marked or inverted structures with the whole predicate fronted.

Consequently, whenever an adverb in the English sentence does not appear in a post-subject position, the sentence is not transferable to Indonesian structure with a one-on-one mechanism. For this reason, only if the T-adverb is in the second position the linear order would favour a T-reading. When the adverb is in clause-initial or clause-final position, a T-interpretation (applying the Indonesian structure Struc$_{IND}$) is less likely since such linear order would be ungrammatical or at least highly marked in Indonesian. As a consequence, the Indonesian representation is not triggered, and the participants arrive at the adverb reading, which is not in competition with T. Since the copula is omitted, the sentence is judged ungrammatical.

What has to be kept in mind is that it is also possible that the whole effect is solely based on the participants' judgment concerning the wrong adverb position. In other words, the participants are unaware that English adverbs allow some variation in linear order and judge the sentence as not grammatical without taking the missing copula into account. In this case, they still apply the Indonesian representation, and since the alleged auxiliary is in the wrong surface position, the sentence is judged as ungrammatical. With the available data, it is impossible to distinguish between these two effects. Interestingly, though, concerning this matter is that sentences with a T-adverb at the clause-initial position have a lower error rate (7%) than sentences with a T-adverb in the clause-final position (14%). However, the clause-initial position is grammatical in Indonesian, while the clause-final position is not. The mean differences are far from significant. We should therefore refrain from drawing any strong conclusions from that. However, if the adverb position were the critical factor, we would expect a significantly higher error rate for sentences with the T-adverb in the clause-initial position. Since even the tendency of the error rate – the error rate of sentences with a T-adverb in clause-initial position is lower than the error rate of sentences with a T-adverb in clause-final position – is not according to this expectation, there is a very weak indication that the wrong surface position of the adverb is less relevant than the matter that the T-interpretation is not triggered.

With the T-effect and the position effect combined, the outcome matches the general pattern for competition, which was outlined at the beginning of this chapter, namely identical/similar linear order but different underlying structures. Only both factors in combination provide an effect. With both languages in contrast having a similar surface structure but two different underlying structures, two competing structures may pop-up in the speaker's mind. If she chooses the L1 structure for the L2 clause, we find competition. Whenever the surface structure of the target sentence is different from the L1-order, the L2 structure has weaker competition from the L1 structure (L1 structure is less likely triggered), and competition is unlikely, however, not completely impossible.

5.3.3 The category of the predicate

After dealing with the influence of adverbs in the first test, the second test concerns the predicate category itself. We saw in the third chapter that Indonesian exploits three different strategies for non-verbal predicates: the no-copula strategy, the *ada*-strategy, and the *adalah*-strategy. Although all strategies can lead to a copulaless structure at the surface, there is an important structural difference between these strategies. While the no-copula type does not even provide a potential position for a copula, the verbal *ada* and the non-verbal *adalah* are optionally realized at PF. However, the structural prerequisites for a copula are given in all cases of the *ada*- and the *adalah*-type. Suppose the predicate category had an influence on the error rate (acceptance of ungrammatical sentences). In that case, we should expect predicates that refer to the no-copula type to provide a higher error rate than predicates that belong to a copular type in Indonesian, either the *ada*-type or the *adalah*-type. Since the adjective category is the only category that is always represented in a no-copula type, adjectival predicates should have a higher error rate than the other three categories (PPs, indefinite DPs, and definite DPs).

The test provides the following results (see Table 27–30). Each test item is represented according to the predicate category. Once again, the error rate is the number of participants that judged the ungrammatical test item as grammatical. Data is provided in an absolute number of positive judgments and as percentages.

Table 27: Error rates for the category adjectives.

Test item	Positive judgments	Error rate in %
Rini exhausted from the race.	8	72.727273
Ridwan tired all day.	7	63.636364
Lizzy angry at her mother	4	36.363636
Ricky happy with his girl-friend.	8	72.727273

Table 28: Error rates for the category definite nouns.

Test item	Positive judgments	Error rate in %
Megan the doctor of my mother.	1	9.090909
Bakti the best student in class.	2	18.181818
Robert the winner of the game	2	18.181818
Nira the most attractive woman.	2	18.181818

Table 29: Error rates for the category indefinite nouns.

Test item	Positive judgments	Error rate in %
Bagus a strong man with a big heart.	2	18.181818
Cindy a businesswoman in Singapore.	5	45.454545
Mega a stewardess of a well-known airline.	5	45.454545
Winston a member of the Nationalist Party.	4	36.363636

Table 30: Error rates for the category preposition phrases.

Test item	Positive judgments	Error rate in %
Mary in her office in Chicago.	1	9.090909
Johnny in Jakarta for a year.	5	45.454545
Udin in America for a visit.	0	0
Siska at the mall in Bandung.	2	18.181818

In summary, this leads to the following mean error rates according to the category presented in Figure 6:

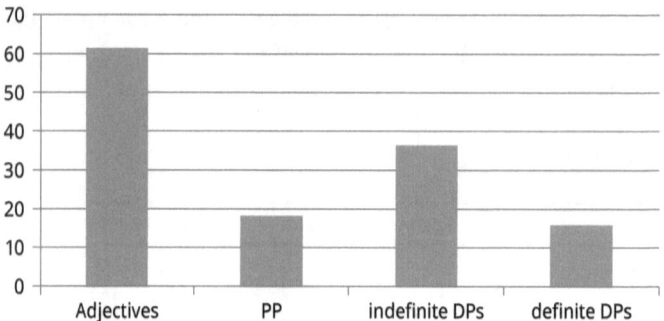

Figure 6: Error rates according to the category of the predicate in %.

The picture meets the expectation. Adjectives provide the highest error rate with more than 50%, while definite DPs are at the lower end with just a bit above 10%. PPs and indefinite DPs are in the middle with about 25% respectively 35%.

Although the means indicate the right tendency, this says nothing about significant differences between their error rates.

A generalized mixed model with the adjective category as intercept (Table 31) provides the following results:

Table 31: Results of the linear mixed model with the predicate category as fixed variable with the adjective category as intercept.

	Estimate	Std. Error	df	t value	Pr(>|t|)
(Intercept)	0.61364	0.09358	18.18196	6.557	3.49e-06***
Definite nouns	−0.45455	0.10415	11.99999	−4.364	0.000921***
Indefinite nouns	−0.25000	0.10415	11.99999	−2.400	0.033495*
Preposition phrases	−0.43182	0.10415	11.99999	−4.146	0.001356**

If we consider the outcome hypothesized above, our expectations have been met. Sentences with adjectival predicates provide a significantly higher error rate than sentences with definite DPs, indefinite DPs, and PPs.

Taking a second look at the mean error rates for the predicate categories (Figure 7), we can see that the error rate of indefinite DPs lies above the general mean of all items (33%).

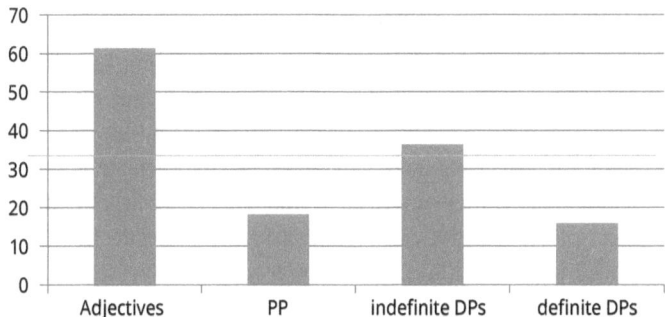

Figure 7: Error rates according to the category of the predicate in % with general mean of all items.

A generalized mixed model with the indefinite DP category as intercept (Table 32) provides the following results:

Table 32: Results of the linear mixed model with the predicate category as fixed variable with the indefinite noun category as intercept.

	Estimate	Std. Error	df	t value	Pr(>|t|)
(Intercept)	0.36364	0.09358	18.18196	3.886	0.00107**
Adjectives	0.25000	0.10415	11.99999	2.400	0.03349*
Definite nouns	−0.20455	0.10415	11.99999	−1.964	0.07313.
Preposition phrases	−0.18182	0.10415	11.99999	−1.746	0.10638

Whereas the contrast with the adjective category still provides a significant effect (threshold <0.05), the contrast to definite nouns is slightly significant (threshold <0.1). This at least indicates that indefinite DPs might have a slight effect in contrast to definite DPs.

To summarize, the data indicates a strong adjective effect and a light effect for indefinite DPs. Let us now take a closer look at this.

The error rate for sentences with adjectives as predicates was significantly higher than for sentences with DPs and PPs. This effect is explainable based on structural differences. In English, there is a structural difference between adjectives and verbs. While Ev, the verb defining head with an event feature, can move into v and consequently become the main predicate of a clause (both semantically and syntactically), the adjective defining head Stat lacks this event feature. Therefore, StatP cannot be selected by v, and another δ-head, namely Mod, must be merged. The ModP cannot become the syntactical main predicate, and a copula (normally *be*) is required if an adjective is used predicatively.

For Indonesian, the two groups (adjectives and verbs) are not separable, at least not by syntactic criteria. Instead of two different class-defining functional heads, such as Ev and Stat for English, in Indonesian, voice (different to v) can select both eventive predicates, Ev as for English verbs, and stative predicates Stat, as for English adjectives,[143] because we have voice-markers that are stative, *ter-* and *ber-*, and voice-markers that are eventive, *meN-* and *di-*. The decisive feature that is checked in voice is not the eventive or stative feature but a specific thematic role. Thus, there is no need for the Indonesian case to group adjectives and verbs into different word classes. As a result, all these forms, including English adjectives and verbs, can move to voice (and under certain circumstances even to T) and become the main predicate, semantically and syntactically, of the clause. We have labeled this the no-copula-type, although it does not differ from any standard clause with a 'verbal' predicate.

For English, we have the underlying structure (714), where the v-position has to be filled with the copula. For Indonesian, we have the underlying structure (715) without a structural position where a copula could be inserted.

(714)

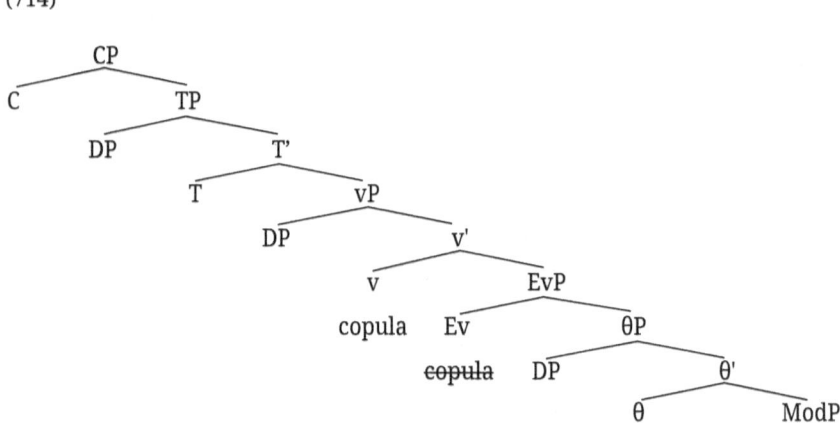

---

[143] This is a simplified approximation.

(715)

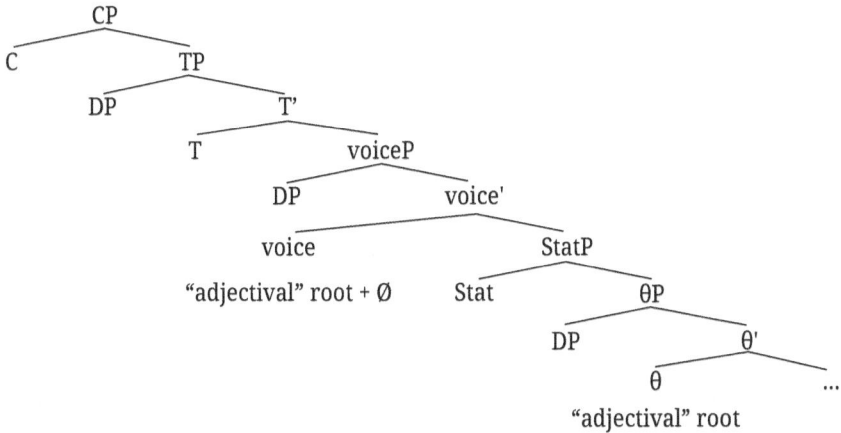

We should apply this to our test items, e.g., a sentence (S_{ENG}*) such as (716).

(716)   *John sad.

There are two possibilities: The participant applies the English structure ($Struc_{ENG}$) or the Indonesian structure ($Struc_{IND}$). In $Struc_{ENG}$, *sad* is realized as ModP, so the copula is required. Therefore, the sentence is judged ungrammatical. If the participant applies the Indonesian structure ($Struc_{IND}$), or at least voice instead of v for S_{ENG}*, *sad* is merged in θ and moves via Stat to voice (717).[144] Since the representation works perfectly fine without a copula, a potential position is not even available. They have no chance to identify the ungrammaticality of the sentence because of the omitted copula.

---

144 If the full Indonesian structure is applied then *sad* is moved to T. If only voice replaces v, voice-to-T-movement might not be available. However, this difference is not relevant for our case.

(717)

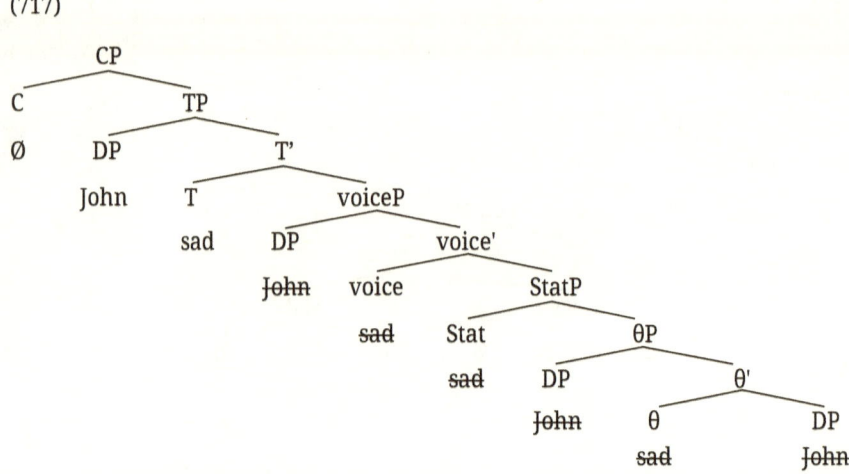

Having dealt with the adjectival case, we now turn to PP- and DP-predicates.

In English, adjectival predicates require not only the same copula as DP- and PP-predicates, but even the structure is comparable in all cases, an asymmetric small clause with the predicate in complement position. Therefore one might expect that Indonesian would do the same, applying one structure for all these cases. However, as we saw in chapter 4, this is not true for Indonesian. While the "adjectival" predicates belong to the no-copula type (clause with a verb-like predicate), PP-predicates belong to the *ada*-type and DP-predicates to the *adalah*-type. The latter two are possible with an overt copula, *ada*, and *adalah*. Therefore, for the *ada*- and the *adalah*-type, we have structures that are far more similar to the English structure than the no-copula structure dealt with above.

Like English, Indonesian PPs and DPs have a distinct category assigning head compared to verbal forms. As a result, they do not have a voice layer and cannot be merged with T but need a copular structure. Here, the basic underlying structure is identical for the two Indonesian types and the English predicational copular construction:

(718)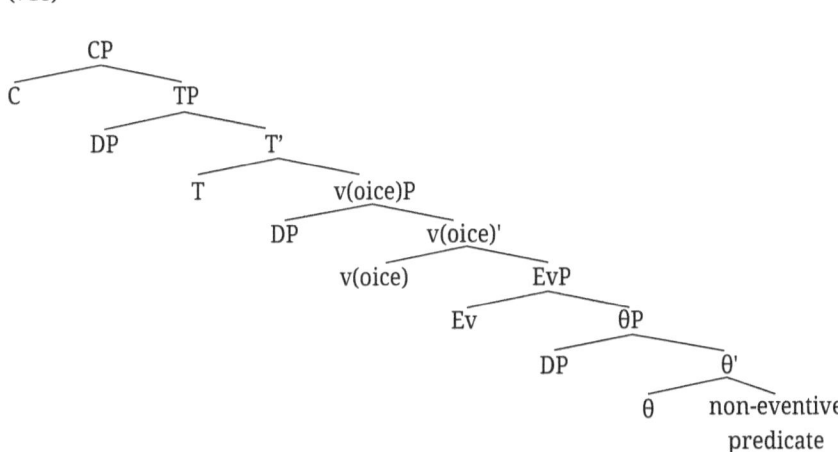

The actual difference between the three copular constructions in question does not lie in the general structure but in the place of insertion of the copula. Since the English copula is no theta-assigner, the copula is not merged in the small clause but later in Ev and v. The Indonesian *ada*-type, relevant for PP-predicates, requires the form *ada*. Since *ada* can be analyzed either as copula or as a full verb with the meaning to exist, it is unclear whether it is (still) a theta-assigner. Consequently, it remains unclear if it has to be base-generated in θ or equivalent to the English structure in Ev[145] and v(oice). The copula *adalah* is not even part of vocabulary insertion but inserted with *adalah*-support in T.

A copula position is available for all the structures dealt with previously in θ, v, or T. The only difference that has to be learned, then, is the position of insertion[146] and that the English copula is not optional but always obligatory. This, however, is a minor problem compared to the structural effect for adjectives where no copula position exists.

Let us consider an example for both PP (719) and definite DP (720) predicates:

(719) *John (is) in Jakarta.*

(720) *John (is) my teacher.*

---

[145] For the Indonesian structure, it would be possible to have a Stat-head instead. However, to have it more comparable to English, I will use the Event head.
[146] With *adalah* we found a T-effect in the previous section.

The English structure should be (721) respectively (722).

(721)

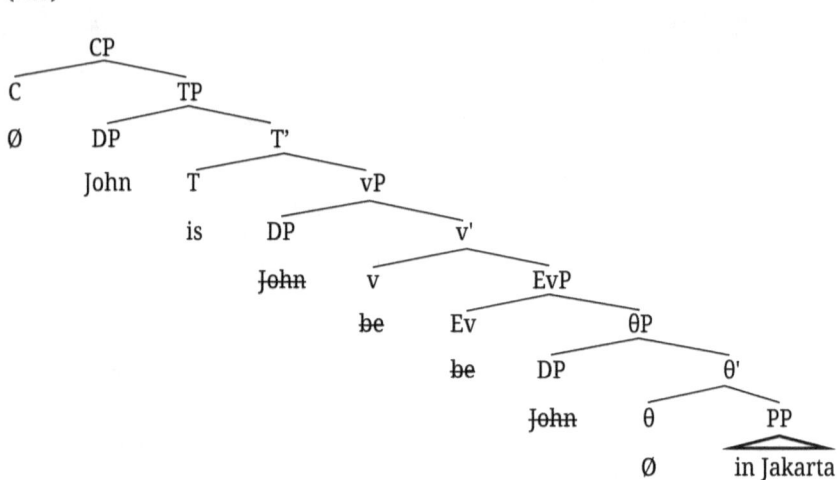

(722)

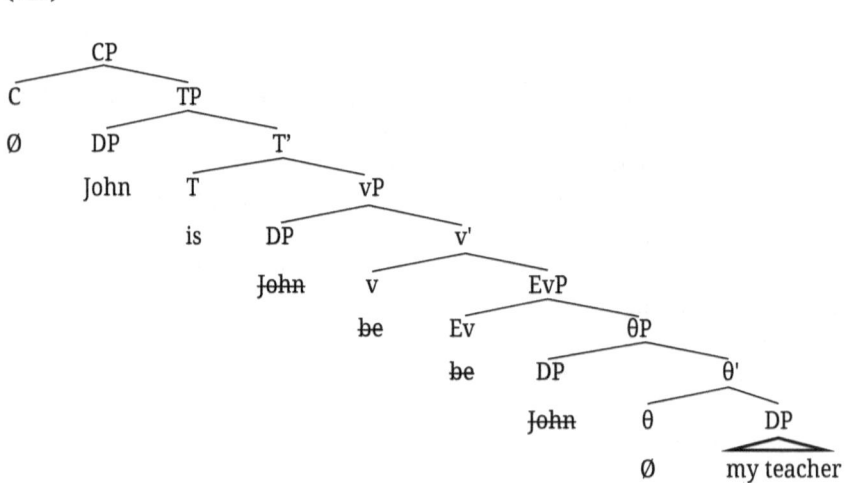

If the speaker applies the Indonesian *ada*-type for the PP-predicate (723) and the *adalah*-type for the DP-predicate (724), the only difference is in the position of the copula. As long as the speaker knows that he is not allowed to set the copula on null-spell out (or she does not want to do so as the indication for *ada*-deletion is weak, or the indication for *adalah*-support strong[147]), this position difference does not affect the linear order. Consequently, she has to judge the sentence with omitted copulas as ungrammatical.

(723)

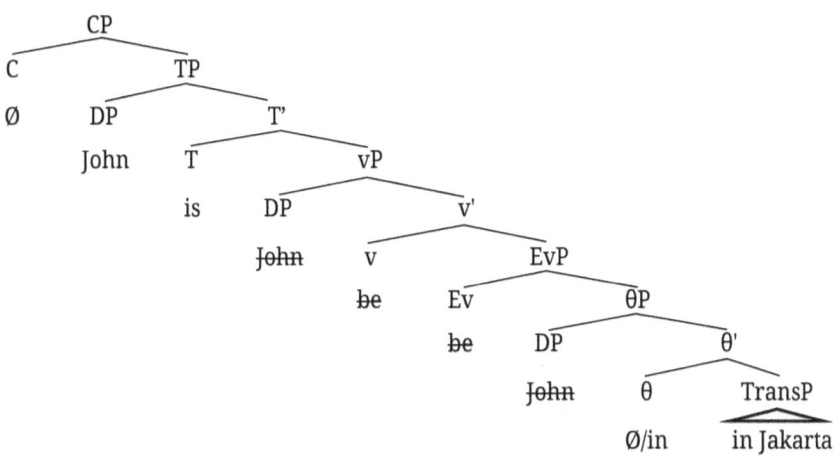

(724)

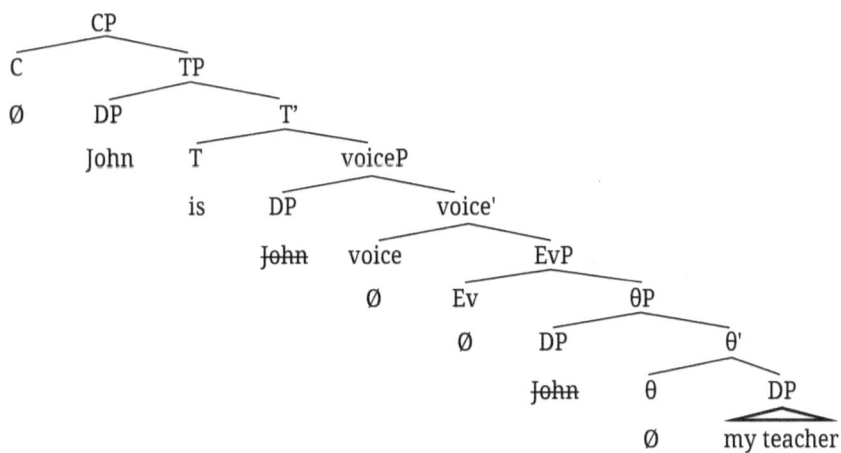

---

147 In these two cases an overt copula would be required in Indonesian. In the *ada*-case, default is with overt *ada*, which can be deleted under certain circumstances. For the *adalah*-type, default is no overt copula, however where required *adalah*-support kicks in.

To sum up, Indonesian has three distinct structures for what we would call adjectival, nominal, and PP-predicates in English, namely the no-copula-type, the *adalah*-type, and the *ada*-type. Although all three types are different in some respect to the English copular structure, only in the no-copula type of the Indonesian language is there no position available where a copula could potentially be inserted. In such a case, no copula is required or not even possible. There is either an overt copula or a null copula in all other structures. Although the copula is realized in different heads, it does not have an effect on linear order. The only relevant difference is the non-obligatoriness in Indonesian as a PF matter. The structural difference in not having a potential copula position triggers much more competition than the PF-difference, which therefore seems to be easier to control.

Thus, adjectival predicates have their extraordinary position amongst the non-verbal predicates if judged by an Indonesian learner of English.

However, that this effect is based on the no-copula structure and not on the adjectival predicate is strengthened by the error rate for indefinite DPs. As shown above, there was a slight significant contrast between indefinite DPs and definite DPs. As outlined in chapter 3, for indefinite DPs (725), there are two competing structures in Indonesian, one following the no-copula structure (726) and one following the adalah-type (727).

(725) Udin   seorang   guru.
      Udin   a/one-CL.HUM   teacher
      'Udin is a teacher.'

(726)

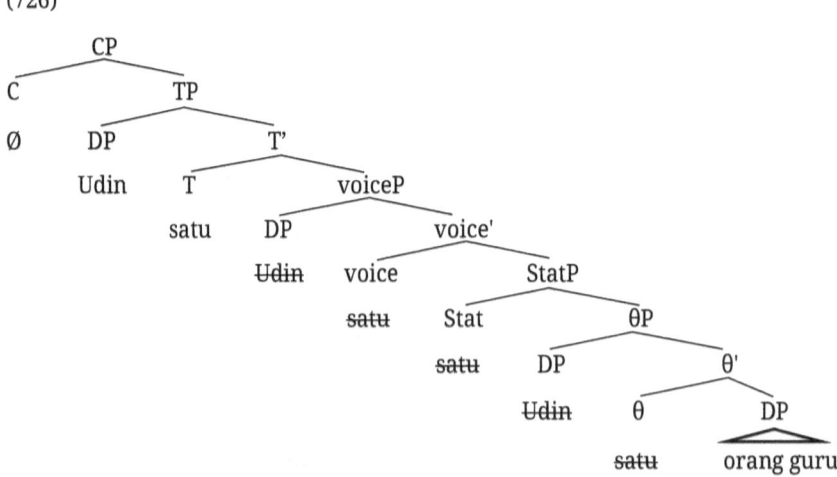

(727)

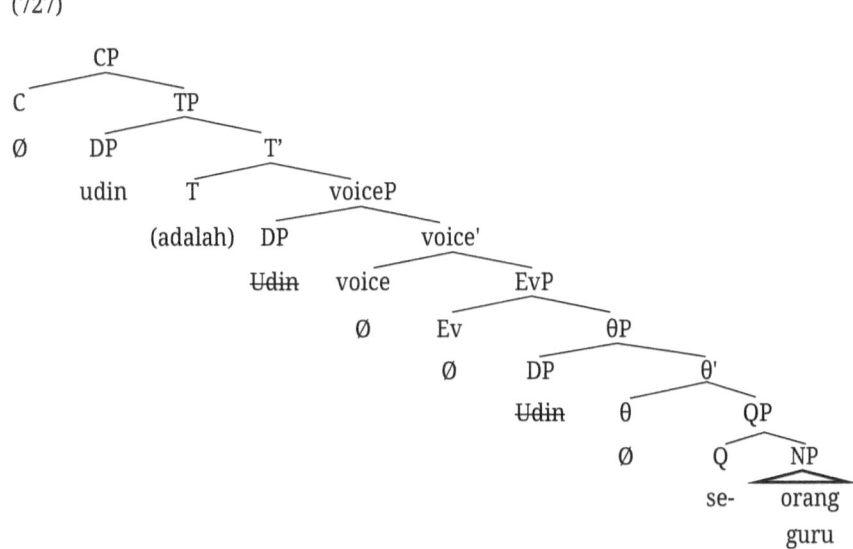

Depending on the underlying structure in Indonesian, competition is likelier (no-copula structure) or less likely (*adalah*-type). Thus, for indefinite DPs, the higher error rate is explainable by the potential no-copula structure. Thus, the reason for competition is the no-copula structure. Still, the error rate for adjectives is the highest, as the no-copula structure is the only possible structure in Indonesian.

5.4 Summary

We have found two major effects in the two tests, a T-effect and a no-copula-structure effect.

1) T-effect

English adverbs that correspond to Indonesian auxiliaries that are either base-generated in T (*already, still*) or move to T (*often, once*, V-adverbs) affect the omission of the copula. Copular constructions with such an adverb in the environment (with omitted copula) are significantly more often judged grammatical than copular constructions without adverbs and copular constructions with sentential adverbs.

Hence, according to this sample, (728) and (729) are more likely to be judged grammatical by Indonesian learners of English than (730) and (731).

(728) *John already a good teacher.*

(729) *John often a good teacher.*

(730) *John a good teacher.*

(731) *John normally a good teacher.*

However, this T-effect is only available if the adverb in question occupies the second position, the position between subject and predicate. Therefore, according to this sample, (732) is more likely to be seen as grammatical than (733).

(732) *John already a good teacher.*

(733) *John a good teacher already.*

There is no second effect traceable for non-T-adverbs, e.g., sentence adverbs. There is no significant difference between clauses with sentence adverbs at sentence-initial (734) and sentence-second position (735).

(734) *Normally John a good teacher.*

(735) *John normally a good teacher.*

2) No-copula-structure-Effect

In the second test, we saw that non-eventive predicates whose Indonesian counterparts have an underlying no-copula structure (no potential position for a copula available) have higher error rates than categories with an underlying copula structure in Indonesian (it does not matter if the copula is realized).

This effect mainly concerns adjectival predicates. Since "adjectival" predicates in Indonesian are always realized as no-copula-construction, copular constructions with adjectival predicates are more likely to be seen as grammatical compared to all other groups of non-verbal predicates, namely definite or indefinite DPs, or PPs, if the copula *be* is omitted. So (736) is more likely to be seen as grammatical compared to (737), (738), or (739).

(736) *John hungry.*

(737) *John in Japan.*

(738) *John a teacher.*

(739) *John the teacher.*

To conclude, both effects, the T-effect and the no-copula-structure effect, fulfill the idea of competition. In the beginning, this work presented three conditions that have to be met for competition:
a) Deviation from the native speaker
b) Structural differences
c) Imitation of L1

All three criteria are met. First, the target items are more often judged grammatical by the participants in contrast to a group of hypothetical native speakers, who should never judge them grammatical (at least in theory). Second, there is a structural difference between English and Indonesian for both effects. In Indonesian, there is a structure where a copula position is either unavailable or already filled by another overt item. For items with these structural differences, error rates are significantly higher than items that miss this structural difference. Third, the effect is only visible if the L1 structure (Indonesian structure) is imitated (see adverb position effect). Therefore, these results strongly suggest competition effects based on the structural differences of T-auxiliaries in Indonesian and adverbs in English in combination with the copulas *adalah* and *be* and based on the different predication structure for "adjectival" predicates.

6 Conclusion

The major question of this work was whether the structural differences between non-verbal predicates in English and Indonesian affect language acquisition. Thus, the first question that had to be answered concerned the structural differences of non-verbal predicates in these two languages.

As pointed out, every verbal form in English bears some event feature either motivated semantically or syntax-internally (the occurrence of a Trans-head). Therefore, all non-eventive forms, which lack such an event feature, are automatically non-verbal. Because of the lack of this event feature, merging v is not possible. As a result, English non-verbal predicates need the support of a copula, the bearer of an abstract event feature. With the help of this abstract event feature, v can be merged in the derivation. The copula itself is base-generated in Ev, consequently head-moves to v, and if finite further to T. Based on the insertion of the copula, the realization of v is possible, and the general sentence structure is reinstalled. Structure-wise, the non-eventive predicate itself has a category-head different from Ev, namely Stat for adjectives and N for nouns, and accordingly a different δ-head, namely Mod for adjectives and D for nouns. The ModP and the DP are complements of a small clause headed by a null θ-head if they are used predicatively. The constituent that will receive subject status later in the derivation is assigned the THEME role. To avoid a clause without a main predicate, the help of the copula is required, which is then merged into Ev. This Ev-head takes the small clause as its complement. With the help of this abstract event feature, we can merge v and consequently, on top of v, merge T. The copula head moves in both heads (at least if finite), and the argument merged in Spec-θP moves via Spec-vP to Spec-TP.

(740)

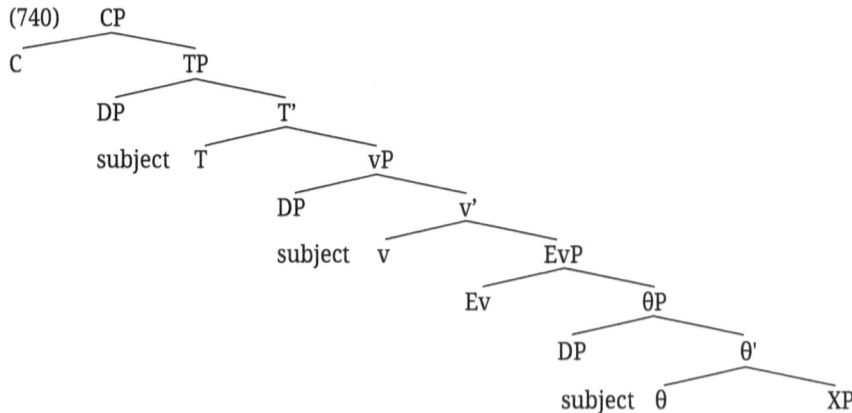

Since prepositions are two-place-predicates, the underlying structure differs in certain aspects. Here, the θ-head, which projects the small clause (takes the second argument in its specifier position), is still the landing position of the preposition. However, since a Stat-head cannot be merged for the second time, the copula must compensate for the missing event feature. After that, the derivation continues, as pointed out for adjectives and nouns.

In contrast to this rather homogenous group of non-eventive predicates in English, the Indonesian group of non-eventive predicates is highly heterogeneous. That category is even not as easily identifiable as in English. The main reason for this is that the Indonesian voice-head is not sensitive to an event feature although position-wise comparable to the English v-head. There is even overt-voice morphology, namely *ter-* and *ber-*, which is specified for resultative and stative, respectively, so in both cases non-eventive. With this peculiarity of the Indonesian voice-head, it is impossible to draw a line between verbs and adjectives based on a syntactic argumentation. Therefore, "adjectival" predicates behave identically to "verbal" predicates. They are merged in θ and move via Stat[148] to voice. As a result, a copula is not only not required but even not possible. The strategy applied here is labeled "no-copula-type". Besides "adjectives", certain bare "nouns", "quantifiers", and for some speakers, even certain "prepositions" can move into voice and follow the no-copula-type.

Although sometimes "prepositions" can follow the no-copula-type, they normally require the copula-like form *ada*. The Indonesian *ada*-type is comparable to the English structure. The PP is the complement of the small clause, which requires the copula *ada* to be merged in Ev and then moved to voice. *Ada* behaves verbally. Nevertheless, *ada* can be omitted. Thus, one must differentiate between two underlying structures for an *ada*-less sentence: structure of the *ada*-type with elided *ada* or the no-copula structure. The data provides a strong tendency towards the *ada*-type.

The third and last strategy found for Indonesian copula clauses is the *adalah*-type. Its general structure is comparable to both the English structure and the *ada*-type since we have a small clause with Ev[149] and voice on top of it. However, the status of *adalah* is substantially different from both *ada* and the English copula *be*. In contrast to *ada* (and English *be*), which are verbal forms (merged into Ev) that can only occur with PP-predicates, *adalah* is a non-verbal form that is not even a part of syntax in its narrow sense. *Adalah* insertion is a PF strategy to avoid ambiguity or provide a better prosodic flow. It is highly optional and normally occurs with DP-predicates. When *adalah* occurs, it is inserted in T.

---

148 For verbal forms we would often find an Ev-head here.
149 For Indonesian, Stat would be possible as well. However, to similize it to the English structure, Ev is chosen.

In conclusion, for Indonesian, there are three different strategies, the no-copula-type (normally for 'adjectives'), the *ada*-type (normally for PPs), and the *adalah*-type (normally for DPs).

These findings were implemented and applied to an experiment with Indonesian learners of English. The goal was to test whether these differences would make competition effects visible in certain error patterns. If the items where Indonesian and English show structural differences show a higher error rate, competition from L1 should be a crucial factor. Since the test was set up so that all test items were ungrammatical English sentences with omitted copula *be*, the major question was in which environment Indonesian competition would lead to higher acceptability of these ungrammatical sentences (more positive grammaticality judgments). Two effects were found: a T-effect caused by T-adverbs and a structural effect produced by underlying no-copula structures in Indonesian.

The first effect, the T-effect, is based on the substantial difference between the English verbal copula *be* and the non-verbal PF-strategy *adalah* in Indonesian; *be* is realized in the v-layer, *adalah* is inserted in T. English adverbs such as *already* or *still* correlate in their translation to Indonesian T-auxiliaries, for instance, *sudah* and *masih*, which are realized in T. As a consequence, these T-adverbs are in complementary distribution to the copula *adalah*, because they compete for the same position, T. Therefore these T-adverbs have an effect on the omission of the copula *be* for Indonesian learners of English. This effect, however, is only detectable if the adverbs occupy the pre-predicate position. In sentence-initial or sentence-final position, no such effect could be found. Hence, the effect must be caused by structural competition for the T-position between adverb and copula; however, it is only available if the identical linear order triggers the T-reading to the Indonesian counterpart, namely at the second position (between subject and predicate).

The second effect is visible when there is an underlying no-copula structure in the Indonesian language. This is generally the case if the predicate is adjectival. Since for PP-and DP-predicates, there are always copula structures (*ada*-type, *adalah*-type) available, and in case of competition with a no-copula-structure, these representations are generally preferable, the omission rate of the copula in English sentences with adjectival predicates was higher than for PP- or DP-predicates.

In general, both effects can and should be explained by the impossibility of inserting a copula in the structure, either because the potential copula position (here T) is filled by an overt item (a T-adverb) or because no copula position is available (no-copula-structure). In conclusion, both effects are based on syntactic differences between English and Indonesian. Therefore, the differences outlined in this work between Indonesian and English non-eventive predicates provide competition for the Indonesian learner of English.

References

Adger, David. 2003. *Core Syntax: A Minimalist Approach.* Oxford: Oxford University Press.
Adger, David and Gillian Ramchand. 2003. Predication and equation. *Linguistic Inquiry* 34(3). 325–359.
Agustin, Yulia. 2015. Kedudukan bahasa Inggris sebagai bahasa pengantar dalam dunia pendidikan [Status of English as the language of instruction in the world of education]. *Deiksis* 3(4). 354–364.
Aldridge, Edith. 2002. Nominalization and wh-movement in Seediq and Tagalog. *Language and Linguistics* 3(2). 393–426.
Alwi, Hasan, Soenjono Dardjowidjojo, Hans Lapoliwa and Anton M. Moeliono. 2003. *Tata Bahasa Baku Bahasa Indonesia* [Grammar of Standard Indonesian]. Jakarta: Balai Pustaka.
Amaral, Luiz and Tom Roeper. 2014. Multiple grammars and second language representation. *Second Language Research* 30(1). 3–36.
An, Duk-Ho. 2007. *Syntax at the PF Interface: Prosodic Mapping, Linear Order, and Deletion.* Storrs, Connecticut: University of Connecticut.
Anwar, Khaidir. 1980. *Indonesian: The Development and Use of a National Language.* Yogyakarta: Gadjah Mada University Press.
Araki, Naoki. 2017. Chomsky's I-language and E-language. *Hiroshima Institute of Technology Research.* 17–24.
Arka, I. Wayan. 2013. On the typology and syntax of TAM in Indonesian. In John Bowden (ed.), *Tense, Aspect, Mood and Evidentiality in Languages of Indonesia*, 23–40. Jakarta: Atma Jaya Catholic University of Indonesia, Pusat Kajian Bahasa dan Budaya.
Arthur, Bradford. 1980. Gauging the boundaries of second language competence: a study of learner judgments. *Language Learning* 30(1). 177–194.
Badan Pusat Statistik. 2010. *Sensus Penduduk 2010* [Census 2010]. Jakarta: BPS.
Baker, Mark C. 1997. Thematic roles and syntactic structure. In Liliane Haegeman (ed.), *Elements of Grammar*, 73–137. Dordrecht: Kluwer.
Baker, Mark C. 2003. *Lexical Categories: Verbs, Nouns and Adjectives*, Cambridge: Cambridge University Press.
Bauke, Leah S. 2018. Exhaustivity interpretations in second language acquisition. In Bart Hollebrandse, Jaiuen Kim, Ana Teresa Pérez Leroux and Petra Schulz (eds.), *TOM and Grammar. Thoughts on Mind and Grammar: A Festschrift in Honor of Tom Roeper*, 15–26. Washington DC: GLSA (Graduate Linguistics Student Association), Department of Linguistics.
Bauke, Leah S. 2020a. A grammar competition analysis of V2 phenomena in second language acquisition. In Horst Lohnstein and Antonios Tsiknakis (eds.), *Verb Second: Grammar Internal and Grammar External Interfaces*, 47–75. Berlin: De Gruyter.
Bauke, Leah S. 2020b. The role of V2 for L2 learners of English with L1 German/Norwegian/Dutch: A grammar competition analysis. In Gunther de Vogelaer, Dietha Koster and Torsten Leuschner (eds.), *German and Dutch in Contrast: Synchronic, Diachronic and Psycholinguistic Perspectives*, 241–270. Berlin: De Gruyter.
Behney, Jennifer and Emma Marsden. 2021. Introduction to SLA. In Susan M. Gass and Alison Mackey, *The Routledge Handbook of Second Language Acquisition and Corpora*, 37–50. Routledge.
Besier, Dominik. 2021. The Indonesian copula adalah: What it is (not) and why we do (not) need it. *NUSA: Linguistic studies of languages in and around Indonesia* (71). 21–40.
Blust, Robert. 2013. *The Austronesian Languages.* Canberra: Australian National University.

Boskovic, Zeljko and Jairo Nunes. 2007. The copy theory of movement: A view from PF. In Norbert Corver and Jairo Nunes (eds.), *The copy theory of movement*, 13–74. Amsterdam: John Benjamins Publishing Company.
Bowers, John. 1993. The syntax of predication. *Linguistic Inquiry* 24(4). 591–656.
Bowers, John. 2001. Predication. In Mark Baltin and Chris Collins (eds.), *The Handbook of Contemporary Syntactic Theory*, 299–333. Oxford: Blackwell Publishing Ltd.
Bowers, John. 2002. Transitivity. *Linguistic Inquiry* 33(2). 183–224.
Breul, Carsten and Dennis Wegner. 2017. German and English past participles in perfect and passive contexts: An identity view. *Sprachwissenschaft* 42(1). 1–58.
Broekhuis, Hans and Leonie Cornips. 2012. The verb krijgen 'to get' as an undative verb. *Linguistics* 50(6). 1205–1249.
Bybee, Joan L., Revere Dale Perkins and William Pagliuca. 1994. *The Evolution of Grammar: Tense, Aspect, and Modality in the Languages of the World*. Chicago: University of Chicago Press.
Carnie, Andrew. 1997. Two types of non-verbal predication in Modern Irish. *Canadian Journal of Linguistics/Revue canadienne de linguistique* 42(1–2). 57–73.
Carnie, Andrew. 2007. *Syntax: A Generative Introduction*. Oxford: Blackwell Publishing.
Carson, Jana Cécile. 2000. *The Semantics of Number in Malay Noun Phrases*. Calgary: University of Calgary, unpublished master thesis.
Chang, Henry Y. 1997. *Voice, Case, and Agreement in Seediq and Kavalan*. Hsinchu, Taiwan: National Tsing Hua University.
Chomsky, Noam. 1957. *Syntactic Structure*. The Hague: Mouton.
Chomsky, Noam. 1965. *Aspects of the Theory of Syntax*, Cambridge, Massachussetts: MIT Press.
Chomsky, Noam. 1968. *Remarks on Nominalization*. Bloomington: Indiana University Linguistics Club.
Chomsky, Noam. 1972. *Language and Mind*, enlarged edn. New York: Harcourt Brace Jovanovich.
Chomsky, Noam. 1982. *Some Concepts and Consequences of the Theory of Government and Binding*. Cambridge, Massachusetts: MIT Press.
Chomsky, Noam. 1986. *Knowledge of Language: Its Nature, Origin, and Use*. Westport, CT: Greenwood Publishing Group.
Chomsky, Noam. 1993. *Lectures on Government and Binding: The Pisa Lectures*. Berlin: Walter de Gruyter.
Chomsky, Noam. 1995. *The Minimalist Program*. Cambridge, Massachusetts: MIT Press.
Chomsky, Noam. 1999. Derivation by phase. *MIT Occasional Papers in Linguistics* 18.
Chomsky, Noam. 2000. Minimalist inquiries: The framework. In Roger Martin, David Michaels and Juan Uriagereka (eds.), *Step by Step: Essays on Minimalist Syntax in Honor of Howard Lasnik*, 89–156. Cambridge, Massachusetts: MIT Press.
Chomsky, Noam. 2008. On phases. *Current Studies in Linguistics Series* 45. 133–166.
Chung, Sandra. 2008. Indonesian clause structure from an Austronesian perspective. *Lingua* 118(10). 1554–1582.
Cinque, Guglielmo. 1999. *Adverbs and Functional Heads: A Cross-linguistic Perspective*. Oxford: Oxford University Press.
Citko, Barbara. 2014. *Phase Theory: An Introduction*. Cambridge: Cambridge University Press.
Cohn, Abigail C. 1989. Stress in Indonesian and bracketing paradoxes. *Natural Language & Linguistic Theory* 7(2). 167–216.
Cole, Peter and Min-Jeong Son. 2004. The argument structure of verbs with the suffix -kan in Indonesian. *Oceanic Linguistics* 43(2). 339–364.
Collins, Chris. 2002. Eliminating labels. In Samuel David Epstein and T. Daniel Seely (eds.), *Derivation and Explanation in the Minimalist Program*, 42–64. Oxford: Blackwell Publishing Ltd.

Comrie, Bernard. 1976. *Aspect: An Introduction to the Study of Verbal Aspect and Related Problems.* Cambridge: Cambridge University Press.
Comrie, Bernard. 1985. *Tense.* Cambridge: Cambridge University Press.
Corder, Stephen Pit. 1967. The significance of learner's errors. *International Review of Applied Linguistics in Language Teaching* 5(1–4). 161–170.
Corder, Stephen Pit. 1971. Describing the language learner's language. *Interdisciplinary Approaches to Language.* 57–64.
Croft, William. 1991. *Syntactic Categories and Grammatical Relations: The Cognitive Organization of Information.* Chicago: University of Chicago Press.
Cumming, Susanna. 1991. *Functional Change: The Case of Malay Constituent Order.* The Hague: Mouton de Gruyter.
Curnow, Timothy Jowan. 2000. Towards a cross-linguistic typology of copula constructions. In John Henderson (ed.), *Proceedings of the 1999 Conference of the Australian Linguistic Society*, Perth.
Dardjowidjojo, Soenjono. 1971. The men-, men-kan and men-i verbs in Indonesian. *Philippine Journal of Linguistics* 2(2). 71–84.
Dardjowidjojo, Soenjono. 1983. A classifier, itu,-nya, or none of the above: the way the Indonesian mind operates. In Soenjono Dardjowidjojo and John W. M. Verhaar (eds.), *Miscellaneous Studies of Indonesian and Other Languages in Indonesia*, 27–40. Jakarta: Science Research Associates.
Dardjowidjojo, Soenjono. 2003. *Rampai Bahasa, Pendidikan, Dan Budaya: Kumpulan Esai Soejono Dardjowidjojo* [Potpourri of language, education and culture: essay collection of Soejono Dardjowijojo]. Jakarta: Yayasan Obor.
Davies, William D. and Craig A. Dresser. 2005. The structure of Javanese and Madurese determiner phrases. In Jeffrey Heinz and Dimitris Ntelitheos (eds.), *Proceedings of AFLA XII*, 57–72. Los Angeles: UCLA Working Papers in Linguistics.
Degraff, Michel Anne Frederic. 1992. *Creole Grammars and Acquisition of Syntax: The Case of Haitian.* Philadelphia: University of Pennsylvania dissertation.
Den Dikken, Marcel. 2006. *Relators and Linkers.* Cambridge, Massachusetts: MIT Press.
Doherty, Cathal. 1996. Clausal structure and the Modern Irish copula. *Natural Language & Linguistic Theory* 14(1). 1–46.
Donnellan, Keith S. 1966. Reference and definite descriptions. *The Philosophical Review* 75(3). 281–304.
Dowty, David. 1979. *Word Meaning and Montague Grammar: The Semantics of Verbs and Times in Generative Semantics and in Montague's PTQ.* Dordrecht: Springer Science & Business Media.
Dowty, David. 1991. Thematic proto-roles and argument selection. *Language* 67(3). 547–619.
Eid, Mushira. 1983. The copula function of pronouns. *Lingua* 59(2–3). 197–207.
Ellis, Rod. 1991. Grammatically judgments and second language acquisition. *Studies in second language acquisition* 13(2), 161–186.
Ellis, Rod. 2004. The definition and measurement of L2 explicit knowledge. *Language learning* 54(2), 227–275.
Ellis, Rod. 2005. Measuring implicit and explicit knowledge of a second language: A psychometric study. *Studies in second language acquisition* 27(2), 141–172.
Ernst, Thomas. 1992. The phrase structure of English negation. *The Linguistic Review* 9(2). 109–144.
Falk, Yehuda N. 2004. The Hebrew present-tense copula as a mixed category. In Miriam Butt and Tracy Holloway King (eds.), *Proceedings of the LFG04 Conference*, 226–246. Canterbury: CSLI Publications.
Ferguson, Charles A. 1959. Diglossia. *Word* 15(2). 325–340.
Feuge, Kerstin. 1991. *Die Dichotomie "Aktiv-Passiv" in Grammatiken und sprachwissenschaftlichen Untersuchungen der Bahasa Indonesia.* Münster: LIT Verlag.

Fishman, Joshua A. 1967. Bilingualism with and without diglossia; diglossia with and without bilingualism. *Journal of Social Issues* 23(2). 29–38.

Fisiak, Jacek. 1980. *Theoretical Issues in Contrastive Linguistics*. Amsterdam: John Benjamins Publishing.

Fisiak, Jacek, Maria Lipińska-Grzegorek and Tadeusz Zabrocki. 1978. *An Introductory English-Polish Contrastive Grammar*. Warsaw: Państ Wydaw Naukowe.

Foley, William A. 1976. *Comparative Syntax in Austronesian*. Berkeley: University of California dissertation.

Foley, William A. and Robert D. van Valin. 1985. Information packaging in the clause. *Language Typology and Syntactic Description* 1. 282–364.

Fortin, Catherine R. 2006. Reconciling meng- and NP movement in Indonesian. In Zhenya Antic, Charles B. Chang, Clare S. Sandy and Maziar Toosarvandani (eds.), *BLS 32: Special Session on the Languages and Linguistics of Oceania*, 47–58. Berkeley: Berkeley Linguistics Society.

Frank, Robert. 2004. *Phrase Structure Composition and Syntactic Dependencies*. Cambridge, Massachusetts: MIT Press.

Fries, Charles C. 1945. *Teaching and Learning English as a Foreign Language*. Ann Arbor: University of Michigan Press.

Furihata, Masashi. 2006. An acoustic study on intonation of nominal sentences in Indonesian. In Yuji Kawaguchi, Ivan Fónagy and Tsunekazu Moriguchi (eds.), *Prosody and Syntax: Cross-linguistic Perspectives*, 303–325. Amsterdam: John Benjamins Publishing.

Gass, Susan M. 1994. The reliability of second language grammaticality judgments. In Elaine E. Tarone, Susan M. Gass and Andrew D. Cohen (eds.), *Research Methodology in Second-language Acquisition*, 303–322. Hillsdale, New Jersey: Lawrence Erlbaum.

Geist, Ljudmila. 2006. *Die Kopula und ihre Komplemente: Zur Kompositionlität in Kopulasätzen*. Tübingen: Max Niemeyer Verlag.

Geist, Ljudmila. 2008. Predication and equation in copular sentences: Russian vs. English. In Ileana Comorovski and Klaus van Heusinger (eds.), *Existence: Semantics and Syntax*, 79–105. Dordrecht: Springer.

Ghomeshi, Jila. 1997. Non-projecting nouns and the ezafe: construction in Persian. *Natural Language & Linguistic Theory* 15(4). 729–788.

Gil, David. 2008. How complex are isolating languages. In Matti Miestamo, Kaius Sinnemäki and Fred Karlsson (eds.), *Language Complexity: Typology, Contact, Change*, 109–131. Amsterdam: John Benjamins Publishing.

Grangé, Philippe. 2011. Aspect in Indonesian: Free markers versus affixed or clitic markers. In Asako Shiohara (ed.), *Proceedings of the International Workshop on TAM and Evidentiality in Indonesian Languages*, 43–63. Fuchu: Research Institute for Languages and Cultures of Asia and Africa Tokyo University of Foreign Studies.

Grangé, Philippe. 2013. Aspect in Indonesian: Free markers versus bound markers. In John Bowden (ed.), *Tense, Aspect, Mood and Evidentiality in Languages of Indonesia*, 57–79. Jakarta: Atma Jaya Catholic University of Indonesia, Pusat Kajian Bahasa dan Budaya.

Grice, Paul. 1975. Logic and conversation. In Peter Cole and Jerry L. Morgan (eds.), *Speech Acts*, 41–58. Leiden: Brill.

Grimshaw, Jane. 1990. *Argument Structure*. Cambridge, Massachusetts: MIT Press..

Guilfoyle, Eithne, Henrietta Hung and Lisa Travis. 1992. Spec of IP and Spec of VP: Two subjects in Austronesian languages. *Natural Language & Linguistic Theory* 10(3). 375–414.

Gutiérrez, Xavier. 2013. The construct validity of grammaticality judgment tests as measures of implicit and explicit knowledge. *Studies in second language acquisition* 35(3). 423–449.

Haegeman, Liliane and Terje Lohndal. 2010. Negative concord and (multiple) agree: A case study of West Flemish. *Linguistic Inquiry* 41(2). 181–211.

Hale, Ken and Samuel Jay Keyser. 1998. The basic elements of argument structure. *MIT Working Papers in Linguistics* 32. 73–118.

Hale, Ken and Samuel Jay Keyser. 2002. *Prolegomenon to a Theory of Argument Structure*. Cambridge, Massachusetts: MIT Press.

Halim, Amran. 1975. *Intonation in Relation to Syntax in Bahasa Indonesia*. Jakarta: Djambatan.

Halle, Morris and Alec Marantz. 1993. Distributed morphology and the pieces of inflection. In Ken Hale and Samuel Jay Keyser (eds.), *The View from Building 20*, 111–176. Cambridge, Massachusetts: MIT Press.

Halle, Morris and Alec Marantz. 1994. Some key features of distributed morphology. *MIT Working Papers in Linguistics* 21. 275–288.

Harley, Heidi. 1995. *Subjects, Events, and Licensing*. Cambridge, Massachusetts: Massachusetts Institute of Technology dissertation.

Harley, Heidi and Rolf Noyer. 1999. Distributed morphology. *Glot International* 4(4). 3–9.

Haspelmath, Martin. 2015. The serial verb construction: Comparative concept and cross-linguistic generalizations. *Language and Linguistics* 17(3). 291–319.

Heggie, Lorie A. 1989. *The Syntax of Copular Structures*. Los Angeles: University of Southern California dissertation.

Hellwig, Birgit. 2010. Meaning and translation in linguistic fieldwork. *Studies in Language: International Journal sponsored by the Foundation "Foundations of Language"* 34(4). 802–831.

Heycock, Caroline. 1991. *Layers of Predication: The Non-lexical Syntax of Clauses*. Philadelphia: University of Pennsylvania dissertation.

Heycock, Caroline. 1994. *Layers of Predication: The Non-Lexical Syntax of Clauses*. New York: Garland.

Heycock, Caroline and Anthony Kroch. 1998. Inversion and equation in copular sentences. *ZAS Papers in Linguistics* 10. 71–87.

Heycock, Caroline and Anthony Kroch. 1999. Pseudocleft connectedness: Implications for the LF interface level. *Linguistic Inquiry* 30(3). 365–397.

Higgins, R. F. 1979. *The Pseudo-Cleft Construction in English*. London: Routledge.

Himmelmann, Nikolaus P. 2008. Lexical categories and voice in Tagalog. In Peter Austin and Simon Musgrave (eds.), *Voice and Grammatical Relations in Austronesian Languages*, 247–293. Stanford: CSLI.

Hopper, Paul J. 1972. Verbless stative sentences in Indonesian. In John W. M. Verhaar (ed.), *The Verb 'Be'and its Synonyms: Part V*, 115–152. Berlin: Springer.

Hopper, Paul J. 1983. Ergative, passive, and active in Malay narrative. In Flora Klein-Andreu (ed.), *Discourse Perspectives on Syntax*, 67–88. New York: Academic Press.

Ionin, Tania. 2013. Morphosyntax. In Julia Herschensohn and Martha Young-Scholten (eds.), *The Cambridge Handbook of Second Language Acquisition*, 505–528. Cambridge: Cambridge University Press.

Isac, Daniela and Allison Kirk. 2008. The split DP hypothesis evidence from Ancient Greek. *Rivista di Grammatica Generativa* 33. 137–155.

Jackendoff, Ray S. 1990. *Semantic Structures*. Cambridge, Massachusetts: MIT Press, Cambridge, MA.

Jenkins, Jennifer. 2003. *World Englishes: A Resource Book for Students*. London: Psychology Press.

Jespersen, Otto. 1968 [1924]. *The Philosophy of Grammar*. London: George Allen and Unwin Ltd.

Johnson, Jacqueline and Elissa Newport. 1989. Critical period effects in second language learning: The influence of maturational state on the acquisition of English as a second language. *Cognitive Psychology* 21(1). 60–99.

Kachru, Braj B. 1992. *The Other Tongue: English across Cultures.* Champaign: University of Illinois Press.
Kähler, Hans. 1965. *Grammatik der Bahasa Indonesia*, 2nd edn. Wiesbaden: Harrassowitz.
Kariaeva, Natalia. 2004. Determiner Spreading in Modern Greek: Split-DP Hypothesis. Paper presented at the workshop on Greek syntax and the minimalist seduction, Reading.
Kartono, Giri. 1976. Kedudukan dan Fungsi Bahasa Asing di Indonesia [Status and function of foreign languages in Indonesia]. In Amran Halim (ed.), *Politik Bahasa Nasional 2*, 117–126. Jakarta: Pusat Pembinaan dan Pengembangan Bahasa, Departemen Pendidikan dan Kebudayaan, Jakarta.
Kaswanti Purwo, Bambang. 1983. Kata yang sebagai pengetat [The word yang as intensifier]. *Majalah Pembinaan Bahasa Indonesia* 4(3). 175–185.
Kaswanti Purwo, Bambang. 1984. The categorial system in contemporary Indonesian: Pronouns. In Bambang Kaswanti Purwo (ed.), *Towards a Description of Contemporary Indonesian: Preliminary Studies*, 55–73. Jakarta: Badan Penyelenggara Seri NUSA, Universitas Atma Jaya, Jakarta.
Kaswanti Purwo, Bambang. 1995. The two proto-types of ditransitive verbs: The Indonesian evidence. In Werner Abraham, Thomas Givón and Sandra A. Thompson (eds.), *Discourse, Grammar and Typology*, 77–99. Amsterdam: John Benjamins Publishing.
Kayne, Robert S. 1994. *The Antisymmetry of Syntax: Vol. 25.* Cambridge, Massachusetts: MIT Press.
KBBI. 2008. *Kamus Besar Bahasa Indonesia.* Jakarta: Balai Pustaka.
Kirk, Allison. 2007. *A Syntactic Account of Split DPs in Herodotus.* Montreal: Concordia University dissertation.
Klein, Wolfgang. 1994. *Time in Language.* London: Routledge.
König, Ekkehard and Bernd Kortmann. 1991. On the reanalysis of verbs as prepositions. In Gisa Rauh (ed.), *Approaches to Prepositions*, 109–125. Tübingen: Narr.
Krashen, Stephen. 1981. *Second Language Acquisition and Second Language Learning.* Pergamon Press Inc.
Kratzer, Angelika. 1996. Severing the external argument from its verb. In Johan Rooryck and Laurie Ann Zaring (eds.), *Phrase Structure and the Lexicon*, 109–137. Heidelberg: Springer.
Kroch, Anthony S. 1994. Morphosyntactic variation. In Katharine Beals (ed.), *Papers from the 30th Regional Meeting of the Chicago Linguistic Society 1994*, 180–201. Chicago: Chicago Linguistic Society.
Kroch, Anthony S. 2001. Syntactic change. In Mark Baltin and Chris Collins (eds.), *The Handbook of Contemporary Syntactic Theory*, 699–229. Malden, Massachusetts: Blackwell.
Kroeger, Paul. 2007. Morphosyntactic vs. morphosemantic functions of Indonesian -kan. In Annie Zaenen (ed.), *Architectures, Rules, and Preferences: Variations on Themes of Joan W. Bresnan*, 229–251. Stanford: CSLI.
Krzeszowski, Tomasz P. 1980. Contrastive generative grammar. In Jacek Fisiak (ed.), *Theoretical Issues in Contrastive Linguistics*, 185–192. Amsterdam: John Benjamins Publishing.
Lado, Robert. 1957. *Linguistics across Cultures: Applied Linguistics for Language Teachers.* Ann Arbor: University of Michigan Press.
Lado, Robert. 1964. *Language teaching: A scientific approach.* New York: McGraw-Hill.
Lahousse, Karen. 2009. Specificational sentences and the influence of information structure on (anti) connectivity effects. *Journal of Linguistics* 45(1). 139–166.
Lakoff, George. 1965. *On the Nature of Syntactic Irregularity.* Cambridge, Massachusetts: Harvard University dissertation.
Laksman, Myrna. 1994. Location of stress in Indonesian words and sentences. In Cecilia Odé and Vincent van Heuven (eds.), *Experimental Studies of Indonesian Prosody*, 108–139. Leiden: Vakgroep Talen en Culturen van Zuidoost-Azië en Oceanié, Leiden University.

Lapoliwa, Hans. 1981. *A Generative Approach to the Phonology of Bahasa Indonesia*. Canberra: Department of Linguistics, Research School of Pacific Studies, Australian National University.
Lardiere, Donna. 2009a. Some thoughts on the contrastive analysis of features in second language acquisition. *Second Language Research* 25(2). 173–227.
Lardiere, Donna. 2009b. Further thoughts on parameters and features in second language acquisition: A reply to peer comments on Lardiere's 'Some thoughts on the contrastive analysis of features in second language acquisition' in SLR 25 (2). *Second Language Research* 25(3). 409–422.
Lauder, Allan. 2010. The status and function of English in Indonesia: A review of key factors. *Hubs-Asia* 12(1). 9–20.
Lee, W. R. 1968. Thoughts on contrastive linguistics in the context of language teaching. In James Alatis (ed.), *19th Annual Round Table: Contrastive Linguistics and its Pedagogical Implications*, 185–194. Washington DC: Georgetown University Press.
Lenneberg, Eric. 1967. The biological foundations of language. *Hospital Practice* 2(12). 59–67.
Leow, Ronald. 1996. Grammaticality judgment tasks and second-language development. *Georgetown University Round Table on Languages and Linguistics*. 126–139.
Levin, Beth and Malka Rappaport Hovav. 1995. *Unaccusativity: At the Syntax-lexical Semantics Interface*. Cambridge, Massachusetts: MIT Press.
Lindblom, Björn. 1990. Explaining phonetic variation: A sketch of the H&H theory. In William J. Hardcastle and Alain Marchal (eds.), *Speech Production and Speech Modelling*, 403–439. Heidelberg: Springer.
Lipinska, Maria. 1980. Contrastive analysis and the modern theory of language. In Jacek Fisiak (ed.), *Theoretical Issues in Contrastive Linguistics*, 127–184. Amsterdam: John Benjamins Publishing.
Löbner, Sebastian. 2013. *Understanding Semantics*. Abingdon: Routledge.
Loewen, Gina. 2011. *The Syntactic Structure of Noun Phrases in Indonesian*. Winnipeg: University of Manitoba master thesis.
Lord, Carol. 1973. Serial verbs in transition. *Studies in African linguistics* 4(3). 269–296.
Lowenberg, Peter H. 1991. English as an additional language in Indonesia. *World Englishes* 10(2). 127–138.
Macdonald, Roderick Ross. 1976. *Indonesian Reference Grammar*. Washington DC: Georgetown University Press.
Mahdi, Waruno. 1981. Some problems of the phonology of metropolitan Indonesian. *Bijdragen tot de Taal-, Land- en Volkenkunde* 137(4). 399–418.
Malinowski, Bronislaw. 1922. *Argonauts of the Western Pacific*. New York: Dutton.
Marantz, Alec. 1997. No escape from syntax: Don't try morphological analysis in the privacy of your own lexicon. *University of Pennsylvania Working Papers in Linguistics* 4(2). 201–225.
Marcellino, Maraden. 2015. English language teaching in Indonesia: A continuous challenge in education and cultural diversity. *TEFLIN Journal* 19(1). 57–69.
Matushansky, Ora. 2006. Head movement in linguistic theory. *Linguistic Inquiry* 37(1). 69–109.
Mead, David E. 1998. *Proto-Bungku-Tolaki: Reconstruction of its Phonology and Aspects of its Morphosyntax*. Houston: Rice University dissertation.
Mees, Constantinus Alting. 1969. *Tata bahasa dan Tata kalimat* [Grammar and Sentence Structure]. Kuala Lumpur: University of Malaya Press.
Meisel, Jürgen. 2011. *First and Second Language Acquisition: Parallels and Differences*. Cambridge: Cambridge University Press.
Meltzer-Asscher, Aya. 2011. *Adjectives and Argument Structure*. Tel Aviv: Tel Aviv University dissertation.
Meltzer-Asscher, Aya. 2012. The subject of adjectives: Syntactic position and semantic interpretation. *The Linguistic Review* 29(2). 149–189.

Merchant, Jason. 2011. Aleut case matters. In Etsuyo Yuasa, Tista Bagchi and Katharine Beals (eds.), *Pragmatics and Autolexical Grammar: In Honor of Jerry Sadock*, 193–210. Amsterdam: John Benjamins Publishing.
Mesthrie, Rajend. 2009. *Introducing Sociolinguistics*. Edinburgh: Edinburgh University Press.
Mikkelsen, Line. 2004. Reexamining Higgins' taxonomy: A split in the identificational class. LSA Annual Meeting, Boston.
Mikkelsen, Line. 2005. *Copular Clauses: Specification, Predication and Equation*. Amsterdam: John Benjamins Publishing.
Moeljadi, David, Francis Bond and Luis Morgado da Costa. 2016. Basic copula clauses in Indonesian. *Proceeding of the Joint 2016 Conference on Head-driven Phrase Structure Grammar and Lexical Functional Grammar*. 442–456.
Mohd Nor, Yusof Md. 1989. *Antologi Enam Hikayat* [Anthology of six Sagas]. Selangor: Fajar Bakti.
Moro, Andrea. 1997. *The Raising of Predicates: Predicative Noun Phrases and the Theory of Clause Structure*. Cambridge: Cambridge University Press.
Musgrave, Simon. 2001. *Non-Subject Arguments in Indonesian*. Melbourne: University of Melbourne dissertation.
Mustaffa, Amir Rashad bin. 2018. Silent syntactic structures in Malay: Copular clauses. *Journal of Modern Languages* 28. 20–43.
Napoli, Donna Jo. 1993. *Syntax: Theory and Oroblems*. Oxford: Oxford University Press.
Nespor, Marina and Irene Vogel. 1986. *Prosodic Phonology*. Dordrecht: Foris.
Nomoto, Hiroki. 2013. On the optionality of grammatical markers: A case study of voice marking in Malay/Indonesian. In K. Alexander Adelaar (ed.), *Voice Variation in Austronesian Languages of Indonesia*, 121–143. Jakarta: Atma Jaya Catholic University of Indonesia, Pusat Kajian Bahasa dan Budaya.
Nuriah, Zahroh. 2004. *The Relation of Verbal IndonesianAaffixes meN- and -kan with Argument Structure*. Utrecht: Utrecht University master thesis.
Odé, Cecilia. 1994. On the perception of prominence in Indonesian. In Cecilia Odé and Vincent van Heuven (eds.), *Experimental Studies of Indonesian Prosody*, 27–107. Leiden: Vakgroep Talen en Culturen van Zuidoost-Azié en Oceanié, Leiden University.
Oetomo, Dede. 1990. The Bahasa Indonesia of the middle class. *Prisma* 50. 68–79.
Pane, Armijn. 1950. *Mencari Sendi Baru Tata Bahasa Indonesia* [Looking for a new joint in Indonesian]. Jakarta: Balai Pustaka.
Perlmutter, David and Paul Postal. 1984. The 1-advancement exclusiveness law. *Studies in Relational Grammar* 2. 81–125.
Pollock, Jean-Yves. 1989. Verb movement, universal grammar, and the structure of IP. *Linguistic Inquiry* 20(3). 365–424.
Pustet, Regina. 2003. *Copulas: Universals in the Categorization of the Lexicon*. Oxford: Oxford University Press.
Radford, Andrew. 2004. *Minimalist Syntax: Exploring the Structure of English*. Cambridge: Cambridge University Press.
Radford, Andrew. 2009. *An Introduction to English Sentence Structure*. Cambridge: Cambridge University Press.
Ramchand, Gillian Catriona. 2008. *Verb Meaning and the Lexicon: A First Phase Syntax*. Cambridge: Cambridge University Press.
Rankin, Tom. 2014. Variational learning in L2: The transfer of L1 syntax and parsing strategies in the interpretation of wh-questions by L1 German learners of L2 English. *Linguistic Approaches to Bilingualism* 4(4). 432–461.

Rauh, Gisa. 1995. *Englische Präpositionen zwischen lexikalischen und funktionalen Kategorien*. Düsseldorf: Sonderforschungsbereich 282.

Rauh, Gisa. 1996. Zur Struktur von Präpositionalphrasen im Englischen. *Zeitschrift für Sprachwissenschaft* 15(2). 178–230.

Rauh, Gisa. 2010. *Syntactic Categories: Their Identification and Description in Linguistic Theories*, Oxford: Oxford University Press.

Rauh, Gisa. 2015. Englische Präpositionen zwischen lexikalischen und funktionalen Kategorien. In Elisabeth Löbel and Gisa Rauh (eds.), *Lexikalische Kategorien und Merkmale*, 125–168. Tübingen: Max Niemeyer Verlag.

Rein, Kurt. 1983. *Einführung in die kontrastive Linguistik*. Darmstadt: WBG.

Reinhart, Tanya. 2003. The theta system: An overview. *Theoretical Linguistics* 28(3). 229–290.

Richards, Jack. 1971. Error analysis and second language strategies. *English Language Teaching* 25. 115–135.

Richards, Norvin. 2001. *Movement in Language: Interactions and Architectures*. Oxford: Oxford Linguistics.

Ringbom, Hakan. 1980. On the distinction between second-language acquisition and foreign-language learning. *AFinLAn vuosikirja*. 37–44.

Rini, Julia Eka. 2014. English in Indonesia. *Beyond Words* 2(2). 19–39.

Rizzi, Luigi. 1990. *Relativized Minimality*. Cambridge, Massachusetts: MIT Press.

Rizzi, Luigi. 1997. The fine structure of the left periphery. In Liliane Haegeman (ed.), *Elements of Grammar: Handbook in Generative Syntax*, 281–337. Heidelberg: Springer.

Roeper, Thomas W. 1999. Universal bilingualism. *Bilingualism: Language and Cognition* 2(3). 169–186.

Roeper, Thomas W. 2016. Multiple grammars and the logic of learnability in second language acquisition. *Frontiers in Psychology* 7.

Rosen, Carol G. 1984. The interface between semantic roles and initial grammatical relations. *Studies in Relational Grammar* 2. 38–77.

Ross, John R. 1967. *Constraints on Variables in Syntax*. Cambridge, Massachusetts: Massachusetts Institute of Technology thesis.

Rothman, Jason. 2008. Aspect selection in adult L2 Spanish and the Competing Systems Hypothesis: When pedagogical and linguistic rules conflict. *Languages in Contrast* 8(1). 74–106.

Rothman, Jason, Jorge Gonzalez Alonso and Eloi Puig-Mayenco. 2019. *Third Language Acquisition and Linguistic Transfer: Vol. 163*. Cambridge: Cambridge University Press.

Rothman, Jason and Roumyana Slabakova. 2018. The generative approach to SLA and its place in modern second language studies. *Studies in Second Language Acquisition* 40(2). 417–442.

Rothstein, Susan. 1983. *The Syntactic Forms of Predication*. Cambridge, Massachusetts: Massachusetts Institute of Technology dissertation.

Rothstein, Susan. 2001. *Predicates and their Subjects*. Dordrecht: Kluwer.

Sadler, Louisa and Douglas J. Arnold. 1994. Prenominal adjectives and the phrasal/lexical distinction. *Journal of Linguistics* 30(1). 187–226.

Sauter, Kim. 2002. *Transfer and Access to Universal Grammar in Adult Second Language Acquisition*. Groningen: University of Groningen dissertation.

Schachter, Paul. 1995. Tagalog. In Joachim Jacobs, Arnim von Stechow, Wolfgang Sternefeld and Theo Vennemann (eds.), *Syntax: An International Handbook of Contemporary Research*, 1418–1430. Berlin: De Gruyter.

Schwartz, Bonnie D. 2004. Why child L2 acquisition?. *LOT Occasional Series* 3. 47–66.

Schwartz, Bonnie D. and Rex A. Sprouse. 1994. Word Order and nominative case in non-native language acquisition: A longitudinal study of (L1 Turkish) German interlanguage. In Teun Hoekstra and Bonnie D. Schwartz (eds.), *Language Acquisition Studies in Generative Grammar*, 317–368. Amsterdam: Benjamins.

Schwartz, Bonnie D. and Rex A. Sprouse. 1996. L2 cognitive states and the full transfer/full access model. *Second Language Research* 12(1). 40–72.

Selinker, Larry. 1969. Language transfer. *General Linguistics* 9(2). 67–92.

Selinker, Larry. 1972. Interlanguage. *International Review of Applied Linguistics in Language Teaching* 10(1–4). 209–232.

Shiohara, Asako. 2012. Applicatives in Standard Indonesian. *Senri Ethnological Studies* 77. 59–76.

Simons, Gary F. and Charles D. Fennig. 2017. *Ethnologue: Languages of the Americas and the Pacific*, 20th edn. Dallas: SIL Academic Publications.

Sirk, Ülo. 1978. Problems of high-level subgrouping in Austronesian. In Stephen A. Wurm and Lois Carrington (eds.), *Second International Conference on Austronesian Linguistics: Proceedings*, 255–273. Canberra: Pacific Linguistics.

Slabakova, Roumyana. 2016. *Second Language Acquisition*. Oxford: Oxford University Press.

Sneddon, James Neil. 1996. *Indonesian: A Comprehensive Grammar*. London: Routledge.

Sneddon, James Neil. 2003a. *The Indonesian Language: Its History and Role in Modern Society*. Sydney: UNSW Press.

Sneddon, James Neil. 2003b. Diglossia in Indonesian. *Bijdragen tot de Taal-, Land- en Volkenkunde* 159(4). 519–549.

Sneddon, James Neil, K. Alexander Adelaar, Dwi N. Djenar and Michael Ewing. 2012. *Indonesian: A Comprehensive Grammar*. London: Routledge.

Soh, Hooi Ling. 2010. Voice and aspect: Some notes from Malay. In Daigaku, Tokyo Gaikokugo Daigaku & Ajia Afurika Gengo Bunka Kenkyūjo. *Proceedings of the workshop on Indonesian-type voice system*, 25–35. Tokyo: Research Institute for Languages and Cultures of Asia and Africa, Tokyo University of Foreign Studies.

Soh, Hooi Ling and Hiroki Nomoto. 2009. Progressive aspect, the verbal prefix meN-, and stative sentences in Malay. *Oceanic Linguistics* 48(1). 148–171.

Soh, Hooi Ling and Hiroki Nomoto. 2011. The Malay verbal prefix meN- and the unergative/unaccusative distinction. *Journal of East Asian Linguistics* 20(1). 77–106.

Son, Minjeong and Peter Cole. 2008. An event-based account of -kan constructions in Standard Indonesian. *Language* 84(1). 120–160.

Stalnaker, Robert. 1974. Pragmatic Presuppositions. in Milton K. Munitz and Peter Unger (eds.), *Semantics and Philosophy*, 197–214. New York: New York University Press.

Stalnaker, Robert. 1978. Assertion. In Peter Cole (ed.), *Syntax and Semantics: Pragmatics*, 315–332. New York: Academic Press.

Stassen, Leon M.H. 2008. Zero copula for predicate nominals. In Martin Haspelmath, Matthews S. Dryer, David Gil and Bernard Comrie (eds.), *The World Atlas of Language Structures*, 486–489. New York: Oxford University Press.

Stowell, Timothy. 1978. What was there before there was there. In Donka Farkas, Wesley M. Jacobsen and Karol W. Todrys (eds.), *Papers from the 14th Regional Meeting of the Chicago Linguistic Society 1978*, 458–471 Chicago: Chicago Linguistic Society.

Stowell, Timothy. 1981. *Origins of Phrase Structure*. Cambridge, Massachusetts: Massachusetts Institute of Technology dissertation.

Suyanto, Suyanto. 2017. Dominasi Pemakaian Bahasa Jawa di Provinsi Lampung Berdasar Data Sensus Penduduk 2010: Ancangan Demografilinguistik [Dominant use of Javanese in Lampung province according to the census 2010: demographilinguistic designation]. In *Prosiding PIBSI XXXIX*, 366–376. Semarang: Fasindo Press.
Tadmor, Uri. 2007. Grammatical borrowing in Indonesian. In Yaron Matras and Jeanette Sakel (eds.), *Grammatical Borrowing in Cross-linguistic Perspective*, 301–328. The Hague: Mouton de Gruyter.
Travis, Lisa. 1984. *Parameters and Effects of Word Order Variation*. Cambridge, Massachusetts: Massachusetts Institute of Technology dissertation.
Travis, Lisa. 1988. The syntax of adverbs. *McGill Working Papers in Linguistics* 20. 280–310.
Tremblay, Annie. 2005. Theoretical and methodological perspectives on the use of grammaticality judgment tasks in linguistic theory. *Second Language Studies* 24(1), 129–167.
Vafaee, Payman, Yuichi Suzuki & Ilina Kachisnke. 2017. Validating grammaticality judgment tests: Evidence from two new psycholinguistic measures. *Studies in Second Language Acquisition* 39(1), 59–95.
Vamarasi, Marit Kana. 1999. *Grammatical Relations in Bahasa Indonesia*. Canberra: Department of Linguistics, Research School of Pacific Studies, Australian National University.
van Buren, Paul. 1980. Contrastive analysis. In Jacek Fisiak (ed.), *Theoretical Issues in Contrastive Linguistics*, 83–118. Amsterdam: John Benjamins Publishing.
van Gerth Wijk, D. 1985. *Spraakleer der Maleische Taal* [Grammar of the Malay language]. reprinted, Batavia: G. Kolff & Co.
van Minde, Don. 2008. The pragmatic function of Malay yang. *Journal of Pragmatics* 40(11). 1982–2001.
van Ophuijsen, Charles Adriaan. 1915. *Maleische Spraakkunst* [Malay Grammar]. Leiden: van Doesburgh.
van Riemsdijk, Henk C. 1990. Functional prepositions. In Harm Pinkster and Inge Genee (eds.), *Unity in Diversity: Papers Presented to Simon C. Dik on his 50th Birthday*, 229–242. The Hague: Mouton de Gruyter.
van Zanten, Ellen and Vincent J. van Heuven. 2004. Word stress in Indonesian: Fixed or free. *NUSA: Linguistic Studies on Indonesian and Other Languages in Indonesia* 53. 1–20.
Vendler, Zeno. 1967. *Linguistics in Philosophy*. Ithaca, New York: Cornell University Press.
Verhaar, John W. M. 1981. *On the Syntax of 'yang' in Indonesia*. Jakarta: National Center for Language Development, Ministry of Education and Culture.
Verhaar, John W. M. 1988. Phrase syntax in contemporary Indonesian: noun phrases. In Bambang Kaswanti Purwo (ed.), *Towards a Description of Contemporary Indonesian: Preliminary Studies III*, 1–45. Jakarta: Badan Penyelenggara Seri NUSA, Universitas Atma Jaya.
Wenguo, Pan and Tham Wai Mun. 2007. *Contrastive Linguistics: History, Philosophy and Methodology*. London: Bloomsbury Academic.
Wurmbrand, Susi. 2012. The syntax of valuation in auxiliary-participle constructions. In Jaehoon Choi (ed.), *Proceeding of the 29th West Coast Conference on Formal Linguistics*, 245–254. Tucson: Cascadilla.
Yap, Foong Ha. 2011. Referential and non-referential uses of nominalization constructions in Malay. In Foong Ha Yap, Karen Grunow-Harsta and Janick Wrona (eds.), *Nominalization in Asian Languages*, 627–658. Amsterdam: John Benjamins Publishing.
Zamparelli, Roberto. 2000. *Layers in the Determiner Phrase*. Leiden: Taylor & Francis Ltd.
Zwarts, Joost. 1992. *X'Syntax – X'Semantics: On the interpretation of lexical and functional heads*. Utrecht: Utrecht University dissertation.

Appendix

Test 1

Kalimat[150]	benar[151]	salah[152]
1. Akik the father of two boys and a girl.	O	O
2. Ashley once belonged to a religious minority.	O	O
3. Barnie refused the fair offer already.	O	O
4. Barry must still do the dishes.	O	O
5. Boas poured the lady out a drink.	O	O
6. Britney quickly a very angry woman.	O	O
7. Bulan already a clever child for her age.	O	O
8. Charlie brought his mother a bunch of flowers round.	O	O
9. Definitely Angie a good mother for her twins.	O	O
10. Finley typed them out the essay.	O	O
11. Freddie handed the children the prizes out.	O	O
12. Harry looked after the annoying child once.	O	O
13. Harto still the most powerful man in Indonesia.	O	O
14. Jason not the first person to cry.	O	O
15. Definitely Mercy likes to smoke cigars.	O	O
16. Jeffrey often the loudest person in class.	O	O
17. Kevin threw the player the ball up.	O	O
18. Kingsley once depressed with his life.	O	O
19. Nicky the best player of her team already.	O	O
20. Often Titus has watched the sports event.	O	O
21. Oscar pinned me a poster up.	O	O
22. Rio wrote her his number down.	O	O
23. Ronny a good math teacher and a nice man.	O	O
24. Thomas rushed his wife down the street.	O	O
25. Tira plays well basketball.	O	O
26. Tulus easily the fastest boy in his class.	O	O
27. Whitney definitely a friendly person with humour.	O	O
28. Wilson supported his children generously to go to university.	O	O
29. Winda shortly hiked on a mountain.	O	O
30. Donald already the worst president of the USA.	O	O
31. Vini worked recently there.	O	O
32. Torie walked his daughter the aisle down.	O	O
33. Thedo lent him some books out.	O	O
34. Taufan not the winner of the election.	O	O
35. Sina brought them the results over.	O	O
36. Shirin handed her the medal down.	O	O
37. Rosie has already walked for hours.	O	O

---

150 *kalimat* = sentence
151 *benar* = correct
152 *salah* = wrong

(continued)

Kalimat	benar	salah
38. Ratu a mother of two children.	O	O
39. Phoebe can definitely sing beautifully.	O	O
40. Pearcy already had breakfast in the kitchen.	O	O
41. Once Marcy left her key on the table.	O	O
42. Often Darma a very nice and friendly person.	O	O
43. Myra plugged my mother in the television set.	O	O
44. Lara sold them back the books.	O	O
45. Lana hooked them up the sink.	O	O
46. Jackson probably the most annoying person here.	O	O
47. Indah often a great help to me.	O	O
48. Homer still works in America.	O	O
49. Gracie gave her last money to the poor freely.	O	O
50. Dewi still angry with her daughter.	O	O
51. Definitely Gary a good husband and loving father.	O	O
52. Certainly Gusti the best player in his team.	O	O
53. Cantik accidentally a mother of a girl.	O	O
54. Bobby went to the cinema often.	O	O
55. Bella not a nice person to talk to.	O	O
56. Bambang once the boyfriend of my sister.	O	O
57. Ashton wants to understand still the world.	O	O
58. Alfi sent the participants the documents out.	O	O
59. Normally Rina looks more beautiful than her friend.	O	O
60. Abbey still an important part of this family.	O	O
61. Abdul already tired after a hard day.	O	O
62. Alo passed the students out the exam papers.	O	O
63. Bettie wrote once a book with her father.	O	O
64. Bintang certainly a faithful friend to everybody.	O	O
65. Daisy the most beautiful person in this room.	O	O
66. Davie a good teacher of biology already.	O	O
67. Greta turned them the lights off.	O	O
68. Jared looks still younger than my younger sister.	O	O
69. Jimboy often drinks milk.	O	O
70. Kiki normally the first to finish an exam.	O	O
71. Lenny fell already in love with her boss.	O	O
72. Lori once a good math teacher in my school.	O	O
73. Nike wrote them out the summary of the novel.	O	O
74. Normally Ratna the teacher in this class.	O	O
75. Often Vera the first in the classroom.	O	O
76. Peter willingly the one to clean up the house.	O	O
77. Prila read the baby out the story.	O	O
78. Quickly Puspa went to Bali.	O	O
79. Refa can swim in the sea certainly.	O	O
80. Rosa handed him over the ball.	O	O

(continued)

Kalimat	benar	salah
81. Sahda willingly bought him the green book.	O	O
82. Tara not a true friend for me.	O	O
83. Terry has travelled often for days.	O	O
84. Tunda messed the parents the bed up.	O	O
85. Uci apparently has an old car.	O	O
86. Vivin cut Frank off a piece of cake.	O	O
87. Wendy often lucky in card games.	O	O

Test 2

Kalimat	benar	salah
1. Carey loves a middle-aged man with glasses.	O	O
2. Bagus a strong man with a big heart.	O	O
3. Mina marries a father of two girls.	O	O
4. Cinta meets the tallest guy she has ever seen.	O	O
5. Megan the doctor of my mother.	O	O
6. Amir calls the wife of his friend.	O	O
7. Chandra painted the wall red.	O	O
8. Penny hits a man naughty.	O	O
9. Intan beats the strongest opponent.	O	O
10. Rini exhausted from the race.	O	O
11. Matthew hated the one pass the exam early.	O	O
12. The issue Tyra stole the money.	O	O
13. Bernie fights a nasty flue for days.	O	O
14. The challenge that Askar cannot eat spicy food.	O	O
15. Mikey defeats his worst enemy.	O	O
16. Mary in her office in Chicago.	O	O
17. Cindy a businesswoman in Singapore.	O	O
18. Tegar sees the one come first.	O	O
19. Hafiz likes mother of twins.	O	O
20. Katie pounded the nail flat.	O	O
21. Ridwan tired all day.	O	O
22. Bakti the best student in class	O	O
23. Novan named I cute little bear.	O	O
24. Our objection that Ranti shouldn't leave London.	O	O
25. Jody hates the neighbour of her friend.	O	O
26. Achi proves she innocent.	O	O
27. Peggy wiped the kitchen table clean.	O	O
28. Johnny in Jakarta for a year.	O	O
29. Simon names her little mouse.	O	O
30. Her fear that Atar will die soon.	O	O
31. Mega a stewardess of a well-known airline.	O	O
32. Firman fought an enemy strong.	O	O
33. My hope that Patty will help me.	O	O
34. Kelly called me a big liar.	O	O
35. Novi married the daughter of his boss.	O	O
36. Lizzy angry at her mother	O	O
37. Howard supported the winner of the Olympic medal.	O	O
38. Dian liked a young lady from Canada.	O	O
39. Joko considered him a good friend	O	O
40. Robert the winner of the game.	O	O
41. The thing that Kolbe cannot come.	O	O
42. Ryan defeated best player in the tournament.	O	O

(continued)

Kalimat	benar	salah
43. Amy hit a very annoying person.	O	O
44. Udin in America for a visit.	O	O
45. His wish Nayla will marry him.	O	O
46. Malcolm met the president of Germany.	O	O
47. Nira the most attractive woman.	O	O
48. Wesley called policeman walking around.	O	O
49. Alif saw a beautiful woman in the garden.	O	O
51. Ricky happy with his girl-friend.	O	O
52. Jamie calls he a cheater.	O	O
53. Winston a member of the Nationalist Party.	O	O
54. Pingkan beated last year's winner.	O	O
55. Sarah loved a handsome prince.	O	O
56. Siska at the mall in Bandung.	O	O
57. Herby makes the floor dirty.	O	O
58. Morgan supports leader of the Democratic Party.	O	O
59. The problem Colin didn't call her.	O	O
60. Sammy considers they good colleagues.	O	O

Index

ada 162, 181–192, 201, 208–211, 215, 217–218, 222–223, 275, 281
ada-type 181–185
adalah 91–92, 162, 171–173, 178–179, 186–189, 190–200, 211–215, 222–223, 227, 245, 251, 254–257
adalah-type 174–176, 180–181, 219–222, 227, 266, 272–273, 276–277
adjectival predicates 154–159, 164–170, 267–268, 272
adjoin 23

ber- (goal voice) 54–55

CatP 29–30, 63, 154, 158
cause 26–27, 33–37, 50–52, 67–69, 144, 153, 203–204
classifier 45, 73, 74
C-layer 39, 115, 121–126
critical period 5
contrastive analysis 6–10
contrastive analysis hypothesis 6–8
copula 128–131, 133, 137–138, 140–141, 146–147, 150, 153–154, 155–159, 160, 162–163, 174–176, 180, 181–182, 184–200, 210–211, 212–215, 222–223, 227
copular clauses 127, 131–142

δP 30–33, 36, 63, 65, 85, 142, 149, 159, 215
determiner 83–87, 149, 147–153, 177
Distributed Morphology 20–21

efficiency tendency 46
EvP 31–32, 34–39, 63–64, 66, 72, 80, 141, 143–154, 158–160, 168, 182, 183, 189–190, 204, 210, 215–216, 227, 269–270
equation 132, 134, 136–140, 142, 162–163

feature reassembly hypothesis 3
focus 39, 101, 115, 118, 121–126, 213–214
full transfer/full access-hypothesis 9, 225
functional head 21–22

goal 26–27, 36–37, 49, 54–55, 59–61, 64–65, 68, 70, 172, 202–205, 209–210
grammar competition 9–10, 224–225
Grammaticality Judgement Task (GJT) 230–232

identificational clauses 132, 134
-i 57–62, 65–66, 203
Indonesian 12–16, 40–126, 161–215
 – Colloquial Indonesian 14–15, 86, 99, 121–122, 194–196, 237
Indonesian intonation 115–120, 121–122, 194–199
ini 67, 75–77, 85–88, 177, 194
itu 67, 77, 85–88, 177, 194

-kan 15, 47–49, 54, 57–62, 65–66, 166–167, 175, 186, 203

lexicon 20–21

masih 91–94, 96, 101–103, 106–108, 113, 123, 126, 172, 177, 185, 187–188, 190–191, 193, 214, 227, 241, 244–245, 251–253, 264, 265, 282
meN- (cause voice) 49–52
merge 21
move 22
ModP 155
multiple grammar 9–10, 224–225

no-copula type 131, 164–170, 172–173, 179–180, 216–217, 266–277, 278–279
nominal morphology in Indonesian 67–70
nominal predicates 147–154, 161–164, 171–176, 179–181, 273–276
non-eventive predicate 10–12, 127, 161–164, 215–222, 227–228, 273
non-verbal predicate 10–12, 37–38, 127, 142–147, 161, 215–222, 227–228, 273
-nya 83–86

PF (Phonological Form) 15, 20, 21, 35–37, 41, 46–47, 62–63, 104, 191–192, 203, 205–206, 209, 211, 216, 223, 256, 264, 281
pivot 31, 39
predication 25–30, 131, 133–134, 136, 140–141

predicational clauses 132
predicate 10–11, 127
PP (preposition phrase) 37–38, 141, 159–160, 181–185, 201–211, 217–218, 267, 281

raising auxiliaries 193, 242 (*see also* verbal auxiliaries)
raising verbs (*see also* verbal auxiliaries)
– CP-embedding raising verbs 244–245
– voiceP-embedding raising verbs 243
referential argument 29, 37, 143, 153,
root 21, 23

secondary pivot 35
second language acquisition 5–6
small clause 132, 135–137, 140, 146
specificational clauses 132–140
StatP 31, 34–38, 63–64, 72, 85, 143, 148, 151, 154–155, 159–160, 168–169, 172, 180, 182–185
subject 10–11, 24–25, 31, 35, 39, 41, 48–49, 54, 60–62, 65, 84, 97, 100, 104, 108, 117–121, 124, 129, 132–137, 140, 143–144, 146, 155, 157–158, 175, 184, 193, 194, 214
sudah 43–46, 89–101, 111–113, 115, 121–123, 214, 227–228, 241, 282

TAM-markers in Indonesian 43–45, 89–115
T-adverb 247–248
T-auxiliaries 111–115, 187–189, 227, 241–242

ter- (theme voice) 52–54
thematic roles 25–28, 48–49, 62–63, 70, 84–85, 133, 142, 155–158, 175, 180, 182, 210
theme 25–27, 31, 33, 35–37, 39, 48–50, 53–54, 57–65, 68–70, 75, 82, 99, 143, 146, 151, 153, 155–160, 168, 172, 175, 202–205, 209, 215
transfer 9–10, 225
topic 87–88, 100, 117–121, 124, 194–195, 197, 214
θP 26–29, 31–36, 39, 62–65, 69–70, 75, 78–80, 85, 104–105, 108, 140, 143–144, 146–147, 151, 153, 157–160, 172, 174–175, 179–180, 182, 184, 190, 202–205, 211, 253, 271, 273, 280–281
T-layer 88–115, 187–188, 190–191, 193, 243–245
TransP 34–35, 38, 65–66, 141

Universal Grammar (UG) 2, 9

verbal auxiliaries 89–109, 243–245
V-layer 25–39, 130–131, 143–144, 223
V 26–27, 29–32, 38, 130–131, 143–144, 270
Voice 26–27, 31, 43, 47–57, 63–65, 70–71, 80, 100, 105, 121, 165–173, 178–180, 182–184, 186, 188–189, 201–207, 211, 216–221, 253, 255, 270–272, 275–277, 281

yang 78–80

zero-nominalizer 81–82
zero-voice 55–56

www.ingramcontent.com/pod-product-compliance
Lightning Source LLC
Chambersburg PA
CBHW030230170426
43201CB00006B/169